Wealth Accumulation & Communities of Color in the United States

CURRENT ISSUES

Jessica Gordon Nembhard & Ngina Chiteji, Editors

THE UNIVERSITY OF MICHIGAN PRESS   *Ann Arbor*

In memory of two giants of African American political economy:

RHONDA M. WILLIAMS (1957–2000): sister scholar, intellectual warrior, mother, colleague, friend; who joined me briefly early on in the journey to produce this book, but couldn't finish with me.

ROBERT S. BROWNE (1924–2004): scholar activist, philanthropist, champion of Black land ownership, father, grandfather, colleague; a pioneer who began the contemporary dialogue about racial wealth inequality, advanced the theory and practice in myriad ways, and led us on the path to remedies.

—Jessica Gordon Nembhard

✿

To my parents: Asante sana kwa vitu vyote.

—Ngina Chiteji

Copyright © by the University of Michigan 2006
All rights reserved
Published in the United States of America by
The University of Michigan Press
Manufactured in the United States of America
♾ Printed on acid-free paper

2009   2008   2007   2006   4   3   2   1

A CIP catalog record for this book is available from the British Library.

Library of Congress Cataloging-in-Publication Data

Wealth accumulation and communities of color in the United States : current issues / [edited by] Jessica Gordon Nembhard and Ngina Chiteji.
    p.   cm.
Includes index.
ISBN-13: 978-0-472-09958-0 (cloth : alk. paper)
ISBN-10: 0-472-09958-2 (cloth : alk. paper)
ISBN-13: 978-0-472-06958-3 (pbk. : alk. paper)
ISBN-10: 0-472-06958-6 (pbk. : alk. paper)
    1. Wealth—United States.   2. Minorities—United States—Economic conditions.   I. Nembhard, Jessica Gordon.   II. Chiteji, Ngina, 1966–

HC110.W4W425   2006
339.2'208900973—dc22   2006015257

Contents

List of Figures

List of Tables

Acknowledgments

Books are always a joint effort. There are many we can thank. We are thankful first to a group of top-notch scholars, our authors, for there would be no book without them: Anthony A. Blasingame, Mariko Lin Chang, Gary Dymski, Yuval Elmelech, Elena Gouskova, Darrick Hamilton, Wilhelmina A. Leigh, Wei Li, Lisa Mohanty, Paul Ong, R. Varisa Patraporn, Bárbara J. Robles, Frank Stafford, Rachael A. Woldoff, and Jay L. Zagorsky. We thank them for their wonderful scholarship, their insights and innovations, and their patience.

We thank several of our colleague friends for their scholarship and sound advice: William Darity, Jr. (who among many things suggested the need for a broad, inclusive book), Patrick Mason (who among other things suggested the University of Michigan Press), Sharon Harley (who provided African American Studies Department support, especially for the conferences and some research assistance). We thank all the participants in the two conferences on wealth organized by Jessica Gordon Nembhard and sponsored by the African American Studies Department at the University of Maryland, College Park—some of whom are also authors. Ngina Chiteji also acknowledges the support of the Skidmore College Dean's Office, which made her pre-tenure sabbatical visit to the University of Maryland possible.

We thank all our assistants. Jason Rotheim graciously and expertly did the bulk of the formatting. Nigel Greaves provided early research assistance. Thanks to our editor at the University of Michigan Press, Raphael Allen. And additional thanks to Ellen McCarthy for her work on the project early in the process.

Jessica Gordon Nembhard also thanks the students in her African American Studies 499E/621 class, fall 2004, "Advanced Topics in Public Policy: Wealth Inequality," for being the first to use the manuscript, giving good feedback, and helping to produce the index. Cheryl Laird completed the final index, and provided essential last minute assistance in the editing process. Many thanks.

Introduction & Overview

JESSICA GORDON NEMBHARD &
NGINA CHITEJI

While wealth clearly has become a popular topic in the social sciences, and while sophisticated research routinely is conducted in this area, mainstream analyses of wealth inequality ignore or minimize many aspects of wealth creation and accumulation. In particular, beyond highlighting the differences between African Americans as a group and Whites, few studies disaggregate families or individuals by race, ethnicity, or gender. This is sometimes a result of data limitations, though it also can stem from apparent lack of interest in other groups. Given the critical role that wealth plays in securing family well-being, the paucity of the extant research is surprising as well as troublesome. We do not yet know much about the aggregate wealth levels, portfolio composition, and asset-ownership patterns of many subgroups in the population, such as Latinos, Pacific Islanders and Asian Americans, Native Americans, and women, nor about the central issues that concern asset accumulation among these groups. We therefore do not have a full understanding of wealth inequality and therefore have little insight into how to increase the well-being of growing segments of the U.S. population, or how to make effective and relevant policies for all U.S. citizens. This volume begins to remedy the lack of such information and analysis.

In many respects *Wealth Accumulation and Communities of Color in the United States* is the first book of its kind. The scope of the populations studied is broad, and the range of assets examined is great. The contributors forge new paths of scholarship in this area, creating new concepts and new knowledge. Much of the richness of the research comes from the innovative and interdisciplinary approaches used. In most cases these authors are the first scholars to tackle their issues from their particular perspectives—be it the perspective of a specific community of color, a perspective focusing on a specific asset that has not received much attention in the existing literature, a perspective that uses the lens of intra-group inequality to make its comparisons, or a perspective emphasizing the community-level effects of wealth inequality in addition to the individual or family-level effects.

THE STUDY OF WEALTH & SPECIFIC LIMITATIONS OF EXISTING STUDIES

Why do social scientists and policymakers care about wealth? Economists define wealth as a stock of resources that is available to a family or individual at any given point in time. It is the total value of a family's savings, or the savings that it has accumulated over its lifetime. As a stock, wealth is distinct from income, which is a flow, although the two are connected because many people accumulate wealth by saving part of the income that they receive. Wealth can be used for a variety of purposes: to finance consumption during retirement, to surmount liquidity constraints, to finance investments in education, and to guarantee that one's offspring are secure after one dies. A family's level of wealth therefore has important implications for its well-being, both contemporaneously and intergenerationally. Wealth is held in a variety of forms, and it grows over time according to both the rate of appreciation of individual assets and the interest rates that are associated with them.

Partly because of the connection between wealth and well-being, the past two decades have been characterized by an explosion of research on wealth inequality. This research has brought several dimensions of wealth inequality to the attention of the academic and policy-making communities. It reveals that there are sharp differences in the amount of wealth held at the top and bottom of the wealth distribution—with the bottom or "poorest" 40 percent of families having only 0.2 percent of the nation's wealth, while the richest 20 percent of the population holds about 83 percent of the nation's wealth (Wolff 2001). It also indicates that there are substantial differences between African American families and White families. For example, the average African American family holds only about 15.7 percent of the wealth of the average White family (Aizcorbe, Kennickell, and Moore 2003). Moreover, existing research suggests that differences by race persist even among families with similar levels of education, income, and occupational status (Oliver and Shapiro 1995; Hurst, Luoh, and Stafford 1998; Wolff 2001; Kunjufu 2002). Finally, the existing research indicates that wealth inequality has been rising over time (Wolff 2001).[1]

While informative, studies such as the ones summarized in the preceding section (and those reviewed in the introduction's appendix) approach distributional questions from a perspective that is rather narrow. *Wealth Accumulation and Communities of Color in the United States* examines wealth accumulation and the connection between wealth and well-being among a wider variety of racial and ethnic communities in the United States. The volume updates the existing research on African Americans while simultaneously extending the examination of wealth inequality and asset ownership to other, understudied groups in the United States. Our book also includes discussion of gender and class issues, with additional analyses of the political, historical, and socioeconomic contexts in which wealth inequalities exist. The aim is to enhance the literature on wealth inequality by offering information about groups that have been overlooked previously, by adding to what is known about African Americans, and by expanding the national dialogue about wealth creation and wealth inequality to include analysis of their implications for communities and democracy. The word *community* is used here in both a literal (spatial-geographic or locational) and a metaphorical sense, with the latter denoting distinct groups of individuals.

There are three major challenges that wealth researchers face. The first is to describe the way wealth is distributed throughout the population, as this descriptive information aids society in its quest to understand the nature of inequality. The second is to explain how families accumulate wealth, so that the different factors that influence families' total wealth and the types of assets they choose to hold, along with the factors that contribute to existing racial/ethnic gaps, can be identified. The third is to ascertain and explain the effects of wealth inequality. Academicians and policymakers have some understanding from existing research of the ways that parents' wealth affects their offspring's outcomes during young adulthood, ideas about the potential benefits of promoting asset ownership among the poor, and knowledge of the ways historical processes and federal policies have shaped the process of wealth accumulation among African Americans and those of European descent. Yet, as noted earlier, most published research covering wealth inequality offers little to address the plight of other racial and ethnic groups, and it has little to say about differences within groups. This is shortsighted. The United States is undergoing substantial changes in the racial and ethnic composition of its population. Accordingly, obtaining information about the aggregate wealth levels and asset-ownership patterns of other subgroups in the population is an urgent priority. Latinos currently represent about 12 percent of the total U.S. population and are expected to grow to be the largest "minority" group by 2010 (U.S. Census Bureau 2004, 14–18). Asian Americans now represent about 4 percent of the population, and estimates suggest that the Native American and Alaska Native population totals over four million people (U.S. Census Bureau 2004, 14). Scholars and policymakers therefore need to know more about the nature of these groups' wealth holdings, about the central factors that influence asset accumulation among these groups, and about any potential consequences of the low levels of wealth held in these communities.

Filling this void is particularly important because different racial and ethnic groups have had different historical experiences in the United States. While many of the outcomes are similar, a variety of historical forces must be studied to understand the problems and challenges facing different racial and ethnic groups. What is known about the history of redlining and the contributory role that it has played in shaping the divide between African American and White families (from treatises such as Oliver and Shapiro's *Black Wealth/White Wealth*), for example, does not necessarily help one understand the causes of low wealth among Native Americans or Native Hawaiians. Also, land loss and asset stripping are significant factors contributing to low levels of wealth in African American, Native American, Native Hawaiian, and even Asian American communities; however, the histories of such losses differ for each group. Native American and Native Hawaiian lands were colonized, and African Americans were kidnapped from Africa and enslaved in the Americas.[2]

The chapters in this volume offer descriptions of different groups' wealth holdings, the factors that influence different groups' wealth accumulation processes, and the implications of low wealth for racial and ethnic minorities. *Wealth Accumulation and Communities of Color in the United States* also examines the consequences that wealth inequality has at the community level, and for political participation and the democratic process, which are aspects of wealth creation and accumulation that have not received sufficient attention to date. Many of our authors recognize the importance of understanding the totality of racial communities, local community economic development, and community wealth in order to understand and research wealth accumulation among different racial and ethnic groups. It is important to this understanding that the impact of wealth (or lack of wealth) on communities, and the impacts of community activity and organization on the process of wealth accumulation, are examined.

The book also includes a discussion of methodological issues, providing both explanations and critiques of the major national data sets that researchers use, to help readers begin to understand the nuances and inherent data limitations of some of the different surveys that are employed in wealth analyses. Moreover, this book presents an assessment of the various empirical strategies that researchers use to examine wealth gaps. While it is not common to find discussions of measurement and methodological matters in books covering inequality, this book addresses such issues because we believe that it is important (1) for readers to understand where the data being presented and analyzed originate and (2) for readers to know how estimates of racial wealth gaps are produced. The accompanying discussion of data collection and methodology from the perspective of race helps one to understand the inherent limitations and challenges confronting wealth researchers and provides opportunities for deeper analysis.

This volume offers scholarship containing analyses of such issues under one cover, using up-to-date data in most instances, therefore providing a comprehensive study of racial and ethnic wealth accumulation and inequality.

ORGANIZATION OF THE VOLUME

This volume is divided into four parts: "Measurement and Methodology," "Intragroup Inequality," "Data and Information about Specific Communities of Color," and "Wealth Effects and Communities."

Section one contains two chapters, each addressing measurement or methodological issues. Chapter 1, "Wealth Measurement: Issues for People of Color in the United States," by Wilhelmina A. Leigh, offers a comprehensive discussion of the six premier data sets that are used most by wealth researchers: the Federal Reserve Board's Survey of Consumer Finances (SCF); the U.S. Census Bureau's Survey of Income and Program Participation (SIPP); the Panel Study of Income Dynamics (PSID), whose data are collected by the Institute for Social Research at the University of Michigan; the Health and Retirement Study (HRS), which is also collected by the University of Michigan's Survey Research Center; the Consumer Expenditure Survey (CEX), conducted by the U.S. Census Bureau (through the Bureau of Labor Statistics [BLS]); and the National Longitudinal Surveys (NLS) (also sponsored by the BLS). Leigh notes that most of the sources providing information about wealth are household survey data; however, the sampling frame, the frequency at which the data are collected, and the range of years for which data are available vary across data sets. Additionally, some of the surveys present cross-sectional data, while others are longitudinal studies. The chapter also explains why there is variation across surveys in the extent to which they can be used to examine populations other than Blacks and Whites. These are issues that individuals may be unaware of if they are not researchers themselves, yet they represent issues that need to be acknowledged and discussed in order for readers who are new to the field to be certain that they fully understand any given author's results.

The discussion in chapter 1 provides essential background concerning where and how researchers get their information, what is generally known about individual wealth holdings, and the limitations of the existing data sets. The chapter delineates and explains the various dimensions of wealth that are measured, the kinds of measures researchers use, and the data available to measure wealth, all while highlighting key differences, strengths and weaknesses, across the premier national data sets used in this field. The chapter also analyzes data from these data sets by race/ethnicity (focusing on the distribution of net worth, frequency with which assets are held, and value of individual assets) and compares results across the data sets from 1989 to 2001.

"Estimating the Effect of Race and Ethnicity on Wealth Accumulation and Asset-Ownership Patterns," by Ngina Chiteji and Darrick Hamilton (chap. 2), provides an overview of the circumstances under which social sciences researchers find wealth gaps and differences in asset-ownership rates to be meaningful. The chapter also discusses the reasons that scholars and policymakers find the existence of substantive differences in the levels of total wealth held by different subgroups of the population and differences in rates of ownership of specific assets troubling. The authors shed light on the debate about the extent to which it is individual characteristics and behavior or structural factors such as discrimination that lead to racial/ethnic and gender wealth inequality. The chapter also explains why several researchers recently have advocated that alternative estimation strategies, such as nonparametric techniques, be used to examine racial wealth gaps. This chapter provides an appreciation of the context in which wealth gaps are evaluated and of the empirical techniques that appear in the literature.

The second section of the book discusses wealth inequality and its measurement from the perspective of intragroup inequality within White, African American, and Latino communities and across gender. In chapter 3, "Determinants of Intragroup Wealth Inequality among Whites, Blacks, and Latinos," Yuval Elmelech recaps some of the current knowledge about differences in asset holdings between Blacks and Whites and then extends the analysis to Latino families. Using data from the Health and Retirement Study (HRS), the author finds that wealth is more highly concentrated among the Black and Latino populations. In addition, while employment and occupational attainment play an important role in understanding wealth inequality, Elmelech demonstrates that marital and immigration statuses are also very significant for African Americans and Latinos.

Chapter 4 begins by presenting an overview of women's wealth holdings and then engages its reader in a discussion of gender differences within different racial/ethnic communities. This chapter, titled "Women and Wealth," by Mariko Lin Chang, explains that little has been written about connections between wealth and gender, or about women as a class, in the literature analyzing wealth inequality.[3] Chang uses the 2001 Survey of Consumer Finances to examine the size of the gender wealth gap, the portfolio allocation decisions of men and women, and the degree to which gender differences differ by race. Perhaps unsurprisingly (given that there are differences in income by gender), the chapter finds that large gender gaps exist between men and women of similar household types and that single parenting poses a significant challenge to women's wealth accumulation. In addition, the data covering women of color suggest that they experience greater barriers to wealth accumulation than White women and that gender wealth inequality may be greater among non-White men and women than among Whites.

The third section, "Data and Information about Specific Communities of Color," contains four chapters that examine data about different racial and ethnic groups, particularly the groups least analyzed, focusing on ownership of specific assets, such as housing, land, business, and pensions. In chapter 5, "Native Americans' Wealth," Jay L. Zagorsky notes that Native American populations are some of the poorest groups in the United States. Wealth among First Nations populations has not been examined previously, largely because most of the premier data sets that wealth researchers rely upon do not include large numbers of Native Americans. However, this is a group whose experience provides an important case study of how history shapes contemporary events. The history of the United States is replete with examples of instances in which Native Americans have been subjected to asset stripping, losing wealth they once had and being clustered onto reservations with limited or no access to wealth-building assets (see Adamson 2003; Henson, Lee, and Nathan 2005). One of the few data sets available that does have information on both Native American status and wealth is the National Longitudinal Survey of Youth (NLSY79). Chapter 5 discusses findings from this data set, definitional questions, and the merits and limitations of the data. Among its many findings, the chapter reveals that Native Americans do not follow the same wealth-building trajectory as Whites. In addition, while there has been much discourse in the public arena about the use of Native American land for gaming purposes, Zagorsky finds that gaming has not enriched the average Native American family.

In "Trouble in Paradise: The Economic Marginalization of Native Hawaiians" (chap. 6), Paul Ong examines business holdings (farm and nonfarm), housing and interest-bearing assets, as well as educational attainment and labor market outcomes of Native Hawaiians. Ong uses census data and data from the 1990 and 2000 Public Use Microdata Samples (PUMS) to explore how earnings and ethnicity affect home ownership probability and home values for Native Hawaiians relative to White non-Hispanics and Japanese Americans born in Hawaii. Ong also provides an important discussion of land ownership, land loss, and lack of home ownership among Native Hawaiians.

"Asian Americans and Wealth," written by Paul Ong and R. Varisa Patraporn (chap. 7), provides insights into the complex way immigration, race, and ethnicity interact in generating Asian American wealth outcomes. The authors use data from the 2001 SIPP wave 3 and PUMS (to study Asian Americans by ethnic group) and find that despite high socioeconomic status and comparable wealth status to White non-Hispanics', Asian Americans experience barriers to wealth accumulation in comparison with Whites. In addition, Asian American intragroup wealth disparity is larger than White intragroup wealth inequality, in great part because of noted ethnic differences within the Asian American population. The authors suggest that more research is needed to examine how the wealth accumulation processes differ by race. Both chapters 7 and 9 (on Asian American banking) highlight the lack of available data on Asian American wealth holdings and the difficulty of making generalizations because of the paucity of data, as well as the great diversity of the Asian American population.

In chapter 8, "Financial Marketplace Participation and Pension Holdings over the Life Course," Ngina Chiteji, Elena Gouskova, and Frank Stafford examine families' portfolios to determine how families in the United States hold their wealth and what role retirement savings in pensions play in the portfolio. The authors argue that it is useful to measure portfolio allocation behavior in two different ways—by looking at the number of different assets that families hold (portfolio span) and the specific combination of assets held (portfolio composition). The chapter analyzes the nature of Black and White families' participation in pension programs, as well as the degree to which pensions are a substitute for other forms of wealth. This research has implications for discussions of the adequacy of retirement savings for African American and White families and for several policy discussions, including debates about the structure of the U.S. pension system and the debate about privatizing Social Security.

In the fourth and final section, the volume provides analyses of wealth's effects on communities. "Banking and Wealth Accumulation in the Asian American Community: Questions and Evidence from Los Angeles," by Gary Dymski, Lisa Mohanty, and Wei Li (chap. 9), investigates wealth building in the Asian American community, particularly Asian American banking. The chapter focuses on the development of the Asian American banking sector in Los Angeles County, the role of banks in community economic development (Chinese American banks in particular), and comparisons with African American–owned banks. The authors find that Asian Americans are at a systematic statistical disadvantage in a model of home-purchase-loan approval but that in some geographic areas Asian-owned banks function as a collective asset for the Asian American community. The authors conclude with a call for organizations to collect more substantial data on the socioeconomic circumstances of Asian Americans.

Chapter 10, "Wealth Creation in Latino Communities: Latino Families, Community Assets, and Cultural Capital," by Bárbara J. Robles, opens with an analysis of the importance of asset ownership in Latino communities and a discussion of reasons that the term *wealth* might need to be viewed differently from the way economists traditionally view it when examining the Latino community. The author highlights the great diversity in Latino communities in the United States (by country of origin, immigrant status, and class status) and provides an overview of Latino family economic indicators, wealth status, and bicultural resources that can be utilized to create asset-building opportunities. The importance of community organizations that understand, support, and promote cultural capital, the financial stability of Latino families, and the sustainable economic development of Latino communities is assessed, as are policies that affect the asset-building opportunities of Latino families and that influence community asset building within Latino communities.

Housing is the focus of "Living Where the Neighbors Are Invested: Wealth and Racial/Ethnic Differences in Individuals' Neighborhood Home Ownership Rates," by Rachael A. Woldoff (chap. 11). This chapter examines the impact of family of origin, wealth, other socioeconomic characteristics, and current family on the neighborhood home ownership rates of Whites, African Americans, and Latinos. Because the location of one's home is important for ensuring high-quality schools, reliable services, stable residents, controlled crime, increased housing values and home equity, and greater life chances for families, racial/ethnic differences in access to good neighborhoods are a key concern. The analysis uncovers that the effect of wealth on neighborhood home ownership is greater for Latinos and African Americans than for Whites. Perhaps surprisingly, Woldoff finds that while Latinos have the closest link between individual characteristics and neighborhood levels of home ownership, African Americans receive the fewest returns to socioeconomic characteristics because of their high levels and long history of discrimination in the housing market.

The final chapter, "Wealth, Civic Engagement, and Democratic Practice," by Jessica Gordon Nembhard and Anthony A. Blasingame (chap. 12), examines the literature and explores many of the ways in which economic activity, status, and interests, as well as political-economic relationships, impact the level or quality of civic engagement, political behavior, and political influence of individuals. Gordon Nembhard and Blasingame note that wealth, socioeconomic inequality, and economic power each matter. This chapter examines, in particular, the ways that wealth ownership impacts the level of charitable giving and volunteering among White and Black households. Using probit and Heckman selection models of estimation, they find that while wealth is significant to Whites' volunteering and not significant to their decision to give to charities (though significant to how much a donation is given), wealth is significant to the African American decision to give a charitable donation but not to Black volunteering. Questions about how to measure such influences and differences across races are addressed. The authors also find that workplace democracy and cooperative business ownership appear to increase wealth and civic participation, and thus democratic practices. They end with a brief discussion about public policies that impact economic democracy and opportunities for wealth accumulation.

Jessica Gordon Nembhard provides an "unorthodox policy guide" in the Afterword. She summarizes the research and policy implications from these studies.

TOPICS THAT ARE NOT COVERED IN THIS VOLUME

For African Americans, there already is a substantial literature addressing various dimensions of asset ownership. Moreover, much has been written about a number of general aspects of wealth accumulation that are relevant for all Americans. Accordingly, this volume does not include chapters on topics and debates such as those surrounding African American entrepreneurship, the implications of wealth inequality for African American children's outcomes, stock market participation rates in the population at large, intergenerational transfers, asset poverty, how wealth accumulation is affected by kin poverty, intergenerational correlations in wealth among African Americans and Whites, and the history and consequences of federal policies such as redlining for African American home ownership rates. (The introduction's appendix reviews each of the major texts covering these issues.) Also outside the scope of this book, albeit interesting, are several current policy debates, including that covering social security reform, financial literacy, federal and state initiatives to promote Individual Development Accounts (IDAs), and Universal Savings Accounts (USA accounts).[4]

CONCLUSION

Wealth inequality exposes the depths of racial and economic inequality in the United States. Browne's (1974) early work on inequality highlighted the importance of looking at wealth rather than only income and education to understand the economic status and well-being of African Americans. Oliver and Shapiro's (1995) pathbreaking book twenty years later refocused attention on wealth and its connection to well-being. Oliver and Shapiro highlighted the role that public policies played throughout U.S. history in creating and perpetuating much of the disparity between African Americans and Whites.

To the existing volumes studying wealth (many of which are briefly described in the appendix), we add our volume. It is designed to serve as a guide for readers who have been searching for a multifaceted discussion of wealth that mirrors the diversity of experience that we see in the U.S. population at large.

Together, these chapters provide an overview of data sources and measurement issues, of what is known and still not known about wealth accumulation, and of issues surrounding wealth and wealth inequality within and among African Americans, Latinos, Asian Americans and Pacific Islanders, Native Americans, and women. While many of the findings confirm the suspicion that most readers undoubtedly will bring to the text prior to reading the volume—that deep, serious, and sometimes growing disparities in wealth exist in the United States—the contributors to this volume provide new evidence and offer new ways to understand wealth in communities of color.

APPENDIX: OTHER BOOKS ABOUT WEALTH

In what follows we discuss some of the recent books contributing to the field's understanding of the distribution of wealth in the United States and the role that wealth plays in individuals' and families' lives. The economics discipline has had a long tradition of examining saving behavior and intergenerational transfers of wealth, with a particular emphasis on the connection between the latter and its implications for the extent to which the life-cycle hypothesis of saving explains actual wealth accumulation in the U.S. population at large. Denis Kessler and Andre Masson's edited volume, titled *Modeling the Accumulation and Distribution of Wealth* (1988), for example, includes a collection of papers from a conference that featured many of the preeminent scholars writing on wealth at the time. The volume contains a number of theoretical contributions that focus on the motives for saving, the motives for making bequests, and modeling the intergenerational transmission process. It also contains the papers representing the famous empirical debate between Kotlikoff, Summers, and Modigliani about the extent to which most individuals' wealth comes from independent saving or from inheritance.

Most books on wealth written prior to the 1990s reflect a similar focus. The early scholarship on wealth had a strong macroeconomic emphasis, and it concentrated on bequests, testing the life-cycle hypothesis, and national balance sheet measures of the aggregate wealth of the household sector. In academia, inequality was largely the domain of those writing about individual earnings and family income (and about residential segregation in sociology), not a subject addressed in the literature on wealth. In popular discourse, wealth and income were used interchangeably, as terms such as *wealthy, rich, high income,* and *upper class* were used to describe the same phenomenon in everyday speech.

Michael Sherraden (1991) strongly emphasizes the importance of drawing a distinction between wealth and income as measures of family resources and injects the concept of wealth into social policy discussions about the poor. Since then, a lively literature that provides some analysis of how wealth is accumulated and appropriated for particular populations, sometimes to the detriment of others, has developed. This literature reveals that laws, policies, ownership patterns, and both the direct and indirect effects of economic discrimination and discriminatory political practices are worthy of exploration when attempting to understand wealth inequality.

Sherraden's *Assets and the Poor: A New American Welfare Policy* takes the role of asset ownership in shaping families' and individuals' outcomes as its subject. Written from a social work perspective, the book contains an extensive discussion of the economic and psychological effects of owning assets. It also discusses the ways that U.S. social welfare policy discouraged asset ownership by the poor, as well as the ways that other federal policies historically have subsidized asset acquisition by the middle class. Sherraden concludes with a call for policy changes specifically designed to promote asset ownership among the nation's poor. This research has led to the development of legislation to promote IDAs, and in 1996 Congress gave states the authority to promote IDAs in the welfare reform legislation. While extremely enlightening, Sherraden focuses heavily on the poor as a group. The book does not undertake the task of trying to analyze the experiences of different racial or ethnic minorities, although many of them are heavily represented among the ranks of the poor.

Assets for the Poor: The Benefits of Spreading Asset Ownership, by Thomas Shapiro and Edward Wolff (2001), is a collection of papers that also focuses largely on the poor and offers interdisciplinary analyses of wealth inequality. The contributors are economists and sociologists. This volume offers an excellent explanation of the reasons that wealth is important. Its chapters provide detailed discussions of the differences between Blacks and Whites, of policies to promote asset ownership among the poor, and of the role of housing as a means of asset accumulation (and the pros and cons of making this a strategy for building the wealth of the poor). This volume also documents changes in the distribution of wealth in the 1980s through the late 1990s. It includes chapters covering public policy topics; the tax code and, for example, the incentives and disincentives for asset accumulation associated with its current structure; and recent state and federal asset-building initiatives. Because it is a collection of papers, this book is able to highlight the variety of data sources that exist for researchers interested in wealth, including nationally representative data sets such as the SCF, the HRS, and the PSID, along with qualitative data from one individual author's independent survey.

The wealth gap that exists between Blacks and Whites and its consequences has, in fact, been explored in several books. Melvin L. Oliver and Thomas M. Shapiro's *Black Wealth/White Wealth: A New Perspective on Racial Inequality* (1995) is a seminal piece that combines sociological ethnographic research and detailed quantitative analysis of cross-sectional data from the 1988 SIPP covering the distribution of household wealth by race. This book compares the aggregate wealth of Black and White families and characterizes the patterns of ownership of individual assets (such as housing) and of broad categories of assets (such as financial assets) among Black and White families. It reveals that there are substantial differences both in the wealth held by Black and White families, on average, and in the composition of their portfolios. It shows that these differences remain even after taking into account several economic and sociodemographic factors normally thought to explain wealth accumulation. Oliver and Shapiro's analysis is supplemented with a discussion of the historical processes and public policy decisions that underlie these differences. This book was pathbreaking and widely acclaimed (deservedly), although its analysis of racial inequality is somewhat narrow because it examines only African Americans compared with European Americans.

One of the major implications of racial wealth differences is the consequence that they have for children. In *Being Black and Living in the Red: Race, Wealth, and Social Policy in America* (1999) sociologist Dalton Conley analyzes the effect of parental wealth on a variety of young adult outcomes, such as teen pregnancy rates, high school graduation rates, and college enrollment. Conley concludes that having wealthy parents has positive and significant effects on an individual's life chances and that one can explain a portion of the gap in outcomes observed for Blacks and Whites during young adulthood by controlling for their parents' wealth. The empirical analysis, which is based on data from the PSID, shows that wealth is an important measure of family background beyond the traditional income, occupational, and educational measures that were once standard in the literature for research seeking to characterize family background. Because the book only focuses on differences between Blacks and Whites, however, it represents only the beginning of an exploration into the implications of racial/ ethnic wealth inequality.

Shapiro's *The Hidden Cost of Being African American: How Wealth Perpetuates Inequality* (2004) continues the theme of exploring the advantages that individuals who come from wealthy families have over individuals from low-wealth families. This book examines the legacy of racial inequality in a Black-White context. Shapiro focuses on one process through which family wealth can affect children's outcomes. In-depth interviews with White middleclass families indicate that the parents often leverage their assets, and the assets of their own parents when possible, to provide advantages to their offspring, by moving to "better" or "safer" neighborhoods with high-quality schools, for example. While middle-income Black families may attempt to do the same with the limited resources that they have, Shapiro notes that many of them do not have the large-asset safety net that middle-class Whites have (since Whites are more likely to have wealthy parents and to inherit wealth). Additionally, a greater proportion of Black families reside in "asset poverty" according to Shapiro. The author argues that because people with access to assets can use their family wealth in this way, inequality in one generation is reproduced in the next.

More general discussions of wealth inequality are provided by scholars such as Wolff in *Top Heavy: The Increasing Inequality of Wealth in America and What Can Be Done about It* (1996, and second edition 2002). Wolff offers an extensive analysis of the size distribution of household wealth in the United States, using data from the SCF to depict the trends in U.S. wealth inequality from the 1960s through the end of the 1980s. *Top Heavy* offers comparisons with the situation in other Western countries. The book provides an excellent discussion of the economic significance of wealth, which clearly explains the economic distinction between wealth and income and reveals that there is significant inequality in the distribution of wealth in the United States by class. However, it only provides a limited amount of information about racial/ethnic wealth inequality; the short section addressing this topic compares "minorities" as a group with Whites. Additionally, there are no comparisons by gender.

Also focusing on the general distribution of wealth, sociologist Lisa Keister's *Wealth in America: Trends in Wealth Inequality* (2000) analyzes the processes underlying the existing distribution, including the role of family structure. Keister uses microsimulation modeling to investigate the forces shaping the distribution of wealth from the 1960s through the 1990s.

Alicia H. Munnell and Annika Sunden's recent volume *Death and Dollars: The Role of Gifts and Bequests in America* (2003) returns scholars to economists' original interest in wealth transfers. Among the topics addressed in this book are inheritances, the theoretical issues surrounding the bequest motive, and connections across generations. This volume also contains discussion of empirical estimates of wealth accumulation over time and among different cohorts and extensive discussion of the estate tax, pensions, and social security (though it does not analyze race/ethnic or gender differences in retirement wealth). The authors contributing to the volume are predominately economists, and they draw on data from national data sets such as the SCF and the HRS.

Should Differences in Income and Wealth Matter (2002), edited by Ellen Frankel Paul, Fred D. Miller, and Jeffrey Paul, presents a collection of papers that offer a discussion of inequality that is largely philosophical. Focusing mostly on income inequality (rather than wealth per se), the contributors discuss the incentive effects of tolerating inequality, distributive justice, and egalitarian thought. While the book raises interesting moral and ethical issues for readers interested in wealth inequality, its subject matter is more philosophical than our volume's. In assessing the implications of wealth inequality *Wealth Accumulation and Communities of Color in the United States* does not ignore questions of fairness; however, it addresses them in the context of social processes and specific policy and historical epochs that have affected different racial and ethnic groups. While a general discussion of philosophical questions surrounding fairness provides food for thought, it inevitably overlooks group-specific details that can have important practical implications in a diverse society.

Sherraden's *Inclusion in the American Dream: Assets, Poverty, and Public Policy* (2005) is an edited volume that contains the most comprehensive discussion of U.S. asset-building policies that is available. The volume contains chapters that discuss several past and present policies to promote asset ownership, the philosophical concerns and political debates surrounding a possible transition from income-based social welfare policies to asset-oriented strategies for aiding the poor (a transition that many deem to be looming on the horizon), and the reasons that asset ownership and development have become important to policymakers. This is an excellent resource for readers interested in contemporary policies such as IDAs, USA accounts, Children's Savings Accounts (CSAs), the history of federal pension policies and the current structure of the U.S. pension system, the federal Thrift Savings Plan (TSP), and the use of the Earned Income Tax Credit (EITC) to promote saving.

NOTES

1. Please note that as we go to press results from the 2004 Survey of Consumer Finances have just been made public (see Bucks, Kennickell, and Moore 2006, and http://www.federalreserve.gov/pubs/oss/oss2/2004/scf2004home.html). Overall the mean value of net worth increased by 6.3 percent while the median value only increased by 1.5 percent. Median wealth declined for families in the bottom 40 percent of the income distribution (Bucks, Kennickell, and Moore). This signals a continued increase in wealth inequality between the wealthiest and the poorest. Bucks, Kennickell, and Moore also note that "the measured gains in wealth in the 2001–2004 period pale in comparison with the much larger increase of the preceding three years," and debt burden increased during this most recent period (A35). For people of color, a similar pattern persists. SCF reports the wealth of two racial/ethnic categories, "White non-Hispanic" families and "nonwhite or Hispanic" families. Nonwhite or Hispanic families' median wealth holdings were only 17.6 percent of total median wealth in 2004—only slightly better than in 2001. In addition, home ownership rates and values continued to lag significantly between the two groups, although they did increase some for both groups of families. For African Americans, however, Bucks, Kennickell, and Moore report that there was virtually no change in median net worth between 2001 and 2004 ($20,300 compared to $20,400, A9).

In terms of the other surveys and studies, the 2003 results from the University of Michigan Institute for Social Research's Panel Study of Income Dynamics (PSID) recently become public (see http://psidonline.isr.umich.edu/). In addition, release of the 2005 PSID data is expected by December 31, 2006. 2001, however, remains the latest year of published information from the U.S. Census Bureau's Survey of Income and Program Participation (SIPP).

Please note that there was no opportunity for our contributors to integrate any of the newer wealth statistics into their studies before this volume went to press. In addition, for those studies that compare across data sets (such as chap. 1), the 2001 SCF is currently still the relevant source to use. This does not diminish our contributors' findings, conclusions, or recommendations, particularly since the 2004 SCF results illustrate that there have not been significant changes in wealth holding or wealth accumulation patterns over the three years since the previous study. The results and analyses in this volume remain relevant, robust, and unique.

2. Ong's chapter (6) provides details about the history of Native Hawaiian colonization and land loss. Native Americans have suffered a gradual erosion of wealth-building opportunities beginning with U.S. confiscation of land and the ceding of a majority of their land to the United States in exchange for treaty-protected rights (see Henson, Lee, and Nathan 2005). In addition, there is documentation of mismanagement and undermanagement of tribal assets by the federal government's trust oversight, as well as restrictions on the transfer of Native trust land, government relocation programs, and failed government interventions (Henson, Lee, and Nathan 2005; Adamson 2003). For African Americans, enslavement restricted owning one's self and any other property; racial land reform never took place as promised after the Civil War; during Jim Crow, Black-owned land was seized violently and records destroyed; and up through the twentieth century Black land loss continued with urbanization, discriminatory public policy and credit policies, and the intestate status of many parcels (see Darity and Nicholson 2005; Winbush 2003; Browne 1973). Asian Americans had land confiscated during their internment in concentration camps during World War II but did eventually receive some reparations.

3. At the time this manuscript went to press, Chang had referenced the most recent literature and used the most current data available. Her chapter stands out as one of the few studies of its kind, particularly on women's wealth in the United States. It has come to our attention that the journal *Feminist Economics* will be publishing a special issue on women's wealth with an international focus, "Women and the Distribution of Wealth" 12, nos. 1–2 (2006), after we go to press. No doubt the research published in that special issue will greatly expand the scholarship in this area.

4. Readers who are interested in these topics can turn to some of the sources listed in the appendix or to scholarly articles by Timothy Bates; Hurst, Luoh, and Stafford (1998); Chiteji and Stafford (1999); Charles and Hurst (2003); Heflin and Pattillo (2002); and Chiteji and Hamilton (2005). For example, Sherraden (2005) offers a comprehensive analysis of recent policy proposals to facilitate asset building in the United States.

REFERENCES

Adamson, Rebecca. 2003. "Land Rich and Dirt Poor—The Story of Indian Assets." *Native Americans,* summer, 26–37.
Aizcorbe, Ana M., Arthur B. Kennickell, and Kevin B. Moore. 2003. "Recent Changes in U.S. Family Finances: Evidence from the 1998 and 2001 Survey of Consumer Finances." *Federal Reserve Bulletin* 89 (January): 1–32.

Barsky, Robert, John Bound, Kerwin Charles, and Joseph Lupton. 2002. "Accounting for the Black-White Wealth Gap: A Non-parametric Approach." *Journal of the American Statistical Association* 97 (459): 663–73.

Browne, Robert S., ed. 1973. *Only Six Million Acres: The Decline of Black Owned Land in the Rural South* (a report sponsored by Clark College of Atlanta, Georgia, and funded by the Rockefeller Brothers Fund). New York: Black Economic Research Center, 1973.

———. 1974. "Wealth Distribution and Its Impact on Minorities." *Review of Black Political Economy* 4: 27–37.

Bucks, Brian K., Arthur B. Kennickell, and Kevin B. Moore. 2006. "Recent Changes in U.S. Family Finances: Evidence from the 2001 and 2004 Survey of Consumer Finances." *Federal Reserve Bulletin* 92 (February 2006), A1–A38. Also at http://www.federalreserve.gov/pubs/oss/oss2/2004/bull0206.pdf (accessed 3-20-06).

Charles, Kerwin Kofi, and Erik Hurst. 2003. "The Correlation of Wealth across Generations." *Journal of Political Economy* 111 (6): 1155–82.

Chiteji, Ngina, and Darrick Hamilton. 2005. "Family Matters: Kin Networks and Asset Accumulation." In *Inclusion in the American Dream: Assets, Poverty, and Public Policy,* ed. Michael Sherraden, 87–111. New York: Oxford University Press. Also Washington University Center for Social Development Working Paper no. 2000.

Chiteji, Ngina, and Frank Stafford. 1999. "Portfolio Choices of Parents and Their Children as Young Adults: Asset Accumulation by African-American Families." *American Economic Review* 89 (2): 377–80.

Conley, Dalton. 1999. *Being Black and Living in the Red: Race, Wealth, and Social Policy in America.* Los Angeles: University of California Press.

Darity, William, Jr., and Melba Nicholson. 2005. "Racial Wealth Inequality and the Black Family." In *African American Family Life: Ecological and Cultural Diversity,* ed. Vonnie McLoyd, Nancy Hill, and Kenneth Dodge, 78–85. New York: Guilford Press.

Deere, Carmen Diana, and Cheryl Doss, eds. 2006. "The Gender Asset Gap: What Do We Know and Why Does It Matter?" Special issue, *Feminist Economics* 12, nos. 1–2.

Dollars and Sense and United for a Fair Economy. 2004. *The Wealth Inequality Reader.* Boston: Dollars and Sense Magazine.

Heflin, Colleen, and Mary Pattillo. 2002. "Kin Effects on Black-White Account and Homeownership," *Sociological Inquiry* 72 (2): 220–29.

Henson, Eric, Anna Lee, and Luxman Nathan. 2005. "Rural Wealth Building." Unpublished manuscript, Harvard Project on American Indian Economic Development and Lexecon—An FTI Company, John F. Kennedy School of Government, Harvard University, Cambridge.

Hurst, Erik, Ming-Ching Luoh, and Frank Stafford. 1998. "The Wealth Dynamics of American Families." *Brookings Papers on Economic Activity* 1: 267–329.

Keister, Lisa. 2000. *Wealth in America: Trends in Wealth Inequality.* New York: Cambridge University Press.

Kessler, Denis, and Andre Masson, eds. 1988. *Modeling the Accumulation and Distribution of Wealth.* Oxford: Clarendon Press.

Kunjufu, Jawanza. 2002. *Black Economics: Solutions for Economic and Community Empowerment.* 2nd ed. Chicago: African American Images.

Mishel, Lawrence, Jared Bernstein, and John Schmitt. 1999. *The State of Working America, 1998–1999.* Washington, DC: Economic Policy Institute.

Munnell, Alicia H., and Annika Sunden, eds. 2003. *Death and Dollars: The Role of Gifts and Bequests in America.* Washington, DC: Brookings Institution Press.

Oliver, Melvin L., and Thomas M. Shapiro, eds. 1995. *Black Wealth/White Wealth: A New Perspective on Racial Inequality.* New York: Routledge.

Orzechowski, S., and P. Sepielli. 2003. "Net Worth and Asset Ownership of Households: 1998 and 2000." Current Population Reports, P70-88. Washington, DC: U.S. Census Bureau. http://www.census.gov/hhes/www/wealth/1998_2000/wealth98_00.html (accessed on 20 August 2004).

Paul, Ellen Frankel, Fred D. Miller, and Jeffrey Paul, eds. 2002. *Should Differences in Income and Wealth Matter.* New York: Cambridge University Press.

Shapiro, Thomas. 2004. *The Hidden Cost of Being African American: How Wealth Perpetuates Inequality.* New York: Oxford University Press.

Shapiro, Thomas, and Edward Wolff, eds. 2001. *Assets for the Poor: The Benefits of Spreading Asset Ownership.* New York: Russell Sage Foundation.

Sherraden, Michael. 1991. *Assets and the Poor: A New American Welfare Policy.* Armonk, NY: ME Sharpe.

———, ed. 2005. *Inclusion in the American Dream: Assets, Poverty, and Public Policy.* New York: Oxford University Press.

U.S. Census Bureau. 2004. *Statistical Abstract of the United States: 2004–2005.* http://www.census.gov/statb/www (accessed on October 10, 2005).

Winbush, Raymond. 2003. "The Earth Moved: Stealing Black Land in the United States." In *Should America Pay? Slavery and the Raging Debate over Reparations,* ed. Raymond Winbush. New York: Harper Collins.

Wolff, Edward N. 1996. *Top Heavy: The Increasing Inequality of Wealth in America and What Can Be Done about It.* New York: New Press. Second, expanded edition, 2002.

———. 2001. "Recent Trends in Wealth Ownership, 1983–1998." In *Assets for the Poor: The Benefits of Spreading Asset Ownership,* ed. Thomas Shapiro and Edward Wolff. New York: Russell Sage Foundation.

I Measurement & Methodology

1 Wealth Measurement

Issues for People of Color in the United States

WILHELMINA A. LEIGH

Although income has long been used to compare the well-being of populations in this country, only since the mid-1960s (toward the end of the civil rights movement) has wealth been used for this purpose as well. The 1967 Survey of Economic Opportunity was the first government survey that allowed an examination of differences in wealth by race. Comparing Blacks and Whites only, the Survey of Economic Opportunity revealed marked disparities that persisted during the remainder of the twentieth century. In 1967 the ratio of mean (or average) Black household wealth, or net worth ($16,972), to mean White household wealth, or net worth ($90,507), was 0.188 (18.8 percent).[1] Net worth for the average Black household had risen to $31,992 in 1984 with the comparable figure for White households at $123,677, for a ratio of 0.259 (25.9 percent). Nearly ten years later, in 1993, the ratio remained virtually unchanged at 0.26 (26 percent), with mean Black household wealth, or net worth, at $34,270 and mean White household wealth, or net worth, at $131,613 (Eller and Fraser 1995; Oliver and Shapiro 1989; Terrell 1971).

In 1998, the ratio of mean wealth for Black non-Latino households to mean wealth for White non-Latino households had fallen to 0.18 (18 percent) again. The comparable ratio for Latino household wealth vis-à-vis wealth for White non-Latino households was 0.25 (25 percent) (Choudhury 2001/2002).[2] In that same year, however, mean wealth for Asian American households was 0.87 (87 percent) of the value held by White households (Wolff 2001).

Explanations for these persistent gaps have included, in particular for the Black-White disparity, the intergenerational consequences of the fact that in 1863 each emancipated slave did not receive the promised "forty acres and a mule." Advocacy for a massive capital transfer or reparations has developed around this historical oversight (Browne 1974; America 1990; Oliver and Shapiro 1995; Ogletree 2004). Limited inheritance of wealth by people of color also is cited to explain this gap (Blau and Graham 1990; Oliver and Shapiro 1995). Another often-suggested explanation is the failure of Blacks (or African Americans), other people of color (i.e., Asian Americans, Native Hawaiians and other Pacific Islanders, American Indians/Alaska Natives, and Hispanics [or Latinos][3]), and immigrants to invest in the stock market, a shortcoming attributed in part to the lack of familiarity with this market and to perceptions of its risk (Brimmer 1988; Wynter 1997). Yet another suggested explanation is the use of measures of wealth that exclude employer pensions and Social Security benefits, both of which are large proportions of the wealth of people of color (Smith 1995).

This chapter provides measures of wealth and details about the distribution of wealth by race/ethnicity to shed light on these summary statistics and the postulated explanations for them. The first section includes measures of, and notes critical distinctions among, these rubrics. Surveys that collect the most commonly cited and readily accessible wealth data also are described in this section. The second section discusses wealth by race/ethnicity—both the frequency with which assets are held and the value of assets. Special emphasis is placed on housing, one of the most frequently held assets and the asset with the greatest value across racial/ethnic groups. The third major section raises issues that arise when measuring wealth and collecting data about it for people of color. The chapter concludes with a summary of its findings.

WEALTH MEASUREMENT

HOW WEALTH IS REPORTED

Gross personal wealth is reported as the gross value of all assets before reduction by the amount of debts.[4] Net personal wealth (or net worth) is the level of wealth (or worth) after all debts have been removed from gross personal wealth (U.S. Census Bureau 1990). Wealth is commonly reported either aggregated for selected population subgroups or per household for each of these groups. Total, or aggregate, net worth for a population group is the sum of the market value of all the assets owned by every member of every household belonging to this group minus the value of the corresponding household debts, or liabilities, both secured and unsecured (Orzechowski and Sepielli 2003).

Aggregate net worth for any population group also can be thought of as the product of multiplying the number of households by the average, or mean, net worth. Put another way, the average, or mean, net worth of a population group is obtained by dividing the total net worth of that group by the number of households in the group. Because of the way it is calculated, mean net worth is affected by all the actually observed values, including very low and very high net worth (known as *outliers*). Median net worth, on the other hand, is the central measure in a distribution of values (i.e., the dollar value that divides all households in a population into two equal-sized groups, one with net worth less than that amount and the other with net worth above that amount). Although mean net worth and median net worth both are used to reflect the wealth of a typical family or household, median net worth is a more appropriate measure for distributions that are skewed. If wealth were evenly distributed across a population, the average, or mean, net worth and the median net worth would be equal, and either could be used. Because wealth distributions generally are skewed, median wealth, or net worth, is reported more frequently in the published research that is the source for this chapter. Means also are provided, however, for comparison since in the social sciences the mean is the most commonly used measure of the central tendency of a distribution of numbers.

HOW WEALTH IS HELD

Social scientists are interested not only in the total amount of wealth held but also in the components of wealth holdings. Net worth, or wealth, is held in a variety of forms, and this mix of wealth holdings is referred to as *portfolio composition* or *portfolio allocation*. In addition to the level and mix of wealth holdings, rates of ownership are reported for assets held. These asset-ownership rates are the percentages of a population that hold any given asset (such as a bank account or a motor vehicle).

Within a wealth portfolio, the assets are commonly distinguished as either housing equity or nonhousing equity (Choudhury 2001/2002). This distinction is made because housing is the major source of wealth for all households in the United States (Caner and Wolff 2004). In addition, nonhousing equity is often characterized as both financial assets and tangible assets, with the major distinction between the two being the degree of liquidity. Financial assets are generally more liquid (i.e., can be converted to cash more easily and quickly) than tangible assets. Commonly used categories of financial and tangible assets are described here:

A. Financial Assets
1. Liquid assets, such as interest-earning assets at financial institutions (e.g., passbook savings accounts, money market deposit accounts, certificates of deposit, and interest-earning checking accounts). Other accounts at financial institutions that are not interest bearing, such as regular checking accounts, also are liquid assets.
2. Stocks and mutual fund shares
3. Bonds—municipal and corporate bonds, as well as U.S. savings bonds
4. IRAs (Individual Retirement Accounts) or Keogh plans[5]
5. Other interest-earning assets, such as money market funds and U.S. government securities, as well as mortgages held from sales of real estate and amounts due from the sale of a business, unit trust, or other financial investments
B. Tangible Assets
1. Equity in motor vehicles
2. Equity in business or profession
3. Other assets (e.g., rental property equity and other real estate equity)

Although some surveys (e.g., the Consumer Expenditure Survey and the Survey of Consumer Finances) collect data on other forms of wealth, such as pensions, these data are not collected in all wealth surveys. Thus, the major forms in which employers provide pensions today (i.e., 401[k], 403[b], and thrift plans[6]) are not included in the preceding list of financial assets. (See discussion of various wealth surveys in this chapter's appendix and in the following section.)

The assets that constitute wealth could alternatively be categorized as either consumable or income producing (Oliver and Shapiro 1989). Consumable assets do not necessarily generate income or future wealth. They include home equity and equity in motor vehicles. Income-producing assets, as the label implies, generate income and potentially generate future wealth. These assets include such items as liquid financial assets, rental property, and net business assets (O'Hare 1983). Net business assets include equity in business or profession, other real estate equity, and possibly "other assets." By either categorization (i.e., housing versus nonhousing equity, or consumable versus income-producing assets), the mix of assets comprising wealth determines likely future wealth accumulation.

WHAT ARE THE MAIN SOURCES OF WEALTH DATA?

The main sources of wealth data for the United States are surveys that have been conducted over time with different populations and differing sample sizes and including somewhat different asset measures. The surveys whose wealth data are most frequently analyzed in published literature include the Consumer Expenditure Survey (CEX), Health and Retirement Study (HRS), National Longitudinal Surveys (NLS), Panel Study of Income Dynamics (PSID), Survey of Consumer Finances (SCF), and Survey of Income and Program Participation (SIPP). Although only one of these (SCF) is designed to be a wealth survey, both the SCF and the PSID are the most widely used data sets for scholarly research about wealth. Each study/survey is described briefly in the appendix to this chapter. A comparison of the surveys follows.

The most commonly used sources of wealth data (CEX, HRS, NLS, PSID, SCF, and SIPP) differ from one another both in the characteristics of the populations from which they collect data and in the type of wealth and other data collected. Thus, for analytical purposes, the choice among wealth survey data sets should be made on the basis of the questions to be addressed. For example, HRS data are most useful for analyzing the wealth holdings of older populations (i.e., those born in 1947 or earlier). The NLS data enable analyses of both mature populations and younger populations (e.g., older men, young men, mature women, and young women). The nationally representative sample surveys (CEX, PSID, SCF, and SIPP) are the best sources for data about the nation as a whole. However, all these surveys tend to underestimate populations difficult to locate such as immigrants and young males, and these frequently excluded populations are likely to include sizable proportions of people of color (Oliver and Shapiro 1995).

The geographic residence of persons eligible to be sampled for the major wealth surveys varies considerably. For example, several surveys (CEX, HRS, and SIPP) exclude from their sampling universe residents of places outside the contiguous United States, such as the Commonwealth of Puerto Rico, U.S. Virgin Islands, and Guam. The HRS draws its samples only from within the forty-eight contiguous states and, thereby, excludes the many people of color in Alaska and Hawai'i and in the U.S. territories. Although the CEX includes all fifty states and the District of Columbia, it excludes the offshore territories from its sampling. The SIPP does not include residents from the Commonwealth of Puerto Rico in its samples. Clearly these sampling design decisions limit the possibility that members of the many diverse subpopulations of color will be represented in the wealth data collected by these surveys.

In the face of geographic sampling decisions that exclude selected populations of color a priori, the major wealth surveys employ various techniques to ensure representation of racial/ethnic subpopulations in their samples. The HRS oversamples African Americans and Hispanics in the forty-eight contiguous states. By oversampling Floridians as well, this survey captures many immigrants and other people of color. During its many years of implementation, the PSID also has oversampled not only for African Americans and Latinos but also for immigrant populations (including Asians), even though these sample sizes are still statistically very small. The SIPP indirectly oversamples racial/ethnic subpopulations because it oversamples for low-income individuals (among whom racial/ethnic subpopulations are overrepresented). In direct opposition to this, however, the SCF oversamples the White population because it oversamples higher-income individuals (who are more likely to be White) in its effort to capture information about all the major forms of wealth. Based on their sampling, the PSID and SIPP would be expected to be the most robust sources of wealth data for people of color (although there are limitations with the use of these data as well).

Differences in the characteristics of the wealth data collected emanate primarily from differences in the purposes of the surveys. For example, the CEX collects data about expenditures, both consumable and durable. Like the CEX, the SIPP and the PSID were not designed primarily to be wealth surveys and, therefore, lack detail about the wealth holdings of persons in the upper tail of the U.S. wealth distribution. Surveys designed primarily to catalog wealth holdings (such as HRS and SCF) include a more comprehensive set of categories for these holdings and sample in such a way as to collect data about wealth in all of these categories. The PSID, for example, reports data for a small fraction of the categories of wealth for which SCF data are provided.

Another difference in the wealth data collected arises from the treatment of nonresponses. The use of bracketed follow-up queries with non-responses has enabled both the HRS and PSID to convert between 75 percent and 80 percent of nonresponses into categorical responses. The SIPP does not use any bracketed questions, the SCF seldom uses them, and the CEX first used them in 2001 (Consumer Expenditure Survey 2003). Thus, the HRS has a much lower conditional nonresponse rate (9 percent) for stock values than other surveys (e.g., the nonresponse rates in SIPP and in the SCF were 42 percent and 26 percent, respectively) (Smith 1995). Table 1.1 summarizes the advantages and disadvantages of the six major data sets.

All of these differences in the populations from which data are collected and in the type of data collected are reflected in the reported values of net worth. If one compares the SCF with the PSID and the SIPP, for example, net worth measures differ for several reasons (Czajka, Jacobson, and Cody 2003). As mentioned previously, median net worth and mean net worth based on data from any single survey conducted in the United States are expected to differ because of the marked, unequal distribution of wealth in this country. However, mean net worth differs for proximate years of data collection from the SCF and from the PSID and the SIPP, with the SCF measure exceeding measures from the other two surveys because of differences in design and implementation. (See tables 1.2a and 1.2b.) The SCF primarily is intended to measure family wealth and thus captures asset holdings more comprehensively than the SIPP and the PSID. Median net worth from the SCF also exceeds these measures for proximate years of PSID and SIPP data. (See tables 1.3a and 1.3b.)

SHARES OF WEALTH BY RACE/ETHNICITY

How does the net wealth of people of color compare with total net wealth in the United States? The earliest and most often available data about wealth, or net worth, of people of color is for Blacks, or African Americans. Since 1967, the share of net wealth holdings by Black households has remained less than the Black share of all U.S. households (which has ranged from 9.4 percent in 1967 to 12.1 percent in 1998 and 12.3 percent in 2000). In 1967, the $101.9 billion in assets held by Blacks constituted 2 percent of the $4,994 billion in total estimated aggregate wealth in the United States (Terrell 1971). By 1979, Blacks reported wealth of $477 billion. Although more than four times aggregate Black wealth in 1967, this figure was only 4.1 percent of total personal wealth in the

TABLE 1.1. Survey Sources of Wealth Data for People of Color

Survey	Sponsoring Entity/ies	Advantages	Disadvantages
Consumer Expenditure Survey (CEX): nationally representative sample survey of U.S. households about their household characteristics, expenditures, income, assets and liabilities	Survey is conducted by the U.S. Census Bureau under contract to the U.S. Bureau of Labor Statistics.	CEX uses bracketed expense categories to avoid nonresponses.	Although information about assets and liabilities is collected as part of CEX, these data often are not deemed as reliable as CEX expenditure data because of unwillingness or inability of respondents to provide accurate information about their assets and liabilities.
Health and Retirement Study (HRS): longitudinal study that asks detailed questions primarily about the health, wealth, retirement, and economic status of age-eligible respondents (i.e., persons born before 1948)	HRS is sponsored by the National Institute on Aging and conducted by the Survey Research Center at the University of Michigan.	HRS oversamples African American and Latino households, as well as residents of Florida (who also are more likely than residents of many other states to be people of color). HRS collects detailed information about assets. HRS uses bracketed expense categories to avoid nonresponses.	Because survey respondents for HRS are older than the sample populations interviewed for other surveys, their wealth is expected to be greater than that of other members of their respective racial/ethnic groups. Sample for survey is drawn from the forty-eight contiguous U.S. states, thus excluding from selection the many people of color who live in Alaska, Hawaii, Puerto Rico, and other U.S. territories.
National Longitudinal Surveys (NLS): longitudinal surveys that collect data about a range of topics (including income and assets) from a variety of populations of different ages (e.g., young women, ages 14–24)	The Bureau of Labor Statistics in the U.S. Department of Labor contracts with a variety of agencies (e.g., Center for Human Resource Research [CHRR] at Ohio State University, U.S. Census Bureau, and National Opinion Research Center [NORC] at the University of Chicago) to conduct the NLS.	NLS can provide data about members of two different age cohorts living in the same household.	Components of the income and asset information in NLS, although available for many years, have changed over time. Thus, comparisons between years are problematic.

Panel Study of Income Dynamics (PSID): longitudinal survey that collects data about demographic characteristics (age, race, sex, marital status), as well as income and wealth for a random sample of individuals and family units (or households)	PSID is collected by the Institute for Social Research at the University of Michigan.	Relative to other surveys, PSID has low nonresponse rates on its wealth questions, presumably because of the rapport developed between the respondents and interviewers over the many years the survey has been conducted (since 1968).	PSID collects data on such small samples of people of color other than African Americans that using data for them is problematic.
Survey of Consumer Finances (SCF): nationally representative interview survey designed to collect wealth data from U.S. families every three years	SCF is sponsored by the Board of Governors of the Federal Reserve System with cooperation from the U.S. Department of Treasury.	SCF is explicitly designed to collect wealth data.	SCF uses a single question to collect information about race and Hispanic origin. SCF oversamples White households because it is designed to collect data about holdings of wealth of all types.
Survey of Income and Program Participation (SIPP): longitudinal survey of the noninstitutionalized, resident adult population in households in the United States; collects wealth and asset data as a supplement to its core questions about labor force participation, income, demographic characteristics, and government program participation	SIPP is conducted by the U.S. Census Bureau.	Emphasis of SIPP on collecting data from low-income households who are eligible for government assistance programs translates into an oversampling of people of color (since many people of color are disproportionately poor).	People living in military barracks and in the Commonwealth of Puerto Rico are excluded from sampling frame. Fact that SIPP emphasizes collecting data from low-income households who are eligible for government assistance programs means that SIPP collects limited detail from households with wealth and that its wealth data are limited in quantity.

United States in 1979 of $11,489 billion (O'Hare 1983).[7] In 1984, the wealth holdings of African Americans ($337.5 billion) were less than their 1979 holdings, and only 3 percent of the $11,204.7 billion of wealth holdings of all U.S. households that year. Wealth holdings by African Americans as a proportion of the wealth of all households fell short of both their share of money income (7.2 percent) and their share of all households (11 percent) in that year (Brimmer 1988).

TABLE 1.2a. Mean Net Worth by Race/Ethnicity, 1989, 1992, 1993, 1994, and 1995 (numbers in thousands of 2001 dollars)

Households/Families[a]	1989 PSID	1992 HRS	1992 SCF	1993 SIPP	1994 PSID	1995 SCF	1995 SIPP
All	185.0		230.5	120.3	180.5	244.8	118.3
White	209.7	338.5		131.6	205.0		130.1
White non-Hispanic			274.8			289.8	
Black/African American	42.8	97.0		34.3	42.2		35.2
Hispanic/Latino[b]		98.6		46.8			45.0
Non-White or Hispanic			95.8			89.1	

Sources: *Cross-Sectional Wealth and Financial Wealth* 2000 for PSID 1989 and 1994; Choudhury 2001/2002 for HRS 1992; Aizcorbe et al. 2003 for SCF 1992 and 1995; Eller and Fraser 1995 (unpublished tabulations) for SIPP 1993; and Davern and Fisher 2001 for SIPP 1995.

[a]Data from the Panel Study of Income Dynamics (PSID) and the Survey of Consumer Finances (SCF) are for families, while data from the Survey of Income and Program Participation (SIPP) are for households. These concepts are similar enough that wealth data from these surveys are comparable. Data from the Health and Retirement Study (HRS) reflect only the net worth of individuals (and the households in which they reside) in various older-age cohorts who are likely to be wealthier than other households of the same racial/ethnic groups.

[b]Hispanics/Latinos may be of any race. Both terms are used here to reflect the variations in usage among the data sources.

TABLE 1.2b. Mean Net Worth by Race/Ethnicity, 1998, 1999, 2000, and 2001 (numbers in thousands of 2001 dollars)

Households/Families[a]	1998 SCF	1998 SIPP	1999 PSID	2000 SIPP	2001 PSID	2001 SCF
All	307.4	162.2	219.0	187.3	248.9	395.5
White		181.2	262.0	209.4	291.8	
White non-Hispanic	363.9	193.9		225.1		482.9
Black/African American		35.0	38.5	40.9	59.1	
Hispanic/Latino[b]		51.4		59.2		
Non-White or Hispanic	109.9					115.3

Sources: Aizcorbe et al. 2003 for SCF 1998 and 2001; Orzechowski and Sepielli (detailed tables) 2003 for SIPP 1998 and 2000; and Gouskova and Stafford 2002 for PSID 1999 and 2001.

[a]Data from the Panel Study of Income Dynamics (PSID) and the Survey of Consumer Finances (SCF) are for families, while data from the Survey of Income and Program Participation (SIPP) are for households. These concepts are similar enough that wealth data from these surveys are comparable.

[b]Hispanics/Latinos may be of any race. Both terms are used here to reflect the variations in usage among the data sources.

By 1993, although total U.S. wealth holdings had grown to $11,607.5 billion, the wealth of African Americans ($385.4 billion) remained 3 percent of the total (Eller and Fraser 1995). African Americans held 7.6 percent of total money income and were 11.6 percent of all households at that time. Viewed differently, if African Americans held a share of wealth comparable to their share of all households (i.e., 11.6 percent), their aggregate net wealth would have been $1,346.5 billion, or $961.1 billion

TABLE 1.3a. Median Net Worth by Race/Ethnicity, 1989, 1992, 1993, 1994, and 1995 (numbers in thousands of 2001 dollars)

Households/Families[a]	1989 PSID	1992 HRS	1992 SCF	1993 SIPP	1994 PSID	1995 SCF	1995 SIPP
All	54.7		61.3	45.3	58.5	66.4	46.4
White	70.0	157.0			55.2	75.2	56.5
White non-Hispanic			86.2			88.5	
Black/African American	7.1	37.7		5.3	8.9		8.2
Hispanic/Latino[b]		44.5		5.6			8.4
Non-White or Hispanic			14.8			18.3	

Sources: *Cross-Sectional Wealth and Financial Wealth* 2000 for PSID 1989 and 1994; Choudhury 2001/2002 for HRS 1992; Aizcorbe et al. 2003 for SCF 1992 and 1995; Eller and Fraser 1995 for SIPP 1993; and Davern and Fisher 2001 for SIPP 1995.

[a]Data from the Panel Study of Income Dynamics (PSID) and the Survey of Consumer Finances (SCF) are for families, while data from the Survey of Income and Program Participation (SIPP) are for households. These concepts are similar enough that wealth data from these surveys are comparable. Data from the Health and Retirement Study (HRS) reflect only the net worth of individuals (and the households in which they reside) in various older-age cohorts who are likely to be wealthier than other households of the same racial/ethnic groups.

[b]Hispanics/Latinos may be of any race. Both terms are used here to reflect the variations in usage among the data sources.

TABLE 1.3b. Median Net Worth by Race/Ethnicity, 1998, 1999, 2000, and 2001 (numbers in thousands of 2001 dollars)

Households/Families[a]	1998 SCF	1998 SIPP	1999 PSID	2000 SIPP	2001 PSID	2001 SCF
All	78.0	51.9	53.1	56.5	63.0	86.1
White		64.6	80.2	70.8	95.0	
White non-Hispanic	103.4	73.8		81.5		120.9
Black/African American		6.4	6.8	7.7	7.5	
Hispanic/Latino[b]		7.5		10.0		
Non-White or Hispanic	17.9					17.1

Sources: Aizcorbe et al. 2003 for SCF 1998 and 2001; Orzechowski and Sepielli (detailed tables) 2003 for SIPP 1998 and 2000; and Gouskova and Stafford 2002 for PSID 1999 and 2001.

[a]Data from the Panel Study of Income Dynamics (PSID) and the Survey of Consumer Finances (SCF) are for families, while data from the Survey of Income and Program Participation (SIPP) are for households. These concepts are similar enough that wealth data from these surveys are comparable.

[b]Hispanics/Latinos may be of any race. Both terms are used here to reflect the variations in usage among the data sources.

greater than their actual 1993 holdings. Thus, African Americans had disproportionately small shares of both income and net wealth through the first half of the 1990s.

In recent years, the proportion that the wealth of Black households was of the wealth of all U.S. households has remained less than the share of Black households out of all U.S. households. The same is true for Latino households. In particular, in 1998, although Black households were 12.1 percent of all households in the United States, the wealth of these households ($439.8 billion) was still only about 3 percent of the wealth of all households ($15,233.8 billion). Latino households were almost 9 percent of all households that year, with their wealth ($465.4 billion) also about 3 percent of the wealth of all U.S. households. By 2000, the wealth and number of households had grown for both Blacks and Latinos, but not enough to alter the relationships identified in 1998. Although Latino households were more than 9 percent of all households and Black households were more than 12 percent of all households that year, their wealth ($594.0 billion for Latino households and $539.0 billion for African American households) was still about 3 percent of the total U.S. wealth ($18,123.3 billion).[8]

LEVELS OF WEALTH

The net worth of persons in the United States as a whole and when examined separately by racial/ethnic group has increased since 1990. This holds true when net worth is measured by either its mean (average) or its median (the level that defines two groups of asset holders: one with more wealth than this level and the other with less wealth than this level). (See tables 1.2a, 1.2b, 1.3a, and 1.3b.) Means and medians from each of the selected data sources show a generally rising trend over the 1989–2001 period. However, as indicated in the description of the most commonly used wealth data sets, wealth (or net worth) measures and values vary greatly by source.

The SCF and the HRS report higher means than the PSID and the SIPP. According to the SCF, mean net worth for all households increased by nearly 72 percent between 1992 and 2001 (from $230,500 to $395,500) (tables 1.2a and 1.2b). In each proximate year, SIPP reported mean net worth significantly less than the SCF values, and PSID values were between the SIPP and SCF levels. Over the 1989–2001 period (and regardless of data source), mean net worth for White or White non-Hispanic households was at least three times that of Black, or African American, households and at least double that of Latino households. In other words, over this period the Black/White mean wealth ratio was one to three or less, and the Latino/White mean wealth ratio was one to two or less. In 2000, the mean net worth of African American households ($40,900) was about a fifth of the mean net worth for White non-Hispanic households ($225,100), and the mean net worth of Hispanic/Latino households ($59,200) was almost a fourth of the mean net worth for White households, according to the SIPP. In 2001, a similar pattern was evident: the average net worth values for non-White or Hispanic households ($115,300 from SCF) and for African American families ($59,100 from PSID) were about a fourth of the corresponding mean wealth for White non-Hispanic households ($482,900 from SCF) and for White families ($291,800 from PSID). (See table 1.2b.)

Median net worth reveals similar patterns in each of the surveys represented and over time. According to the SCF, median net wealth for all households increased by 40 percent between 1992 and 2001 (from $61,300 to $86,100) (tables 1.3a and 1.3b). The SIPP data reveal that median net worth for Blacks increased from $5,300 in 1993 to $7,700 in 2000 (or by 45 percent). For Hispanics over the same period and also using SIPP data, median net worth was comparable in 1993 at $5,600 but increased by nearly 80 percent (to $10,000) by 2000. Although in published SCF data non-Whites and Hispanics are combined into a single category "non-White or Hispanic," the median net worth for households in this category increased from only $14,800 in 1992 to $17,100 in 2001 (nearly a 16 percent increase). In addition, the respective wealth ratios are about one to six for the 1992 median net worth for non-White or Hispanic households relative to White non-Hispanic households and one to seven in 2001 for the median net worth of non-White or Hispanic households when compared with White non-Hispanic households.

These huge gaps in median net worth between people of color and Whites are explained in part by the large shares of African American households and of Latino households (compared with White non-Hispanic households) that report zero or negative net worth and the small shares that report high net worth. The 2000 SIPP reports that 29 percent of Black households and 28 percent of Hispanic-origin households have zero or negative net worth. These shares are more than double the 11 percent of White non-Hispanic households and the 13 percent of White households that are similarly without assets (Orzechowski and Sepielli 2003). This pattern is confirmed at the upper end of the distribution where we find that one in every five (or 20 percent of) White and White non-Hispanic households has a net worth of $250,000 or greater, while only 3 percent of Black households and 5 percent of Hispanic households report this much net worth.

ASSET-OWNERSHIP RATES

As noted previously, asset-ownership rates represent the frequency with which various assets are held. When analyzed by the frequency with which they are reported, the four most frequently held assets are common across racial/ethnic groups. The asset category in which the largest proportion of households reported holdings in 2000 was "equity in motor vehicles," followed by "equity in own home," "interest-earning assets at financial institutions," and, finally, "regular checking accounts" (i.e., checking accounts on which interest is not earned) (table 1.4). Among all U.S. households, 86 percent reported equity in motor vehicles, 67 percent reported equity in own home, 65 percent reported interest-earning assets at financial institutions, and 38 percent reported having regular checking accounts.[9] Shares among White non-Hispanic households by type of asset are slightly larger than for all households—89 percent have motor vehicles, 73 percent have home equity, 71 percent have interest-earning assets at financial institutions, and 39 percent have regular checking accounts.

Shares of Black and Hispanic-origin households with the four most frequently held assets are markedly lower than the shares among White households. Among Black households, 70 percent have equity in motor vehicles, 47 percent have home equity, 42 percent have interest-earning

TABLE 1.4. Percentage of Households, by Race/Ethnicity, with Most Frequently Held Assets (2000)

	Black	Hispanic-Origin[a]	White	White Non-Hispanic	All
Equity in motor vehicles	70	78	88	89	86
Equity in own home	47	48	71	73	67
Interest-earning assets at financial institutions[b]	42	45	69	71	65
Regular checking accounts[b]	30	32	38	39	38

Source: Detailed tables from Orzechowski and Sepielli 2003.

[a]The term *Hispanic-origin* (rather than *Latino*) is used here because data were reported thus by Orzechowski and Sepielli 2003.

[b]The category "interest-earning assets at financial institutions" includes passbook savings accounts, money market deposit accounts, certificates of deposit (CDs), and interest-earning checking accounts. "Regular checking accounts" are reported separately because they are not interest-earning accounts.

assets at financial institutions, and 30 percent have regular checking accounts. (See table 1.4.) Hispanic-origin households are more likely than Black households (but less likely than White households) to have equity in motor vehicles (78 percent), although the frequency with which African American and Hispanic-origin households report having home equity, interest-earning assets at financial institutions, and regular checking accounts is comparable.

Two of the four most frequently held assets are consumable, and one of these—equity in motor vehicles—is the asset most frequently reported by households of all racial/ethnic groups. The other most frequently held consumable asset is home equity, with nearly half of Black and Hispanic-origin households and nearly three-fourths (73 percent) of White non-Latino households reporting this asset.

The remaining two most frequently held assets—interest-earning assets at financial institutions and regular checking accounts—are treated differently in the various wealth data sets. In addition, the major data sets do not categorize the assets held by consumers at financial institutions in such a way that one can determine at a glance ownership rates for the generic "bank account" or "transactions account" among people of color. The various surveys reveal, however, that people of color are less likely to own any of the accounts (e.g., savings accounts or regular checking accounts) commonly subsumed under these generic labels. Being less likely to have bank accounts or transactions accounts at financial institutions translates into people of color being more likely to incur additional expenses (i.e., fees associated with purchasing money orders rather than using personal checks to pay bills) to meet their ongoing financial obligations.

In particular, the SIPP data do not include, as a unified category, ownership rates for bank accounts or transactions accounts. However, SIPP data do provide ownership rates for passbook savings accounts and regular checking accounts separately. Both the SCF and PSID surveys provide data comparable to the familiar terms *bank accounts* or *transactions accounts*. In 2001, for example, the SCF indicated that "transactions account" ownership rates were 91 percent nationally (Aizcorbe et al. 2003), while the PSID reported "bank account" ownership rates (i.e., checking accounts and savings accounts) of 82.3 percent (Gouskova and Stafford 2002). Rates of account ownership for non-Whites are much lower than they are for Whites. Based on an analysis of SCF data, Aizcorbe and others (2003) report that about 21 percent of non-White or Latino families do not have transactions accounts, compared with the only about 5 percent of White non-Hispanic families without such accounts. Looking at Blacks specifically, PSID data suggest that about 44 percent of Black families do not have a bank account, while the comparable figure for Whites is only 12 percent (Gouskova and Stafford, 2002).

The SIPP data reveal that the dominant form of interest-earning assets at financial institutions is passbook savings accounts. Passbook savings accounts are held by 51 percent of all asset-holding households, 55 percent of asset-holding White non-Latino households, 37 percent of asset-holding Hispanic-origin households, and 35 percent of asset-holding Black households (Orzechowski and Sepielli 2003). The other financial asset in the top four—regular checking accounts—is held with less frequency than passbook savings accounts: roughly between a third (33 percent) and two-fifths (40 percent) of African American, Hispanic-origin, and White households have regular checking accounts (table 1.4). However, a larger percentage of African American, Latino, and White households have checking accounts (either interest earning or regular) than have passbook savings accounts. The shares of African American households, Latino households, and White non-Hispanic households that owned either type of checking account in 2000 were 48 percent, 49 percent, and 76 percent, respectively (Orzechowski and Sepielli 2003).

Looking beyond the four most frequently held assets to the less frequently held, all are found to be potentially income producing, and greater diversity emerges in the asset-ownership rates by race/ethnicity of household. "Stocks and mutual fund shares" was the asset category most likely to be held in 2000. However, the share of households with stocks and mutual fund shares ranged from about 10 percent of Black and Hispanic households to nearly a third of White and White non-Hispanic households, and more than a fourth of the households of all racial/ethnic groups combined. (See tables 1.5a–1.5d.) In the early 1990s, among the less frequently held assets, the major ones held were U.S. savings bonds (for Black and Hispanic-origin households) and IRAs and Keogh plans (for White households and households of all racial/ethnic groups combined). The run-up in stock values during the 1990s may be evident in this shift in the ranking of less frequently held assets. In 2000, U.S. savings bonds were the second most frequently held of the assets in table 1.5a for Blacks, being held by 7 percent. Only 4 percent of Hispanic households held U.S. savings bonds (fourth ranked) (table 1.5b). However, U.S. savings bonds were held by a higher percentage of Whites (16

TABLE 1.5a. Percentage of Black Households with Less Frequently Held Assets (2000)

Stocks and mutual fund shares	10.2
U.S. savings bonds	6.9
IRAs or Keogh plans	6.5
Equity in business or profession	4.7
Other real estate equity	2.3
Rental property equity	2.2
Other assets	0.9
Other interest-earning assets	0.8

Source: Detailed tables from Orzechowski and Sepielli 2003.

TABLE 1.5b. Percentage of Hispanic-Origin Households with Less Frequently Held Assets (2000)

Stocks and mutual fund shares	9.2
Equity in business or profession	8.1
IRAs or Keogh plans	8.1
U.S. savings bonds	3.9
Rental property equity	3.0
Other real estate equity	2.6
Other assets	2.2
Other interest-earning assets	0.4

Source: Detailed tables from Orzechowski and Sepielli 2003.
Note: The term *Hispanic-origin* (rather than *Latino*) is used here because data were reported thus by Orzechowski and Sepielli 2003.

TABLE 1.5c. Percentage of White and White Non-Hispanic Households with Less Frequently Held Assets (2000)

	White	White Non-Hispanic
Stocks and mutual fund shares	29.7	31.9
IRAs or Keogh plans	25.7	27.5
U.S. savings bonds	16.1	17.3
Equity in business or profession	11.6	12.0
Other real estate equity	7.3	7.8
Rental property equity	5.2	5.4
Other assets	4.4	4.6
Other interest-earning assets	3.7	4.1

Source: Detailed tables from Orzechowski and Sepielli 2003.

percent) than by either Blacks or Hispanics, even though they are third ranked among these less frequently held assets for Whites, behind stocks and mutual fund shares, and IRAs or Keogh plans.

Equity in business or profession is another asset ranked differently by race/ethnicity. Nearly 5 percent of Black households reported having this asset, the fourth of the eight assets ranked in decreasing order of frequency held in table 1.5a. However, equity in business or profession is the second most frequently held asset (among the eight assets being considered here) by Hispanic-origin households (8 percent) and the fourth most frequently held asset among White households (12 percent). (See tables 1.5b and 1.5c.) Although the shares reported by asset-holding households of all racial/ethnic groups (table 1.5d) are somewhat smaller than those for White households (table 1.5c), the rank orderings of assets are the same.

VALUES OF INDIVIDUAL ASSETS HELD

Among racial/ethnic groups, the most commonly held assets (featured in table 1.4; see also tables 1.5a–1.5d) do not necessarily have the greatest median or mean values. In addition, differences in the value of asset holdings by race/ethnicity are marked.

By median asset value in 2000, the highest-ranking category of net worth for all the racial/ethnic groups except Blacks was rental property equity, followed by home equity, other real estate equity, other interest-earning assets, IRAs or Keogh plans, other assets, and 401(k) and Thrift Savings plans. (See table 1.6.) Of these assets, the ranking for Blacks in decreasing order of value is as follows: home equity, rental property equity, other real estate equity, 401(k) and Thrift Savings plans, and,

TABLE 1.5d. Percentage of All Households with Less Frequently Held Assets (2000)

Stocks and mutual fund shares	27.1
IRAs or Keogh plans	23.1
U.S. savings bonds	14.7
Equity in business or profession	10.8
Other real estate equity	6.6
Rental property equity	4.9
Other assets	3.9
Other interest-earning assets	3.3

Source: Detailed tables from Orzechowski and Sepielli 2003.

finally, IRAs or Keogh plans. African Americans have greater median equity in business or profession ($10,270) than in either IRAs or Keogh plans, or 401(k) and thrift plans. Their holdings of stocks and mutual fund shares ($8,216) equal the value of their IRAs or Keogh plans. Although the top-ranking category is the same for Hispanic-origin and White households, the magnitudes of the asset values differ. White households have $74,458 in median rental property equity, compared with $63,674 for Hispanic households. Median net value of rental property equity for Black households is $30,810, second in value to their $35,945 in home equity. This pattern of asset values contrasts with the ranking for Blacks, Whites, and Hispanics in 1993, when home equity was the greatest-valued asset for all three groups, followed by rental property equity, other assets, and other real estate equity (Leigh 2003).

By mean asset value in 2000, although rankings differ for Black households and for Hispanic-origin households, the highest-ranking categories of wealth for households of all racial/ethnic groups and for White and for White non-Hispanic households in decreasing order of value are rental property equity, equity in business or profession, stocks and mutual fund shares, other real estate equity, other interest-earning assets, and home equity. (See table 1.7.) The rankings by value for equity in business or profession and other real estate equity differ for the four groups of households. For White households the mean value of rental property equity exceeds that of all other assets, while for African American asset-holding households, mean equity in business or profession ($103,413) exceeds two similarly valued assets: equity in own home ($47,292) and rental

TABLE 1.6. Assets with Largest Median Net Values in Asset-Holding Households, by Race/Ethnicity (2000, in 2001 dollars)

	Black	Hispanic-Origin[a]	White	White Non-Hispanic	All
Rental property equity	30,810	63,674	74,458	75,998	71,890
Equity in own home	35,945	39,026	61,620	65,933	60,593
Other real estate equity	13,351	30,810	41,080	41,080	41,080
Other interest-earning assets	NA	NA	29,796	30,273	29,796
IRAs or Keogh plans	8,216	15,405	25,675	26,240	24,648
Other assets	NA	6,213	24,648	25,675	22,594
401(k) and thrift plans	9,243	12,324	22,286	23,313	20,540

Source: Detailed tables from Orzechowski and Sepielli 2003.

Note: NA = not available.

[a]The term *Hispanic-origin* (rather than *Latino*) is used here because data were reported thus by Orzechowski and Sepielli 2003.

property equity ($47,237). Other real estate ($98,896) is the asset with the greatest average value for Hispanics, followed by rental property equity ($92,437). Holdings of other real estate equity also exceed mean equity in business or profession ($76,461) and mean equity in own home ($62,902) among Hispanics.

The income-producing, financial assets among the highest-valued assets for any of the racial/ethnic groups in 2000 included stocks and mutual fund shares, IRAs or Keogh plans, 401(k) and Thrift Savings plans (median values), and other interest-earning assets (mean values). (See tables 1.6 and 1.7.) Generally, White households and White non-Hispanic households have greater net financial wealth of these types than either African American or Hispanic-origin households. For example, the median and mean values for stocks and mutual funds held by Whites ($20,540 and $112,164, respectively) greatly exceed these values for African Americans ($8,216 and $39,724, respectively) and Hispanics ($10,270 and $53,532, respectively). (See table 1.8.)

TABLE 1.7. Assets with Largest Mean Net Values in Asset-Holding Households, by Race/Ethnicity (2000, in 2001 dollars)

	Black	Hispanic-Origin[a]	White	White Non-Hispanic	All
Rental property equity	47,237	92,437	145,257	148,467	143,065
Equity in business or profession	103,413	76,461	139,825	143,371	133,353
Stocks and mutual fund shares	39,724	53,532	112,164	113,969	107,830
Other real estate equity	30,898	98,896	105,424	105,587	101,681
Other interest-earning assets	NA	NA	100,494	100,773	99,118
Equity in own home	47,292	62,902	93,490	95,658	89,968

Source: Detailed tables from Orzechowski and Sepielli 2003.
Note: NA = not available.
[a]The term *Hispanic-origin* (rather than *Latino*) is used here because data were reported thus by Orzechowski and Sepielli 2003.

TABLE 1.8. Median and Mean Values of Stocks and Mutual Fund Shares in Asset-Holding Households, by Race/Ethnicity (2000, in 2001 dollars)

	Black	Hispanic-Origin[a]	White	White Non-Hispanic	All
Median values	8,216	10,270	20,540	20,540	19,788
Mean values	39,724	53,532	112,164	113,969	107,830

Source: Detailed tables from Orzechowski and Sepielli 2003.
[a]The term *Hispanic-origin* (rather than *Latino*) is used here because data were reported thus by Orzechowski and Sepielli 2003.

Home equity is the only asset that is highly ranked by both its value and its ownership rate. Home ownership is associated with greater wealth holding in the United States, although the direction of causality is unclear. In addition, such factors as the lower incomes and adverse locational characteristics of homes purchased by African Americans have been found to account for only 22 percent of the racial wealth gap (Blau and Graham 1990). The major role of home ownership in wealth is suggested by comparisons of the median net wealth of owners and renters. According to the 2001 SCF, the median net wealth of owners far exceeds the median net wealth of renters for Black non-Hispanic, Hispanic-origin, and White non-Hispanic households (*State of the Nation's Housing* 2003). In 2001, Black owners reported median net wealth of $69,000 versus median net wealth among Black renters of $1,890. Hispanic-origin owner households reported median net wealth of $70,560, versus $2,650 for renter households. Similarly, White owner households reported median net wealth of $198,900, in contrast to $8,120 for White renter households.

As the preceding text indicates, both the value of home equity and the relative wealth of owners and renters reflect a persistent racial disparity, with holdings by Whites far in excess of the holdings by African Americans and Hispanics. What explains these disparities? How are these disparities reconciled with research findings such as the following: savings rates for Blacks and Whites approach equality as income rises, and Blacks (more than Whites) tend to concentrate their wealth in home equity as income rises (Long and Caudill 1992; Oliver and Shapiro 1995)? In addition, independent of income level, home equity constitutes a larger proportion of the net wealth of Blacks than of Whites. The 1967 Survey of Economic Opportunity revealed that equity in a home constituted 67 percent of the net worth of Black households but only 40 percent of the net worth of White households (Kain and Quigley 1972). In 1988, home equity accounted for 63 percent of the net worth of Blacks but only 43 percent of the net worth of Whites (Oliver and Shapiro 1995). In 2000, this share remained constant for Blacks (62 percent), although it had declined to 31 percent for White non-Hispanic households at that time (Orzechowski and Sepielli 2003).

Home equity dominates the wealth of Black households, even though Whites have higher home ownership rates and generally own more valuable homes than African Americans (O'Hare 1983). In 2002, the home ownership rate for Whites was 74.7 percent and ranged from a low of 48 percent for persons younger than age 35, to 86 percent among persons ages 65 to 74. That same year, the rate for Blacks was 48.9 percent (with a range from 26 percent among persons younger than age 35, to 74 percent for persons ages 75 and older). For Hispanic-origin households, the home ownership rate was 47.4 percent, reflecting a range from 30 percent (persons younger than age 35) to 69 percent (persons ages 65 to 74). Asian and "Other" (Pacific Islander, Aleut, and Native American) households combined were more likely to own homes (53.9 percent) than either Black or Hispanic households, but less likely than White households. The lowest Asian and Other home ownership rate (31 percent) was for householders under the age of 35, and the age cohort most likely to own was 55 to 64 years of age (*State of the Nation's Housing* 2003). See appendix 2 for discussion of racial disparities in home ownership.

ISSUES: PEOPLE OF COLOR & WEALTH

One of the purposes of this chapter is to assess the nature and availability of data about the wealth, or net worth, of people of color in published and otherwise readily accessible sources (such as Web sites). Although a variety of sources for wealth data were identified, all of the data were collected using somewhat different measures for wealth, or net worth. In addition, often the samples drawn of survey populations are so small that they limit the racial/ethnic and gender detail that the wealth data can provide. These definitional and survey issues are discussed next along with issues specific to the various racial/ethnic groups.

DEFINITIONS & SAMPLES

Definitional issues related to the wealth holdings of people of color transcend the arithmetic concerns about the use of mean or median, noted earlier in this chapter. More problematic for people of color are the components included in and excluded from net worth measures. For example, two populations of color—recent immigrants and older African Americans—are generally believed to retain substantial cash holdings. These populations are believed to be more likely than other people of color to avoid storing their wealth in vehicles that are captured in the most common wealth measures for two main reasons—unfamiliarity with the financial system of the United States and the legacy of having lived through the Depression. Other examples are provided in the section entitled "Racial/Ethnic Groups."

In addition to not capturing all the forms in which people of color may hold assets, the sample surveys conducted to collect wealth and other data seldom include large enough samples of all the racial/ethnic groups of interest to allow detailed analyses for them. For example, because the SCF wants to capture the least frequently held assets (such as closely held businesses) in its measure of wealth, or net worth, this survey oversamples wealthier people, who generally are less likely to be people of color. On the other hand, the SIPP is more likely to include people of color because it oversamples lower-income populations (among whom people of color are overrepresented) and individuals who are eligible to participate in the programs in which the SIPP has an interest. However, even with this oversampling of low-income people, the SIPP does not use samples large enough to produce reliable wealth estimates for populations other than White, White non-Hispanic, Black, Hispanic-origin (of any race), and not Hispanic-origin (Orzechowski and Sepielli 2003). In addition, although SIPP data are robust enough to provide median net worth by type of household (married couple, male householder, and female householder), as well as for the racial/ethnic groups noted here, these data are not robust enough to also provide statistics for Black female householders. Analyses by Altonji, Doraszelski, and Segal (2000) suggest that the notable differences among the wealth holdings of Black married couples, White married couples, Black females, Black males, White females, and White males evident in PSID data could be unraveled if larger sample sizes were used to generate robust net worth estimates by race/ethnicity and gender simultaneously.

RACIAL/ETHNIC GROUPS

One measurement issue has the potential to affect wealth data for members of all racial/ethnic groups, especially those who marry across racial/ethnic lines. Although the race/ethnicity of members of a single family/household may vary, the SCF (and other surveys in which the family or household is the unit of observation) assigns each family as a whole the self-identified race/ethnicity of the interview respondent (Aizcorbe et al. 2003). Depending on the race/ethnicity of members of the affected families and whether family asset accretion for mixed-race families is markedly different from that for racially homogeneous families, this racial/ethnic assignation rule may bias wealth estimates. The direction of bias would depend on whether the mixed-race or the racially homogeneous family was likely to have greater wealth.

Another measurement issue that affects most subpopulations of color is the exclusion of proceeds from rotating credit associations from discussions of wealth. This wealth enhancement tradition is found among several racial/ethnic populations: Asian Americans, Black non-Spanish-speaking immigrants to the United States from the West Indies (e.g., Jamaica or Trinidad) and Africa (e.g., Nigeria or Sierra Leone), and Latinos (e.g., persons from the Dominican Republic). Although it has numerous labels,[10] regardless of the moniker, the system operates the same. At some regular interval, most often weekly or monthly, each member of the network will pay a fixed amount of money to an individual who is the "banker." The proceeds of this pool are given by the banker to one member of the association on a rotating schedule. For example, if each of twelve members of a rotating credit association contributes $100 monthly, each member would receive $1,200 once a year. Although the concept is seldom (if ever) queried about in wealth surveys and its prevalence within U.S. society is unknown, this system is sometimes employed as an alternative means to meet one's financial obligations. In addition, sums accumulated via these associations are used for such things as down payments on homes and businesses (Hafford 2003).[11]

Asset accumulation issues also exist for individual racial/ethnic populations among the major groups. Some of these are noted in the following.

American Indians/Alaska Natives. The treaty relationships between the federal government and American Indian/Alaska Native nations make it difficult to determine and/or acquire ownership of reservation land to develop for housing or business purposes (U.S. General Accounting Office 2002). However, because more than half of American Indians/Alaska Natives (56 percent) live in metropolitan areas and not on reservations or trust lands, this fact has not constrained home ownership rates among these populations any more than for other people of color (Forquera 2001). A 55 percent majority of American Indians/Alaska Natives owned their homes in 2000, a somewhat larger share than among Black or Latino households (U.S. Census Bureau 2000). Also, as measured by dissimilarity scores,[12] American Indians/Alaska Natives in metropolitan areas are less segregated from Whites than are either Blacks or

Latinos, a fact that suggests that their housing choices and wealth accumulation thereby may be more volitional than for other people of color (Iceland, Weinberg, and Steinmetz 2002).

The major issue for American Indians/Alaska Natives is how infrequently data about their wealth holdings are collected and reported. Surveys (such as the HRS) that limit their sampling to the forty-eight contiguous states by definition limit the likelihood of interviewing Alaska Natives. Because American Indians/Alaska Natives are a small population (i.e., 4.1 million persons identified themselves as American Indians/Alaska Natives either alone or in combination with one or more other race[s] in the 2000 census), selecting them for survey samples is unlikely without oversampling for them and targeting the western states, where 43 percent of them live (Ogunwole 2002).* Because a fourth of American Indians/Alaska Natives live in California and Oklahoma combined, conducting a wealth survey in these two states would be a cost-effective way to collect data about them. Without targeted surveying such as this, wealth data for American Indians/Alaska Natives will remain irretrievably subsumed in categories such as "Non-White or Hispanic" (as in tables 1.2a, 1.2b, 1.3a, and 1.3b) or "Asian and Other."

Asian Americans. As for American Indians/Alaska Natives, little information is available in the published literature about the net worth of Asian Americans. Limiting the sampling for surveys such as the HRS (to the forty-eight contiguous states) and the CEX (to exclude offshore U.S. territories such as Guam) lessens the likelihood that Asian American subpopulations would be included in the wealth data ultimately collected. Available data suggest, however, that Asian Americans may be somewhat wealthier than other racial/ethnic populations. Using SCF data, Wolff (1998) shows that between 1983 and 1995 the proportion of Asian and other populations (including American Indians/Alaska Natives and other racial groups) among the top 1 percent of wealth holders more than doubled (to 3.9 percent) so that it equaled the proportion of Asians and others in the U.S. population in 1995. The category "Asian Americans (and Others)" is the only population grouping equally represented among the top 1 percent of U.S. wealth holders and among the entire U.S. population. Although American Indians/Alaska Natives are included

*Zagorsky (chap. 5) specifically addresses issues about wealth creation and how to find data on wealth holdings for Native Americans. Ong (chap. 6) also finds innovative ways to explore the wealth of Native Hawaiians [*Editors*].

in this category, their small population size relative to Asian Americans suggests that these wealth data primarily reflect Asian Americans.*

Deciding that Asian Americans collectively are a relatively wealthy population, however, may obscure the variation in wealth among sub-populations of Asian Americans. Asian populations resident in the United States the longest (such as Chinese and Japanese) may be wealthier than newcomers such as Vietnamese or Hmong, who are likely to have come to the United States as refugees. In addition, the longer-term residents clearly have had more time to establish themselves and build assets in the United States. However, to the extent that the more recent Asian immigrants have come to the United States under the ten thousand investor (EB-5) visas made available annually, these newcomers, particularly from India and China (the second- and third-ranked countries after Mexico in number of immigrants to the United States in 2001), may be wealthier than other Asian immigrants (U.S. Census Bureau 2003). Immigrants with EB-5 visas must bring with them at least $500,000 to invest in a business in the United States, after they arrive (U.S. Citizenship and Immigration Services 2003).

Where Asian Americans settle in the United States also may influence their accumulation of wealth. Many Asian Americans live in western states (such as California and Hawai'i) and in some of the most expensive cities in the United States (e.g., Honolulu, Los Angeles, and San Francisco) (Barnes and Bennett 2002). Living in expensive places such as these may influence wealth accumulation in two ways. It may limit the likelihood of home ownership because of its cost. Since home equity is the major form of wealth for all U.S. households, having a reduced probability of ownership can translate into holding less wealth. However, those households able to own homes in these high-cost places are more likely to see these assets appreciate in value and, therefore, have more housing wealth than populations living in other parts of the United States. Thus, the effect of living in high-cost areas on the value of housing wealth is indeterminate. In addition to its expensiveness, though, in 2000, the San Francisco metropolitan area had the distinction of being the place in which Asians and Pacific Islanders were more segregated from Whites than in any other locality (Iceland, Weinberg, and Steinmetz 2002). Although the dissimilarity scores that measure the segrega-

*Ong and Prataporn (chap. 7) and Dymski, Mohanty, and Li (chap. 9) further explore issues of measuring and understanding the wealth of Asian Americans. Ong (chap. 6) explores similar issues for Native Hawaiians [*Editors*].

tion of Asian Americans from other racial/ethnic groups are smaller than for Blacks and Latinos, if segregation lessens housing values for Asians in the same manner as it does for other groups, another factor may operate to reduce the housing wealth and thereby the total wealth of Asian Americans.

Blacks/African Americans. Among people of color, the most data are available for and the most research has been conducted about issues related to wealth among the population known as Black or African American. Most of the research has had as its objective to identify the determinants of the Black-White wealth gap using a variety of techniques (such as simple OLS [ordinary least squares] regressions, median regressions, nonparametric estimation techniques, or "decomposition analysis").* Such things as income level, on the one hand, and housing market discrimination and segregation, on the other, are examined as potential determinants.

In general, the Black-White wealth gap has been demonstrated to reflect factors beyond the lower income levels of African Americans (Blau and Graham 1990; Smith 1995; Altonji, Doraszelski, and Segal 2000). Researchers disagree, however, in their assessments of the causes of this gap. For example, Blau and Graham (1990) drew different conclusions about the major causes of this gap than did Altonji, Doraszelski, and Segal (2000). Blau and Graham (1990) considered three potential and fairly standard explanations (differences in inherited wealth [or other intergenerational transfers], rates of return on investments, and previous savings) and determined that differences in inherited wealth or intergenerational transfers is the most likely of the three standard explanations to account for the wealth differences between Black and White households. Their work suggests that attributes of wealth associated with race (e.g., discrimination and its influence on income and thereby on wealth accretion) play a prominent role in explaining these disparities.

Altonji, Doraszelski, and Segal (2000), on the other hand, found that Blacks would have wealth levels comparable to Whites' if the relationship between wealth and income and demographics for Blacks were the same as it is for Whites, and if Blacks and Whites had the same income and demographic characteristics. Their analysis found that much of the difference between Blacks and Whites in the effect of income and

*Chiteji and Hamilton (chap. 2) examine estimation techniques in more detail [*Editors*].

demographics on wealth is due to differences in savings behavior and/or in the rates of return on assets, rather than to differences in inter vivos transfers and inheritances.*

Historically and at present, African Americans are the subpopulation most residentially segregated from all others in the United States (Iceland, Weinberg, and Steinmetz 2002). Residential segregation of African Americans generally means that when Blacks own homes, they live in neighborhoods/areas with lower property values and earn less appreciation in these values relative to properties in White neighborhoods. Thus, home equity, this key component of net worth, has less value among African Americans than it would if the United States were less segregated by race/ethnicity. The low home ownership rate of African Americans when compared with other groups merely compounds this wealth gap.

Hispanics/Latinos. Data about Hispanics, or Latinos, in wealth surveys are influenced by three main definitional issues. The first is how being of Hispanic origin is captured in surveys. For example, the SCF queries about race and ethnicity in a single question and, since 1998, has given respondents the option to choose as many as seven responses to this item. Thus, it may be less easy in the SCF to identify that someone is of Latino origin than it would be in a survey that asks about race and ethnicity in separate questions (such as the SIPP, whose queries are modeled after the Current Population Survey [CPS]) (Aizcorbe et al. 2003; Kennickell et al. 2000). The population share of Hispanics in the SCF and in the SIPP (and the CPS) do not match, a fact that poses a concern for the reliability of wealth data about this group (Czajka, Jacobson, and Cody 2003).

Another definitional issue that influences wealth data for the Latino population is the exclusion from the CEX, the HRS, and the SIPP of people living in the Commonwealth of Puerto Rico and in other offshore territories of the United States where Latinos may be a large proportion of the population. The influence of this exclusion on wealth estimates is indeterminate. Puerto Ricans residing in Puerto Rico either may have more wealth (which they do not want to move away from by moving to the mainland United States) or less wealth (and are unable to afford to move to the mainland United States) than their state-side counterparts.

The third issue is the omission of remittances from the measurement

*Also see Chiteji and Hamilton (chap. 2) and Chiteji, Gouskova, and Stafford (chap. 8) for more discussion of Black-White differences, particularly in portfolio composition, and how to interpret them [*Editors*].

of wealth for Latino populations. The Inter-American Development Bank estimated that, in 2004, Latin American migrants living in the United States sent $30 billion (2004 dollars) back to their countries of origin.[13] Although remittances may be used to support family members back home, they also may be sent to invest in a homestead for retirement in the future, a use that certainly qualifies as wealth accumulation for a current resident of the United States.

More than three-fourths (75 percent) of Latinos reside in seven states (Arizona, California, Florida, Illinois, New Jersey, New York, and Texas), some of which contain the most expensive housing markets in the United States (e.g., Los Angeles and New York City) (Guzman 2001). How does this geographic reality influence both the ability of Latinos to become home owners and the value of the homes owned by this population? Although segregation of Latinos from Whites is less intense than that of African Americans, to what degree do segregation and discrimination limit the housing options and, thereby, the opportunities for Latinos to accumulate home equity (Iceland, Weinberg, and Steinmetz 2002; Turner et al. 2002)? Although the answers to these questions probably vary by Latino subpopulation, housing was a key component (51 percent) of the net worth of Latino households in 2000 (Orzechowski and Sepielli 2003). Thus, these questions warrant answers if we are to have a fuller understanding of wealth holdings among Latinos in the United States.*

SUMMARY & CONCLUSIONS

Since the mid-1960s, questions about the wealth of persons, families, and households in the United States have been included in a variety of ongoing surveys. These surveys differ in the characteristics of both the populations interviewed (age, race/ethnicity, and residence) and the wealth measures employed. Their major findings also vary by race/ethnicity.

Although the rankings of assets by ownership rates and by value are similar for African American, Latino-origin, and White households, these rankings differ in some ways from one another. In addition, asset values consistently are greater for White households than for either Black households or Hispanic-origin households. The most frequently held assets for African American, Hispanic-origin, and White households alike

---

*Robles (chap. 10) specifically examines Latino wealth accumulation. Woldoff (chap. 11) and Elmelech (chap. 3) include Latinos in their studies of locational effects on home ownership and intragroup wealth inequality, respectively [Editors].

are motor vehicles, interest-earning assets at financial institutions, home equity, and regular checking accounts. However, the rank orderings of these four most frequently held assets differ when their median values and mean values are compared. Rental property equity and home equity are the first- and second-ranked assets by median value, and only home equity is highly ranked both by its ownership rate and by its median and mean values. Income-producing assets, such as stocks and mutual fund shares, are not a major source of investment for households of any racial/ethnic group, although White households have larger holdings than either African Americans or Hispanics.

This dominance of home equity as both a frequently held and highly valued asset is examined in the relevant research literature because it exists along with a persistent gap between the home ownership rates of and amounts of housing equity held by Whites and members of the major racial/ethnic groups. Some research finds that differences in permanent income and intergenerational transfers account for these findings, in part. However, in most of the research reviewed, a substantial unexplained residual remains. The failure to fully explain these differentials using income, sociodemographic, preference, and locational variables suggests that racially discriminatory market mechanisms and policy practices may be responsible for the remaining observed gaps in wealth holdings—as much as 78 percent of the total gap in one study (Blau and Graham 1990)—among racial/ethnic subpopulations.

Other factors, such as the measurement of wealth and the exclusion of selected populations from the groups sampled for wealth surveys, also influence the wealth data reported for people of color. Foremost among these factors is the size of the samples of racial/ethnic populations interviewed for wealth surveys. These samples often are so small as to make tabulations of race by gender or race by income impossible.

In addition, in terms of published and readily accessible wealth data, we are constrained in what we can say about people of color other than Hispanics/Latinos and Blacks/African Americans. Seldom are data for groups other than these robust enough to be reported. In addition, data about subgroups (e.g., Puerto Ricans or African immigrants to the United States) of these two populations do not exist.

Thus, knowledge about the wealth holdings of people of color is spotty. We have much more complete information than in 1967 when the Survey of Economic Opportunity first collected wealth data about Blacks and Whites only. However, as the United States becomes more racially and ethnically diverse, the wealth data collected by our nation need to become more expansive to capture the full scope of wealth held by the U.S. population: its measure, type, value, and frequency held.

APPENDIX 1: DESCRIPTIONS OF THE SIX DATA SETS

CONSUMER EXPENDITURE SURVEY

The Consumer Expenditure Survey (CEX) collects information from a nationally representative sample of U.S. households (termed *consumer units* in the survey) on their buying habits (expenditures), income, and household characteristics. A consumer unit consists of any of the following: (1) all members of a particular household related by blood, marriage, adoption, or other legal arrangements; (2) a person living alone or sharing a household with others or living as a roomer in a private home or lodging house or in permanent living quarters in a hotel or motel, but who is financially independent; or (3) two or more persons living together who use their incomes to make joint expenditure decisions. To be financially independent, a respondent must cover at least two of the three major expense categories (housing, food, and other living expenses) for himself/herself.

Conducted by the Census Bureau under contract to the Bureau of Labor Statistics (in the U.S. Department of Labor), the CEX has two components (a quarterly Interview Survey and a weekly Diary Survey), each with its own questionnaire and sample. Data from both survey components are provided in the CEX Annual Report and the CEX Biennial Report. Prior to 1980, the CEX was conducted about once every ten years. Since 1980, it has been an ongoing survey (Consumer Expenditure Survey 2003).

The two components of the CEX are designed to collect data about different types of expenditures. The Interview Survey is administered once per quarter for five consecutive quarters to collect data about relatively large expenditures, such as automobiles, property, and major durable goods, and about recurring expenditures such as rent and utilities. In the fifth administration of the Interview Survey, data are collected about changes in assets and liabilities over a one-year period. Beginning in 2001, the CEX included information collected from respondents to the Interview Survey using income ranges or brackets ($2,000 to $2,499, for example). Bracketed income categories as response options are employed to avert potential nonresponses. The weekly Diary Survey, on the other hand, is designed to obtain expenditure information about frequently purchased smaller items. Respondents are asked to report in their diaries all expenses incurred for two consecutive one-week periods.

Although information about assets and liabilities is collected as part of the CEX, these data are generally not deemed as reliable as the expenditure data from this survey because of the unwillingness or inability of respondents to provide accurate information about their assets and liabilities. Data on net changes in assets and liabilities are reported in the CEX Biennial Report. In addition to asset and liability information, this report presents data in selected expenditure categories by a standard set of characteristics including race and Hispanic origin of the reference person for the consumer unit. The biennial report includes the same data as the annual report, but with greater detail.

The Health and Retirement Study (HRS) is a longitudinal study of health, retirement, and aging sponsored by the National Institute on Aging and conducted by the Survey Research Center at the University of Michigan. The survey, which oversamples Black and Hispanic households and residents of Florida (presumably because of the survey's interest in retirement), asks questions primarily about respondents' health, wealth, retirement, and economic status. The HRS core sample is augmented by the following three supplements: a 1.86:1 oversample of African Americans, a 1.72:1 oversample of Hispanics, and a 2:1 oversample of Floridians (Health and Retirement Study 1999).

Study data have been collected from four age cohorts of individuals who constitute what the HRS terms as eligible household financial units (i.e., either a single unmarried age-eligible person, a married couple in which both persons are age eligible, or a married couple in which only one spouse is age eligible). To be age eligible, persons must be in one of the following four age cohorts: persons born in 1923 or earlier (in the Asset and Health Dynamics [AHEAD] among the Oldest Old Study), persons born in the 1924–30 cohort (known as the Children of the Depression sample), persons born between 1931 and 1941 (known as the HRS sample), and persons born between 1942 and 1947 (known as the War Babies sample). In general, survey respondents are noninstitutionalized; however, respondents are followed over time if they move into institutions such as nursing homes. Because survey respondents for the HRS are older than the sample populations interviewed for other wealth surveys, their wealth is expected to be greater than that of other members of their respective racial/ethnic groups.

The HRS has been conducted with the sample populations in several waves between 1992 and 2000. Modules about the following topics collect data related to net worth: employment (including questions about pension and retirement plans), net worth (including questions mainly about financial assets such as bonds and IRAs), and income (including questions about annuities and lump sum payments). In addition, the HRS uses a separate housing module to query the respondent about the existence and value of housing in these forms: house or apartment, second homes, farm or ranch, and mobile home (Smith 1995). Data are obtained about values of first mortgages, second mortgages, home equity loans, and all mortgages on second homes, all of which are housing liabilities. Other asset categories in the HRS include other real estate; vehicles; business equity; IRAs or Keogh plans; stocks, trusts, or mutual funds; checking accounts, savings accounts, and money market funds; CDs, government savings bonds, or Treasury bills;

other bonds; and other savings and assets (Smith 1995). In later waves of the study, asset and income data are collected in a single module, and a module with questions about widowhood/divorce and asset change has been added.

The modules that collect data about Social Security and employer pension wealth are among the most detailed in the HRS (Smith 1995). Respondents are asked their current accumulation for their defined contribution plans (such as IRAs, 401[k] plans, and 403[b] plans) and their expected initial income flow and age of receipt for defined benefit plans (such as Social Security and selected employer pension plans). Once benefit levels are estimated, assumptions are made about real interest rates, expected inflation (for plans without COLAs, or cost-of-living adjustments), and expected mortality to translate these estimates into pension wealth values.

To enhance the information available about financial assets, the HRS uses unfolding bracket questions to solicit information after an initial nonresponse (Smith 1995; Choudhury 2001/2002). For example, bracket questions for the initial query, "Are your assets more than $1,000?" would be asked to place responses within categories such as 0 to $1,000, $1,000 to $5,000, and so on, up to a bracket of over $50,000. The use of different bracket intervals for different asset categories reduced nonresponse rates notably (as much as 75 percent) for many financial assets (Smith 1995).

NATIONAL LONGITUDINAL SURVEYS

Since the mid-1960s, the National Longitudinal Surveys (NLS) have collected data from a variety of populations of different ages: young men (ages 14 to 24 years), older men (ages 45 to 59 years), young women (ages 14 to 24 years), and mature women (ages 30 to 44 years). The Bureau of Labor Statistics in the U.S. Department of Labor contracts with a variety of agencies (e.g., the Center for Human Resource Research [CHRR] at Ohio State University, the Census Bureau, and the National Opinion Research Center [NORC] at the University of Chicago) to conduct these surveys. The NLS has as its primary focus employment patterns, such as leaving and re-entering the labor force due to events such as childbearing (primarily women), or after initial retirement (primarily men).

The core set of questions in the NLS may vary from year to year and among the populations interviewed (U.S. Department of Labor 2003). For example, because the 5,020 older men (ages 45–59) initially interviewed in 1966 were well into their careers and were on the threshold of making decisions about the timing and extent of labor force withdrawal, data collected from them focused on topics such as work and nonwork experiences, retirement planning and expectations, midlife job changes, and insurance coverage. The older men's cohort of the NLS was last conducted in 1990, when these men were between the ages of 69 and 83 years. The 5,225 young men (ages 14–24), also first interviewed in 1966, were queried about educational experiences, career choices, and their marital and fertility histories. Interviews with the cohort of young men ceased in 1981, when the youngest turned age 29 and the oldest age 39. Both of these surveys were terminated due to attrition from their respective panels.

The NLS mature women cohort (5,083 women ages 30–44) was first interviewed in 1967, when many in this group were reentering the workforce and balancing the roles of homemaker, mother, and labor force participant. This survey is ongoing, last conducted in 2003 with 2,318 interviewees (U.S. Department of Labor 2003). The NLS cohort of 5,159 young women (ages 14–24), initially interviewed in 1968, was leaving their parents' homes, making initial career and job decisions, and beginning families of their own. This survey was last conducted in 2001 with 2,806 interviewees (U.S. Department of Labor 2003). Three basic types of information are collected for both cohorts of women: core data about work experiences, training, school, family income and assets, physical well-being, and geographic residence; marital and fertility history; and supplemental data specific to age, stage of life, or labor market attachment. All but two of the surveys of women conducted since 1977 have collected data about retirement and pensions. Future collection of these NLS surveys is not planned at this time.

In 1979, the National Longitudinal Survey of Youth (NLSY79) was fielded to collect information from 12,686 individuals born between 1957 and 1964 and, thus, ages 14–21 years when first interviewed. (Ages were as of December 31, 1978.) The NLSY79 interviewees were a national probability sample (1) of civilian young men and women with overrepresentation of Blacks and Latinos and (2) of economically disadvantaged non-Black non-Hispanics. Funding from the U.S. Department of Defense allowed sampling of a group of young persons in the military for interviewing. The military sample was dropped in 1984, and the sample of economically disadvantaged non-Black non-Hispanics was dropped in 1990, both due to lack of funding. Data about the offspring of the NLSY79 sample also are collected as are data about these offspring when they become young adults. The NLSY79 was conducted annually through 1994 but has been conducted biennially since then. Last conducted in 2002, the NLSY79 is a continuing survey, as is the NLSY97. The National Longitudinal Survey of Youth 1997 (NLSY97) targets the 12-to-16-year-old age cohort (with age reckoned as of December 31, 1996), or persons born between 1980 and 1984. First fielded in 1997, the NLSY97 is a continuing survey that was last conducted in fall 2003 through spring 2004 (U.S. Department of Labor 2003).

A unique feature of the NLS is the fact that households can contain members of two age cohorts. For example, a single household could contain both an older man and a young woman (his daughter). This allows intrahousehold comparisons of members from different cohorts and also enables one to examine intergenerational transfers of assets.

Although data about income and assets have long been collected in the NLS, the components of the asset information have changed. Asset information available from the NLSY79 includes the types and total market value of property owned by the respondents (e.g., real estate, farm, and business), the value of other assets including vehicles and savings accounts, as well as total debts owed including mortgages, back taxes, and debts exceeding $500.

These data were collected for 1985–1990 and in 1992. Data about net savings and dissavings are available beginning with the 1989 survey (U.S. Department of Labor 2003).

Annually from 1968 through 1997, the Panel Study of Income Dynamics (PSID) was conducted by the University of Michigan's Institute for Social Research with a random sample of individuals and family units, and a separate sample of low-income households. The low-income sample is based on about 2,000 low-income families with heads under the age of 60 who were interviewed in the Survey of Economic Opportunity in 1967 and is known as the SEO sample (Panel Study of Income Dynamics n.d.). This sampling resulted in a large representation of African American families in the surveys conducted between 1968 and 1997. Because of the lengthy time period during which annual data were collected for this sample (which had grown from 4,800 households in 1968 to 8,500 households in 1996), the PSID is a rich source of longitudinal data about demographic characteristics (age, race, sex, marital status), as well as about income and wealth for households in the United States.

In 1997, the PSID was redesigned in several ways. It shifted from annual to biennial data collection. Its core sample was reduced (to 6,168 in 1997 and to more than 7,000 families in 2001), and a refresher sample of post-1968 immigrant families and their adult children was added. Although a sample of 2,000 Latino households (from Mexico, Puerto Rico, and Cuba) had been added in 1990, it was dropped in 1995 (due both to a lack of funding and to the failure to include Asian immigrants in the sample). The Latinos included in the core PSID in 1994 were not interviewed for the wealth supplement. A 441-family sample of immigrants (both Latino and Asian) was added to the PSID core sample in 1997, with this sample projected to reach nearly 7,400 families by 2005. The SEO sample of low-income families was reduced dramatically in 1997 to 609 families headed by an African American individual and containing at least one child age 12 or under, in 1996 (Panel Study of Income Dynamics n.d.).

Wealth data were collected in special supplemental surveys conducted with the 1984, 1989, 1994, 1999, 2001, and 2003 PSID. (A wealth file currently is available with data for all years except 2003.) These supplements collected data about major categories of net worth noted in the section "How Wealth Is Held "(Panel Study of Income Dynamics n.d.). Wealth-related data also are available in the Active Saving File for 1984–89 and 1989–94. This file contains data measuring flows of money into and out of different assets, such as putting money into or taking it out of the stock market and putting money into annuities or cashing them in.

Relative to other surveys, the PSID has low nonresponse rates to wealth questions, presumably because of the rapport developed between the respondents and interviewers over the many years the survey has been conducted. In addition, by using queries with bracketed response categories (similar to those in the HRS) to follow up on nonresponses, the PSID has been able to convert between 75 percent and 80 percent of nonresponses into categorical responses (Smith 1995).

SURVEY OF CONSUMER FINANCES

The Survey of Consumer Finances (SCF) is a nationally representative interview survey of U.S. families conducted every three years. The SCF is sponsored by the Board of Governors of the Federal Reserve System with the cooperation of the U.S. Department of the Treasury. The five most recent surveys were conducted in 1992, 1995, 1998, 2001, and 2004 (which just became public as we go to press). For comparability with other wealth surveys this chapter features 2001 data. Since 1992, the SCF has been conducted by the National Opinion Research Center (NORC) at the University of Chicago, generally between May and December of the survey year. The survey is designed to provide detailed information about the balance sheets of and the use of financial services by U.S. families. In addition, the SCF collects information from families about topics such as pensions, labor force participation, and demographic characteristics.

As a survey purposely designed to collect wealth data, the SCF is expected to provide reliable information both for attributes that are broadly distributed in the population (such as home ownership) and for attributes highly concentrated in a relatively small part of the population (such as closely held businesses). Thus, the survey employs a two-part sample design that has been largely unchanged since 1989, including a geographically based random sample and an oversample of relatively wealthy families (i.e., a high-income supplement).

The unit of observation for the SCF, a family or primary economic unit, is defined as the economically dominant single individual or couple in the household and all other persons in the household who are financially dependent on that person or those persons. In recent years, a total of between 4,300 and 4,450 families have been included in the survey. Each of the most recent surveys represents an increasing number of families: 95.9 million families in 1992, 99 million in 1995, 102.6 million in 1998, and 106.5 million in 2001.

The SCF uses a single question that includes race categories along with the category "Hispanic" to collect data for the following groups: White non-Hispanic, Black non-Hispanic, Hispanic, Asians, American Indians and Alaska Natives, and Others. In the 1998 SCF, when respondents were allowed to provide multiple responses, very few (56 out of 4,390) did so, with the most common combination being White and American Indian/Alaska Native (twenty-one responses) (Kennickell 1999). However, tabulations of the SCF seldom present data for these groups separately. The presentation of wealth data for families in the racial/ethnic categories "non-White or Hispanic," "White non-Hispanic," and "all" in a major source document based on 1998 and 2001 SCF data (Aizcorbe et al. 2003) is a standard one, dictated in part by the overrepresentation of White families that results because the

SCF oversamples wealthy families. An article by Wolff (1998) provides an exception, though, because it presents 1983 and 1995 SCF data for the distribution of wealth among the top 1 percent of wealth holders along with the distribution of the population by major racial/ethnic groups, defined as White non-Hispanic, Black non-Hispanic, Hispanic, and Asians and Others.

Bracketed category questions are seldom used to follow up on nonresponses in the SCF, thus yielding higher nonresponse rates for selected asset categories than surveys such as the HRS that employ this technique (Smith 1995). Although SCF data are available before 1983, this is the earliest year for which wealth analyses customarily are conducted because, prior to that date, the number of wealth questions was limited and a high-income supplement was not part of the survey (Wolff 1998).

SURVEY OF INCOME & PROGRAM PARTICIPATION

The Survey of Income and Program Participation (SIPP), first conducted in 1984, is a longitudinal survey of the noninstitutionalized, resident adult population (i.e., 15 years or older) in households in the United States. Conducted by the U.S. Bureau of the Census, the SIPP collects wealth and asset data as a supplement to its core questions about labor force participation, income, demographic characteristics, and program participation. The large sample sizes of the SIPP (e.g., 37,000 households in the 1996 panel) enable one to compare assets of groups such as low-income households who might participate in government assistance programs and who tend to be underrepresented in other surveys.

For the purposes of the SIPP, a household is defined as all the people who occupy a housing unit (Orzechowski and Sepielli 2003). Residents of group quarters and of institutions (such as dormitories or nursing homes) and people living in military barracks and in the Commonwealth of Puerto Rico are excluded from data collection for the SIPP. Households are selected for interview in the SIPP using sampling methodology similar to that used for the Current Population Survey, another survey conducted by the U.S. Bureau of the Census. A new sample or panel is introduced at the beginning of a calendar year. This sample of households is divided into four interview groups called "rotation groups," and each month one of the four rotation groups is interviewed about the previous four months (known as "the reference period"). A complete cycle of interviews for the four rotation groups is termed "a wave," and each panel is interviewed for multiple waves (i.e., three or four years).

The emphasis of the SIPP on lower-income households who would be eligible to participate in government assistance programs limits the wealth detail collected in this survey. For example, the SIPP does not measure equities in pension plans, cash surrender value of life insurance policies, and the value of household furnishings such as antiques, art, and jewelry, all of which would be included in a survey (such as the SCF) that sought to comprehensively measure family wealth (Orzechowski and Sepielli 2003). In addition, the SIPP does not employ bracketed follow-up questions to gather data about asset categories that are nonresponses, a technique found to decrease non-responses markedly in the HRS (Smith 1995).

Since the 1970s, researchers have attempted to explain the racial disparities (initially identified between African Americans and Whites only) in the rates of home ownership, the value of home equity, and net wealth. Terrell (1971) links the poorer net wealth position of African Americans to the fact that at any observed income level, African American households have had a past history of lower average incomes than White families at that same income level. Income is, of course, the source of savings for down payments for homes and to acquire other assets. Kain and Quigley (1972) attribute the home ownership wealth gap among Black households to supply constraints (such as real estate industry practices and barriers in access to credit) on the choice of housing available to Black households.

Parcel (1982) proffers three reasons for Whites being favored in the accumulation of housing equity. The first is the fact that immediately after World War II the Veterans Administration (VA) and the Federal Housing Administration (FHA) generally provided their guaranteed/insured loans to Whites but not to Blacks, giving Whites a "head start" in equity accumulation. Other practices of the VA and FHA, such as not counting all of a wife's income when determining mortgage eligibility for a husband-wife household also limited the access of Black households to home mortgage loans (Leigh 1992a). The historically greater labor force participation of Black women (when compared with White women) makes policies such as these more of a barrier to home ownership among Black households than among White households (Leigh and Simms 1998). The second reason is mechanisms of institutional discrimination, such as the steering by real estate professionals of African Americans and Whites to separate housing markets. Law suits filed and settled in favor of the plaintiffs during the 1970s, 1980s, and 1990s give ample evidence that continued housing market discrimination limits Blacks in their choice of housing and, thereby, also limits the accretion of wealth this housing provides (Leigh 1992b; Turner et al. 2002). The third reason is the fact that, even if both Black and White households owned a home, housing values in areas in which Whites live generally increase more rapidly than in areas in which Blacks live, in the dual real estate markets maintained in most places in the United States. Based on his analysis of data for Black and White men 35 to 54 years of age, however, Parcel concludes that the major explanatory factor for the racial difference in the accumulation of housing equity is the fact that Blacks are less able than Whites to rely upon returns to their earnings and their age to bolster net wealth through the acquisition of housing or other assets.

Using data from the 1986 Current Population Survey and from the 1970 and 1980 census public use samples, Long and Caudill (1992) developed models to estimate both the probability of home ownership and the value of home equity among African American husband-and-wife households and among White husband-and-wife households in which the household head was at least 20 years of age. They found that the racial gap in home ownership was strongly associated with differences between the races in permanent income and in central city residence. The primary factors found to contribute to the relatively low Black housing wealth also included lower permanent income of Black home owners, compared with White home owners, and the fact that houses owned by African Americans are physically smaller (in number of rooms and number of baths), older, and less apt to be located in metropolitan areas in the West (where housing values skyrocketed during the 1970s and 1980s).

Oliver and Shapiro (1995) offer three reasons for the limited accumulation of housing wealth by Black households, relative to White households. All three explanations relate to institutional and policy discrimination that restrict the access to housing by Black households, and the authors found evidence to support all potential explanations. The first explanation is access to credit, considered important "because whom banks deem to be credit worthy and whom they reject may delineate a crucial moment of institutional racial bias occurring in access to home mortgages." (Oliver and Shapiro 1995, 137). The second area of potential discrimination noted is interest rates on loans made to those approved for home purchases. The final factor noted is that when housing values increased sharply and at rates exceeding the overall rate of inflation during the 1970s and 1980s, this created a large pool of assets for those who already owned homes. Because historical barriers to acquiring home ownership in place prior to the 1970s reduced the likelihood of home ownership among Black households (relative to White households), African Americans were, therefore, less likely than Whites to benefit from the increase in house values that took place during these decades.

NOTES

The author thanks Kelley D. Coleman for valuable research assistance. The views in this chapter are the author's and do not necessarily reflect the views of the Joint Center for Political and Economic Studies or its board of governors.

1. Unless otherwise noted, all the dollar amounts in this chapter have been indexed to 2001 as the base year.

2. The ratios are from Wolff 2000, as cited in Choudhury 2001/2002, 13, n. 3.

3. Although the sources of wealth data generally report information for the Hispanic or Hispanic-origin population, both the terms *Hispanic* and *Latino* are used interchangeably in this chapter.

4. Gross personal wealth also is defined to include the full face value of life insurance (reduced by any policy loans).

5. IRAs and Keogh plans are tax-favored retirement savings plans. In a given year, individuals enrolled in any of the several types of IRAs or Keoghs are allowed to contribute up to a specified amount of money to be invested

in instruments such as mutual funds, annuities, stocks, bonds, and certificates of deposit. Amounts invested in IRAs (except Roth IRAs) and Keoghs are tax deductible and untaxed until their withdrawal, which can occur after age 59½, when the investor is presumably in a lower tax bracket. With the Roth IRA, however, contributions are not tax deductible, but proceeds from investment contributions are not taxed, and withdrawals are tax-free after age 59½. The main differences between IRAs and Keoghs are their contribution limits and the participant eligibility for Keoghs. Keoghs are retirement plans for self-employed professionals or owners and employees of small businesses such as partnerships, sole proprietorships, and LLCs (limited liability companies). The maximum annual contribution in Keogh plans is $30,000, and the employer makes 100 percent of the contributions. The maximum annual IRA contribution is $3,000 (or $3,500 in 2004 for individuals older than age 50). Business owners, self-employed individuals, and independent contractors, however, also may invest in the SEP (Simplified Employer Pension) IRA, which allows annual contributions greater than $3,000.

6. The 401(k), 403(b), and Thrift (or Thrift Savings) plans are tax-sheltered annuities (TSAs), or tax-advantaged retirement savings plans, made available, respectively, by private corporations, nonprofit organizations, and government agencies for their employees. Sponsored by employers, these plans allow employees and employers (if they choose) to make pre-tax contributions for their retirement. In a given year, employees may contribute to these plans 100 percent of their compensation up to a maximum amount (e.g., $13,000 in 2004 for 401[k] plans). Earnings on investments in these TSAs grow tax deferred until they may be withdrawn at age 59½. Although investment proceeds may be first tapped without penalty at age 59½, these proceeds are taxed upon withdrawal.

7. The percentages for 1967 and 1979 are computed with Black wealth as a percentage of the sum of Black wealth and White wealth, excluding the holdings of the then very small non-Black minority population.

8. Household totals by race are taken from the Current Population Survey and are somewhat less than the totals from Census 2000, especially for Latinos. See http://www.census.gov/hhes/income/histinc/h05.html.

9. Asset-ownership rates reflect the percentage of a group of households that own a given asset, regardless whether they simultaneously own other assets. Thus, the asset-ownership rates for subcategories of interest-earning assets at financial institutions will not sum to 100 percent; persons reporting that they own a certificate of deposit (CD) also may report having a passbook savings account, for example.

10. The labels include *san* or *sociedad* among persons from the Dominican Republic, *sou sou* or *susu* among Trinidadians, *len' han'* among Jamaicans, *box* among Guyanese, *osusu* among persons from Sierra Leone, and *ajo* among Yorubas from Nigeria. Aracelis Gray (from the Dominican Republic) provided information about *jugando un san* (playing a san) or *tiene un san* (having a san) and about *sociedad* during an e-mail exchange on May 18, 2004. Liselle Yorke (from Trinidad and Tobago) provided the information about *sou sou, len' han',* and *box* in an interview on May 18, 2004. Hafford

(2003) is the source for the term *susu*. Aramidé Kazeem (from Nigeria) provided information about *ajo* in an interview on May 27, 2004. Winston Allen (from Sierra Leone) provided the term *osusu* via e-mail on August 4, 2004.

11. Classic texts about rotating credit associations as cited in Hafford 2003 include Bonnet 1980 and Vélez-Ibañez 1983.

12. The dissimilarity score indicates the percentage of a given population that would have to move so that its population share within each geographic unit within a locality would equal the share of the total population in this locality that this group constitutes.

13. This estimate excludes remittances to Haiti and to the English-speaking Caribbean countries (http://www.iadb.org).

REFERENCES

Aizcorbe, A. M., A. B. Kennickell, and K. B. Moore, with R. M. Bledsoe, G. Fries, and L. B. Wells. 2003. "Recent Changes in U.S. Family Finances: Evidence from the 1998 and 2001 Survey of Consumer Finances." *Federal Reserve Bulletin* 89: 1–32.

Altonji, J., U. Doraszelski, and L. Segal. 2000. "Black/White Differences in Wealth." *Economic Perspectives* 24: 38–50.

America, R. 1990. *The Wealth of Races.* Westport, CT: Greenwood Press.

Barnes, J. S., and C. E. Bennett. 2002. "The Asian Population: 2000." *Census 2000 Brief.* Washington, DC: U.S. Census Bureau.

Blau, F. D., and J. W. Graham. 1990. "Black-White Differences in Wealth and Asset Composition." *Quarterly Journal of Economics* 105: 321–39.

Bonnet, A. W. 1980. "An Examination of Rotating Credit Systems among Black West Indian Immigrants in Brooklyn." In *Sourcebook on the New Immigration: Implications for the United States and the International Community,* ed. R. S. Bryce-Laporte. New Brunswick, NJ: Transactions Publishers.

Brimmer, A. F. 1988. "Income, Wealth, and Investment Behavior in the Black Community." *American Economic Review (Papers and Proceedings)* 78: 151–55.

Browne, R. S. 1974. "Wealth Distribution and Its Impact on Minorities." *Review of Black Political Economy* 4: 27–37.

Caner, A., and E. N. Wolff. 2004. "Asset Poverty in the United States: Its Persistence in an Expansionary Economy." In *Public Policy Brief,* no. 76. Annandale-on-Hudson, NY: Levy Economics Institute of Bard College.

Choudhury, S. 2001/2002. "Racial and Ethnic Differences in Wealth and Asset Choices. *Social Security Bulletin* 64: 1–15.

Consumer Expenditure Survey. 2003. "Frequently Asked Questions" (U.S. Department of Labor, Bureau of Labor Statistics). http://www.bls.gov/cex/csxfaqs.htm (accessed on April 14, 2004).

Cross-Sectional Wealth and Financial Wealth. 2000. http://psidonline.isr.umich.edu (accessed on July 24, 2004).

Czajka, J. L., J. E. Jacobson, and S. Cody. 2003. *Survey Estimates of Wealth: A Comparative Analysis and Review of the Survey of Income and Program Participation (Final Report)*. Washington, DC: Submitted by Mathematica Policy Research to the Social Security Administration.

Davern, M. E., and P. J. Fisher. 2001. *Household Net Worth and Asset Ownership: 1995*. Current Population Reports, P70-71. Washington, DC: U.S. Census Bureau and U.S. Government Printing Office.

Eller, T. J., and W. Fraser. 1995. *Asset Ownership of Households: 1993*. Current Population Reports, P70-47. Washington, DC: U.S. Census Bureau and U.S. Government Printing Office. http://www.census.gov/prod/1/pop/p70-47.pdf (accessed on March 24, 2000, and March 28, 2000).

Forquera, R. 2001. *Urban Indian Health* (issue brief). Menlo Park, CA: Henry J. Kaiser Family Foundation.

Gouskova, E., and F. Stafford. 2002. *Trends in Household Wealth Dynamics, 1999–2001*. http://psidonline.isr.umich.edu (accessed on July 24, 2004).

Guzman, B. 2001. "The Hispanic Population: 2000." *Census 2000 Brief*. Washington, DC: U.S. Census Bureau.

Hafford, C. A. 2003. "Between Sisters and Cousins: Child Caretaking and the Reproduction of Familial Interdependence across Dominican Migrant Households." Unpublished doctoral dissertation, Columbia University.

Health and Retirement Study. 1999. http://hrsonline.isr.umich.edu/intro/sho_uinfo.php?hfyle=design&xtyp=2 (accessed on April 14, 2004).

Iceland, J., D. H. Weinberg, and E. Steinmetz. 2002. *Racial and Ethnic Residential Segregation in the United States*. Series CENSR-3. Washington, DC: U.S. Census Bureau and U.S. Government Printing Office. http://www.census.gov/hhes/www/housing/resseg/front_toc.html (accessed on May 18, 2004).

Kain, J. F., and J. M. Quigley. 1972. "Housing Market Discrimination, Homeownership, and Savings Behavior." *American Economic Review* 62: 263–77.

Kennickell, A. B. 1999. *Revisions to the SCF Weighting Methodology: Accounting for Race/Ethnicity and Homeownership*. Board of Governors of the Federal Reserve System. http://www.federalreserve.gov/pubs/oss/oss2/method.html.

Kennickell, A. B., M. Starr-McCluer, and B. J. Surette, with G. Fries, A. K. Li, and A. L. Lytle. 2000. "Recent Changes in U.S. Family Finances: Results from the 1998 Survey of Consumer Finances." *Federal Reserve Bulletin* 86: 1–29.

Leigh, W. A. 1992a. "Attitudes toward Fair Housing as Barriers to Housing Equity Accumulation by Black Americans." *Research on Economic Inequality* 2: 89–103.

———. 1992b. "Civil Rights Legislation and the Housing Status of Black Americans: An Overview." *The Housing Status of Black Americans,* ed. W. A. Leigh and J. B. Stewart, 5–28. New Brunswick, NJ: Transaction Publishers.

———. 2003. "Implications of Social Security Reform for Wealth Development among African Americans." In *African-American Social Workers and Social Policy,* ed. T. Bent-Goodly. Binghamton, NY: Hearth Press.

Leigh, W. A., and M. C. Simms. 1998. *The Black Worker in the 21st Century:*

Job Creation Prospects and Strategies. Lanham, MD: University Press of America.

Long, J. E., and S. B. Caudill. 1992. "Racial Differences in Homeownership and Housing Wealth, 1970–1986." *Economic Inquiry* 30: 83–100.

Ogletree, C. J., Jr. 2004. *All Deliberate Speed.* New York City: W. W. Norton and Co.

Ogunwole, S. U. 2002. "The American Indian and Alaska Native Population: 2000." *Census 2000 Brief.* Washington, DC: U.S. Census Bureau.

O'Hare, W. P. 1983. *Wealth and Economic Status: A Perspective on Racial Inequity.* Washington, DC: Joint Center for Political Studies.

Oliver, M. L., and T. M. Shapiro. 1989. "Race and Wealth." *Review of Black Political Economy* 17: 5–25.

———. 1995. *Black Wealth/White Wealth: A New Perspective on Racial Inequality.* New York: Routledge.

Orzechowski, S., and P. Sepielli. 2003. "Net Worth and Asset Ownership of Households: 1998 and 2000." Current Population Reports, P70-88, U.S. Census Bureau, Washington, DC. http://www.census.gov/hhes/www/wealth/1998_2000/wealth98_00.html (accessed on April 6, 2004).

Panel Study of Income Dynamics. n.d. http://psidonline.isr.umich.edu/Guide/Overview.html (accessed May 3, 2004).

Parcel, T. L. 1982. "Wealth Accumulation of Black and White Men: The Case of Housing Equity." *Social Problems* 30: 199–211.

Smith, J. P. 1995. "Racial and Ethnic Differences in Wealth in the Health and Retirement Study." *Journal of Human Resources* (special issue on the Health and Retirement Study: data quality and early results) 30: S158–S183.

State of the Nation's Housing, 2003. 2003. Cambridge, MA: Joint Center for Housing Studies of Harvard University. http://jchs.harvard.edu (accessed on May 18, 2004).

Terrell, H. S. 1971. "Wealth Accumulation of Black and White Families: The Empirical Evidence." *Journal of Finance* 26: 363–77.

Turner, M. A., S. L. Ross, G. C. Galster, and J. Yinger, with E. B. Godfrey, B. A. Bednarz, C. Herbig, S. J. Lee, AKM R. Hossain, and B. Zhao. 2002. *Discrimination in Metropolitan Housing Markets: National Results from Phase I of HDS2000.* Washington, DC: Office of Policy Development and Research, U.S. Department of Housing and Urban Development.

U.S. Census Bureau. 1990. *Statistical Abstract of the United States: 1990.* 110th ed. Washington, DC: U.S. Government Printing Office.

———. 2000. *American FactFinder.* http://factfinder.census.gov (accessed on May 26, 2004).

———. 2003. *Statistical Abstract of the United States: 2003.* http://www.census.gov/prod/www/statistical-abstract-03.html (accessed on April 20, 2004).

U.S. Citizenship and Immigration Services. 2003. *Immigration through Investment.* http://uscis.gov/graphics/exec/prnfriendly.asp (accessed on April 20, 2004).

U.S. Department of Labor. 2003. *NLS Handbook, 2003.* Washington, DC: Bureau of Labor Statistics, U.S. Department of Labor.

U.S. General Accounting Office. 2002. *Native American Housing: VA Could Address Some Barriers to Participation in Direct Loan Program.* GAO-02-654. Washington, DC: U.S. General Accounting Office. http://www.gao.gov (accessed on May 26, 2004).

Vélez-Ibañez, C. G. 1983. *Bonds of Mutual Trust: The Cultural Systems of Rotating Credit Associations among Urban Mexicans and Chicanos.* New Brunswick, NJ: Rutgers University Press.

Wolff, E. N. 1998. "Recent Trends in the Size Distribution of Household Wealth." *Journal of Economic Perspectives* 12: 131–50.

———. 2000. "Recent Trends in Wealth Ownership." Working Paper no. 300, Levy Economics Institute, New York.

———. 2001. Recent Trends in Wealth Ownership, from 1983 to 1998. In *Assets for the Poor: The Benefits of Spreading Asset Ownership,* ed. Thomas M. Shapiro and Edward N. Wolff, 34–73. New York: Russell Sage Foundation.

Wynter, L. E. 1997. "Black Households Play It Safe with Investments" (Business and Race column). *Wall Street Journal,* May 8, 1997.

2 Estimating the Effect of Race & Ethnicity on Wealth Accumulation & Asset-Ownership Patterns

NGINA CHITEJI & DARRICK HAMILTON

How different are White and non-White wealth holdings and why are there differences between Whites and non-Whites? Several scholars attempt to answer this question. To fully understand what the existing research reveals, one must understand the different empirical techniques employed in the literature. This chapter discusses such methodological matters, identifying the standard techniques used, their merits and limitations, and current debates about different estimation strategies.

COMPARISON OF AVERAGE DIFFERENCES IN OUTCOMES BETWEEN TWO GROUPS

One popular way to look for differences across groups is to compare the average outcome in some variable of interest for each group. For example, with a continuous variable such as wealth, researchers often compute the mean level of wealth for Whites, which then is interpreted as the outcome of the typical or average White family or individual, and then compare it to the mean for non-Whites (or the mean for a particular group of non-Whites). Provided that the difference is a statistically significant one, a difference in the means suggests the presence of a wealth gap, albeit an "unadjusted" gap in statistical parlance.[1] For wealth in particular, because its distribution is highly skewed, it is also common to examine differences measured at some percentile, most commonly the median. The median is more representative of the average or typical family than the arithmetic mean when a distribution contains a few outliers with extremely large values, as the distribution of wealth does.

With a dichotomous outcome variable, such as whether a family holds a specific asset (like a bank account) or not, the approach is similar. Asset ownership is typically measured by a dummy variable that takes on a value of zero if the family does not own the asset in question and a value of one if the family does own the asset. Researchers then compute the mean value (or "share") of this variable for each racial/ethnic group. It can be interpreted as a rate of asset ownership for the group, and the rates of ownership for the different groups can be compared to determine whether there are meaningful differences between them.[2] While the mathematical procedure is the same as it is for wealth, the interpretation of the "mean" is slightly different for dichotomous variables. When contemplating ownership of different assets, the mean is often interpreted as the proportion of families in each group that holds the asset in question, or as the probability of asset ownership for an individual in the group.[3]

What does a difference in average outcomes tell us? Social science researchers' interest in racial or ethnic differences in average outcomes for variables such as wealth and asset-ownership rates often stems from a desire to understand whether some racial/ethnic groups are disadvantaged relative to others, as well as from concerns that the differences may indicate the presence of discrimination (or disparate treatment) in U.S. society.[4] It is common to pose questions about the conditions of non-Whites using implicit or explicit comparisons with the situation of White Americans.[5] Accordingly, scholars' research questions often are framed so as to ask not only how non-Whites fare on a wide variety of outcome measures but how they fare compared with Whites. In instances in which non-Whites are deemed to fare poorly relative to Whites, the standard follow-up question is whether this is because of race/ethnicity and, if race is found to be the reason, whether its relevance signals the presence of discrimination.

To determine whether non-Whites fare differently from Whites, it suffices to ask whether there are differences in mean (or median) outcomes between non-Whites and Whites that are statistically significant. Accordingly, to assess the degree of disadvantage that non-Whites experience—in terms of lower levels of family resources, for example—an unadjusted gap for a variable like wealth suffices to provide the information that a researcher needs. However, to determine whether a gap reflects discrimination or disparate treatment, the researcher must be sure that the difference in outcomes that he or she is scrutinizing is attributable to race or ethnicity. And then the researcher is obligated to establish that race/ethnicity plays a role because Blacks are treated differently from Whites and not because they make different choices voluntarily.

To make these assessments, the researcher is required to assess the role of race *net* of other factors that affect the outcome variable. Why? If there are factors that affect the outcome variable independent of race/ethnicity that also happen to be correlated with race/ethnicity, a simple comparison of average differences between two racial or ethnic groups does not indicate that the observed gap between two racial/ethnic groups is actually attributable to race. When other factors that affect the outcome variable also differ by race, the influence of these variables will be confounded with those of race when one looks at a simple bivariate association between the outcome variable and race/ethnicity. To determine whether the "gap" of interest is truly attributable to race/ethnicity, and not to some other variable, one must separate out the independent effects of these other variables.

For example, theory indicates that a family's wealth will be affected by the structure of the family. Consider two couples, a couple that is married and residing together and an unmarried couple that resides separately. Suppose both couples have a combined income of $20,000 and that everyone faces the same housing costs in the amount of $10,000. The married couple residing together clearly will have $10,000 above their housing costs, and this could be saved, perhaps by putting it into the stock market. The second couple will not have the $10,000 to spare since each individual in the second couple would have to spend his or her entire income on housing. So, based on this example, if Black couples are less likely to be married and residing together, they will face higher total housing costs, and hence Blacks will have less available to save and will consequently accumulate less wealth than an otherwise comparable White couple.[6] However, we know that the resulting difference in wealth is not directly attributable to race; instead, it stems from the marital status of the couples and the effect that this has on expenditures and saving rates. Similarly, theory suggests that, on average, families with children will have greater expenditures and therefore fewer dollars to save than those without children. If there are sizeable differences across racial or ethnic groups in either marriage rates or family size, these will be expected to manifest themselves as a difference in wealth levels between the two racial/ethnic groups being compared if the researcher does not take care to account for or "control" for their effects.

CONTROLLING FOR FACTORS OTHER
THAN RACE/ETHNICITY THAT AFFECT WEALTH &
ASSET OWNERSHIP

How does one control for the influence of factors other than race or ethnicity when analyzing wealth holdings and asset-ownership patterns? It is standard for researchers to use multivariate regression analysis to identify and isolate the independent effects of different causal variables on the outcome of interest. Continuing with levels of wealth as our example, a regression for wealth in which race/ethnicity and other factors—such as marital status, number of children, labor income, education, and age—are specified as independent or control variables will produce an estimate of the effect of race/ethnicity that is much smaller than one would infer by looking simply at an unadjusted wealth gap.[7] This is because a regression adjusts for differences in average characteristics across the racial/ethnic groups being compared. For example, research shows that Blacks typically have lower rates of marriage and lower levels of income and education than White families do. Because each of these variables is likely to depress a family's level of wealth, Blacks would be expected to have lower wealth than Whites when one is making a simple comparison between averages of the two groups, even if there were no independent effect of race. To determine what the independent (or direct) effect of race is, one has to separate out the effects of these additional factors.[8]

INTERPRETING THE RACE COEFFICIENT IN A
MULTIVARIATE REGRESSION

A multivariate regression adjusts for differences in average characteristics that exist between Blacks and Whites so as to "net out" the influence of the other causal factors and to allow one to produce an estimate of the effect of race/ethnicity by itself. For this reason it is common for researchers to speak of an "adjusted" or "net" wealth gap, in comparison with an "unadjusted" or "gross" wealth gap. The adjusted gap is represented by the coefficient on the race variable in a multivariate regression. This captures the effect of race/ethnicity independent of the other control variables.

Table 2.1 shows unadjusted wealth gaps along with the net effect of race found in a few seminal papers in the literature on wealth inequality. As shown in the table, the estimated effects of race are often substantially smaller than the mean (or median) differences in wealth.[9] Hurst, Luoh, and Stafford (1998), for example, find that the mean level of net worth for Black families is $37,457, while the mean for White families is $177,952.[10] The associated gap in Black and White wealth therefore is $140,495—indicating that, on average, their analysis suggests that White families have over $100,000 more than Black families. Once other factors that affect wealth levels are taken into consideration however, the authors find that the estimated gap between Black and White families falls to $27,408. Being Black still has an effect on one's wealth level; however, the estimated effect for the typical family is smaller when one accounts for differences in education, average labor income, age, family size, marital status, and gender than it is when one simply examines the bivariate association between race and wealth. This shows that some of the difference that one finds between the national averages for Blacks and Whites is attributable to lower levels of education and other individual or family characteristics. These factors affect wealth accumulation, but they do not represent a direct effect of race on wealth. One therefore can interpret estimates such as Hurst, Luoh, and Stafford's as indicating that there is wealth disparity between Black and White families, but disparity that is not due simply to race. Instead, much of the disparity has to do with differences in sociodemographic and economic characteristics, such as education and earnings, which can naturally lead to lower

TABLE 2.1. Comparison of Unadjusted and Adjusted Wealth Gaps

	Hurst, Luoh, and Stafford 1998	Oliver and Shapiro 1995
Black mean wealth	$37,457	$23,818
White mean wealth	$177,952	$95,667
Unadjusted gap (mean)	$140,495	$71,849
Adjusted gap (mean)	$27,408	$27,075
Black/White wealth ratio	.21	.25
Black median wealth	$8,470	$3,700
White median wealth	$63,522	$43,800
Unadjusted gap (median)	$55,052	$40,100
Adjusted gap (median)	$2,815	Not provided

Sources: The Hurst, Luoh, and Stafford (1998) results are based on an analysis of data from the Panel Study of Income Dynamics. Oliver and Shapiro (1995) use data from the 1988 Survey of Income and Program Participation.

levels of saving and ultimately wealth. This discussion indicates how comparisons of simple averages between groups can be misleading.

As noted earlier, researchers are only partly interested in wealth and asset-ownership differences for the specific purpose of knowing what resources different families have available to them. And not all researchers are content to identify or "explain" the sociodemographic and economic factors that cause wealth gaps and asset-ownership rate differences. Many researchers also examine gaps in outcomes between Whites and non-Whites in an effort to determine whether discrimination still exists and how it may be operating. The logic here is that if differences in outcomes are driven by structural barriers to success faced by non-Whites, racial/ethnic disparity will signal or serve as evidence for the existence of discrimination (Darity and Mason 1998, for example). However, because it is difficult to directly measure discrimination, a researcher often has to indirectly measure discrimination based on racial/ethnic residual differences in wealth after controlling for all nondiscrimination-based factors that affect that outcome. Relying on this residual estimation requires that he or she eliminate all other potential explanations for racial/ethnic differences besides market-based discrimination in order to claim that discrimination is present. In particular, to strengthen his or her findings or claims of discrimination, the researcher should establish that the differences between Whites and non-Whites are not attributable to differences in voluntary choices (preferences or behavior) across groups.[11]

Controversy naturally can emerge as a result. There is sometimes debate about whether all relevant differences in preferences across groups have been controlled for in empirical research. For example, attitudes toward saving naturally affect how much one saves, and attitudes toward risk affect the decisions that people make about which assets they will choose to store their wealth. Yet preferences toward saving and risk tolerance are difficult to measure. Because of this, few data sets contain measures that can be used to control for these influences.[12]

STANDARD ESTIMATION STRATEGIES

What options does a researcher have who wants to employ multivariate regression techniques to estimate the effects of race/ethnicity? To run a regression, one must specify an empirical model and estimate it using appropriate statistical techniques. To obtain an estimate of the net gap for wealth, it is common (1) to specify an equation relating wealth to independent variables such as age, age squared (to get at quadratic effects associated with age), marital status, gender of the family head, labor income, and education of the family head, in addition to race, and (2) to use ordinary least squares (OLS) to estimate the model. Formally, a regression equation such as the following,

$$\text{Wealth} = \beta_0 + \beta_1 \text{ age} + \beta_2 \text{ age}^2 + \beta_3 \text{ marital status}$$
$$+ \beta_4 \text{ gender} + \beta_5 \text{ race} + \beta_6 \text{ number of children}$$
$$+ \beta_7 \text{ income} + \beta_8 \text{ education} + \varepsilon,$$

where ε represents a normally distributed error term, would be estimated using OLS procedures, which minimize the sum of squared deviations from the mean.[13]

How does one understand the results of an OLS regression? A regression can be thought of as describing how the average or expected value of the outcome variable (the left-hand-side variable) varies as any of the independent variables (right-hand-side variables) change. More formally, an OLS regression relates the mean of the dependent variable to the mean of each independent variable, and the estimated coefficients give the effect that changing the independent variable by one unit has on the outcome variable. Another way to think about the coefficient estimates that OLS produces is to think of each coefficient as giving the effect of a unit change in the independent variable on the conditional expectation of Y. In fact, it is common to call the conditional mean function—$E(Y|X)$—the regression of Y on X.

SPECIAL CONSIDERATIONS ASSOCIATED WITH OLS ESTIMATION OF THE WEALTH EQUATION

Because the distribution of wealth is highly skewed, the embedded assumption of a normally distributed dependent variable—which follows from the assumption of a normally distributed error term (ε)—is slightly tenuous. To cope with this feature, it is common to trim the distribution— to trim the upper and lower tails (outliers) of the wealth distribution— so that the resulting coefficient estimate is purged of the potential influence of the extreme values. Another way to contend with a skewed distribution is to transform the dependent variable into its logged form. However, because net worth can take on negative values (which cannot be logged), this approach—while commonly employed for estimating earnings—is not as common in the literature on wealth.[14] (It would require one to eliminate or transform an entire portion of the actual wealth distribution and virtually ignore the effects associated with being a net debtor by eliminating or reassigning all negative and zero values.)

ESTIMATION WITH OWNERSHIP OF AN ASSET AS THE
DEPENDENT VARIABLE

When examining individual assets, such as a bank account or a home, and the effects of different variables in determining whether a family owns the asset, an equation similar to the preceding one typically is specified.[15] However, because the outcome variable of interest is dichotomous in this case, a qualitative response model estimation strategy such as probit or logit often is preferred to OLS.

Why? There is first the issue of how one interprets the outcome of the estimation process. It is common to think about a regression as "explaining" some outcome variable of interest. Explaining whether an individual has an asset or not is like attempting to explain whether that person will buy something given his or her individual characteristics, which means that in this instance the regression equation is essentially estimating a probability that something will occur (that a specific outcome will prevail) given the characteristics of the person or family in question. One reason that OLS estimation is deemed undesirable in this situation is that it can generate nonsensical predicted values for these probabilities. In estimating the coefficient for any independent variable in a regression, OLS essentially seeks to fit a line between all the points associated with the observed Y and X values.[16] For an outcome variable that *only* takes on values of zero or one (see fig. 2.1, where for each explanatory variable value [X] on the horizontal axis there is a corresponding *actual* outcome variable value [Y] that is either zero or one), OLS estimation estimates a line that may very well extend beyond the *actual* zero to one range. This means that OLS estimation will arrive at predicted probabilities of ownership greater than one for some individuals and predicted probabilities that are negative for others. This is a drawback of the "linear probability model," as it is called. In practice it makes little sense to talk about negative probabilities and probabilities greater than one. Even if one reassigns "zero" values to the negative probabilities and a value of "one" to those predicted to be greater than one, the model is still unsatisfactory because some outcomes predicted to occur with certainty may very well not occur, and likewise some outcomes predicted not to occur with certainty may very well occur. Consider point X_T in figure 2.1, for example,

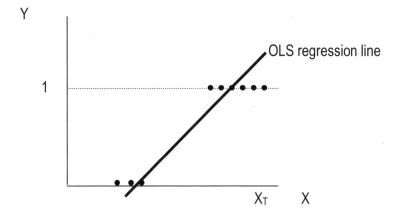

Fig. 2.1. OLS line. (From Kennedy 1985)

where the predicted value of Y lies above one. Even if one reassigns a value of one—indicating that one predicts certain ownership—there are likely to be individuals with characteristics X_T in the sample who do not own the asset in question. Accordingly, many researchers prefer to work with a functional form that confines itself within the dependent variable's limited range, without actually ever generating predicted values exactly equal to zero or one. This requires the specification of a nonlinear regression equation. Researchers typically use probit or logistic regression techniques to estimate the model (to produce the coefficients that are used to draw inferences about the effects of the different independent variables).

A second issue is that of the heteroskedasticity of the error term. If the variance of the error term in a regression is not the same across all observations, then heteroskedasticity is said to be present, and one of the assumptions of the classical linear regression model is violated.[17] In such an instance, the OLS coefficient estimates will not be efficient. This is not to say that the linear probability model is useless. Despite its drawbacks, it remains a viable way of detecting the presence of an association between two variables. Nonlinear estimation procedures can produce better estimates, however. This represents another advantage of the probit and logit models.

When using a probit model, the researcher is essentially conceptualizing families' characteristics as defining a buying index for them and assuming that if this index exceeds some (unknown) critical value, the asset will be bought. One then makes an assumption about the distribution of the critical values—that they are distributed normally—and the researcher can then specify a likelihood function that is used to obtain estimates of the marginal effect that any independent variable of interest has on the outcome variable. With the logit model the logic is similar to what has been described for a probit regression. The difference is that the critical values are presumed to be distributed according to a logistic function.

MEDIAN OR QUANTILE REGRESSIONS

Recall that by definition an OLS estimator chooses the coefficient estimates for the independent variables by minimizing the sum of squared residuals. Because the residuals are squared, large deviations from the regression line or large residuals have magnified effects in OLS regressions since they are squared. This renders OLS sensitive to outliers. Because of the skewness of the distribution of wealth (more specifically, the existence of the high wealth outliers in the right tail), one can argue that a regression technique that is less sensitive to outliers is more appropriate. Running a median regression offers a potential solution to this problem.[18] The objective of a median regression is to estimate the median of the outcome variable conditional on the values of the independent variables (much like an ordinary regression estimates the conditional mean of the dependent variable). The "least absolute deviation (LAD) estimator," as it is called, fits the median to a linear function of the independent variables and is viewed as being attractive for the same reason that the median is often viewed as a better measure than the mean. (See Buschinsky 1998 for additional discussion.)

While there is a valid theoretical argument for using median regressions when working with the distribution of wealth, in practice they are not that common. Instead, it is more common to trim the sample as discussed earlier. One paper that does present a median regression for wealth was written by Hurst, Luoh, and Stafford (1998). The first column of table 2.1 shows their results and indicates that the effect of race on wealth at the median—a little less than $3,000 (shown in the bottom row)—is much smaller than it is at the mean. When the OLS regression is used, one finds that the effect of being Black is to reduce wealth by about $27,408 instead.

DECOMPOSITION ANALYSIS

Another way to assess the effects of different independent variables on an outcome variable is to perform a decomposition analysis.[19] This is a technique that allows one to take a gap observed between two groups and to determine the portion of it that is explained by different independent variables, such as education or income. The procedure decomposes the observed racial/ethnic wealth gap into two parts—the first part is explained by the independent variables included in the regression that theory suggests predict the dependent variable (called the portion of the gap that is "explained"). This portion is a weighted difference in the average values of the independent (explanatory) variables of the two groups; hence, it is the racial/ethnic difference in wealth that is attributable to (explained by) differences in the way that wealth-generating characteristics (independent variables) are distributed across the two groups being compared. For example, theory suggests that education and age are predictors of wealth, so to the extent that Blacks and Whites differ in education and age, these differences in characteristics will be captured by the explained portion of the wage gap.

The second portion of the observed wealth gap, the "unexplained" portion, is the weighted difference between the rates of return (or coefficients) of the independent variables in the wealth regression. This portion compares differences in racial/ethnic rates of return (i.e., the ability to translate wealth-generating characteristics into wealth, or—in mathematical parlance—the difference between the conditional expected wealth functions for each group). For example, both the respective rates of return of education and age to wealth may differ across races (i.e., an additional year of schooling might predict a different level of wealth for Whites than it does for Blacks, and the same may be true for an additional rise in age). The "unexplained" portion is often used to measure "treatment" (or discriminatory) differences in wealth. It can be interpreted as the portion of the racial/ethnic wealth gap that is explained by differential treatment in the financial marketplace that prevents Blacks from accumulating wealth. However, to the extent that there exist other uncontrolled characteristics that vary across the groups and are not included in the model, the "unexplained" portion would be misinterpreted as treatment differentials because these additional uncontrolled characteristics would be captured by different group rates of returns (or regression coefficients) and be measured by the "unexplained" portion of the wealth gap. This potential for misinterpreting differences due to discrimination in decomposition analyses is similar to the potential problem that prevails using a dummy variable for race in OLS, probit, and logit, as described earlier, in that the culprit for both approaches is omitted variable bias.

A potential advantage of the decomposition approach toward measuring discrimination versus the dummy variable approach is that the former allows for differential treatment to manifest directly via race, but also indirectly via differential ability to translate wealth-generating characteristics into wealth. The decomposition approach allows for all of the regression coefficients to differ across race and hence indicates differential abilities of the groups to translate wealth-generating characteristics into wealth, while the dummy variable approach constrains the coefficients to be the same across race, unless interaction terms are included. And, to the extent that the races differ in their abilities to translate wealth-generating characteristics into wealth, the exclusion of relevant interaction terms leads to misspecification error in the dummy variable approach.

The "explained" and "unexplained" portions of the observed wealth gap are both dependent on their mutual choices of weights. In the case of the "explained" portion, the group differences in the independent variables are weighted by some corresponding regression coefficients of the independent variables. In the case of the "unexplained" portion, the group differences in rates of returns (regression coefficients) of the independent variables are weighted by some corresponding wealth-generating characteristics. The choice of weighting coefficients and weighting characteristics are typically generated from one of the racial groups— that is, Black (White) group coefficients and White (Black) group characteristics, respectively. Alternatively, the weights may come from some combination of the groups such as coefficients generated from a regression that includes both Blacks and Whites (the entire population) and characteristics computed from average levels of the independent variables that include both Black and White observations. Depending on which weights are chosen, the decomposition results will generally differ. Table 2.2 illustrates this point. In the Altonji et. al. (2000) data, for example, the unexplained gap ranges from 33 percent, when the White coefficients are used to weight the mean values of the explanatory variables, to 94 percent, when the Black coefficients are used to weight the difference in average characteristics.

There is no statistical theory to suggest which weights should be chosen to perform the decomposition; instead researchers may report multiple decomposition results based on multiple choices of weights (as shown in table 2.2). Then the reader is able to discern how sensitive the decomposition results are to the choice of weights. In addition, reporting multiple results can yield a lower and upper bound on both, the "explained" and "unexplained" predicted gaps.

The choice of weights also may be dictated by data concerns. For example, suppose a researcher is using a national probability sample and trying to perform Black/White wealth decompositions for those earning above $100,000 a year. Since relative to Whites there are so few Blacks earning $100,000 a year, such a stratification from a national probability sample may not yield enough observations to generate a Black wealth regression with an acceptable amount of statistical power on which to base out-of-sample predictions. As a result, it would be more appropriate to use weighting coefficients from the White wealth regression when predicting the Black/White "explained" portion of the wealth gap.

Finally, the choice of weights may depend on analytical reasoning or some perspective that the researchers are attempting to put forth. For

TABLE 2.2. Examples of Decomposition Analysis Results

	Altonji et al.[a]	Oliver and Shapiro-1[b]	Oliver and Shapiro-2[c]	Blau and Graham[d]
Unadjusted gap (mean)	−$152,029	−$71,849	−$47,587	−$20,829
Black wealth—mean	$54,357	$23,818	$17,434	$6,210
White wealth—mean	$206,386	$95,667	$65,024	$27,039
Predicted Black wealth	$53,213	$25,629	$38,121	NA
Predicted White wealth	$203,869	$86,229	$100,491	NA
Unadjusted gap (predicted values unless otherwise indicated)	$150,656	$60,600	$62,370	$20,829 (actual gap)
Explained gap (using White coefficients)	Amount = $101,391 Percent = 67 of predicted gap	Amount = $34,958 Percent = 57.7	Amount = $31,733 Percent = 50.9	Amount = $15,335 Percent = 73.6 of actual gap
Unexplained gap (using White coefficients)	33%	42.3%	49.1%	26.4%
Explained gap (using Black coefficients)	Amount = $9,220 Percent = 6	Amount = $17,459 Percent = 28.8	Amount = $16,076 Percent = 25.8	Amount = $4,545 Percent = 21.8
Unexplained gap (using Black coefficients)	94%	71.2%	74.2%	78.2%

Note: The Altonji et al. data come from a pooled sample from the 1984, 1988, and 1994 Panel Study of Income Dynamics (PSID) and are reported in 1989 dollars. Oliver and Shapiro (1995) use data from the 1988 Survey of Income and Program Participation (SIPP). Blau and Graham use data from the 1976/78 National Longitudinal Surveys of Youth (NLSY) and report figures using 1976 dollars.

[a]Data are for married couples sample from tables 1 and 3.
[b]Data are for full sample from tables 4.4 and A6.2.
[c]Data are for married households from table 5.2.
[d]Data are for married couples sample from table 5.

example, if a researcher wanted to address the hypothetical, "How much would the wealth gap fall if Blacks had the same wealth-generating *characteristics* as Whites?" then the mean characteristics from the White sample would be used to compare differences in Black and White wealth-generating *coefficients*. (For a more detailed discussion of decomposition techniques, see Blinder 1973, Oaxaca 1973, Jones and Kelley 1984, and Oaxaca and Ransom 1999)

NONPARAMETRIC ESTIMATION TECHNIQUES

Part of the reason that there are differences in the portion of the gap found to be explained when using the White and Black coefficients to weight the mean differences in characteristics is because of differences in the role attributed to earnings when explaining wealth differences. Barsky et al. (2002) show that, for this particular explanatory variable, the Black coefficient resulting from an OLS regression will always be smaller than the coefficient generated from a similar regression for Whites.[20] This obtains because the true relationship between wealth and earnings is non-linear, which means that the "rate of return" to earnings, or the effect that earnings have on wealth accumulation, varies across the earnings distribution. Barsky et al. show that in such a situation the OLS coefficients generated in a regression for Blacks inherently come from a regression run over the portion of the earnings distribution where the relationship between wealth and earnings is weak—where the conditional distribution of wealth given earnings is relatively flat. Contrarily, because White earnings span a greater range of values, the White distribution undoubtedly extends into a range of earnings in which the conditional wealth function has a steeper slope, resulting in an OLS coefficient that "averages" information from both ends of the distribution, which necessarily will be greater than that produced from a regression over a range of incomes where the conditional expectations function is relatively flat. Figures 2.2a and 2.2b show two different, hypothetical distributions that illustrate these points

Barsky et al. also note that in instances in which one has an explanatory variable whose relationship to wealth is nonlinear, decompositions based on OLS are likely to involve specification error, ensuring that the decomposition will miscalculate the portion of the wealth gap that is unexplained, regardless of which set of coefficients (White or Black) the researcher chooses to use.

Why does this occur? To properly decompose the gap in mean wealth,

Wealth

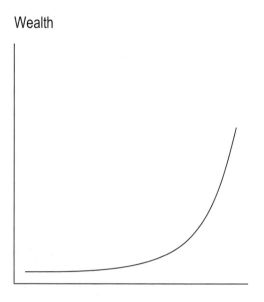

Earnings

Fig. 2.2a. Hypothetical White wealth distribution

Wealth

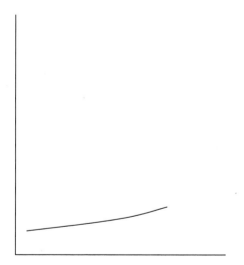

Earnings

Fig. 2.2b. Hypothetical Black wealth distribution

one must be able to divide the difference in means into two parts—one associated with the difference in the distributions of the characteristics of the two populations and a second reflecting differences in the conditional expectations functions of the two groups.[21] Barsky et al. find that if the true relationship between wealth and a characteristic that is relevant for wealth accumulation—earnings, for example—is nonlinear, OLS will give incorrect information about the difference between the two groups' conditional expectations functions (because of specification error).

To understand this point intuitively, recall that it is common for researchers to perform decompositions in two different ways. A researcher might use coefficients from a regression for Blacks to weight the differences in average characteristics, which can be described as asking what Black wealth would be if Blacks' earnings were to rise to the level of Whites' earnings. Alternatively, a researcher might use the White coefficients to weight the differences in average characteristics, which is akin to asking what would happen to White wealth if Whites' earnings were to fall to the level of Blacks'. Either method involves the construction of an estimate for a hypothetical or "counterfactual" case (as Black and White earnings are not distributed the same in practice). In the first instance, the counterfactual exercise involves predicting or estimating Black mean wealth based on the White earnings distribution. In the second instance, the counterfactual exercise involves predicting White mean wealth over the Black earnings distribution. Barsky et al. show that OLS estimation cannot arrive at the correct value for the counterfactual exercise in either case.

The problem lies in attempting to generate the right conditional expectations function for the group whose earnings distribution is not being used to weight the distance between the two groups' conditional expectations functions. When viewed intuitively, the problem is that when one tries to ask what wealth Whites would have if Whites had the Black earnings distribution, one is guaranteed to get an answer that is not correct when using OLS. (Barsky et al. prove this.) Similarly, if one were to opt for doing one's decomposition by using the White earnings distribution to weight the difference between the Black and White conditional expectations functions, the value computed for Blacks' expected wealth, assuming their earnings were distributed like Whites', would be wrong.[22] This, in turn, means that one will miscalculate the unexplained portion of the wealth gap, since the portion that researchers deem to be "unexplained" is the portion attributable to differences in the conditional expectations function (the part represented by the co-efficients).

Barsky et al. show that using a nonparametric technique, which does not assume a particular functional form as OLS does, is preferable to OLS. For this reason, many researchers have begun to advocate the use of this technique to decompose racial/ethnic wealth gaps, although the approach is relatively new to the social sciences.

CONCLUSION

There are a variety of empirical techniques that can be employed to analyze racial and ethnic wealth gaps and patterns of asset ownership. However, to impart meaning to observed differences (i.e., to go beyond merely characterizing differences between non-Whites and Whites so that one can explain why the differences exist), a researcher must be prepared to undertake analyses that distinguish between (1) factors contributing to the differences that stem from individual behavior and (2) those that are due to structural features of U.S. society. This is not always easy, as some methods require assumptions that researchers can always debate and new methods are constantly under development. While useful for identifying the presence of wealth differences that are directly attributable to race, for example, OLS regressions have the drawback of assuming and constraining the effects of variables other than race to be the same for Blacks and Whites. Alternatively, decompositions allow one to examine the role of differences in rates of return (to wealth-generating characteristics) in generating wealth gaps, but the effect of differences in coefficients by race is difficult to estimate precisely. This technique also can involve loss of degrees of freedom, and—depending on data set limitations—researchers sometimes do not have a sufficient number of observations to employ it as it commonly requires that separate regressions be run by race. Another drawback of standard decomposition techniques is that they assume a linear relationship between the outcome variable and the explanatory variables. Nonparametric estimation offers a possible solution to this quandary, yet this empirical technique is difficult and not free of limitations of its own.

Because of these issues a researcher must choose judiciously when deciding on an empirical strategy for assessing the role of race in generating wealth or asset-ownership rate gaps, as well as when interpreting results and attempting to discern the reasons that race is relevant. As shown in this chapter, the methods available vary in degrees of statistical sophistication, and there are pros and cons to each.

1. For the difference in the mean values of two groups to be considered significantly different from a statistical standpoint, it is not enough for the means to be different. Information about different subgroups of the U.S. population typically is obtained from surveys that sample a subset of the population. Means and medians for each subgroup are then computed from the sample. The researcher then uses information about the sample to draw inferences about the population. The means and medians computed for each subgroup therefore are only estimates of the true values one would find if one were to survey the entire population. Accordingly, the standard error for each calculated mean, which combines information about the variance and sample size, must be examined too. The standard errors must be small enough to rule out the possibility that the calculated means (the estimates of the true means for each of the two groups) could have come from the same distribution.

2. As with the case for continuous variables, to be "meaningful" the differences must be both statistically significant and sizeable (or economically relevant). See Ziliak and McCloskey 2004 for further discussion of this issue.

3. When the data are not coded with zeroes for lack of ownership and a one for any family that does own the asset, it is standard procedure to recode them accordingly in order to make interpretation easier.

4. Why does a gap suggest disadvantage? In practice, when racial gaps do exist, they typically reveal that non-Whites have less wealth and lower rates of asset ownership, on average, than Whites. Because wealth is a measure of the total stock of resources that a family has at its disposal, this implies that non-Whites have fewer resources than Whites do, hence putting them at a disadvantage in our society in which most goods and services must be privately purchased. For individual assets, such as bank accounts, stocks, or homes, lower rates of asset ownership are considered disadvantageous either because they serve as further examples of non-Whites' low wealth status or—for assets with functional uses beyond their store of value function—because lack of ownership suggests that non-Whites may be likely to be foregoing some service that other members of society take for granted. For example, in addition to representing an asset where wealth is stored, bank accounts are used to make and process payments, so families that do not have a bank account must turn elsewhere for transactions services (often to higher per-unit-cost providers, Caskey 1994).

5. The convention in the United States is to establish the White group as the reference or baseline group and to compare others with it. This means that an alternative interpretation of the inequality described in the preceding note is that it represents White advantage rather than a non-White dis-

84 - ✿ -   Wealth Accumulation & Communities of Color in the United States

advantage. The choice of Whites as the baseline is generally a subjective one, and for convention, we adopt it as well for this chapter.

6. In general, married couples benefit from economies of scale and are thus positioned to be able to accumulate greater wealth than single individuals, an empirical finding that is robust throughout the literature. (See Blau and Graham 1990, for example.)

7. Economic and social science theory identifies several candidates for control variables. This list is not exhaustive. Instead it is representative of the types of regressors that one is apt to find in the literature and in the other chapters of this volume.

8. Note that it is possible that discrimination may manifest in the acquisition of wealth-generating characteristics. In the literature, this typically is referred to as "premarket" discrimination. In general, this chapter is discussing "in-market" forms of discrimination. Its analysis does not attempt to address debates about whether there is racial/ethnic discrimination that affects the acquisition of characteristics that lead to high levels of wealth. For example, high labor income and high levels of education both boost wealth, so if there is discrimination in the labor market or the educational arena—so-called premarket factors in the market for wealth accumulation—these forms of discrimination are not accounted for in the standard analyses of wealth and asset-ownership gaps.

9. Most of the existing literature focuses on differences between Blacks and Whites, or Whites and non-Whites, and does not present estimates of the effect of being in other racial or ethnic minority groups. Readers who are interested in what is known about the effect of being in other racial/ethnic groups should consult other chapters in this volume.

10. These figures, which come from PSID data, are for the year 1994 and are reported in 1996 dollars.

11. Among scholars this essentially is a debate about whether all relevant factors have been controlled for in a regression so that the race coefficient can truly be interpreted as reflecting the presence of discrimination, as opposed to the presence of "cultural" differences, for example. (Becker [1991] is one proponent of the argument that differences in "culture" may explain some differences that are observed across families.)

12. In technical terms, there is a problem of omitted variable bias. A priori, the bias could lead to either over- or underestimates of discrimination. If there are strong reasons to believe that preferences may be different across racial/ethnic groups, a researcher has to accept the possibility that the race effect that he or she finds in a regression that does not control for preferences actually may not represent discrimination. However, if there is no theoretical reason to expect a difference in preferences toward the outcome variable of interest, then the criticism may not apply. Note, additionally, that having a measure of preferences would introduce complications of its own. The endogenous nature of such a variable can introduce other problems into the estimation process.

13. Additional discussion of OLS estimation can be found in any statistics or econometrics textbook. See Greene 1997, for example.

14. See Charles and Hurst 2003 for an example of the application of the method.

15. Though one or two regressors may be different. For example, some researchers argue that an equation for stock ownership should include the family's level of wealth as a regressor.

16. Where we said earlier that OLS minimizes the sum of squared residuals, we can now add that this is equivalent to attempting to minimize the distance between actual observations of Y, X pairs measured by a line given by the estimated regression equation.

17. See Greene 1997 or Maddala 1983 for an explicit mathematical representation of the problem.

18. A median regression is one type of a more general class of regressions—quantile regression.

19. Because most published decomposition analyses focus on Black-White differences, this section refers repeatedly to these two groups. However, the insights can be extended to other racial/ethnic groups too.

20. Taking the case of only one explanatory variable for simplicity, recall that the portion of the gap that was attributed to differences in characteristics is computed as B^i $(\bar{X}^{white} - \bar{X}^{black})$ and that researchers typically report two estimates for this value. The first takes B from the regression for Whites (i = Whites). The second takes B from the regression for Blacks (i = Blacks). And from table 2.2 it is clear that the latter route always yields a smaller portion explained and a larger portion unexplained than the former does.

21. In the context of the linear model estimated by OLS (discussed in the previous section covering decomposition analysis), the first part is represented by the (weighted) differences in the average value of the characteristics, or the means of the distributions of characteristics, and the second part is represented by the (weighted) difference in the regression coefficients.

22. Barsky et al. (2002) offer a strong argument for not choosing this particular counterfactual exercise however.

REFERENCES

Altonji, Joseph, Ulrich Doraszelski, and Lewis Segal. 2000. "Black/White Differences in Wealth." *Federal Reserve Bank of Chicago Economic Perspectives* 24 (1): 38–50.

Barsky, Robert, John Bound, Kerwin Kofi Charles, and Joseph P. Lupton. 2002. "Accounting for the Black-White Wealth Gap: A Nonparametric Approach." *Journal of the American Statistical Association* 97 (459): 663–73.

Becker, Gary. 1991. *A Treatise on the Family.* Cambridge: Harvard University Press.

Blau, Francine, and John W. Graham. 1990. "Black-White Differences in Wealth and Asset Composition." *Quarterly Journal of Economics* 105 (2): 321–39.

Blinder, Alan. 1973. "Wage Discrimination: Reduced Form and Structural Estimates." *Journal of Human Resources* 8 (4): 436–55.

Buschinsky, Moshe. 1998. "Recent Advances in Quantile Regression Models: A Practical Guideline for Empirical Research." *Journal of Human Resources* 33 (1): 88–126.

Caskey, John P. 1994. *Fringe Banking: Check-Cashing Outlets, Pawnshops, and the Poor.* New York: Russell Sage Foundation.

Charles, Kerwin Kofi, and Erik Hurst. 2003. "The Correlation of Wealth across Generations." *Journal of Political Economy* 111 (6): 1155–82.

Darity, William, Jr. 2003. "Will the Poor Always Be with Us?" *Review of Social Economy* 61 (4): 471–77.

Darity, William, Jr., and Patrick L. Mason. 1998. "Evidence on Discrimination in Employment: Codes of Color, Codes of Gender." *Journal of Economic Perspectives* 12 (2): 63–90.

Gittleman, Maury, and Edward Wolff. 2004. "Racial Differences in Patterns of Wealth Accumulation." *Journal of Human Resources* 39 (1): 193–277.

Greene, William. 1997. *Econometric Analysis.* 3rd ed. Upper Saddle River, NJ: Prentice Hall.

Hurst, Erik, Ming Ching Luoh, and Frank Stafford. 1998. "The Wealth Dynamics of American Families, 1984–94." *Brookings Papers on Economic Activity* 1: 267–392.

Jones, F. L., and Jonathan Kelley. 1984. "Decomposing Differences between Groups: A Cautionary Note on Measuring Discrimination." *Sociological Methods and Research* 12 (3): 323–43.

Kennedy, Peter. 1985. *A Guide to Econometrics.* 2nd ed. Cambridge: MIT Press.

Maddala, G. S. 1983. *Limited-Dependent and Qualitative Variables in Econometrics.* Cambridge: Cambridge University Press.

Oaxaca, Ronald. 1973. "Male-Female Wage Differentials in Urban Labor Markets." *International Economic Review* 14 (3): 693–709.

Oaxaca, Ronald, and Michael Ransom. 1999. "Identification in Detailed Wage Decompositions." *Review of Economics and Statistics* 81 (1): 154–57.

Oliver, Melvin, and Thomas Shapiro. 1995. *Black Wealth/White Wealth: A New Perspective On Racial Inequality.* New York: Routledge.

Ziliak, Stephen T., and Deirdre N. McCloskey. 2004. "Size Matters: The Standard Error of Regressions in the *American Economic Review.*" *Journal of Socio-Economics* 33 (5): 527–46.

II Intragroup Inequality

3 Determinants of Intragroup Wealth Inequality among Whites, Blacks, & Latinos

YUVAL ELMELECH

Since the late 1970s, research on racial inequality has documented growing intragroup economic divisions among racial and ethnic groups. In his influential book *The Declining Significance of Race: Blacks and Changing American Institutions,* Wilson (1980) claims that the Black population has become stratified into groups whose members range from those who are highly educated and affluent to those who are marginalized and impoverished. These deepening intragroup economic disparities, Wilson argues, represent a trend toward the declining significance of race and the growing importance of class as a factor determining the life chances of Blacks in contemporary U.S. society. Recent evidence confirms the growing economic disparities among Blacks (see Gordon Nembhard, Pitts, and Mason 2005). Most previous studies on intragroup economic inequality and the race-class nexus have focused on the Black community while emphasizing differentials in educational attainment and labor market attributes. Less attention was given to intragroup wealth disparities within communities of color.

Compared with the more common measures of economic well-being (e.g., education, poverty, earnings, and occupational status), household net worth encompasses a broad notion of socioeconomic inequality, which is more closely related in meaning to the concepts of living standards and life chance. Studies report that assets, as a "stock" of material resources, increase personal control and security, improve household stability, promote development of human capital among offspring, increase social status and social influence, and generate social capital in the form of contacts and social networks (see review in Page-Adams and Sherraden 1997). As such, the study of wealth is key to an understanding of intragroup economic stratification and its perpetuation.

The purpose of this chapter is to illuminate the social and economic determinants of intragroup wealth inequality among Whites, Blacks, and Latinos. Data for this study were derived from the Health and Retirement Survey (HRS92), which covers middle-aged American households born between 1931 and 1941. This age cohort has benefited from the unprecedented economic growth and the antidiscrimination legislation after World War II, which coincided with the expansion of the Black middle class on the 1950s and 1960s. By studying the determinants of intragroup wealth inequality among Whites and non-Whites, this chapter questions the declining-significance-of-race thesis while shedding new light on the race-class debate.

THEORETICAL FRAMEWORK: INTRAGROUP DIFFERENTIALS IN HOUSEHOLD NET WORTH

Data on wealth inequality in the United States reveal that household net worth is more unevenly distributed among Latinos and Blacks than among Whites: the median net worth held by White households at the highest income quintile is 16.2 times greater than the median net worth of the wealth held by households at the lowest income quintile, and is 3.3 times greater than the amount held by the middle (third) quintile. The comparable figures for Blacks and Latinos are 180 and 5.3 (among Blacks), and 112 and 8.8 (among Latinos), respectively (U.S. Department of Commerce 1995b). Using data from the Survey of Consumer Finances (SCF) collected during three points in time—1962, 1983, and 1989—and comparing the mean and the median value of wealth of Whites and non-Whites, Wolff (1994) concludes that the distribution of wealth is more unequal among non-Whites than Whites and the gaps have increased over time. While this pattern corroborates the copious evidence on the increasing polarization in education and labor market remuneration among non-White populations, we know very little about the demographic and socioeconomic determinants of intragroup wealth disparity among non-White populations.

The literature on wealth identifies three critical explanations of inequality: human capital and labor market characteristics, family structure, and intergenerational transfers. The classical economic view attributes wealth inequality to human capital and labor market differentials. According to this framework, education and occupational attainment are strongly correlated with ownership of assets such as home, business, and bank accounts (see review in Heflin and Pattillo-McCoy 2002). This pattern is consistent with the Life-Cycle Hypothesis (LCH) of wealth accumulation (Osberg 1984, quoted in Spilerman 2000, 507), according to which, household wealth follows the course of labor market participation, linking increasing income with increasing wealth, followed by spending down of assets during the years after retirement. Labor market characteristics, however, provide merely a partial explanation to wealth inequality. Contrary to common belief, wealth and income are not strongly correlated. Previous research has produced estimates of the correlation between income and wealth that range from a low of 0.26 to a high of 0.5 (Keister and Moller 2000), and the correlation between the two variables is especially small among those at the top of the income bracket (Inhaber and Carroll 1992, 91, fig. 5.3; Wolff 2001, 61, table 2.12). However, the association between labor market attainment and household net worth is likely to differ across racial and ethnic lines.

First, because racial and ethnic non-White groups have, on average, lower levels of wealth, and are more dependent on labor market remuneration as a source of economic security, human capital and occupational attainment are likely to have a stronger effect on intragroup wealth inequality among Blacks and Latinos. Second, the socioeconomic circumstances and the opportunity structure faced by various groups vary. Research on the changing economic conditions of Blacks since the early 1960s suggests that while some segments of the population remain trapped within the inner city, where education and employment opportunities are limited, others have taken advantage of the opportunities opened up by the civil rights movement and are experiencing socioeconomic mobility (see Wilson 1980, 1987; Patillo-McCoy 1999). While the Black middle class has clearly grown since the 1960s, critics of the declining-significance-of-race thesis report persistent economic gaps between middle-class Whites and non-Whites and argue that this respective inequality reflects racial differences in both the development and the characteristics of class structure. While the White middle class, for example, has historically contained more upper- than lower-middle-class workers, the opposite is true among Blacks, who have had less access to the types of jobs that facilitate socioeconomic mobility (see review in Pattillo-McCoy 1999; see also Son, Model, and Fisher 1989; Gates 2004). Based on these observations, Ogbu (1987) concludes that the economic and education problems of Black Americans do not result merely from lower-class status.

> Instead they are consequences of the double stratification of class and racial caste. As a result, lower-class Blacks share certain attributes common to all lower-class people everywhere, but they also have distinctive attributes because they belong to a subordinate racial caste. (Ogbu 1987, 239–40)

While Latinos possess relatively inferior positions in the labor market, the factors responsible for their socioeconomic disadvantage are much different from those that determine Black economic circumstances. Specifically, the foreign nativity of many Latinos has been cited as a major cause of their limited access to jobs and wealth. National figures show that among men and women alike, the foreign-born are more heavily concentrated in service jobs and have the lowest representation in managerial and sales jobs (Chiswick and Sullivan 1995; Waters and Esbach 1995). Research on home ownership—one of the major components of household net worth—has found that home ownership is strongly associated with immigration status and labor market advancement (Alba and Logan 1992). With the passage of time, the economic hardship faced by newcomers is often alleviated, and immigrants tend to experience occupational mobility (Neidert and Farley 1985; Portes and Rumbaut 1990), which in turn translates into higher home ownership rates.

In addition to labor market attainment, a major demographic trend affecting the distribution of wealth in the United States is the changing pattern of the American family. Data on wealth inequality show that the amount of net worth among households maintained by married couples is about four times greater than that of households maintained by either women or men (U.S. Department of Commerce 1995b). This pattern is attributed to several factors (see Waite and Gallagher 2000; Hao 1996). First, the division of labor among couples and the benefits of economies of scale—the sharing of house, car, and domestic commodities—enable married couples to maintain higher standards of living than do single people with similar socioeconomic characteristics. Second, married couples have the propensity to save and invest a higher proportion of their income for unforeseen events, such as death and unemployment, that may leave their spouse and children without sufficient material resources. Third, the likelihood of receiving financial assets increases as a result of the expansion of family and social networks. Given the distinct racial/ethnic patterns of family structure, socioeconomic returns on marriage are likely to vary by racial and ethnic origin. Since Latino families are larger, and demonstrate a high propensity to rely on extended family members as a source of social and economic support, the expansion of social networks is likely to play a critical role in determining wealth inequality between Latino families (also see chap. 10). While marriage is associated with wealth, divorce and widowhood have strong negative impacts on the accumulation of assets. Holden and Kuo (1996) report that couples in which at least one spouse had experienced divorce or widowhood have significantly lower incomes and assets than couples in first-time marriages (also see chap. 4). The higher incidence of marital disruption and the breakup of the husband-wife family among Blacks has been cited as a major factor in differential rates of poverty and wealth between Blacks and Whites (Farley 1984; Bianchi 1999; Rodgers 1987; Smith and Ward 1989; Keister 2004).

   A third explanation of variation in asset holdings views the transfers of intergenerational resources in the form of inter vivos (transfers that people made during their lifetime) and bequests as a major source of household net worth (Langbein 1991; Gale and Scholtz 1994; McNamee and Miller 1998; Wilhelm 2001). Studies report that inherited wealth is often used as a means of mobilization in the housing market and is associated with both the ownership of businesses and the amount of capital employed in a new enterprise (Henretta 1984; Holtz-Eakin, Joulfaian, and Rosen 1994; Lindh and Ohlsson 1998). While some scholars have predicted that the continuing decrease in family size, changing women's roles, rising incidence of divorce, and the survival of more parents to old age will reduce intergenerational contacts, data collected in recent years found no evidence to indicate a decline of supportive relationships between the generations (Logan and Spitze 1996; Attias-Donfut and Arber 2000). Because individuals live longer and are likely to share more years and experiences with other generations, intergenerational transfers of financial resources may be more important today than in earlier decades (Lowenstein and Bengtson 2003, 372). The distribution of inherited wealth is highly unequal and has a strong polarizing effect on socioeconomic inequality (Smith 1997). Consequently, neglect of intergenerational transmission of material advantage is becoming harder to justify in stratification research in general (Kotlikoff and Summers 1989; Spilerman, Lewin-Epstein, and

Semyonov 1993) and in the context of racial and ethnic inequality in particular (Avery and Rendell 2002; Shapiro 2004). Because non-White households have, on average, fewer material resources, intergenerational financial assistance is a critical determinant of economic mobility among non-White families (McAdoo 1997). In addition, research emphasizes the distinct pattern of family transfers among Black and Latino families as compared with Whites and suggests that non-White parents have stronger investment and exchange motives and are likely to give more to adult children with higher education and economic resources (Lee and Aytac 1998). This finding implies that family transfers may have a more polarizing effect on the distribution of economic resources among Blacks and Latinos.

In line with the preceding considerations, the aims of the present investigation are to describe intragroup racial/ethnic variation in the distribution of household net worth and to analyze the extent to which demographic and human capital characteristics shape these differentials. First, I expected to find substantial intragroup wealth disparities within the three racial categories, although these gaps are likely to be greater within the two non-White groups. Second, I hypothesized that education and labor market attributes, as well as family structure and intergenerational wealth transfers, play an important role in determining intragroup inequality in household net worth among Black, White, and Latino populations. However, these factors are likely to have a more polarizing effect among the two non-White groups. Finally, I predicted that immigration status is a critical determinant of wealth among Latinos.*

POPULATION & DATA

This chapter uses data from the Health and Retirement Study (HRS) 1992 (wave 1). The data include a sample of about 12,600 persons in 7,600 households for the 1931–41 birth cohort (and their spouses, if married, regardless of age). The sample design is a multistage area probability sample of households, with oversamples of Latinos, Blacks, and

---

*Other authors in this volume find immigration status to be an important explanatory variable for Latino and Asian American wealth disparity. See Ong and Patraporn (chap. 7) and Dymski, Mohanty, and Li (chap. 9) for Asian Americans and Pacific Islanders and Robles (chap. 10) for Latinos. In addition, we had hoped to have a chapter on wealth differences in African American communities by immigration status, but that article did not come through [Editors].

Florida residents. The HRS is an exceptional source of data suitable for the current analyses because it contains detailed information on household net worth, intergenerational transfers, and marital history. Research indicates that the most crucial age cohort in terms of wealth accumulation, its transmission, and its socioeconomic impact on cross-generational relations includes persons on the verge of retirement. Household net worth and the income derived from financial assets are critical factors determining the economic well-being of people in retirement (Angel and Angel 1997). Also, with the increase in life expectancy, bequests are being transferred at later stages of the life cycle, namely, when the heirs are entering the "third age" (Laslett 1987). The variables included in the analyses are described in the appendix to this chapter.

FINDINGS

Table 3.1 displays descriptive statistics on household net worth and demographic and socioeconomic characteristics by racial/ethnic origin. The data reveal substantial racial inequality in household net worth. Whereas the net worth held by an average White household is $278,000, the net worth held by the average Black or Latino households is almost one-third of that amount. This gap is substantially larger than the racial/ethnic variation in income; the average annual amount of labor-related income for a White household is nearly two times greater than that of either a Black or Latino household. These figures support the assumption that accumulated wealth is not a mere reflection of labor market attainment. Since the wealth distribution is skewed to the right, table 3.1 also reports the median net worth of the three groups: while the median White household holds $127,000 in net worth, the median Black and Latino households hold $28,500 and $31,500, respectively.

The data reveal substantial interracial/ethnic variation in education and labor market attributes. While 44 percent of the White householders have high (more than twelve years) education, the comparable figures for Blacks and Latinos are 29.6 and 21, respectively. The data also indicate that 69.4 percent of White respondents are employed, while 58.7 of Black respondents and 52.9 percent of Latino respondents are employed. In terms of family structure characteristics, the racial variation is apparent: while 70 percent of the White householders and 59 percent of the Latino householders are married, less than half (41.5 percent) of the Black householders are married. In addition, Latinos seem to experience more

TABLE 3.1. Mean Characteristics (standard deviation) of Households by Racial/Ethnic Origin (weighted)

	Whites	Blacks	Latinos
Net worth (in thousand $)	277.8	83.5	105.3
	(560.0)	(243.5)	(403.3)
Median net worth (in thousand $)	127.0	28.5	31.5
Resources received			
Transfers (%)	35.6	10.7	10.0
	(47.8)	(30.9)	(30.0)
Inheritance (%)	24.5	4.7	5.0
	(43.4)	(21.2)	(21.9)
Gifts (%)	9.4	2.2	2.0
	(29.2)	(14.9)	(14.1)
Life insurance benefits (%)	5.7	4.3	3.1
	(23.3)	(20.3)	(17.5)
Labor income (in thousand $)	41.8	24.9	21.3
	(47.7)	(27.8)	(28.9)
Education			
Less than high school (0–11 years)	18.9	41.6	61.4
	(39.2)	(49.3)	(48.7)
High school (12 years)	36.9	28.7	17.5
	(48.2)	(45.2)	(38.0)
More than high school (13+ years)	44.0	29.6	21.0
	(49.6)	(45.6)	(40.7)
Occupation			
Managerial/professional	33.6	15.8	12.1
	(47.2)	(36.5)	(32.6)
Sales/clerical/support	25.8	14.7	15.4
	(43.7)	(35.4)	(36.1)
Other (service/operators/no occupation/	40.5	69.4	72.4
farming)	(49.1)	(46.0)	(44.7)
Currently employed	69.4	58.7	52.9
	(46.0)	(49.2)	(49.9)
Marital status			
Married	69.9	41.5	59.0
	(44.8)	(49.2)	(49.1)
First marriage	48.9	28.7	44.8
	(49.9)	(45.2)	(49.7)
Married before	21.0	12.8	14.2
	(40.7)	(33.4)	(34.9)
Divorced	14.6	19.0	15.0
	(35.3)	(39.2)	(36.6)
Widowed	7.1	14.9	8.8
	(25.8)	(35.6)	(28.4)
Other (never married/separated/living	8.2	24.5	16.0
with a partner)	(27.4)	(43.0)	(36.7)
Native-born	95.5	95.3	47.0
	(20.6)	(20.9)	(49.9)
Gender (male)	55.0	40.7	48.9
	(49.7)	(49.1)	(49.9)
Age	56.1	55.8	55.9
	(4.9)	(4.6)	(5.1)

TABLE 3.1.—*Continued*

	Whites	**Blacks**	**Latinos**
Household size	2.4	2.5	3.3
	(1.1)	(2.6)	(1.9)
Region (South)	32.2	49.8	39.3
	(46.7)	(50.0)	(48.8)
Metropolitan area	72.1	86.9	83.8
	(44.8)	(33.6)	(33.6)
Children	2.9	3.5	3.7
	(1.9)	(2.5)	(2.7)
N	5,297	1,424	714

Note: Total *N* = 7,605 households.

stable marriages: two-thirds of the Latino couples live in intact families. At almost 40 percent, Black households are more likely to be headed by females. Intergenerational transfers of wealth are distributed unequally across racial and ethnic lines. While more than one-third (35.6 percent) of White householders received intergenerational transfers, the comparable figures for Blacks and Latinos are 10.7 and 10, respectively. Table 3.1 shows that the White–non-White gap in inheritance and inter vivos gifts is substantially large. For example, about a quarter (24.5 percent) of the White households received inheritance, while only 5 percent of the non-White households report the receipt of inheritance.

WEALTH INEQUALITY AMONG BLACKS, LATINOS, & WHITES

Since this chapter focuses on intragroup variations in wealth, table 3.2 provides information on how wealth is distributed among the three racial/ethnic groups. The total household net worth in each group was divided into five categories (quintiles), each quintile represents 20 percent of the population. Two findings merit attention. First, the data show substantial racial and ethnic inequality: the typical White household in each net worth quintile has higher median net worth than a similar-quintile non-White household. The median Black household at the top fifth of the wealth distribution, for example, holds $167,000 in net worth, which is about 70 percent of the amount held by a typical White household at the fourth quintile of the distribution ($236,100). Note also that the amount of wealth held by the median non-White household at the lower fifth of the distribution is zero.

TABLE 3.2. Median Measured Net Worth by Racial/Ethnic Origin: Distribution and Ratio between Quintiles

Quintiles	White	Black	Latino
Bottom quintile (0–20%)	6,500	00	00
Ratio to top quintile	90.8	167,000[a]	213,835[a]
Second quintile (20–40%)	61,000	2,700	3,000
Ratio to top quintile	9.7	61.8	71.2
Third quintile (40–60%)	126,912	28,650	31,500
Ratio to top quintile	4.6	5.8	6.8
Fourth quintile (60–80%)	236,100	66,600	79,700
Ratio to top quintile	2.5	2.5	2.7
Top quintile (80–100%)	590,500	167,000	213,835

[a]Assuming that the median net worth of households in the bottom quintile is 1.

Second, a substantial intragroup polarization between non-White households who are well off and those who are not is also apparent. To illuminate this point, table 3.2 displays the ratio of the median net worth between the top quintile and each of the four quintiles below it by racial/ethnic category. In line with the previously mentioned hypotheses, the data reveal that the intragroup differences between the lower and the upper quintiles are more substantial among the non-White populations. For example, while the gap (ratio) between the median net worth of the top fifth and the second-lowest fifth is 9.7 among Whites, the figures for Blacks and Latinos are 61.8 and 71.2, respectively.

MULTIVARIATE ANALYSIS: DETERMINANTS OF INTRAGROUP WEALTH INEQUALITY

This section tests the previously mentioned hypotheses and estimates the extent to which socioeconomic and demographic determinants affect net worth among White, Black, and Latino households. Because the right-hand skew of the net worth distribution creates complications in regression analysis, the dependent variable (net worth) was transformed by taking natural logarithms. However, the log transformation cannot be applied to those households with zero or negative net worth. Furthermore, the least squares estimation of a regression model for a truncated sample, which includes only those households with positive net worth, or a censored sample in which an arbitrary zero value is used for those households with a nonpositive value, leads to biased and inconsistent regression estimators (Amemiya 1985, chap. 10; Land and Russell 1996; Long 1997). Hao (2004) adds that the effects of demographic and socioeconomic determinants of household net worth are likely to be in the same direction for positive and negative values compared with the category zero net worth, leading to bias in ordinary least squares results. For these reasons, the multivariate analysis presented in the following table 3.3 and figure 3.1 is based on a lower-bound Tobit regression model (see Land and Russell 1996; Hao 2004).[1]

Table 3.3 reports findings on the distinct effect that labor market attainment, marital status, and intergenerational transfers have on household net worth among each of the three groups under study. Since the dependent variable is the natural logarithm of net worth, the coefficients can be transformed using the natural logarithm to indicate a percentage increase in net worth. For example, in the White model, the effect of being employed is 1.73 times that of unemployed (exp .55 = 1.73). Applying the McDonald and Moffitt correction factor (1980; see also Roncek

TABLE 3.3.   Unstandardized Regression Coefficients from Tobit Analysis Predicting Logged Total Household Net Worth by Racial Category

	Net Worth White	Net Worth Black	Net Worth Latino
Marital status[a]			
Married, intact	1.62***	2.88***	2.84***
	(.152)	(.472)	(.690)
Married, married before	1.21***	2.22***	2.86***
	(.166)	(.539)	(.781)
Divorced	−.652***	.166	−1.01
	(.183)	(.489)	(.767)
Other	−.016	−1.00*	−1.15
	(.206)	(.469)	(.760)
Received family transfers[b]	.783***	2.33***	2.13***
	(.079)	(.434)	(.574)
Education[c]			
High school	.938***	.749*	1.01*
	(.108)	(.341)	(.475)
More than high school	1.11***	1.43***	1.23*
	(.119)	(.417)	(.513)
Occupation[d]			
Professional/managerial	.545***	.873	1.21*
	(.102)	(.475)	(.609)
Sales/clerical	.350**	1.02*	.736
	(.101)	(.417)	(.504)
Employed[e]	.550***	2.19***	1.43***
	(.086)	(.305)	(.366)
Income (/1000)	.008***	.042***	.018*
	(.000)	(.006)	(.008)
			(continued)

TABLE 3.3.—*Continued*

	Net Worth White	Net Worth Black	Net Worth Latino
Native-born[f]	−.380*	.692	1.96***
	(.190)	(.632)	(.359)
Region: South[g]	−.296***	.075	.463
	(.077)	(.291)	(.343)
Metropolitan area[h]	−.105	−1.03*	.099
	(.084)	(.424)	(.459)
Age	.068***	.136***	.025
	(.008)	(.029)	(.033)
Sex (male)[i]	.126	.205	−.223
	(.085)	(.303)	(.379)
Size of household	−.114**	−.193*	.099
	(.037)	(.091)	(.097)
Number of children	−.053*	.067	.017
	(.021)	(.056)	(.066)
Constant	4.97	−5.32	.506
	(.538)	(1.91)	(2.00)
log-likelihood	−12,619	−3,629	−1,830
N censored	256	332	132
Total *N*	5,297	1,424	714

[a]Marital status: omitted term is for "widowed."
[b]Family transfers: omitted term is for "no transfers received."
[c]Education: omitted term is for "less than high school."
[d]Occupation: omitted term is for "other."
[e]Employment: omitted term is for "unemployed/not in labor force."
[f]Native-born: omitted term is for "foreign-born."
[g]Region: omitted term is for "other region."
[h]Metropolitan area: omitted term is for "nonmetropolitan area."
[i]Sex: omitted term is for "female."
*$p > .05$ **$p > .01$ ***$p > .001$

1992) enables us to illustrate the differential effects that the independent variables have on wealth for cases with positive net worth (see fig. 3.1).[2]

The analysis reveals that intergenerational transmission of financial resources enhances wealth inequality within all three groups under study. Specifically, among the non-White populations, within which wealth is more highly concentrated, private transfers of wealth have a strong and significant effect on the reproduction of intragroup inequality. For example, within the White population, the effect of receipt of family transfers on wealth is 1.9. That is, all things equal, the amount of net worth held by a White household who received family transfers is 90 percent higher than the amount held by a White household who has not received family transfers. The comparable effects for Blacks and Latinos

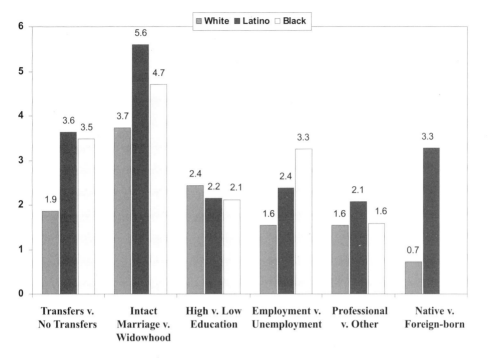

Fig. 3.1. Coefficient estimates from Tobit analysis by racial/ethnic category (with correction factor). (Based on data from the Health and Retirement Survey.)

are greater—3.6 and 3.5, respectively. A similar pattern is found when comparing the effect that marriage exerts on accumulated assets. While being married is strongly associated with the level of a household's net worth, the effect of an intact marriage (relative to widowhood) on household net assets varies across racial and ethnic lines and is particularly strong among the Latino population. Further, in accordance with the evidence on the increasing effect that labor market characteristics has on intragroup socioeconomic polarization among Blacks, the analysis shows that employment status exerts a strong effect on net worth within the Black sample. Another finding that merits attention is the unique effect that immigration status has on household net worth among Latinos. The net worth held by native-born Latinos is about three times greater than the amount held by foreign-born Latinos, even after controlling for education and labor market characteristics.

The literature on the relationship between race and wealth tends to focus on Black/White inequality and is motivated by concerns about the impact of wealth on the reproduction of inequality across racial lines. Wealth inequality among non-Black minorities as well as intragroup wealth differentials have been understudied. Building on theoretical ideas and empirical evidence in the contemporary research on wealth, this chapter studies the determinants of inequality in household net worth among middle-aged Blacks, Whites, and Latinos. The data utilized in this chapter show two key findings. First, Blacks and Latinos are worse off than Whites in terms of educational attainment and other measures of economic well-being such as employment, occupational attainment and income, and net worth. Indeed, when the focus of the analysis shifts from labor market remuneration to accumulated wealth, the White–non-White disparities are particularly substantial. Specifically, the median Black and Latino households at each quintile of the wealth distribution lag behind their White counterparts (table 3.2). The racial/ethnic inequality in wealth reported in this chapter is especially alarming because the focus of the analysis is on households on the verge of retirement, a stage in which the prospects for increasing income are slim and reliance on household net worth is critical, particularly for middle-aged Blacks and Latinos (Angel and Angel 1997). Second, intragroup wealth inequality is greater among Blacks and Latinos than Whites. The extreme economic divide within Black and Latino populations in conjunction with the substantial racial and ethnic wealth disparities, seem to reflect a persistent "double jeopardy" of both class and racial/ethnic stratification.

Results from multivariate analyses that aim to explore the socioeconomic and demographic determinants of wealth among racial and ethnic groups confirm that (in accordance with expectations) educational attainment, employment, and occupational status play an important role in shaping intragroup wealth inequality. In particular, employment status has a strong effect on inequality within the Black population. However, while labor market success is key to understanding wealth inequality, it illuminates only part of the picture. When we consider the extraindividual determinants of wealth inequality, it becomes evident that marital status, immigrant status, and intergenerational transfers are also significant factors explaining such intragroup inequality.

Marital status is critical to an understanding of the production and reproduction of economic polarization among non-White groups.* Specifically, an intact marriage is a significant predictor of wealth for Black and Latino households. One possible explanation for the strong effect that marital status has on wealth is that among non-White households, for whom family support systems play an important role in determining economic well-being and life chances (Mutran 1985; McAdoo 1997; Robles, this volume), the status of not being married carries a higher financial cost. Another finding that merits attention is the critical role that immigration status plays in shaping wealth differentials among Latinos. The large number of foreign-born Latino householders affects the relatively low rates of wealth and high level of inequality among this group. Because educational attainment and labor market attributes are controlled for in the models, the effect of immigration may be attributed to other factors such as institutional discrimination, as well as lack of language skills and information, which may hinder access to housing and other desirable assets (Alba and Logan 1992; Krivo 1995). Finally, the analysis supports the hypothesis that intergenerational transfers of wealth are key to an understanding of intragroup class divisions among Blacks and Latinos. While receipt of material resources enhances wealth inequality within all three racial/ethnic groups, cross-generational transfers of wealth seem to replicate the extreme wealth inequality within the Black and Latino populations, further polarizing the non-White communities.

By analyzing the cumulative, cross-generational dimension of household net worth, these findings question previous explanations of socioeconomic polarization that focus on the more traditional measures of economic status (e.g., earnings, income or poverty, occupation, and employment). The picture that emerges from this chapter suggests that a more coherent understanding of intragroup socioeconomic divisions necessitates the consideration of wealth and its intergenerational transmission. Accordingly, policies that aim to reduce wealth differentials by enhancing human capital and occupational mobility of less privileged groups will have a limited success. These policies need to take into account the different social and demographic mechanisms responsible for wealth inequality among distinct racial and ethnic groups and to adopt specific strategies based on these considerations.

*Chang (chap. 4) finds marital status to be crucial to an understanding of gender wealth disparities in White as well as African American communities [Editors].

Variable	Description
Race/ethnicity	Three dummy variables: White, Black, Latino
Household net worth	Total sum of marketable net worth (wealth minus debts) held by the household. This measure includes home, other real estate, business, IRA and Keogh account, vehicle, bank accounts, stocks, bonds, mutual funds, and other sources.
Household labor income	Annual income of the respondent and spouse from earnings, pension, and annuity income
Transfers received	Measures whether the respondent received (1) inheritance, (2) other transfers from relatives in the amount of $10,000 or more, (3) life insurance payments. Coded 1 if received transfers and 0 if not.
Age	Measured in years
Sex	Sex of primary respondent is male (versus female)
Education	Three dummy variables: less than high school (0–11 years); high school (12 years); more than high school (more than 12 years)
Marital status	A set of dummy variables: coded 1 if respondent is married, marriage intact; remarried; divorced; widowed; other (living with a partner/separated/never married)
Employment status	Coded 1 if the respondent is currently working
Occupation	A set of dummy variables; coded 1 if respondent is in specific occupational category: managerial/professional; sales/clerical/administrative support; other (e.g., operators, no occupation, farming, service, construction)
Household size	Number of additional members, except for respondent and spouse/partner, age 15 and older
Region: South	Coded 1 if living in the southern region of the United States; 0 if other
Metropolitan area	Coded 1 if living in metropolitan area; 0 if other
Number of Children	Number of children
Nativity status	Coded 1 if native-born

NOTES

This study was supported by grants from (1) the Ford Foundation to the Center for the Study of Wealth and Inequality at Columbia University (1040–1239) and (2) the National Science Foundation (SES-9906969).

1. The Tobit regression model can be described as

$$y^*i = xi\beta + ui,$$

Where $\quad yi = y^*i \quad$ if $\quad y^*i > 0$

$$= 0 \quad \text{if} \quad y^*i < 0.$$

Where the xs are observed for all cases, y^* is a latent variable (net worth) that is observed for values greater than 0 and is censored for values less than or equal to zero. The Tobit model yields estimates of the effects of the regressors that have good statistical properties in the presence of all observations (i.e., households with positive, zero, and negative net worth) (see Amemiya 1985; Land and Russell 1996; Long 1997).

2. The McDonald and Moffitt (1980) formula was utilized to calculate the effect of the coefficients on the dependent variable for uncensored cases (with positive net worth). Applying this technique, the calculated magnitudes of the correction factor for the White, Black, and Latino models were .81, .54, and .61, respectively. In other words, the component of the effect of the independent variables on net worth among Whites, for those cases with positive net worth, is .81 of the total coefficient estimates (also see Roncek 1992). In the White model, for example, the effect of being employed is .81 * .55 = .445. Since the dependent variable is the natural logarithm of net worth, this coefficient represents a percentage increase in wealth of exp .44 = 1.56. Thus, in the White model, the effect of being employed is 1.56 times that of being unemployed.

REFERENCES

Alba, Richard D., and John R. Logan. 1992. "Assimilation and Stratification in the Homeownership Patterns of Racial and Ethnic Groups." *International Migration Review* 26: 1314–41.

Amemyia, Takeshi. 1985. *Advanced Econometrics.* Boston: Harvard University Press.

Angel, Ronald J., and Jacqueline L. Angel. 1997. *Who Will Care for Us? Aging and Long-Term Care in Multicultural America.* New York: New York University Press.

Attias-Donfut, Claudine, and Sara Arber. 2000. "Equity and Solidarity across the Generations." In *The Myth of Generational Conflict: The Family and State in Ageing Societies,* ed. Arber Sara and Claudine Attias-Donfut. New York: Routledge.

Avery, Robert B., and Michael S. Rendell. 2002. "Lifetime Inheritances of Three Generations of Whites and Blacks." *American Journal of Sociology* 107 (5): 1300–1346.

Caner, Asena, and Edward Wolff. 2004. *Asset Poverty in the United States: Its Persistence in an Expansionary Economy.* Levy Economics Institute, Public Policy Brief, 76.

Chiswick, Barry R., and Teresa A. Sullivan. 1995. "The New Immigrants." In *State of the Union: America in the 1990's,* ed. Reynolds Farley, vol. 2, 211–70. New York: Russell Sage Foundation.

Clignet, Remi P. 1998. "Ethnicity and Inheritance." In *Inheritance and Wealth in America,* ed. R. K. Miller and S. J. McNamee, 119–38. New York: Plenum Press.

Conley, Dalton C. 1999. *Being Black, Living in the Red.* Berkeley: University of California Press.

Durkheim, Emile. 1992. *Professional Ethics and Civic Morals.* New York: Routledge.

Farley, Reynolds. 1984. *Blacks and Whites: Narrowing the Gap?* Cambridge: Harvard University Press.

Furstenberg, Frank F., Saul Hoffman, and Laura Shrestha. 1995. "The Effect of Divorce on Intergenerational Transfers: New Evidence." *Demography* 32 (3): 319–33.

Gale, W. G., and J. K. Scholtz. 1994. "Intergenerational Transfers and the Accumulation of Wealth." *Journal of Economic Perspectives* 8: 145–60.

Gates, Henry Louis, Jr. 2004. *America behind the Color Line: Dialogues with African Americans.* New York: Warner Books.

Gordon Nembhard, Jessica, Steven C. Pitts, and Patrick L. Mason. 2005. "African-American Intra-Group Inequality and Corporate Globalization." In *African Americans in the United States Economy,* ed. Conrad Cecilia, John Whitehead, Patrick Mason, and James Stewart, 208–22. New York: Rowman and Littlefield Publishers.

Gratton, B. 1987. "Familism among Black and Mexican American Elderly: Myth or Reality?" *Journal of Aging Studies* 1: 1932.

Glick, Paul C. 1997. "Demographic Pictures of African American Families." In *Black Families,* ed. Harriette P. McAdoo, 118–39. New York: Sage Publications.

Hao, Lingxin. 1996. "Family Structure, Private Transfers, and the Economic Well-Being Of Families with Children." *Social Forces* 75 (1): 269–92.

———. 2004. "Wealth of Immigrant and Native-Born Americans." *International Migration Review* 38: 518–46.

Heflin, Colleen M., and Mary Pattillo-McCoy. 2002. "Kin Effects on Black-White Account and Home Ownership." *Sociological Inquiry* 72 (2): 220–39.

Henretta, John C. 1984. "Parental Status and Child's Home Ownership." *American Sociological Review* 49: 131–40.

Holden, K. C., and H. H. Kuo. 1996. "Complex Marital Histories and Economic Well-Being: The Continuing Legacy of Divorce and Widowhood as the HRS Cohort Approaches Retirement." *Gerontologist* 36: 383–90.

Holtz-Eakin, Douglas, David Joulfaian, and Harvey S. Rosen. 1994. Sticking It Out: Entrepreneurial Survival and Liquidity Constraints. *Journal of Political Economy* 102 (1): 53–75.

Inhaber, Herbert, and Sidney Carroll. 1992. *How Rich Is Too Rich?* New York: Praeger Publishers.

Keister, Lisa A. 2004. "Family Structure, Race, and Wealth Ownership: A Longitudinal Exploration of Wealth Accumulation Processes." *Sociological Perspectives* 47: 161–87.

Keister, Lisa A., and Stephanie Moller. 2000. "Wealth Inequality in the United States." *Annual Review of Sociology* 26: 63–81.

Kotlikoff, Laurence J., and Lawrence H. Summers. 1989. "The Role of Inter-generational Transfers in Aggregate Capital Accumulation." In *What Determines Savings?* ed. Laurence J. Kotlikoff, 43–68. Cambridge: MIT Press.

Krivo, Lauren J. 1995. "Immigrant Characteristics and Hispanic-Anglo Housing Inequality." *Demography* 32 (4): 599–616.

Land, Kenneth C., and Stephen Russell. 1996. "Wealth Accumulation across the Adult Life Course: Stability and Change in Sociodemographic Covariate Structures of Net Worth Data in the Survey of Income and Program Participation, 1984–1991." *Social Science Research* 25 (4): 423–62.

Langbein, John H. 1991. "The Inheritance Revolution." *Public Interest* 102: 15–32.

Laslett, Peter. 1987. "The Emergence of the Third Age." *Ageing and Society* 7: 133–60.

Lee, Yean-Ju, and Isik A. Aytac. 1998. "Intergenerational Financial Support among Whites, African-Americans, and Latinos." *Journal of Marriage and the Family* 60: 426–41.

Lindh, T., and H. Ohlsson. 1998. "Self-Employment and Wealth Inequality." *Review of Income and Wealth* 44: 25–42.

Logan, John R., and Glenna D. Spitze. 1996. *Family Ties: Enduring Relations between Parents and Their Grown Children.* Philadelphia: Temple University Press.

Long, J. S. 1997. *Regression Models for Categorical and Limited Dependent Variables.* Advanced Quantitative Techniques in the Social Sciences Number 7. Thousand Oaks, CA: Sage Publications.

Lowenstein, Ariela, and Vern L. Bengtson. 2003. "Challenges of Global Aging to Families in the Twenty-First Century." In *Global Aging and Challenges to Families,* ed. V. L. Bengtson and A. Lowenstein, 371–79. New York: Aldine de Gruyter.

McAdoo, Harriette P. 1997. "Upward Mobility across Generations in African American Families." In *Black Families,* ed. Harriette P. McAdoo, 139–62. Thousand Oaks, CA: Sage Publications.

McDonald, John F., and Robert M. Moffitt. 1980. "The Use of Tobit Analysis." *Review of Economics and Statistics* 62: 18–21.

McNamee, Stephen J., and Robert K. Miller, Jr. 1998. "Inheritance and Stratification." In *Inheritance and Wealth in America,* ed. R. K. Miller and S. J. McNamee, 193–211. New York: Plenum Press.

Mutran, E. 1985. "Intergenerational Family Support among Blacks and Whites: Response to Culture or to Socioeconomic Differences." *Journal of Gerontology* 40: 382–89.

Neidert, Lisa J., and Reynolds Farley 1985. "Assimilation in the United States: An Analysis of Ethnic and Generation Differences in Status and Achievement." *American Sociological Review* 50: 840–50.

Ogbu, John U. 1987. "African American Education: A Cultural-Ecological Perspective." In *Black Families,* 3rd ed., ed. Harriette P. McAdoo, 234–51. Thousand Oaks, CA: Sage Publications.

Oliver, Melvin L., and Thomas M. Shapiro. 1995. *Black Wealth/White Wealth.* New York: Routledge.

Orzechowski, Shawna, and Peter Sepielli. 2003. "Net Worth and Asset Ownership of Households: 1998 and 2000." *Household Economics Studies.* P70-88. U.S. Department of Commerce, U.S. Census Bureau.

Page-Adams, Deborah, and Michael Sherraden. 1997. "Asset Building as a Community Revitalization Strategy." *Social Work* 42 (5): 423–35.

Patillo-McCoy, Mary. 1999. *Black Picket Fences.* Chicago. University of Chicago Press.

Phillips, Julie A., and Douglas S. Massey. 1999. "The New Labor Market: Immigrants and Wages after IRCA." *Demography* 36 (2): 233–46.

Portes, Alejandro, and Ruben G. Rumbaut. 1990. *Immigrant America: A Portrait.* Berkeley: University California Press.

Roncek, Dennis W. 1992. "Learning More from Tobit Coefficients: Extending a Comparative Analysis of Political Protest." *American Sociological Review* 57: 503–7.

Sakamoto, A., H. H. Wu, and J. Tzeng. 2000. "The Declining Significance of Race among American Men during the Latter Half of the 20th Century." *Demography* 37 (1): 41–51.

Shapiro, H. D. 1994. "The Coming Inheritance Bonanza." *Institutional Investor* 28: 143–48.

Shapiro, Thomas. 2004. *The Hidden Cost of Being African American: How Wealth Perpetuates Inequality.* New York: Oxford University Press.

Smith, James P. 1997. "Wealth Inequality among Older Americans." *Journals of Gerontology Series B—Psychological Sciences and Social Sciences* 52: 74–81

Sobol, Marion Gross. 1979. "Factors Influencing Private Capital Accumulation on the 'Eve of Retirement.'" *Review of Economics and Statistics* 61 (4): 585–93.

Son, In Soo, Suzanne W. Model, and Gene A. Fisher. 1989. "Polarization and Progress in the Black Community: Earnings and Status Gains for Young Black Males in the Era of Affirmative Action." *Sociological Forum* 4 (3) 309–27.

Spilerman, Seymour. 2000. "Wealth and Stratification Processes." *Annual Review of Sociology* 26: 497–524.

Spilerman, Seymour, Noah Lewin-Epstein, and Moshe Semyonov. 1993. "Wealth, Intergenerational Transfers and Life Chances." In *Social Theory and Social Policy,* ed. A. Sorensen and S. Spilerman, 165–85. Westport, CT: Praeger.

U.S. Department of Commerce. 1995a. *Assets Ownership of Households: 1993.* Current Population Reports, Household Economic Studies, P70-47, Bureau of the Census.

———. 1995b. *What We're Worth—Asset Ownership of Households: 1993.* Bureau of Census, SB/95-26.

Waite, Linda J., and Maggie Gallagher. 2000. *The Case for Marriage: Why Married People Are Happier, Healthier, and Better Off Financially.* New York: Broadway Books.

Waters, Mary C., and Karl Eschbach. 1995. "Immigration and Ethnic and

Racial Inequality in the United States." *Annual Review of Sociology* 21: 419–46.

Wilhelm, Mark O. 2001. "The Role of Intergenerational Transfers on Spreading Asset Ownership." In *Assets for the Poor: The Benefits of Spreading Asset Ownership,* ed. Thomas M. Shapiro and Edward N. Wolff, 132–65. New York: Russell Sage Foundation.

Wilson, William Julius. 1980. *The Declining Significance of Race: Blacks and Changing American Institutions.* Chicago: University of Chicago Press.

———. 1987. *The Truly Disadvantaged: The Inner City, the Underclass, and Public Policy.* Chicago: University of Chicago Press.

Wolff, Edward N. 1994. "Trends in Household Wealth in the United States, 1962–83 and 1983–89. *Review of Income and Wealth* 40 (2): 143–75.

———. 2001. "Recent Trends in Wealth Ownership, from 1983 to 1998." In *Assets for the Poor: The Benefits of Spreading Asset Ownership,* ed. Thomas M. Shapiro and Edward N. Wolff, 34–74. New York. Russell Sage Foundation.

———. 2002. *Top Heavy.* New York: New Press.

4 Women & Wealth

MARIKO LIN CHANG

Our current understanding of women's economic status has been derived almost exclusively through the lens of earnings. Yet wealth confers many benefits that earnings do not: wealth can be transferred to others, can generate income (through interest, capital gains, and rent, for example), can be used as collateral for loans, and provides the ability to weather common financial crises, such as spells of unemployment or illness, in which income is temporarily cut or disrupted.

The lack of research on gender inequality in wealth is particularly troubling given that wealth inequality is much greater than income inequality (Keister 2000b; Shapiro and Wolff 2001; Sherraden 1991; Spilerman 2000; Wolff 1995). In 1998, the top 1 percent of the population earned 16.6 percent of the total income (in comparison with 38.1 percent of the total wealth), and the bottom 80 percent of the population earned 43 percent of the total income (in comparison with less than 20 percent of the total wealth). In that same year, the wealthiest 20 percent of households held 83 percent of the total wealth, whereas the bottom 40 percent of the population held less than 1 percent of the total wealth (Wolff 2001).

Despite the importance of wealth in shaping life chances, we know little about the extent to which women have access to and control over wealth. Perhaps the gender wealth gap has evaded attention because gender is an individual-level characteristic, whereas wealth is considered to be a household-level characteristic. As such, gender is considered salient only for nonmarried households. But this is no small number: nonmarried households comprise 47 percent of all households (U.S. Bureau of the Census 1998).

To the extent that gender differences in wealth have been examined, they have typically been explored by contrasting single-female-headed households with other households, most often as a control variable in regression equations predicting household wealth. Female-headed households do have less wealth than male-headed households; however, aggregating never-married, divorced, and widowed households into a single category conceals the contours of the gender wealth gap for different household types. A first step toward understanding the gender wealth gap is to take into account how gender intersects with marital status to shape the distribution of wealth.

For example, marriage impacts men's and women's labor market participation differently. For example, in 2002 61 percent of married women were in the labor market, compared with 67.4 percent of never-married women (U.S. Census Bureau 2003c). Marriage does not have similar consequences for men's labor force participation. In fact, men's labor market commitment often increases upon marriage (Nock 1998). If the marriage ends in divorce, women often return to the labor market full-time but often earn less than their ex-husbands who have worked full-time continuously during marriage.

Another reason why we might expect wealth differences between those who have never been married and those who are divorced is the economic consequences of divorce. Divorce comes with a hefty economic price tag for both partners, but research suggests that women's economic status suffers most upon divorce (Duncan and Hoffman 1985; Holden and Smock 1991; Peterson 1989, 1996). Consequently, we would expect to find gender differences in the wealth of divorced men in comparison with divorced women *and* we would also expect that the wealth of divorced men and women may differ from their same-sex counterparts who have not experienced the financial toll of divorce.

The failure to distinguish widowed individuals from never-married and divorced individuals is also problematic for understanding the ways that gender and marital status impact wealth. Upon the death of a spouse, all household wealth generally passes to the surviving spouse. Since marital wealth is not split in two, widows may have more wealth than those who have never been married or who have been divorced.

Because gender and marital status intersect to impact household wealth, this chapter examines gender differences separately for the following types of nonmarried households: never married, divorced, and widowed.

DATA

I use data from the 2001 Survey of Consumer Finances (SCF), a comprehensive triennial national survey of households carried out by the Federal Reserve Board. Households for the main survey are selected from a multistage area probability design. The SCF also contains an oversample of high-income households who are less likely to show up in the main sample. (See Aizcorbe, Kennickell, and Moore 2003 for an overview of the SCF.)

The SCF is considered to be the best source of survey data on the *distribution* of wealth because it oversamples high-income households,[1] who are much less likely to appear in representative samples because they form such a small percentage of the population.[2] The oversample of high-income households allows for the most accurate picture of wealth inequality because it captures wealth at the very top of the distribution, where the families holding the bulk of the nation's wealth reside. Sample weights are used in all calculations so that the data represent the wealth distribution of the U.S. population.

Respondent's marital status was determined from the survey question that asks, "Are you currently married or living with a partner, separated, divorced, widowed, or have you never been married?" Due to sample size, separated and divorced respondents were combined into a single category. And, because it was not always possible to disentangle the wealth of two individuals who were cohabitating, cohabitating households were treated as a separate category.

DEFINING WEALTH

Wealth is defined as net worth: the value of one's assets minus liabilities. I use the definition of net worth suggested in the SCF 2001 codebook, except that I do not include the market value of vehicles in the calculation of assets.[3] Assets include money in checking and savings accounts (including money market accounts), mutual funds, stocks, certificates of deposit, bonds, call accounts at brokerages, the cash value of whole life insurance, the market value of one's home and of other real estate, business assets, certain retirement assets,[4] and other financial and nonfinancial assets (trusts, annuities, royalties, jewelry, art objects, etc.). Debts include all real estate debt (mortgages, home equity loans, etc.), credit card debt, installment loans (such as car loans), loans from individuals, and loans taken against pension or life insurance accounts.

THE GENDER WEALTH GAP

Median wealth across household types and by gender is presented in table 4.1. The gender gap is the proportion of the median wealth held by women in comparison with men, within nonmarried household types. Significant differences in wealth exist across household types and also between men and women within the same household type.

Married households are the wealthiest, with a median wealth of $148,700, far above the median of all other household types. The greater wealth of married couples is most likely a result of the differential selection of individuals into marriage as well as the wealth-enhancing benefits of marriage (Waite and Gallagher 2000).

In contrast, never-married women have the least wealth of all household types, with a median net worth of only $2,500. Never-married women also fare worst with respect to the gender wealth gap, owning only 23¢ in wealth for every dollar owned by never-married men. Divorced women do better than never-married women, with a median wealth of $19,380 and a gender wealth gap of 44 percent. Widowed women fare best out of all female-headed households, but they still have only 59¢ for every dollar of wealth owned by widowed men.

TABLE 4.1. Median Wealth by Household Type and Gender, 2000

Household Type	All Ages		Under Age 65	
	Median ($)	Gender Gap (%)	Median ($)	Gender Gap (%)
Married	148,700		121,800	
Cohabitating	9,320		8,000	
Separated				
Male	44,000		35,650	
Female	19,380	44.0	15,695	44.0
Widowed				
Male	125,000		212,900	
Female	73,400	58.7	54,700	25.7
Never married				
Male	10,700		8,000	
Female	2,500	23.4	1,200	15.0
All households	74,600		52,700	

Source: Author's calculations of the 2001 Survey of Consumer Finances.

When restricting the sample to households younger than age 65,[5] the gender gap in wealth remains at 44 percent for divorced households, but the gender gap widens substantially to 26 percent for widowed households and 15 percent for never-married households, suggesting that wealth is even more unequally distributed between men and women who have not yet reached retirement.

Table 4.2 presents the distribution of households by gender and marital status across five wealth quintiles. As expected, married households do best overall and never-married households do the worst. However, striking gender differences are also evident, particularly when comparing the composition of the top and bottom quintiles.

Households in the first quintile are the most economically disadvantaged, with a median net worth of −$2,300. Women of all nonmarried household types are more likely than their male counterparts to be found in the bottom quintile. Never-married women are particularly disadvantaged, as almost half of all never-married women are in the bottom wealth quintile. In fact, more than two-thirds of never-married women are located in the bottom two quintiles, underscoring their vulnerable economic situation. Divorced women fare slightly better, with only 31 percent located in the bottom quintile, but nevertheless, more than half of divorced women are found in the lowest two quintiles. Of all female-headed households, widows fare best, which is most likely due to the positive relationship between wealth and age and because they have benefited from the wealth advantages of marriage and did not experience the division of marital assets that occurs when a marriage ends in divorce.

TABLE 4.2.   Distribution of Households across Wealth Quintiles, 2000

	1st Quintile (−$2,300)	2nd Quintile ($12,030)	3rd Quintile ($74,500)	4th Quintile ($208,670)	5th Quintile ($719,000)	Total (%)
Married	11.2	15.1	19.6	24.5	29.6	100
Living with partner	33.3	29.3	18.0	10.3	9.1	100
Divorced						
Men	20.3	26.5	20.4	19.5	13.3	100
Women	31.0	27.6	20.7	13.2	7.5	100
Widowed						
Men	10.5	16.7	22.5	31.8	18.5	100
Women	14.6	21.3	30.7	20.6	12.8	100
Never married						
Men	36.0	22.3	19.4	13.2	9.1	100
Women	43.6	27.6	14.2	10.7	3.9	100

Source: Author's calculations of the 2001 Survey of Consumer Finances.
Note: Median wealth is listed for each quintile.

An extreme gender gap is also evident at the very top of the wealth distribution. Within each household type women are less likely than men to belong to the top quintile. Widows generally fare best, with close to 13 percent of widows belonging to the top quintile (in comparison with almost 19 percent of widowers), and never-married women fare the worst, with only 4 percent belonging to the top quintile (in comparison with 9 percent of never-married men).

In summary, gender wealth inequality exists for each type of female-headed household. However, the largest gender gaps are found among never-married households. Never-married women own only one-quarter of the wealth of never-married men and are heavily concentrated at the very bottom of the wealth distribution, with no wealth. Of all female-headed households, widows fare best, with the highest median wealth and the smallest gender gap; however, widowed women still own only 59 percent of the wealth of widowed men.

THE INTERSECTION OF GENDER, RACE, & HOUSEHOLD TYPE

I now turn to the question of whether the gender wealth gaps observed in table 4.1 are consistent for different racial groups. Table 4.3 provides the median wealth by gender and household type for Whites, Blacks, and people of other racial backgrounds.[6]

Table 4.3 reveals that non-White households do hold less wealth than

TABLE 4.3. Gender Differences in Median Wealth by Race, 2000

	White	Black	Other
Separated			
Men	$57,470	$22,700	$10,600
Women	$42,500	$3,050	$1,720
Gender gap	74.0%	10.4%	16.2%
Widowed			
Men	$149,000	NA[a]	NA[a]
Women	$91,400	NA[a]	NA[a]
Gender gap	61.3%		
Never married			
Men	$28,500	$120	$3,800
Women	$11,400	$50	$1
Gender gap	40.0%	41.7%	.03%

Source: Author's calculations of the 2001 Survey of Consumer Finances.
[a]Sample size too small to provide reliable estimates.

Whites among the divorced, widowed, and never married. However, equally striking is that the gender wealth gaps are even more pronounced for non-Whites. Although the gender wealth gap between never-married Blacks and Whites is similar, the gender wealth gap for divorced Blacks is much larger, with divorced Black women holding only 10 percent of the median wealth of their male counterparts. Women of other racial backgrounds also fare much worse than Whites, with divorced women owning only 16 percent of the wealth of divorced men and never-married women owning a paltry 0.03 percent of the wealth of never-married men. These data suggest that not only is the gender wealth gap persistent across racial categories but it is actually much larger for non White households.

GENDER & TYPES OF WEALTH

Not all wealth is identical; assets vary according to their liquidity, risk, and average rates of return. During the 1989–98 period, for example, cash accounts (savings accounts, money market funds, and certificates of deposit) had an average annual rate of return of 1.41 percent, whereas bonds had an average annual rate of return of 4.66 percent and stocks had an average annual rate of return of 9.92 percent (Wolff 2000). Consequently, gender differences in types of assets owned are likely to impact gender differences in wealth over time.

Table 4.4 presents household differences in the ownership (and median value, if owned) of the four most commonly held assets: (1) bank accounts (savings and checking accounts, certificates of deposit), (2) homes, (3) stocks, bonds, and other financial assets, and (4) retirement assets (Individual Retirement Accounts [IRAs], Keoghs, 401[k], 403[b], and certain future pensions—see n. 4). Because individuals typically begin to spend down some of their wealth upon retirement, table 4.4 provides an overview of asset ownership for those households under age 65; however, the substantive conclusions were similar when data contained all households.

Cash reserves form the base of a household's financial pyramid. As shown in table 4.4, almost all households have a bank account of some form, most commonly a checking or savings account. However, differences among households and between men and women are evident. With the exception of widowed households, women are less likely than their male counterparts to own a bank account. Given the centrality of a savings or checking account to economic participation in society, it is particularly troubling that 23 percent of never-married women do not posses even this basic financial asset. Households without savings are the most vulnerable and are continually at risk of failing to meet basic needs and are vulnerable to the "rent-to-own" industry where they may end up paying three to five times the price of an item (Hudson 1996). Those without a bank account are also often dependent upon check-cashing outlets that typically charge high rates for cashing checks (Caskey 1994).

The second most commonly owned asset is one's own home. The majority of married, divorced, and widowed households own their own homes, but once again divorced and widowed women are less likely to own their own homes than their male counterparts. Interestingly, never-married women are slightly *more* likely to be home owners than never-married men, although the median home equity held by never-married women who do own their own homes is lower than the median home equity of never-married male home owners. Nevertheless, home

TABLE 4.4. Asset Ownership—and Median Value, If Owned—by Household Type and Gender, 2000

	Bank Accounts		Home		Stocks, Bonds, Other Financial Assets		Retirement	
	% Own	Median Value ($)	% Own	Median Equity ($)	% Own	Median Value ($)	% Own	Median Value ($)
Married	95.0	5,000	80.6	66,000	66.1	15,000	68.5	38,000
Cohabitating	89.5	2,400	49.7	32,000	46.4	5,250	50.0	10,000
Divorced								
Men	89.8	2,300	58.5	40,000	56.3	7,000	52.6	20,000
Women	87.2	1,200	50.1	45,000	48.0	4,000	43.1	11,000
Widowed								
Men	78.2	10,200	89.1	83,000	64.2	15,000	60.4	60,000
Women	85.7	1,700	77.2	51,000	51.1	15,300	42.2	41,000
Never married								
Men	89.3	2,500	30.6	45,000	55.1	5,000	40.2	9,200
Women	77.0	1,300	31.9	40,000	36.6	2,800	35.6	5,400
All households	90.7	3,150	64.4	60,000	57.5	10,000	56.9	26,900

Source: Author's calculations of the 2001 Survey of Consumer Finances.
Note: Bank accounts include money held in savings accounts, checking accounts (including money market accounts), and certificates of deposit. Retirement accounts include the market value of IRAs, Keoghs, 401(k), 403(b), and certain future pensions but *exclude* social security and employer-sponsored defined-benefit plans (see n. 4). Stocks, bonds, and other financial assets include stocks, bonds, mutual funds, savings bonds, cash value of whole life insurance, call accounts at brokerages, other managed assets (trusts, annuities, etc.), and other financial assets (future proceeds, royalties, etc.) and exclude any assets held in retirement accounts. Homes include one's primary residence (houses, condos, farms, mobile homes, etc.), and the median value refers to the net equity (market value minus any housing debt).

ownership is the one area in which never-married women compare favorably with never-married men.

Stocks, bonds, and other financial assets are owned by 57.5 percent of households under age 65.[7] However, women in each household category are less likely to own these assets than their male counterparts. The wealth that women lack in bank accounts and in homes is unfortunately not being compensated for with stocks, bonds, and other financial assets.

The fourth most commonly held asset is retirement accounts (IRAs, Keoghs, 401[k], 403[b], future pensions, etc.). Once again, women are both less likely to have any retirement savings accounts, and those who do have less money than their male counterparts. Unfortunately, women also receive less social security than men due to their generally lower lifetime earnings and differences in labor force participation. When it comes to retirement, women are therefore doubly disadvantaged.

In summary, table 4.4 reveals that women are less likely than their male counterparts to own almost every type of asset. Furthermore, for those women and men who do own each type of asset, the median value of the asset is almost always lower for women than it is for men. The gender gaps in asset ownership are particularly large for never-married and divorced women, paralleling findings from the gender gap overall. However, of the various assets examined here, home ownership is the most evenly distributed across gender lines. Further research is necessary to understand how men and women build their financial portfolios and why gender gaps differ with respect to the ownership of different types of assets.

INCOME VERSUS WEALTH

In 2000, the gender income gap for year-round full-time workers ages 18–64 was 74 percent; however, the gap differs dramatically across marital status categories (see table 4.5). The gender income gap is the smallest for never-married individuals, with never-married women earning 97 percent of the incomes of never-married men. Divorced and widowed women face a larger gender gap of 84 percent and 78 percent, respectively. But married women face the largest gender income gap, receiving incomes of only 67 percent of married men.

Comparisons of the gender income and wealth gaps have important implications. First and most simply, the gender wealth gap is much larger than the gender income gap. For example, divorced women receive an average 84 percent of the incomes of divorced men, but divorced women under age 65 own only 44 percent of the wealth of divorced men. The re-liance on income as an indicator of women's economic status has painted a much rosier picture of women's economic status than the sta-tistics on wealth inequality suggest.

Second, the gender gaps in income and wealth provide contradictory information regarding which groups of women fare best (and worst). To elaborate, the smallest gender income gap exists for never-married women, whose incomes are 97 percent of the incomes of their male counterparts. Yet, with respect to wealth, never-married women of that same age group experience the largest gender gap of any of the marital status groups, with only 15 percent of the wealth of their male counter-parts. In contrast, married women experience the largest gender income gap, but if we assume that marital wealth is shared equally, then married women experience no gender wealth gap.[8]

The comparison of the gender income and wealth gaps across marital

TABLE 4.5. Median Annual Income for Year-Round Full-Time Workers, Ages 18–64, by Marital Status and Gender in 2000

Household Type	Median
Never married	
Women	$26,116
Men	$26,886
Gender gap	97.1%
Divorced	
Women	$31,092
Men	$36,981
Gender gap	84.1%
Widowed	
Women	$28,192
Men	$36,217
Gender gap	77.8%
Married[a]	
Women	$30,021
Men	$44,433
Gender gap	67.6%
All households	
Women	$28,762
Men	$38,834
Gender gap	74.1%

Source: Data are from the 2000 March sup-plement of the Current Population Survey.
[a]Married, spouse present.

status categories reveals that wealth and income are distinct dimensions of gender inequality and both must be examined in order to understand women's economic status. The tremendous wealth gap for never-married women is particularly puzzling given that never-married women's incomes are so close to equaling those of never-married men. To understand this discrepancy, research must address the causes of the gender wealth gap and seek to discover why the comparatively low gender income gap for never-married women does not translate into a low gender wealth gap.

LIKELY CAUSES OF THE GENDER WEALTH GAP

Although research on the causes of the gender wealth gap has not yet been conducted, this section explores some of the likely causes: the gender earnings gap, gender differences in labor market characteristics, the financial toll of single parenthood, gender differences in financial risk tolerance (and hence saving and investment decisions), and the impact that marriage has on women's human capital.

GENDER EARNINGS GAP

Earnings are the primary source of income for the majority of households, and earnings are one of the strongest determinants of wealth (Keister 2000b; Oliver and Shapiro 1995). Consequently, the gender earnings gap is likely to play a key role in explaining the gender wealth gap. Since women earn on average only 73¢ for every dollar earned by men (U.S. Department of Labor 2000), it is not surprising that women are unable to accumulate the same amounts of wealth.

No doubt, the gender earnings gap is likely to be a critical component of the gender wealth gap. However, earnings cannot be the only answer since the gender income gap does not necessarily correspond with the gender wealth gap in ways that we would expect. As already discussed, the gender income gap is smallest for never-married individuals, yet these individuals have the largest gender wealth gap. Consequently, it is likely that other factors also play a role in explaining the gender wealth gap.

GENDER DIFFERENCES IN LABOR MARKET CHARACTERISTICS

Women and men work in different occupations and industries and often have different patterns of labor force participation. These differences in labor market characteristics affect not only their earnings but also their access to pensions and the value of their pensions. The probability of pension coverage increases with job tenure, full-time work status, public sector or unionized employment, and firm size (Even and Macpherson 1994). Because women often have less job tenure and are less likely to work full-time, to work in unionized jobs, and to work at large firms, they are less likely to be covered by pensions. For these same reasons, women often have less pension wealth as well, even if they are covered by pensions (Even and Macpherson 1994; McGarry and Davenport 1998).

THE COSTS OF SINGLE PARENTHOOD

The ability to accumulate wealth is not only a factor of resources flowing into the household (such as earnings) but also a function of a household's living expenses. Research on consumption differences between women and men is scarce but suggests that men and women with similar financial means spend similar proportions of their incomes on nonessential expenses (Brown 1998; Paulin and Lee 2002). However, among nonmarried households, there is a considerable expense that is shouldered disproportionately by women: the costs of raising children. Children are a drain on financial resources,[9] and because nonmarried women are more likely to have custody of minor children than nonmarried men, women have less disposable income to save and invest, all else being equal. Further exacerbating the economic situation of custodial mothers is that many do not receive adequate child support. Of those custodial mothers awarded child support during the 1994–2002 period, only 37 percent received the full amount of support due, and 25 percent received nothing (U.S. Census Bureau 2003b).

FINANCIAL RISK TOLERANCE

Another aspect of wealth accumulation is deciding how to save and invest. As mentioned, the choice of saving and investment vehicles impacts the eventual rate of return and hence the accumulation of wealth across households. Research suggests that women are more financially risk averse than men (Bajtelsmit and VanDerhei 1997; Hinz, McCarthy, and Turner 1997, but see Papke 1998), often preferring less volatile investment options. Risk aversion is not inherently positive or negative, but because riskier investments have performed better historically, gender differences in financial risk tolerance should contribute to gender differences in wealth. Explanations for women's generally lower risk tolerance include gender differences in access to financial information, confidence in economic matters, and gender socialization (Barber and Odean 2001; Estes and Hosseini 1998; Newcomb and Rabow 1999). Further research is needed regarding possible gender differences in saving and investment decisions to disentangle the ways in which the wealth accumulation process may be gendered and why.

HOW MARRIAGE IMPACTS WOMEN'S HUMAN CAPITAL

Another potential cause of the gender wealth gap is that marriage affects men and women's human capital development differently and in ways that may impact the gender wealth gap if the marriage ends. Married men are more likely to work full-time than nonmarried men, have higher incomes, and report higher levels of commitment to the labor market (for a summary of research findings, see Nock 1998 and Waite and Gallagher 2000). In contrast, marriage often has a negative impact upon the human capital development of women. For example, during marriage, women are more likely than men to exit the labor force or to work part-time to tend to caregiving responsibilities. Married women are also more likely to limit their career aspirations in favor of their husbands' careers (Bielby and Bielby 1992). These decisions often have negative consequences for women's earnings and wealth should the marriage end in divorce. All else being equal, women with fewer years of full-time labor force participation, or women who have placed their husbands' career advancements over their own, will find it difficult to earn wages (and pensions) equal to a comparable man or woman who has worked continuously for his or her adult life. Consequently, when a marriage ends in divorce, men are often better equipped to support themselves on a single income than women.

CONCLUSION

Large gender wealth gaps exist between men and women of similar household types. Widowed women fare better than other nonmarried women: widowed women have the highest median wealth of all groups of female-headed households, and the gender gap between widowed women and men is the smallest of all household types. However, even so, widowed women own only slightly more than half of the wealth of their male counterparts. Never-married women clearly fare worst of all female-headed households.[10] Women who have never been married own only about $2,500 in wealth, and they own only 23¢ for every dollar of wealth owned by never-married men. And almost half of all never-married women are located at the bottom wealth quintile.

Racial disparities in the magnitude of the gender wealth gap are striking and suggest that women of color are particularly disadvantaged. Although the gender wealth gap for never-married Blacks and Whites is similar, gender wealth gaps for all other household types are much larger for Blacks and people of other racial backgrounds, revealing that women of color may experience even greater barriers to wealth accumulation than White women. These findings echo other findings in this volume, demonstrating that differences in intragroup racial wealth inequality are mirrored by differences in gender wealth inequality across racial groups. In other words, not only is wealth inequality greater among non-White families, but gender wealth inequality is also greater among non-White men and women than it is among Whites.

This chapter also establishes that the gender wealth gap is much larger than the gender income gap. Because wealth provides a more comprehensive description of economic status, the reliance on income as an indicator of women's economic status has been misleading. Women are more economically vulnerable than the gender income gap implies. But wealth inequality is more than simply an exaggeration of income inequality. Gender wealth gaps suggest that the most economically vulnerable segment of the population is never-married women, a vulnerability that is concealed by income data, which reveals that never-married women receive 97 percent of the incomes of never-married men.

The severity of the gender wealth gap suggests that we must focus new attention on understanding its causes. I have identified some of the likely causes here: the gender earnings gap, gender differences in labor market characteristics, the likelihood that children of nonmarried parents will live with their mothers, gender differences in financial risk tolerance, and the effects that marital status may have on women's human capital development. However, further research is needed to empirically examine these potential causal factors. And it is likely that an important component of the causal story may be found in the interrelationships between these different factors. For example, mothers often receive a wage penalty that is not reducible to differences in human capital or other measured characteristics (Budig and England 2001; Waldfogel 1997). As a result, being a custodial parent most likely affects women's wealth by impacting the ability to save *and* by affecting earnings. Likewise, it is possible that some women may invest in lower-risk investments in part because they feel more economically vulnerable due to their status as single parents. Therefore, when theorizing the ways that the wealth accumulation process is gendered, researchers will need to take into consideration the reciprocal relationships between many of these causal factors.

Future research should also investigate the consequences of the gender wealth gap. Wealth inequality no doubt impacts women's quality of life, their health, and their power within the family and the broader society. However, the gender wealth gap also has profound implications for the well-being and future life chances of children, since 23 percent of children live in single-mother families and 52 percent of single-mother families are below the poverty line (U.S. Census Bureau 2003a). Therefore, the consequences of wealth inequality are likely to be broad and experienced throughout many social institutions, ranging from the family to the economy.

Previous research has demonstrated that wealth inequality across class and racial lines is dramatic.[11] We now know that wealth inequality by gender is just as dramatic. Research regarding the benefits of spreading asset ownership can no longer be confined to scholars interested in reducing class-based and race-based inequalities but should also be a central component of research seeking to reduce gender-based inequalities as well.

NOTES

1. Although not all high-income households are wealthy (and vice versa), the oversample of high-income households brings in substantially more wealthy households than would appear in a strictly representative sample.

2. For further information comparing the SCF with other household surveys of wealth, see Curtin, Juster, and Morgan 1989 and Wolff 1995 (appendix).

3. Vehicles are excluded because, like other durable goods, they are not a financial investment (they do not hold their value, and there is no possibility of monetary return, such as interest income or capital gains). For similar treatment of vehicles in the calculation of net worth, see Wolff 2001.

4. Retirement wealth includes IRAs, Keogh accounts, and the following employer-sponsored accounts: 401(k), 403(b), thrift savings accounts from current or past jobs, other current job plans from which loans or withdrawals can be made, and accounts from past jobs from which one expects to receive the account balance in the future. Retirement wealth excludes social security and employer-sponsored defined benefit plans. See Aizcorbe, Kennickell, and Moore 2003 for further details on the definition of retirement wealth in the SCF. For the SCF's calculation of retirement wealth, see http://www

.federalreserve.gov/pubs/OSS/oss2/bulletin.macro.txt. For a more detailed general discussion of varieties of pension plans, see chapters 1 and 8.

5. For married households, the age of the household was determined by the age of the oldest spouse.

6. Unfortunately, the "other" racial category could not be disaggregated further due to sample size limitations.

7. Other financial assets include mutual funds, savings bonds, cash value of whole life insurance, call accounts at brokerages, other managed assets (trusts, annuities, etc.), and other financial assets (future proceeds, royalties, etc.).

8. Although husbands and wives do not always share equal control over household wealth (Blumstein and Schwartz 1985; Burgoyne 1990; England and Kilbourne 1990; Hertz 1986; Pahl 1983; Zelizer 1997), unless one assumes a *vast* disparity in control over wealth for married couples, married women have access to more wealth than nonmarried women.

9. Although children provide a motivation to save (Fisher 1930), single parents are often unable to fulfill this desire because the costs of providing for children on a single income tend to utilize all of their economic resources.

10. The comparative wealth disadvantage experienced by never-married women holds across age groups (results not shown), suggesting that their comparatively poor economic situation is not simply an artifact of the generally younger ages of individuals who have never been married.

11. See Avery and Rendall 2002; Blau and Graham 1990; Conley 1999; Keister 2000a, 2000b; Keister and Moller 2000; Oliver and Shapiro 1995; Shapiro 2004; Shapiro and Wolff 2001; Shapiro 2004; Sherraden 1991; Spilerman 2000; Wolff 1995.

REFERENCES

Aizcorbe, Ana M., Arthur B. Kennickell, and Kevin B. Moore. 2003. "Recent Changes in U.S. Family Finances: Evidence from the 1998 and 2001 Survey of Consumer Finances." *Federal Reserve Bulletin* 89: 1–32.

Avery, Robert B., and Michael S. Rendall. 2002. "Lifetime Inheritances of Three Generations of Whites and Blacks." *American Journal of Sociology* 107: 1300–1346.

Bajtelsmit, Vickie L., and Jack L. VanDerhei. 1997. "Risk Aversion and Pension Investment Choices." In *Positioning Pensions for the Twenty-First Century,* ed. Michael S. Gordon, Olivia S. Mitchell, and Marc M. Twinney, 45–66. Philadelphia: University of Pennsylvania Press.

Barber, Brad M., and Terrance Odean. 2001. "Boys Will Be Boys: Gender, Overconfidence, and Common Stock Investment." *Quarterly Journal of Economics* 116: 261–92.

Bielby, Denise D., and William T. Bielby. 1992. "I Will Follow Him: Family Ties, Gender Role Beliefs, and Reluctance to Relocate for a Better Job." *American Journal of Sociology* 97: 1241–67.

Blau, Francine D., and John W. Graham. 1990. "Black-White Differences in Wealth and Asset Composition." *Quarterly Journal of Economics* 105: 321–39.

Blumstein, Phillip, and Pepper Schwartz. 1985. *American Couples: Money, Work, Sex.* New York: Pocket Books.

Brown, Ralph J. 1998. "Saving Rate Estimates for Single Persons by Income, Age, and Gender." *Journal of Legal Economics* 8: 49–62.

Budig, Michelle J., and Paula England. 2001. "The Wage Penalty for Motherhood." *American Sociological Review* 66: 204–25.

Burgoyne, Carole B. 1990. "Money in Marriage: How Patterns of Allocation Both Reflect and Conceal Power." *Sociological Review* 38: 634–65.

Caskey, John P. 1994. *Fringe Banking: Check-Cashing Outlets, Pawnshops, and the Poor.* New York: Russell Sage Foundation.

Conley, Dalton. 1999. *Being Black, Living in the Red: Race, Wealth, and Social Policy in America.* Berkeley: University of California Press.

Curtin, Richard F., Thomas Juster, and James Morgan. 1989. "Survey Estimates of Wealth: An Assessment of Quality." *The Measurement of Savings, Investment, and Wealth,* ed. R. Lipsey and H. S. Tice, 473–551. Chicago: University of Chicago Press.

Duncan, Greg J., and Saul D. Hoffman. 1985. "A Reconsideration of the Economic Consequences of Marital Dissolution." *Demography* 22: 485–97.

England, Paula, and Barbara Stanek Kilbourne. 1990. "Markets, Marriages, and Other Mates: The Problem of Power." *Beyond the Marketplace: Rethinking Economy and Society,* ed. Roger Friedland and A. F. Robertson, chap. 6. New York: Aldine de Gruyter.

Estes, Ralph, and Jinoos Hosseini. 1998. "The Gender Gap on Wall Street: An Empirical Analysis of Confidence in Investment Decision Making." *Journal of Psychology* 122: 577–90.

Even, William E., and David A. Macpherson. 1994. "Gender Differences in Pensions." *Journal of Human Resources* 29: 555–87.

Fisher, Irving. 1930. *The Theory of Interest.* New York: MacMillan.

Hertz, Rosanna. 1986. *More Equal than Others: Women and Men in Dual-Career Marriages.* Berkeley: University of California Press.

Hinz, Richard P., David D. McCarthy, and John A. Turner. 1997. "Are Women Conservative Investors? Gender Differences in Participant-Directed Pension Investments." In *Positioning Pensions for the Twenty-First Century,* ed. Michael S. Gordon, Olivia S. Mitchell, and Marc M. Twinney, 91–103. Philadelphia: Pension Research Council and the University of Pennsylvania Press.

Holden, Karen C., and Pamela J. Smock. 1991. "The Economic Costs of Marital Dissolution: Why Do Women Bear a Disproportionate Cost?" *Annual Review of Sociology* 17: 51–78.

Hudson, Michael. 1996. *Merchants of Misery: How Corporate America Profits from Poverty.* Monroe, ME: Common Courage Press.

Keister, Lisa A. 2000a. "Race and Wealth Inequality: The Impact of Racial Differences in Asset Ownership on the Distribution of Household Wealth." *Social Science Research* 29: 477–502.

———. 2000b. *Wealth in America: Trends in Wealth Inequality.* New York: Cambridge University Press.

Keister, Lisa A., and Stephanie Moller. 2000. "Wealth Inequality in the United States." *Annual Review of Sociology* 26: 63–81.

McGarry, Kathleen, and Andrew Davenport. 1998. "Pensions and the Distribution of Wealth." In *Frontiers in the Economics of Aging,* ed. David A. Wise, chap. 11. Chicago: University of Chicago Press.

Newcomb, Michael D., and Jerome Rabow. 1999. "Gender, Socialization, and Money." *Journal of Applied Social Psychology* 29: 852–69.

Nock, Steven L. 1998. *Marriage in Men's Lives.* New York: Oxford University Press.

Oliver, Melvin L., and Thomas M. Shapiro. 1995. *Black Wealth, White Wealth: A New Perspective on Racial Inequality.* New York: Routledge.

Pahl, Jan. 1983. "The Allocation of Money and the Structuring of Inequality within Marriage." *Sociological Review* 31: 237–62.

Papke, Leslie E. 1998. "How Are Participants Investing Their Accounts in Participant-Directed Individual Account Pension Plans?" *American Economic Review* 88: 212–16.

Paulin, Geoffrey D., and Yoon G. Lee. 2002. "Expenditures of Single Parents: How Does Gender Figure In?" *Monthly Labor Review* 125: 16–37.

Peterson, Richard R. 1989. *Women, Work, and Divorce.* Albany, NY: SUNY Press.

———. 1996. "A Re-Evaluation of the Economic Consequences of Divorce." *American Sociological Review* 61: 528–36.

Shapiro, Thomas M. 2004. *The Hidden Cost of Being African American: How Wealth Perpetuates Inequality.* New York: Oxford University Press.

Shapiro, Thomas M., and Edward N. Wolff, eds. 2001. *Assets for the Poor: The Benefits of Spreading Asset Ownership.* New York: Russell Sage Foundation.

Sherraden, Michael. 1991. *Assets and the Poor: A New American Welfare Policy.* Armonk, NY: M.E. Sharpe.

Spilerman, Seymour. 2000. "Wealth and Stratification Processes." *Annual Review of Sociology* 26: 497–524.

U.S. Census Bureau. 1998. *Statistical Abstract of the United States.* Washington, DC: Government Printing Office.

———. 2003a. "Children's Living Arrangements and Characteristics: March 2002." Current Population Reports, P20-547. Washington, DC.

———. 2003b. "Custodial Mothers and Fathers and Their Child Support: 2001." Current Population Reports, P60-225. Washington, DC.

———. 2003c. *Statistical Abstract of the United States.* Washington, DC: Government Printing Office.

U.S. Department of Labor, Women's Bureau. 2000. "Earnings Differences between Women and Men." http://www.dol.gov/dol/wb/public/wb_pubs/wagegap2000.htm.

Waite, Linda J., and Maggie Gallagher. 2000. *The Case for Marriage: Why Married People Are Happier, Healthier, and Better Off Financially.* New York: Broadway Books.

Waldfogel, Jane. 1997. "The Effects of Children on Women's Wages." *American Sociological Review* 62: 209–17.

Wolff, Edward N. 1995. *Top Heavy: The Increasing Inequality of Wealth in America and What Can Be Done about It.* New York: New Press.

———. 2000. "Why Has Median Wealth Grown So Slowly in the 1990s?" Unpublished manuscript, New York University.

————. 2001. "Recent Trends in Wealth Ownership, from 1983 to 1998." In *Assets for the Poor: The Benefits of Spreading Asset Ownership,* ed. Thomas M. Shapiro and Edward N. Wolff, chap. 2. New York: Russell Sage Foundation.

Zelizer, Viviana. 1997. *The Social Meaning of Money.* Princeton, NJ: Princeton University Press.

III Data & Information about Specific Communities of Color

5 Native Americans' Wealth

JAY L. ZAGORSKY

The United States at the beginning of the twenty-first century is an extraordinarily rich country. Data compiled by the Federal Reserve show that the average household has a net worth of over $370,000 in 2000.[1] Moreover, even after adjusting for inflation this wealth has been steadily growing by over 2 percentage points a year since the mid-1950s.[2] While overall the United States is a wealthy country, there are many groups that do not share in this bounty. This chapter examines the wealth of Native Americans and finds that along this important economic dimension they are extremely disadvantaged.

Income data show Native Americans are one of the poorest groups in the United States. Information from the 2000 census shows that the median Asian family earns the most at $59,324, White non-Hispanic families earn the second most with $54,698, Hispanics follow with $34,397, Blacks are in second to last place with $33,255, and Native Americans with $33,144 bring up the rear.[3]

While many Native Americans are currently poor, the relatively recent introduction of casino gambling on Indian lands has the potential for dramatically boosting both income and wealth. The financial expectations surrounding gambling are very high, with the California Nations Indian Gaming Association stating, "Indian gaming is the first—and only—economic development tool that has ever worked on reservations."[4]

Since Congress passed the Indian Gaming Regulatory Act in 1988, gambling on protected Indian lands has exploded. Net revenue in 1988, primarily from high-stakes bingo, was $500 million. By 1996 the introduction of casino-style games had boosted revenue to $6.3 billion, and in 2002 the commission calculates Indian gaming generated $14.5 billion of revenue, which is one-fifth of the country's gambling industry.[5] In addition to gambling profits Native American casinos and bingo halls provide employment to roughly one hundred thousand Native Americans and three hundred thousand other individuals.[6]

Given that the regulatory act specifies standard management fees cannot exceed 30 percent and special management fees that include capital investment cannot exceed 40 percent of revenues, the dollars flowing to Native American communities are substantial.[7] However, since one purpose of the act is to channel gambling funds to general tribal development, not for the enrichment of individuals, there is no direct linkage between higher gambling revenues and higher Native American personal wealth and income.[8]

Given that gambling has clearly enriched some tribes, has the typical Native American's economic situation improved? Census income data clearly show the average Native American family has not been enriched. While income is important, wealth, which is another key financial indicator, has not been investigated. This chapter examines wealth holdings by contrasting the amounts held by all young baby boomers with the amounts held by Native Americans. This other financial indicator is important to understand because gambling's benefits might be boosting wealth instead of income. Additionally, wealth is important to study because higher levels are correlated with better health, more education (Henretta and Campbell 1978), and greater happiness (Gardner and Oswald 2001). By understanding wealth holdings, readers gain insight into how Native Americans fare along a key but unexplored socioeconomic dimension.

Previous researchers were stymied in studying Native American's wealth because until recently few wealth data sets were available that specifically tracked this group. The premier source of individual wealth data in the United States is the Survey of Consumer Finances, sponsored every three years by the Federal Reserve. While this survey provides exceptional detail on families' wealth and debt holdings, it provides relatively little detail on the respondents' racial background. In particular, while the survey asks respondents if they are "American Indian" or "Alaska Native," the public data release combines Asians, Native Americans, Native Hawaiians, and the catchall "other" individuals into a single category, preventing researchers from using this preeminent source to study Native Americans.[9]

One of the few data sets available that have detailed information on both Native American status and wealth is the National Longitudinal Survey of Youth (NLSY79). This survey is a nationally representative panel survey of young baby boomers that started in 1979. While a survey that tracked all ages would clearly be better for understanding Native American wealth, given the dearth of data and dearth of previous research, understanding young baby boomers is a key first step.

The rest of this chapter describes the data in more detail, discusses who is a Native American, examines wealth holdings, and finds Native Americans have little wealth. The chapter then investigates other data that provide information on Native American wealth and shows this additional information corroborates the NLSY79 findings. The research concludes with an investigation into why Native American wealth holdings are much lower than those of other young baby boomers.

THE DATA

One source of wealth information for Native Americans is the National Longitudinal Survey of Youth (NLSY79). The NLSY79, from its inception to present, has questioned the same group of people nineteen times. This repetitive surveying provides an in-depth picture of how young baby boomers are aging over time.[10] While the NLSY79 began in 1979, the research for this chapter starts its focus in 1985, which was the first survey that included wealth questions, and ends in 2000, the latest publicly available year of wealth data. Additional survey details are found in Zagorsky 1997.

The primary goal of the NLSY79 is neither to track Native Americans nor to track wealth. Instead the survey was created to understand how the education and training backgrounds of individuals affected their labor market outcomes. Fortunately, wealth questions were added to expand the list of outcomes researchers could monitor. Beyond the survey's longitudinal aspects the NLSY79 also oversampled poor individuals, Blacks, and Hispanics to ensure more accurate research results for these groups.[11]

Not all NLSY79 respondents are used in the research for this chapter. To ensure wealth is precisely tracked, a simple sample selection criterion was used. All individuals used in the research for this chapter needed to participate in more than half (more than six) of the NLSY79 surveys since a wealth module was first fielded in 1985. This criterion ensures a detailed history is available for every respondent, and the noise caused by respondents with irregular participation is attenuated. The two key data series used in this research are the respondent's Native American status and net worth. Creation of both series is described in the next sections.

WHO IS A NATIVE AMERICAN?

Who is a Native American? Individuals belonging and living together on tribal lands, such as the Burns Paiute tribe of Oregon with about three hundred individuals, or in close physical proximity, such as the Cherokee in central Oklahoma with over three hundred thousand individuals, are well defined. However, not all Native Americans belong to clearly defined groups that live together. Instead of geographic location, ancestry and race define this segment of the U.S. population.

When asked about their ancestry, many individuals define themselves as "native to America." The 2000 decennial census question on ancestry found over 7.3 percent of the population (20.6 million out of 281.4 million) stated their ancestors were either U.S. or American.[12] Race data from the same census, however, show that only 1.5 percent of the population (4.1 million) state their race is either American Indian or Alaska Native.[13]

In the research for this chapter, determining who is a Native American in the NLSY79 is done by combining information on ancestry and race. In the survey's first round individuals were asked to provide up to six different ancestries. One choice on the list was "Indian-American or Native American," which was selected by 6 percent of all individuals as either their only or most important ancestry. Three criteria were then applied to this set of individuals. First, all respondents who stated more than two different ancestries were not considered Native American. This eliminated individuals with less than one-half Native American bloodlines.

Second, after each face-to-face survey, interviewers marked down if they thought the respondent was White, Black, or other race. All individuals who claimed they were "Indian-American or Native American" but were never once classified in the nineteen NLSY79 interviews since 1979 as being in the "other race" category were removed. Last, the sample selection criterion (more than six surveys since 1985) was applied. This resulted in eighty-three respondents being labeled Native Americans, which, after weighting, represent almost 1 percent of all U.S. young baby boomers.

One drawback to this research is the small sample size. If wealth, from gambling and other sources, is distributed unevenly among Native Americans, a small sample makes it likely that the rich will be underrepresented. To remedy this problem a later section in this chapter looks at wealth data from other sources and confirms the findings of low Native American wealth.

Table 5.1 shows the demographics from the 2000 survey of both the overall young baby boomer population and among the Native American subgroup. The top section of the table tracks standard demographic indicators like age, marital status, and gender, while the bottom investigates the key issues facing Native Americans today as defined by *The National Congress of American Indians.*[14] The key issues are education, health, employment training, veterans, disabilities, welfare reform, adoption care, foster care, alcohol abuse, and substance abuse.

The table's top section shows that in the 2000 survey the typical young baby boomer was slightly more than 38 years old. While the majority of both Native American and all boomers were married (54.5 percent versus 70.7 percent overall), Native Americans have higher divorce rates and greater numbers of never-married individuals than the overall population.

TABLE 5.1. Demographics of All Young Baby Boomers and
Native Americans in 2000

	Overall	Native American
Average age in years	38.7	38.5
Marital status (%)		
Single	16.1	22.1
Married	70.7	54.5
Divorced	13.2	23.4
Gender (%)		
Male	48.6	49.5
Female	51.4	50.5
Highest grade completed (%)		
<12th grade	15.4	26.5
12th grade	35.0	40.5
>12th grade	49.6	33.1
Health problems (%)	39.4	52.7
Vocational training (%)	66.7	74.1
In military (%)	9.8	17.8
Handicapped (%)	3.2	5.4
Ever on welfare (%)	25.1	52.3
Adopted/foster care (%)	2.9	6.2
Ever heavy drug user (%)	6.1	22.2
Ever heavy alcohol user (%)	7.1	11.0
Ever heavy smoker (%)	22.3	43.0

The table's bottom section shows why *The National Congress of American Indians* defined these as key issues. Native Americans have lower educational attainment (67 percent twelfth-grade education or less) than the overall population (50.4 percent twelfth-grade education or less). Health problems, indicated by the respondents stating in any NLSY79 survey since 1985 that they were limited in the kind or amount of work they could do by health reasons, affect Native Americans (52.7 percent) more than the overall population (39.4 percent).

Native Americans (74.1 percent) are slightly more likely to receive some form of training from 1985 to 2000 than the general population (66.7 percent) and are also much more likely to belong to the military (17.8 percent versus 9.8 percent overall).[15] Being handicapped, which is based on the interviewer's observation,[16] is also more prevalent among Native Americans (5.4 percent versus 3.2 percent overall). The ever-on-welfare line tracks respondents who received income from Aid to Families with Dependent Children (AFDC), Temporary Assistance to Needy Families (TANF), Supplemental Security Income (SSI), or other similar government programs from 1985 to 2000. Native American rates for ever being on welfare are double (52.3 percent) that of the overall populations (25.1 percent).

Native Americans (6.2 percent) are also much more likely either to be adopted or to grow up in foster care sometime from birth to age 18 than other baby boomers (2.9 percent overall). The last three lines of the table track the prevalence of drug,[17] alcohol[18] and smoking[19] abuse. Overall, Native American young baby boomers are much more likely to ever be a heavy user of drugs (22.2 percent versus 6.1 percent overall) and cigarettes (43 percent versus 22.3 percent overall) and slightly more likely to drink heavily (11 percent versus 7.1 percent) than the general boomer population.

HOW MUCH WEALTH?

How much wealth do Native Americans hold? How has the ratio of Native American to overall wealth changed over time? This section shows that the net worth held by the typical Native American is roughly one-quarter to one-half that of the typical family overall. More importantly, while the typical boomer's wealth grows steadily over time, the typical Native American's wealth does not.

How wealthy or poor are young baby boomers? The NLSY79 asked

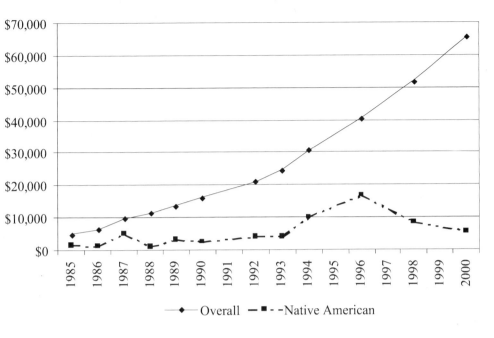

Fig. 5.1. Median young baby boomer wealth (2000 dollars)

each respondent a variety of detailed asset and debt questions in eleven out of the thirteen surveys fielded from 1985 to 2000. These eleven wealth modules all follow the same pattern. Respondents are first asked if they or their spouse currently owe a debt or have an asset. If they answer yes, the interviewer asks them to state the current value. By summing all the asset answers and subtracting from that total all debt answers, a respondent's total net worth was created for each survey year. Repeating this procedure for all eleven surveys created a net worth series for each respondent. While complete details of constructing the net worth series are described in Zagorsky 1999, the key formula sums ten asset and subtracts five debt categories.[20] After creating each series, all net worth values are adjusted and reported in 2000 dollars to account for inflation.

Figure 5.1 shows the median net worth held overall by young baby boomers and among just those who are Native American. The median is used instead of the mean to avoid the dramatic fluctuations caused by the presence or absence of the very rich. The figure is missing data for 1991 because the survey did not ask wealth questions in that year. There are no data for 1995, 1997, and 1999 since the NLSY79 switched from interviewing respondents every year to every other year in 1994 to lower the survey's cost.

In general the figure shows the median boomer starts off with relatively little net worth (1985 $5,055) but steadily builds wealth over time. By 2000, the median young baby boomer amassed $65,500, a thirteen-fold increase in wealth. Native Americans, however, do not follow the same wealth-building trajectory. In 1985 the median Native American's net worth was almost $1,700, or one-third the overall level. Then, instead of steadily building, over the next fifteen years the median Native American's wealth fluctuates in a relatively narrow band that peaks in 1996 ($16,986) and then steadily declines (2000 value $5,700).

Table 5.2 breaks down net worth from the 2000 survey into a variety of percentiles. The richest NLSY79 respondent had approximately $12 million in wealth, while the richest Native American respondent's net worth was $310,000. To be in the richest 5 percent of all families, a respondent needed over $600,000, but a Native American needed slightly more than $200,000. The rows labeled *maximum* (one hundredth percentile) down to the fiftieth percentile show the typical Native American's wealth ranges from 2.6 percent to 52 percent and on average is approximately one-quarter of the overall total.

At the bottom of the distribution, Native Americans are also in worse financial shape. Twenty-five percent of all Native Americans have zero net worth or are in debt compared with just 10 percent of all boomers. Having a net worth of negative $30,000 ranks a family in the bottom 5

TABLE 5.2.   Net Worth of Native American and All Young Baby Boomers in 2000

	Overall[a] ($)	Native American[b] ($)	Ratio (%) (native/all)
Maximum	11,850,001	310,000	2.6
99%	2,161,002	310,000	14.3
95%	634,000	229,500	36.2
90%	387,000	201,300	52.0
75%	177,000	58,500	33.1
50%	65,500	5,700	8.7
25%	10,000	0	0.0
10%	0	−595	Undefined
5%	−2,700	−30,000	1,111.1
1%	−31,500	−30,000	95.2
Minimum	−999,000	−30,000	3.0

[a]Number of observations = 7,905.

[b]Number of observations = 53.

percent of all Native Americans, compared with the bottom 1 percent of all young baby boomers. Overall, at both the upper and lower ends of the wealth spectrum, Native Americans are financially behind.

How does the composition of Native American wealth change over time? Table 5.3 breaks down assets and debts into three major categories: financial, or liquid, wealth holdings; home, or residential equity; and illiquid, which includes assets difficult to sell quickly. The table tracks the mean percentage of net worth held in each category by respondents whose net worth is not zero. To understand the financial status of Native Americans, all three indicators are computed both for all young baby boomers and just for Native American respondents.

The table's first two columns show the percentage of net worth held as financial wealth.[21] For the mean young baby boomer this category comprises roughly one-fifth (21.2 percent) of net worth, while for Native Americans financial wealth comprises one-sixth (15.7 percent). The next two columns track the percentage of net worth held in illiquid forms,[22] such as cars, trucks, and businesses. This series, which is trending downward as boomers age, comprises almost three-quarters (71.7 percent) of Native Americans net worth but a little more than half (56.4 percent) for all young baby boomers. The table's final category, home, tracks the net value of the respondent's primary residence as a

TABLE 5.3. Mean Percentage of Net Worth Held in Financial, Illiquid, and Home Forms

	Financial		Illiquid		Home	
	Overall	Native American	Overall	Native American	Overall	Native American
1985	20.0	9.4	70.0	98.4	10.0	−7.9
1986	18.3	7.9	69.9	74.6	11.6	17.5
1987	17.3	11.0	66.7	73.3	15.8	17.8
1988	17.8	18.9	63.4	82.1	17.9	−1.0
1989	18.8	14.4	61.2	70.1	19.7	15.5
1990	19.8	13.7	57.7	72.5	22.0	13.8
1992	21.3	14.0	54.8	65.4	24.3	20.6
1993	20.4	15.0	54.4	66.4	25.5	18.6
1994	21.9	19.4	50.6	76.2	27.5	4.4
1996	23.7	19.0	47.2	66.1	28.2	14.9
1998	26.5	22.7	43.1	61.3	30.2	16.0
2000	29.0	22.5	37.6	54.2	33.6	23.3
Average	21.2	15.7	56.4	71.7	22.2	12.8

Note: Calculations based on individuals who have nonzero net worth. Negative numbers occur when debts are greater than assets for a category.

percentage of net worth.[23] This series shows that residences are slowly becoming a larger portion of the portfolio of both the typical boomer (10 percent in 1985 to 33.6 percent in 2000) and Native American (−7.9 percent in 1985 to 23.3 percent in 2000).

What does the portfolio of assets and debts held by Native American and all families look like? Table 5.4 shows the percentage that own a particular asset, or owe a particular debt, the mean value of these assets and debts, and the percentage each particular asset or debt value makes up of the typical family's total assets or total debts from the 2000 NLSY survey.

Columns 1 and 2 show that a car or truck is the most widely held asset, with 75.6 percent of all young baby boomers and 67.8 percent of all Native Americans owning a vehicle. The second most widely held asset is a checking or savings account, with 64.6 percent of all young baby boomers and 43.4 percent of all Native Americans having these types of accounts. Wilhelmina Leigh points out in chapter 1 of this volume that low rates of bank account ownership are not limited to just Native Americans but also to Blacks and Hispanics. Caskey (2002) finds

TABLE 5.4. Percentage Owning, Mean Value, and Percentage of Portfolio for Specific Categories 2000

	(1)	(2)	(3)	(4)	(5)	(6)
	Percentage Owning		Mean Value ($)		Percentage of Portfolio	
	Overall	Native	Overall	Native	Overall	Native
Assets						
Vehicles	75.6	67.8	14,659	9,688	20.5	37.5
Homes	57.4	33.2	111,924	43,544	43.9	28.9
Gross business value	7.2	4.5	27,220	7,049	3.1	3.8
Possessions	56.4	40.6	14,754	4,605	9.4	15.3
Checking/savings/money market	64.6	43.4	16,198	2,578	7.1	5.5
Stocks/bonds/mutual funds	21.5	6.3	26,316	1,336	3.2	2.4
Trusts	2.5	0.0	10,546	0	1.3	0.0
IRAs	20.8	10.5	11,872	2,350	3.1	1.2
401(k)s	37.2	25.1	22,637	8,561	8.0	5.4
Certificates of deposit	5.2	0.0	2,139	0	0.5	0.0
Debts						
Mortgages	49.3	28.0	55,695	20,669	60.0	36.0
Other residential	3.5	0.0	664	0	0.9	0.0
Business	4.3	5.7	7,362	3,318	3.1	3.7
Credit card	39.7	39.4	5,694	4,420	20.1	28.6
Other debt	31.0	34.7	4,414	4,754	16.0	31.8

that many people do not have bank accounts because "they do not need an account, generally because they have almost no month-to-month savings." Thus, these low rates are a concern because they signal problems in building up savings.

Among all boomers the third and fourth most held assets are a home (57.4 percent) and expensive possessions, like jewelry (56.4 percent). For Native Americans the order is reversed, with more respondents holding expensive possessions (40.6 percent) and fewer owning homes (33.2 percent).[24] Among these four asset categories Native American ownership rates are much lower than the overall totals. Many other asset categories have even wider disparities than these top groups. For example, stock ownership is three times as likely overall (21.5 percent) as among Native Americans (6.3 percent).

The bottom of the table shows the percentage holding various debts. The top three types of debts are mortgages (49.3 percent overall; 28 percent Native American), credit card balances (39.7 percent overall; 39.4 percent Native American), and other debt such as installment loans (31 percent overall; 34.7 percent Native American). In every *asset* category there are fewer Native American holders than found among the overall population. The reverse occurs in the debt section, where the percentage of Native Americans holding *debts* is larger in three out of the five cases.

The middle columns (3 and 4) show the average (mean) assets held by Native Americans is much smaller than the overall total. While most families own a vehicle, Native American cars and trucks ($9,688) are worth less than the overall figure ($14,659). The overall average ($16,198) amount of money held in a checking or savings account is six times larger than the typical Native American amount ($2,578). Native American housing values ($43,544) are less than half the level of the overall home's value ($111,924). Financial assets like stocks, bonds, and mutual funds ($26,316 overall, $1,336 Native American) also show a very large difference.

In the debt section, except for mortgages ($55,695 overall and $20,669 Native American), the differences are much smaller. Overall, boomers held $5,694 in credit card debt in 2000, while Native Americans held slightly less ($4,420). Comparing other debt (the last line) shows Native Americans ($4,754) have slightly *more* than the overall average ($4,414).

The final two columns show the percentage of the asset and debt portfolio each category makes up.[25] Overall, three-quarters of all young baby boomers' assets are composed of their homes (43.9 percent), vehicles (20.5 percent), and expensive possessions (9.4 percent). While these three categories are also important for Native Americans, the table shows that vehicles (37.5 percent) and possessions (15.3 percent) make up a much larger percentage of their assets. In the debt section, mortgages are the largest category, comprising 60 percent of all debt overall and 36 percent among Native Americans. Credit card debt (20.1 percent overall and 28.6 percent Native American) and other debt (16 percent overall and 31.8 percent Native American) are also important components, but business and other residential debt is not.

Overall, this table shows that Native Americans have much lower home ownership rates and home values than the overall population. In addition, Native Americans' wealth is skewed much more toward vehicles than the overall population's. On the debt side Native American credit card, business, and other debt values are not dramatically different from overall figures. However, on the asset side Native Americans hold significantly fewer financial and retirement resources than the overall population.

OTHER WEALTH DATA

While the NLSY79 provides detailed data, one significant drawback is that it captures only one segment of the population. This section examines other sources of Native American wealth information such as business, home, and vehicle ownership, that track all ages, not just young baby boomers.

BUSINESS OWNERSHIP

The Census Bureau runs a census of business every five years. Since the 1972 census the bureau has provided details on the race and ethnicity of business owners. Businesses are broadly defined in the census and include everything from individuals who file a 1040 schedule C to large, multinational corporations.[26]

Table 5.5 shows trends in Native American business ownership from 1972 to 1997.[27] While the total number of firms in the United States has grown 2.5 times over this twenty-five-year period, Native American–owned firms have grown one-hundred-fold, starting at fewer than two thousand in 1972 to almost two hundred thousand by 1997. While this growth is dramatic, since Native Americans comprise roughly 1.5 percent of the U.S. population, they are still underrepresented in the business community.

The table also tracks the number of Native American firms with paid employees. The number of firms in this category has grown 120-fold, and employment by these firms has increased by 230 times since 1972. While again this is explosive growth, the last column shows the vast majority of Native American businesses continue to employ no workers outside of the owner.

Going beyond the data in table 5.5, Census Bureau statistics reveal that many Native American businesses are smaller than other firms. The average firm in the United States with paid employees had sales of $3.4 million, twenty workers, and a $500,000 payroll in 1997. The typical Native American firm with paid employees had sales of $880,000, nine workers, and a $200,000 payroll. Among all firms without paid employees, average sales in 1997 were $41,500, while Native American sales averaged $31,200, or three-quarters the overall size (U.S. Bureau of the Census 2001).

Over time, sales at Native American firms have been converging toward overall values. Comparing all firms (both with and without paid employees) to Native American firms in 1972 shows Native American firms' sales were seven times smaller. By 1997, however, this difference had shrunk to a factor of five. Combining the above information shows that from 1972 to 1997 Native American business has experienced explosive growth in terms of number of firms, sales, and employment. Nevertheless, without additional growth typical Native American–owned businesses will continue to lag the average U.S. firm.

TABLE 5.5. Native American Business Ownership

	Total U.S. Firms	All Native American Firms	Percentage of Native American Firms	Native American Firms with Paid Employees	Number of Employees at Native American Firms	Percentage of No-Employee Firms
1972	8,730,000	1,819	0.02	278	1,297	84.7
1977	9,833,000	5,679	0.06	1,145	7,513	79.8
1982	12,059,950	14,844	0.12	1,462	7,158	90.2
1987	13,695,500	21,380	0.16	3,739	8,956	82.5
1992	17,253,143	102,271	0.59	NA	NA	NA
1997	20,821,934	197,300	0.95	33,277	298,661	83.1

Source: U.S. Bureau of the Census 1971, 1975, 1980, 1986, 1991, 1996, and 2001.

Note: NA means not available, because the 1992 publication combined American Indian and Asian business ownership for these categories.

What percentage of Native Americans own homes and vehicles? Data from the decennial census answer these questions. Overall, roughly two-thirds of all U.S. households own their homes.[28] Native Americans' home ownership rates follow national trends from 1980 to 2000 but are on average 10 percentage points lower. In 1980 slightly more than 53 percent of Native American households owned their homes, a rate 11 points lower than the overall population. By 2000, almost 60 percent of Native Americans owned their homes, and the gap had shrunk to 8.7 percentage points. Both of these gaps in home ownership rates are similar in direction but much smaller in size than those found in the NLSY79.

The census data on housing values not only confirm the gap between Native Americans and all young boomers found in the NLSY79 but also show the gap is widening over time. In the 1980 census the median Native American home was worth $35,400, which was approximately three-quarters the overall U.S. value. Twenty years later the median Native American home had jumped to $81,000. However, because the average U.S. home's value had climbed even further in that period to $119,600, the typical Native American home was worth just two-thirds the overall average.

Census figures that track vehicle ownership show vehicles are more widely held in the overall population than among NLSY79 baby boomers.[29] Combining the data for 1980 to 2000 shows 88.4 percent of all households own at least one vehicle, while the corresponding figure for Native Americans is almost 5 points lower at 83.7 percent. The gap in vehicle ownership rates shrank slightly from 1980 to 1990 but showed no change in the 2000 census. As with business ownership, national data show that Native Americans lag the overall population in home ownership, home value, and vehicle ownership.

WHAT EXPLAINS THESE WEALTH DIFFERENCES?

Why do Native Americans have so little wealth? There are three possibilities. Wealth is created primarily by saving, receiving transfers, or having capital assets appreciate. Saving increases wealth when people spend less than their current income. By definition the residual not spent increases their wealth holdings. Transfers, which are gifts from outside the household, increase wealth if the transfer is not completely spent. Last, capital appreciation increases wealth since increasing asset values result in a larger net worth. This section examines each of these three areas and suggests the most likely cause is that Native Americans' low incomes result in little savings.*

The simplest case to handle is capital appreciation. For some groups, capital appreciation is extremely important. For example, Wolff (2001) attributes most of the recent rise in wealth to changes in stock market values. As the stock market rose in the late 1990s, wealthy households holding lots of stock became significantly wealthier. This factor is not important for young baby boomers because both the overall population and Native Americans hold little financial wealth. Capital appreciation is important only when wealth reaches a relatively large level.

For example, an investment of $100 with a consistent 25 percent return becomes $8,700 if all interest is reinvested annually for twenty years. While this is a phenomenal percentage growth, in absolute terms the $8,700 does little to change a person's net worth ranking. Given that the peak Native American's median net worth was slightly less than $17,000, it would take very high and consistent appreciation rates to have almost any effect on total wealth.

The second major method of gaining or losing wealth is via transfers. Charles Dickens popularized the story of the poor orphan who is suddenly transformed into a man of means when he received a large inheritance. Wealth transfers are not just storybook fiction but are a major source of transferring wealth from generation to generation. Wilhelm's (2001) work shows that inheritances are not just the province of rich White families but that minorities also receive inheritances. More importantly, he finds individuals who received a medium (> $8,896) or large inheritance had a significantly higher probability of being self-employed. This suggests inheritances have a positive feedback effect on wealth beyond the initial generational transfer of wealth.

Transfers are tracked in the NLSY79 with each survey asking respon-

*Several studies note that lack and loss of wealth in Native American and Native Hawaiian—and even African American, Asian American, and Latino—communities are in great part a result of land confiscation and asset-stripping policies throughout U.S. history. Ong addresses this in chapter 6, detailing the history for Native Hawaiians. Our introduction also directs readers to additional sources on these issues, as well as issues of U.S. federal government mismanagement of assets held in trust for First Nations (see Henson et. al. 2005 and Adamson 2003 in the "Introduction and Overview," for example) [Editors].

dents if they have received an inheritance or gift in the last year worth more than $500 and, if so, the amount. Combining the data from all surveys shows that, overall, 46.3 percent of all young baby boomers received a gift or inheritance compared with 51.3 percent of Native Americans. While more Native Americans received gifts, the amount they received ($4,100 median, $20,161 mean) was slightly less than the overall values ($5,300 median, $28,885 mean). Given the dramatic differences between Native American wealth levels and those seen overall, these slight differences in the amounts and reception rates make it unlikely that transfers explain the wealth gap.

The last method of creating wealth is by saving. When people spend less than their after-tax income, the residual accrues to their wealth. Conversely, when people spend more than their income, their savings are negative, and their wealth decreases. Hence, to understand if Native American wealth is created or destroyed by savings, it is important to first track how their income has changed over time. While the causes are still uncertain, recent work by Dynan, Skinner, and Zeldes (2004) shows that savings rates in the overall population tend to rise as permanent income rises. Their work suggests that permanent growth in Native Americans' income should lead to more savings.

Calculating yearly median total family income shows the typical Native American's income was much less than the overall young baby boomer average.[30] In the NLSY79 the average Native American's income was 75¢ for every $1 of income received by the typical boomer. Additionally, Native American baby boomers experienced real annual income growth of 1.4 percent, which is roughly half the 2.7 percent growth rate experienced by the entire cohort. Data from the 2000 decennial census, which covers all ages, corroborates the low median income found among Native American young baby boomers. In the census the overall median household income was $41,994, but the median Native American household's $30,599 was just 73 percent of the overall figure (U.S. Bureau of the Census 2003a, table 10).

Even among tribes with very large gambling operations, income is not inordinately high. Two of the most prosperous Indian gaming casinos are Foxwoods Casino, run by the Mashantucket-Pequot Tribal Nation, and the Mohegan Sun Casino, run by the Mohegan Tribe. The 2000 census shows median household income of Connecticut's Mashantucket-Pequot was $60,132 and Mohegan was $70,104 (U.S. Bureau of the Census

2003a, table 50). While these figures are higher than the U.S. average, the tribes' median incomes aren't as high when compared only with other Connecticut households. Connecticut's overall median income of $53,935, which ranks second in the nation, was just $6,000 less than the Mashantucket-Pequot amount and $16,000 less than the Mohegan (U.S. Bureau of the Census 2003b).

More importantly, not all tribal households receive high income. Twenty percent of the Mashantucket-Pequot and 25 percent of Mohegan households reported incomes of less than $25,000 in 2000. In the Mohegan's case gambling has clearly improved many members' incomes. The 1990 census, which occurred five years before the casino opened, found a median household income of just $25,375, almost $45,000 lower than the 2000 figure. These figures show that even among small nations gambling improves the economic position of many but does not provide exceptionally high income to all.

While these figures indicate lower income is an important cause of lower wealth, it is important to check consumption. If Native Americans spend much less than the overall boomer, even though they have smaller incomes, they potentially can still increase their wealth by saving. Unfortunately the NLSY79 neither tracks total spending nor housing expenditures. The only category tracked is a brief series from 1990 to 1994 when the survey asked respondents how much money they spent on four different food categories. Using these data, total food spending per year per person was calculated by summing the four food categories from each survey and dividing by each family's size.

In the early 1990s the overall young baby boomer spent an average (mean) of $2,000 per person per year on food. Average Native American food spending is roughly similar to this overall figure since in two of the years the average Native American spent less, in two years the average Native American spent more, and in one year the average Native American spent an equal amount on food. These limited data suggest Native Americans spend similar amounts on food, but since they have lower incomes, they are saving less than the typical household.

Overall, the data in this section suggest that low Native American incomes are the primary reason why their wealth is smaller than the overall young baby boomers'. Information on transfers and capital appreciation and limited data on expenditure patterns indicate none of these factors are important reasons for explaining the wealth gap.

CONCLUSION

How wealthy is a particular social, religious, or ethnic group? Is the group's wealth growing, shrinking, or staying unchanged over time? These are key questions in the United States since higher wealth is associated with better health, more education, and improvement in other socioeconomic variables. This chapter investigates the wealth of Native Americans and finds a relatively bleak picture.

The key facts laid out in this chapter are straightforward. Among young baby boomers the typical Native American's wealth is between one-half and one-quarter the overall average. More importantly, while the median baby boomer starts off with relatively little net worth and then steadily builds wealth over time, the median Native American does not. Instead, Native American wealth has moved around in a small range without any trend. Looking at the composition of Native American wealth shows that it is skewed much more toward vehicles and that Native Americans have lower home ownership rates than the overall baby boomer population.

Wealth information that covers the entire age distribution shows a similar picture. Compared with U.S. residents overall, Native Americans own fewer businesses, have lower rates of home ownership, have lower rates of vehicle ownership, and reside in homes worth significantly less.

Income data, like wealth data, present similar findings. Among all racial groups in the 2000 census, Native American families have the lowest income, earning roughly 60 percent of what White families earn. This is the same ratio determined by the 1990 census. Examining data for just young baby boomers shows a slightly smaller gap, with the typical Native American's income about three-quarters of the overall average.

In summary, Native Americans are not wealthy along any of the key financial dimensions, and outside of business ownership, Native American wealth is not showing much growth. What will improve Native Americans' wealth? This research suggests the primary reason for low Native American wealth is low income. Programs devoted to raising salaries and employment opportunities for Native Americans, such as casino gambling, may boost income and by extension should improve Native American wealth. Because of casino gambling's potentially large impact, more research needs to be done to understand how the financial picture of Native Americans changes as new jobs and income flow into their communities. If casinos bring sustainable economic development to relatively large groups of Native Americans, future research should find a more positive financial picture than the bleak one presented in this chapter.

1. Data are from the flow of funds accounts of the U.S. historical releases, which are online at http://www.federalreserve.gov/releases. The figure is calculated by subtracting household balance sheet (table B.100) liabilities from assets, removing the net worth of nonprofit organizations, and then dividing the result by the number of U.S. households.

2. Adjusting all figures into 2000 dollars shows in 1955 the average household had a net worth of $176,000.

3. Similar income patterns are seen in the 1990 census data (U.S. Bureau of the Census 1993), with the median Asian family earning $41,258, White non-Hispanic families $40,370, Hispanics $25,394, Native Americans $24,798, and Blacks $23,161. The primary difference between the two years is that in 1990 Native Americans were slightly higher than Blacks but in 2000 were slightly lower. The 2000 data are from http://www.factfinder .census.gov, tables entitled "Median Family Income in 1999 Dollars."

4. Quote from http://www.cniga.com/facts/qanda.php.

5. Data from National Indian Gaming Commission 2000 and http://www .nigc.gov.

6. Data from the National Indian Gaming Association (http://www .indiangaming.org).

7. Native American gambling operations have numerous other expenses besides management fees. Some revenue is shared with states in lieu of taxation, and other business expenses, such as advertising and promotions, reduce profits.

8. The act specifies funds are used for five purposes "(i) to fund tribal government operations or programs; (ii) to provide for the general welfare of the Indian tribe and its members; (iii) to promote tribal economic development; (iv) to donate to charitable organizations; or (v) to help fund operations of local government agencies."

9. See, for example, variable X6809 in the 2001 codebook.

10. Young baby boomers are individuals who were between the ages of 14 and 22 in 1979.

11. Given this oversampling, all results are reported after being adjusted by the survey weights, which removes the oversampling effects and allows the answers to be considered national totals. The 1979 survey weights found on the data CD-ROM as variable R02161.00 adjust all data.

12. Data from http://www.factfinder.census.gov, table QT-P13, entitled "Ancestry: 2000."

13. Data from table QT-P5, entitled "Race Alone or in Combination: 2000."

14. The list is found online under the "Human Resources" heading at http://www.ncai.org. The list also contains an item labeled "Elders," but the

Native Americans' Wealth - ✿ - 151

NLSY79 provides no information to track individuals who are not young baby boomers.

15. The "in military" flag tracks respondents who signed up for either active duty or the reserves at any time in life.

16. Interviewers fill in a brief questionnaire about their perception of the respondent after each survey to guide staff in deciding if an interviewer with special characteristics, such as the ability to speak American Sign Language, is needed in the future. This questionnaire identifies special characteristics that created problems while interviewing respondents, such as being blind, deaf, or mentally or physically handicapped. This procedure is a lower-bound estimate since handicaps not affecting a sit-down interview are overlooked.

17. Heavy drug users are determined from NLSY79 supplements fielded in 1984, 1988, 1992, and 1994, which ask about the quantity and frequency of drugs used. Since the supplements focus primarily on marijuana, cocaine, and crack, abusers of other drugs like heroin are not counted as drug users. Additionally, since only the 1984 survey included questions on how drugs affected respondents' lives, abusers are primarily determined by frequency of use. In this research heavy drug users are individuals using crack, cocaine, or marijuana more than three times per week over the last thirty days in the 1994, 1990, and 1988 surveys. Respondents who used drugs at work in 1984 were also classified as heavy users. To avoid including reformed drug users, the most recent data (1994 if possible) determined drug status.

18. Heavy drinkers are defined in a two-step process. First, all people who told the interviewer they had six or more drinks on at least two occasions in the last month were identified. Then such individuals were questioned to see if drinking caused serious problems. If these drinkers had at least twelve times in the past year faced a serious drink-induced problem such as arrest, staying away from work, hurting their chances for a raise, or losing ties with family, they were considered heavy drinkers. To avoid penalizing reformed drinkers, the most recent data (1994) were used unless they were missing.

19. Heavy smokers are defined as people who in any one of the 1998, 1994, 1992, or 1984 cigarette supplements ever stated that they smoked more than a pack a day.

20. Net worth is obtained by summing the current market value of the respondent's home; cash savings; stocks, bonds, and mutual funds; trusts; equity in businesses, farms, and investment real estate; vehicles; possessions and jewelry; IRAs; 401(k)s; and certificates of deposit. Subtracted from the asset total are the current values of mortgages; other property debt; business, farm, and other real estate debt; vehicle debt; and credit card, installment, and other debts. Missing wealth values were imputed using the procedure described by Camphuis (1993) for the Netherlands Socio-Economic Panel. Camphuis' technique causes some data smoothing, but the high response rates to wealth questions result in little imputation being needed.

21. Financial Percentage = (Cash Savings + Stock + Trusts + IRA + 401[k] + CD) / Net Worth.

22. Illiquid Percentage = (Business Equity − Business Debt + Car Value − Car Debt + Possessions − Other Debt) / Net Worth.

23. Home Percentage = (Home Value − Mortgage − Property Debt) / Net Worth.

24. The year 2000 gap in home ownership rates is wider than in most other years. From 1985 to 2000 the average difference in Native American and overall home ownership rates is 13.9 percentage points.

25. Families whose total assets or debts were zero are not included in the calculations.

26. The Census Bureau classifies businesses based on surveys, which ask owners about their sex, race, and ethnicity. The bureau creates part of its sample by combining IRS data with the race and ethnicity questions filled out by people when they requested their social security numbers. Race and ethnicity data are also available from a trial survey done in 1969. While this survey included a category for American Indians on the forms, so few Indian businesses were found they were consolidated into the "other" category.

27. The 2002 data are not available until 2006.

28. Overall home ownership rates in the United States from 1980 to 2000 are 64.4, 64.2, and 68.3 percent. Among Native Americans the figures are 53.4, 52.9, and 59.6 percent.

29. Overall vehicle ownership rates in the United States from 1980 to 2000 are 87.1, 88.5, and 89.7 percent. Among Native Americans the figures are 82.1, 83.9, and 85.1 percent.

30. The two exceptions in the NLSY79 are 1983 and 1985.

REFERENCES

Camphuis, H. 1993. *Checking, Editing and Imputation of Wealth Data of the Netherlands Socio-Economic Panel for the Period '87–'89.* Progress Report 10. VSB-CentER Savings Project, Tilburg University, Netherlands.

Caskey, John. 2002. "Check-Cashing Outlets in a Changing Financial System." Working Paper no. 02-4, Federal Reserve Bank of Philadelphia.

Dynan, Karen, Jonathan Skinner, and Stephen Zeldes. 2004. "Do the Rich Save More?" *Journal of Political Economy* 112 (2): 397–444.

Gardner, Jonathan, and Andrew Oswald. 2001. "Does Money Buy Happiness? A Longitudinal Study Using Data on Windfalls." University of Warwick Working Paper. http://www.warwick.ac.uk/fac/soc/Economics/oswald/marchwindfallsGO.pdf.

Henretta, John, and Richard Campbell. 1978. "Net Worth as an Aspect of Status." *American Journal of Sociology* 83 (5): 1204–23.

National Indian Gaming Commission. 2000. *Biennial Report of the National Indian Gaming Commission, 1998–2000.* Washington, DC.

U.S. Bureau of the Census. 1971. *Minority-Owned Businesses, 1969.* Report MB-1. August, Washington, DC.

———. 1975. *1972 Survey of Minority-Owned Business Enterprises.* Report MB72-3. February, Washington, DC.

———. 1980. *1977 Survey of Minority-Owned Business Enterprises.* Report MB77-3. November, Washington, DC.

———. 1985. *Statistical Abstract of United States: 1985*. Table 1313. Washington, DC.

———. 1986. *1982 Survey of Minority-Owned Business Enterprises*. Report MB82-3. October, Washington, DC.

———. 1991. *Survey of Minority-Owned Business Enterprises; 1987 Economic Census*. Report MB87-3. June, Washington, DC.

———. 1993. *1990 Census of Population: Social and Economic Characteristics, United States*. Washington, DC.

———. 1994. *1990 Census of Population: Characteristics of American Indians by Tribe and Language*. Report CP-3-7. Washington, DC.

———. 1996. *Survey of Minority-Owned Business Enterprises; 1992 Economic Census*. Report MB92-4. September, Washington, DC.

———. 2001. *Survey of Minority-Owned Business Enterprises; 1997 Economic Census*. Report EC97CS-1. September, Washington, DC.

———. 2003a. *Characteristics of American Indians and Alaska Natives by Tribe and Language: 2000*. Report PHC-5. December, Washington, DC.

———. 2003b. *Statistical Abstract of United States: 2003*. Table 682. Washington, DC.

Wilhelm, Mark. 2001. "The Role of Intergenerational Transfers in Spreading Asset Ownership." In *Assets for the Poor: The Benefits of Spreading Asset Ownership,* ed. Thomas Shapiro and Edward Wolff, 132–64. New York: Russell Sage Press.

Wolff, Edward. 2001. "Recent Trends in Wealth Ownership, from 1983 to 1998." In *Assets for the Poor: The Benefits of Spreading Asset Ownership,* ed. Thomas Shapiro and Edward Wolff, 34–73. New York: Russell Sage Press.

Zagorsky, Jay L. 1997. *NLSY79 Users' Guide*. Columbus, OH: Center for Human Resource Research, Ohio State University.

———. 1999. "Young Baby Boomers Wealth." *Review of Income and Wealth* 45: 135–56.

6 Trouble in Paradise

The Economic Marginalization of Native Hawaiians

PAUL ONG

This chapter examines the wealth holdings of the indigenous population in the state of Hawai'i, home to three-fifths of all Native Hawaiians in the United States.[1] About a quarter million Native Hawaiians live on the islands, comprising about a fifth of the state's total population, and two out of three are only part Native Hawaiian. Like many indigenous people, Native Hawaiians are economically marginalized in their own homelands as a result of a long history of subjugation. They suffered from near genocide in the face of colonialism, lost much of their lands, and were nearly robbed of their culture. After initial contact in 1778 with the coming of Captain James Cook and his crew, Native Hawaiians progressively lost control of the islands as Westerners, often led by Americans, seized economic and political power. During the nineteenth century, epidemics caused by newly introduced diseases decimated the indigenous population, making them a minority within their own lands. Prior to Western contact, the estimated size of the Native Hawaiian population was at least three hundred thousand, but by the end of the nineteenth century, Native Hawaiians numbered less than forty thousand and comprised only a quarter of the total population.[2] While the population decline stopped after the islands were annexed as an American territory in 1898, the indigenous population continued to lose ground as it remained marginalized in the developing plantation economy, which was built on the backs of exploited immigrant labor, particularly from Asia.[3]

The economic marginalization continued after Hawai'i became the fiftieth state of the United States in 1959. The state has failed to prepare Native Hawaiians to compete in an increasingly modernized economy.[4] By the start of the twenty-first century, when a four-year college education is the most important indicator of educational attainment (and socioeconomic success), the indigenous population lacked the human capital to be competitive in a globalized, high-tech world. Among those born in the state, just 16 percent of Native Hawaiians between the ages of 25 and 39 have attained this level of education, compared with nearly 50 percent of Japanese Americans and over 40 percent of White non-Hispanics.

One of the consequences of the historical and contemporary processes is a relative lack of wealth in the hands of Native Hawaiians. The remainder of this chapter examines this topic by focusing on two types of assets. The first is business holdings, which includes farms and non-farm operations. The second type of asset is household holdings, and the analysis focuses on housing and income-bearing assets. Unfortunately, the major data sets frequently used to examine the wealth holdings (Survey of Consumer Finances, Panel Study of Income Dynamics, National Longitudinal Survey of Youth, and Home Mortgage Disclosure Act) do not identify Native Hawaiian respondents, largely because they comprise an insignificant subsample. The available evidence comes primarily from the U.S. Bureau of the Census and includes its censuses or surveys of agriculture, population, housing, and businesses. Much of the information is published as aggregated statistics, which limits econometric modeling of many of the outcomes related to wealth. Moreover, there are inconsistencies in the way that race data are collected, making it difficult to compare statistics from different sources. While the decennial census allowed respondents to report more than one race, other data sources limited respondents to only one choice. This has a substantial impact on the counts of Native Hawaiians because a large majority is multiracial. When forced to choose only one race, many multiracial Native Hawaiians opt for a non-Native Hawaiian category.[5] Because of these limitations, the available data provide only a partial and often imprecise picture. Despite these flaws, the major conclusion is nonetheless robust. Native Hawaiians are severely disadvantaged when it comes to wealth.

BUSINESS HOLDINGS

Ownership of businesses, the very means of production, is the quintessential form of wealth in our capitalist economy, and this section analyzes Native Hawaiian business holdings in two parts: farms and all businesses. The analysis of farms relies on both historical and recent data. Ownership of farms is important because the land is a tangible asset, but also because land is central to the Native Hawaiian culture. The importance of land was recognized in a 1993 congressional resolution that stated that the "well-being of the Native Hawaiian people is intrinsically tied to their deep feelings and attachment to the land."[6] Returning to the productive, agricultural use of the land is seen as a way of promoting economic and community development. Despite the centrality of land, little is currently held by the indigenous population.*

Colonization robbed the Native Hawaiians of their land. Prior to Western contact, the indigenous population had a communal land tenure system under control of a royalty class. Under pressure from Westerners, the then sovereign Hawaiian Kingdom privatized ownership of land in 1848 through the "Great Mahele," or the division of the land. The vast majority of the land initially went to Hawaiian royalty and to the government of the Hawaiian Kingdom and was to be held for the benefit of all Native Hawaiians.[7] During the latter part of the nineteenth century, an ever-increasing share of the land owned by royalty fell into the hands of Westerners, a process that continued under colonial rule. The single largest loss occurred after the Hawaiian Kingdom was overthrown in 1893. Those who took power later ceded 1.8 million acres of crown, government, and public lands to the United States, an act that was done without the approval of Native Hawaiians. A minority share of the land previously held by royalty is now controlled by foundations that use the income derived from the holdings to support programs for Native Hawaiians.[8]

The privatization of land left the vast majority of Hawaiians landless. Hawaiian commoners were largely excluded from the distribution of land through the Great Mahele, receiving less than 1 percent of all lands, which rendered the large majority landless.[9] Much of the land that they received was comprised of the least desirable parcels. The legacy of the land grab on Native Hawaiians can be seen in table 6.1, which is based on Census of Agriculture statistics on farms by the race of the primary operator. The statistics reported are for farms owned by Native Hawaiians

---

*The question of land ownership—lack of land ownership and land confiscation—is also important for Native Americans and African Americans. See the "Introduction and Overview" for a short discussion, as well as references to Henson et. al. 2005 and Adamson 2003 for Native Americans and Darity and Nicholson 2005, Winbush 2003, Oliver and Shapiro 1995, and Browne 1973 for African Americans [Editors].

and farms operated by Native Hawaiians as managers. In 1930, when agriculture was the backbone of the state's economy, Whites controlled or managed 92 percent of the agricultural lands, which accounted for 85 percent of the total value of land and buildings.[10] At that time, Whites accounted for less than one-eighth of the total population. On the other hand, Native Hawaiians accounted for about one-seventh of the islands' total population, but they owned only a twentieth of the farms and a fiftieth of the agricultural lands. The value of the land and buildings was even smaller, roughly 1 percent of the total. In other words, Native Hawaiians had a disproportionately small share of the farms, and the farms they owned were small and less valuable. Native Hawaiians also managed farms that were typically larger and more valuable than the farms owned by Native Hawaiians. Even including these farms, however, does not change the conclusion that Native Hawaiians were marginalized in terms of land holdings.

The inequality in agricultural land holding continues today. According to the most recent data, Whites continue to be dominant, owning or managing three-quarters of the land. On the other hand, Native Hawaiians own less than 5 percent.[11] The indigenous population controls more lands when farms with Native Hawaiian managers are included, but this more inclusive collection of farms tends to be less productive than average. Consequently, Native Hawaiians produce less than 3 percent of the value of all agricultural products. The 2002 Census of Agriculture does not report the value of land by race, so there are no statistics on the agricultural-based wealth held by Native Hawaiians. However, the existing statistics on the distribution of land and products can provide a reasonable range. The value of the property held or managed by Native Hawaiians as

TABLE 6.1. Farmland Assets

	Total	% Native Hawaiian Owned	% Native Hawaiian Owned and/or Managed
1930			
Farms	5,955	5.1	8.5
Acres	2,815,026	2.0	5.6
Value of land and buildings	$111,780,432	1.1	3.6
2002			
Farms	5,398	4.5	7.9
Acres	1,300,499	4.9	8.5
Value of goods (×1,000)	$534,309	NA	2.7

Source: 1930 Census of Agriculture; 2002 Census of Agriculture.

a percent of all farm property value is likely to be between 8 percent (their share of the land) and 3 percent (their share of the value of products). For Native Hawaiian–owned farms, the range is likely to be only 4 to 2 percent. These estimates show that the indigenous population controls very little of the contemporary wealth tied to agricultural lands.

While the relative lack of ownership of agricultural land remains culturally and symbolically important to Native Hawaiians, the agricultural sector has declined in economic importance for the whole state. This is evident in the dramatic decrease in total farmland acreage between 1930 and 2002. According to the most recent estimates from the Bureau of Economic Analysis, farming produced only 0.8 percent of Hawai'i's gross state product, compared with 0.9 percent of the national gross domestic product.[12] In other words, farming accounts for only a minuscule part of business wealth.

An analysis of the available statistics on all businesses leads to the same conclusion: Native Hawaiians own a disproportionately small share of the wealth. The primary data source for analyzing racial patterns of business ownership is the 1997 Survey of Minority-Owned Businesses (SMOB).[13] The firms represented by this survey account for a vast majority (96 percent) of all businesses in the state but generate only half (50 percent) of all revenues. The other half of the revenues is controlled by large corporations, which are not or cannot be classified by the race of individually identifiable owners or partners. The available information indicates that Native Hawaiians are largely excluded from management control over and ownership of the large corporations. In the private sector, Native Hawaiians make up only 11 percent of the top executives, 6 percent of the chief executives, and 4 percent of the highly paid chief executives.[14] It is likely that Native Hawaiians are disproportionately underrepresented among the stockholders of the large public corporations, and the next section presents indirect evidence of this. The bottom line, then, is that Native Hawaiians have little accumulated wealth through control of or investment in large corporations.

Even among the firms included in the SMOB, Native Hawaiians are extremely underrepresented. Table 6.2 reports the summary statistics for Native Hawaiians and the two other major racial/ethnic groups, Japanese Americans and White non-Hispanics. Ideally, the Native Hawaiians' share of businesses should be compared with their share of the population to assess the degree of underrepresentation. Because the SMOB does not allow for reporting more than one racial category, the racial distribution of the population as reported in the 2000 census has to be adjusted. The adjusted counts indicate that White non-Hispanics account for about three-tenths of the total population, Japanese Americans account for about one-fifth, and Native Hawaiians account for about one-seventh.[15] A comparison of the business and population statistics shows that White non-Hispanics and Japanese Americans are overrepresented among business owners. Moreover, their firms tend to be larger than average, so they are even more overrepresented in terms of sales and employee payroll. On the other hand, Native Hawaiians are extremely underrepresented among business owners. The number of Native Hawaiian firms would have to double to bring their business ownership rates to parity with their share of the population. The disparity is even greater when looking at sales and employee payroll.

Unfortunately, the SMOB does not contain information on the value of businesses, but it is reasonable to assume that the value of a firm is roughly proportionate to its revenues. This relationship can be seen in the data on participants in the Small Business Administration's 8(a) program for minority firms. One measure of the value of a firm is its net assets (gross assets minus liabilities), and that measure is highly correlated with revenues.[16] Given that Native Hawaiian firms generate only 3 percent of the total revenue for firms represented by the SMOB, it is likely that they hold only 3 percent of the wealth tied up in businesses. Total net assets held by Native Hawaiians would have to increase by four- to fivefold to achieve parity with their proportion of the total population.

One of the ironic consequences of a relative lack of business wealth is an inability to take advantage of programs for minority-owned businesses. This can be seen in the listing of firms certified for government contracts set aside for socially and economically disadvantaged businesses. The State of Hawai'i Department of Transportation is a leading agency in the certification process. Native Hawaiians own less than one-tenth of the certified businesses listed in the department's most recent directory.[17]

TABLE 6.2. Racial Distribution of Businesses, 1997 (percent)

	Firms	Sales	Payroll
White Non-Hispanics	39	46	46
Japanese Americans	24	35	36
Native Hawaiians	7	3	3

Source: 1997 Survey of Minority-Owned Business.

This section focuses on contemporary wealth holdings of households by analyzing home ownership and income-bearing assets. The primary source is the 5 percent Public Use Microdata Sample (PUMS) from the 2000 census, which contains socioeconomic, demographic, and housing information.[18] Unfortunately, the PUMS has limited information on wealth. Only personal real estate in the form of home ownership can be directly observed. Savings, stocks, and rental property can be indirectly observed from income derived from these assets. Despite these limitations, the available data provide insights into the size of household assets held by Native Hawaiians relative to other groups.

The analysis excludes two groups. The first group is made up of military households. This is done because most of those in the service are in Hawai'i only temporarily and the state has a disproportionately large military sector.[19] The second group is made up of those in group quarters, which includes those in college dormitories and group homes. The unit of analysis is the household rather than the individual because personal assets are jointly held. A household is classified according to the demographic characteristics of the head of the household.

To simplify the reporting, three subpopulations are used: Native Hawaiians, all others born in Hawai'i, and those born outside the state. Each group is likely to experience unique opportunities and barriers that affect wealth accumulation and its composition. Those born in Hawai'i, for example, would be more willing to invest in less liquid real property because they are more likely to be committed to staying on the islands. On the other hand, those not born in the state have fewer social and other ties and consequently are more likely to invest in assets not tied to the islands. Moreover, members of this group have spent only a part of their lives on the islands. This shortens the time period that they could have been in the local housing market and therefore lowers their odds of having purchased a home.

Because wealth accumulation is tied to life cycle and typically increases with age, outcomes are examined by the age of the head of the household.[20] Four age categories are used: under 30 years, 30 to 47 years old, 48 to 64 years old, and 65 and older.

Income from household assets is defined as the total from interest, dividends, and net rental income. Unfortunately, the PUMS does not report the income from each component. The underlying assets include "savings or bonds, stockholdings or membership in associations, net income from rental of property to others and receipts from boarders or lodgers, net royalties, and periodic payments from an estate or trust fund." This type of income is reported for individuals, and the amount for a household is the summation of the reported asset-based income for all individuals in that household. For all households in the sample, the average (mean) income from household assets is about $5,000; however, there is enormous variation, as indicated by a standard deviation of over $18,000. Moreover, only 45.6 percent of households have any reported income from household assets.

The variation by age and population groups can be seen in statistics in the top half of table 6.3. For all groups, income from household assets and the proportion of households with reported income increase with age, indicating that the underlying wealth is also increasing with age.[21] The analysis also shows substantial group variation, with those not born in Hawai'i with the highest average (mean). This may be due to a portfolio choice in favor of assets that are not state specific. Native Hawaiians are at the other end of the statistics, reporting asset-based incomes that are less than half of the incomes for the other two groups.

The other asset held by households is from home ownership, and this is the most important source of wealth accumulation for people of color.[22] While the ideal measure of wealth from home ownership is the

TABLE 6.3. Household Assets by Age Groups

	Under 30	30–47	48–64	65+
Average income from assets				
Native Hawaiian	$268	$1,187	$2,362	$4,477
Other born in Hawai'i	$625	$2,374	$4,754	$9,674
Other	$707	$2,833	$6,899	$11,128
Percentage with nonzero asset income				
Native Hawaiian	12.4	25.5	38.1	44.9
Other born in Hawai'i	23.3	47.3	58.4	67.8
Other	17.5	33.9	48.8	59.2
Average housing asset				
Native Hawaiian	$45,700	$107,600	$168,300	$211,600
Other born in Hawai'i	$62,300	$177,200	$251,200	$252,000
Other	$28,500	$115,000	$201,600	$218,500
Percentage with housing asset				
Native Hawaiian	18.1	45.7	63.8	74.0
Other born in Hawai'i	26.5	64.4	77.9	80.2
Other	13.0	43.4	63.0	66.6

Source: Compiled by author from 2000 PUMS.

equity held by owners, the census does not collect that information. What is available is reported property values, which are based on the responses from home owners to the following question: "how much do you think this house and lot, apartment, or mobile home and lot would sell for if it were for sale?" The question is for the place of residence. For all households in the sample (regardless of housing tenure), the average (mean) value is about $175,000; however, there is enormous variation, as indicated by a standard deviation of over $226,600.[23] Moreover, only 58.9 percent of households were home owners.

The average (mean) values of homes by age and population groups are listed in table 6.3. For all groups, the averages increase with age, indicating that the underlying wealth is also increasing with age.[24] The analysis also shows substantial variation by subpopulation, with non-Native Hawaiians born in the state with the highest averages (means) and highest ownership rates. These outcomes may be due to a portfolio choice in favor of fixed real assets that are tied to the state, such as homes. Native Hawaiians are at the other end of the statistics, with average home values about two-thirds of those for the group composed of others born in Hawai'i. Home ownership rates are from 6 to 18 percentage points lower.

Lower household earnings[25] for Native Hawaiians ($44,000 for Native Hawaiians and $48,700 for all other households, not age adjusted) contribute to some of the disparity because the ability to save and purchase a home is tied to earning power. Table 6.4 reports household earnings by age groups, and Native Hawaiians consistently earn less than others born in Hawai'i and those born off the islands. The lower earnings of Native

TABLE 6.4. Housing Characteristics

	Under 30	30–47	48–64	65+
Average household earnings				
Native Hawaiian	$31,400	$47,600	$55,100	$22,900
Other born in Hawai'i	$35,700	$62,400	$67,700	$18,100
Other	$32,800	$55,900	$63,100	$23,300
Percentage of persons with earnings				
Native Hawaiian	1.55	1.74	1.93	0.98
Other born in Hawai'i	1.58	1.72	1.88	0.72
Other	1.60	1.69	1.80	0.86
Percentage of persons per household				
Native Hawaiian	3.23	3.80	3.34	2.74
Other born in Hawai'i	2.67	3.13	2.85	2.27
Other	2.59	3.21	2.85	2.35

Source: Compiled by author from 2000 PUMS.

Hawaiian households are not due to a lack of work effort. The number of persons with earnings per household is roughly comparable for all three groups. Native Hawaiians earn less because their salaries and wages are lower.

Group disparities in household assets, however, are not due just to variations in earnings. For example, demographic differences (beyond the age of the head of a household) also contribute to the disparities. Native Hawaiians tend to have larger households, which means they spend proportionately more of their income on daily necessities and are less able to invest. Other factors are likely to affect wealth accumulation, and the next section examines them in more detail.

DETERMINANTS OF ASSET ACCUMULATION

The analysis to this point measures the business and household wealth held by Native Hawaiians, albeit only partially and often indirectly. Despite the limitations, there is little doubt that Native Hawaiians suffer from low wealth holding. A part of the explanation is the legacy of racism, but contemporary processes work to maintain and reproduce race-based wealth inequality. The PUMS data can be used to estimate the direct role of race after accounting for other factors that influence income from assets and home values. As mentioned earlier, earnings, as well as sources of income, strongly influence asset accumulation. Current income, however, can include transitory elements such as a temporary windfall or unexpected loss in earnings. Including educational status in the analysis helps to account for longer-term earning capacity. Demographic factors also affect assets, such as the age, gender, place of birth (Hawai'i-born, born elsewhere in the United States, or born abroad), and marital status of the head of the household, as well as the size of the household. Geographic location (residing in the state's only metropolitan area of Honolulu on the island of Oahu, in the rest of the island of Oahu, or on one of the other islands) affects the cost of living and housing prices and thus affects asset accumulation. An important question is whether these factors can account for the observed (or unadjusted) disparities by race. In other words, does being Native Hawaiian play a role that cannot be explained by the other factors?

Multivariate analysis of the PUMS data is used to estimate the independent contributions of the factors listed here. The analysis is limited to nonmilitary households. Logit regressions are used to model the dichotomous outcome of whether a household has reported any income from assets and whether it owns its place of residence. Ordinary least squares (OLS) regressions are used to estimate the amount of asset-based income and home values for owners. While all nonmilitary households are included, the analysis focuses on comparing Native Hawaiians with the two groups at the top of the economic (and political) ladder: Japanese Americans and White non-Hispanics. Table 6.5 summarizes the key outcomes for these three groups. The rankings are not consistent. Japanese Americans fare best in terms of the percentage with some reported income from household assets, and White non-Hispanics fare best in terms of average income for household assets (both for the average for all households and the average for those with income). Japanese Americans fare best in terms of home ownership rates, and White non-Hispanics fare best in terms of housing value among owners. There is, however, one consistent pattern. For all indicators, Native Hawaiians are at the bottom.

Table 6.6 reports the contributions of clusters of factors to the disparities between Native Hawaiians and Japanese Americans, and between Native Hawaiians and White non-Hispanics. The observed differences are the unadjusted differences in the percentages and averages listed in table 6.5. For example, there is an unadjusted difference of −33.5 percentage points between the percentage of Native Hawaiians with asset income and the percentage of Japanese Americans with asset income (30.8 percent minus 64.3 percent). The regression results and the group differences in the independent (or causal) factors are used to decompose the disparity.[26]

The estimates in table 6.6 reveal that group differences in observed personal and household characteristics contribute to the disparities between Native Hawaiians and Japanese. For example, Native Hawaiians tend to be

TABLE 6.5.   Asset Income and Home Values by Race

	Native Hawaiians	Japanese Americans	White Non-Hispanics
Asset income			
Overall average (all households)	$2,090	$6,190	$8,430
Percentage with asset income	30.8	64.3	49.2
Conditional average (with assets)	$6,790	$9,630	$17,160
Home value			
Overall average (all households)	$135,000	$229,300	$183,200
Percentage of home owners	52.3	76.4	54.3
Conditional average (owners)	$258,100	$300,100	$337,300

Source: Compiled by author from 2000 PUMS data.

younger, have larger households, live outside the metropolitan area, and have less income and education. These factors influence the odds of having asset income and a home, as well as the amount of asset income and value of a home. What is interesting is the large residual race effect (the difference not explained by the other variables) on the percentage of the population with asset income and a home. On the other hand, the race residual is smaller in the estimates of the income from assets and home values.

The estimates also show that personal and household characteristics contribute to the disparities between Native Hawaiians and White non-Hispanics. These factors adversely affect outcomes for Native Hawaiians. In this comparison, the residual race effect is sizeable for the proportion of the population with asset income and a home, as well as the income from assets and home values.

Taken together, the findings suggest that racial disparities are produced in complicated ways. The residual race effects are difficult to explain, but they do point to additional unobserved factors and processes that disadvantage the indigenous population. The results from the logit regressions indicate that there are barriers to accumulating assets at a

TABLE 6.6. Decomposition of Group Disparities

	Native Hawaiian—Japanese		Native Hawaiian—White Non-Hispanics	
	Percentage point difference in the proportion of the population with assets	Dollar difference among those with assets (in $1,000s)	Percentage point difference in the proportion of the population with assets	Dollar difference among those with assets (in $1,000s)
Asset income				
Observed	−33.5	−2.84	−18.4	−10.37
Demographic	−8.2	−2.74	1.1	−1.80
Location	−1.0	−0.18	−0.1	−0.31
Income	−1.6	0.07	−0.4	0.01
Education	−3.3	−0.51	−6.3	−1.86
Race residual	−19.4	0.51	−12.7	−6.42
Housing value				
Observed	−24.1	−42.0	−2.0	−79.2
Demographic	−7.6	−9.1	6.3	20.9
Location	3.9	−16.7	0.8	−1.7
Income	−3.3	−7.2	−2.2	−16.6
Education	−1.8	−7.7	−2.7	−17.4
Race residual	−15.3	−1.2	−4.2	−64.4

Source: Simulation by author from regression results of 2000 PUMS data.

very early stage, precluding many Native Hawaiians from even participating in the process of wealth building. These potentially include discriminatory practices by financial and real estate institutions. The results from the OLS regressions indicate that Native Hawaiians who
overcome the initial hurdle are still disadvantaged compared with White
non-Hispanics. The impact of race is further complicated by the fact that
overt and institutionalized discrimination in the school system and labor
market also creates race inequalities in education and income and thus
has an indirect adverse impact on asset accumulation.

CONCLUSION

This chapter documents the relatively low wealth holding of Native
Hawaiians and identifies some of the contributing factors. Data limitations prevent a more detailed understanding of the mechanisms generating the racial disparities, but there is no doubting that Native Hawaiians
are severely disadvantaged. The inequality is the result of complex forces
and societal structures. Today's outcomes are the cumulative results of a
historical racial oppression that systematically stripped the indigenous
population of their resources. The injustices have been perpetuated by
contemporary institutions and practices that reinforce and reproduce
the inequality.

The U.S. government bears a large part of the responsibility. In many
ways, Native Hawaiians share a common historical fate with American
Indians.[27] The government has played a pivotal role in marginalizing
both populations. In the case of Native Hawaiians, territorial rule by the
United States failed to fairly incorporate the indigenous people into a
market economy, and the State of Hawai'i has continued this failure. The
government has a moral obligation, and perhaps a legal one also, to re-
dress the wrongs of the past. In 1993, Congress passed and President
Clinton signed a bill apologizing for this nation's role in the overthrow of
the Hawaiian Kingdom and the deprivation of Native Hawaiian self-deter-
mination. That is a start, but much more is needed.

Unlike American Indians, Native Hawaiians do not have a "nation-
to-nation" relationship with the United States, and this has weakened
their ability to secure justice and control their future. Instead, they are
treated as another disadvantaged minority group, and the programs designed to help Native Hawaiians have been attacked for reverse discrimination.[28] The future hinges in part on whether Congress and the

president are willing to extend limited sovereignty to this indigenous population.[29] Even then, there are enormous social and economic problems to overcome before Native Hawaiians can regain control over the stolen resources that are the foundation for wealth.

NOTES

I am indebted to Jonathan Ong, Margaret Johnson, and Lucy Tran for assisting in the preparation of this manuscript and to Davianna McGregor for her advice. I alone am responsible for any errors.

1. In 1960, 95 percent of this group lived in Hawai'i. Because of limited opportunities, large numbers of Native Hawaiians moved to the U.S. mainland in search of economic and educational opportunities.

2. The Office of Hawaiian Affairs (OHA) estimates the Native Hawaiian population at the low end, while David Stannard estimates eight hundred thousand (personal correspondence, Davianna McGregor, September 26, 2002, citing David Stannard, *Before the Horror: The Population of Hawai'i before Western Contact* [Honolulu: Social Science Research Institute, University of Hawai'i, 1989]). Historical population data in this section come primarily from the OHA (1998). Data for the year 2000 come from the demographic files from the U.S. Bureau of the Census.

3. See Takai 1984. Importing labor dramatically altered the population. From 1910 to 1930, the number of non-Native Hawaiians grew by thirty times, from about 10,000 to 314,000. By 1930, Native Hawaiians constituted less than one-sixth (14 percent) of the islands' population.

4. The growing gap in human capital occurred throughout the twentieth century. Just after annexation, the 1900 census data show that Native Hawaiians had a substantially higher literacy rate than did Whites or Japanese, the two most important ethnic groups in the islands. According to the census publication, "The Census Bureau classifies as illiterate any person 10 years of age or over who is unable to write, regardless of ability to read" (U.S. Bureau of the Census 1913). By the middle of the twentieth century, White adults emerged on top in terms of educational attainment, with about a quarter having some college training, compared with only one-twentieth of Native Hawaiians and Japanese (U.S. Bureau of the Census 1950). The statistics in the text are based on the author's tabulations of the 5 percent Public Use Microdata Sample of the 2000 census. Recent analysis of students in Hawai'i's public school shows that Native Hawaiian children are faring poorly (Kanaiaupuni and Ishibashi 2003).

5. Ong and Leung 2003, 7–16.

6. This statement is from U.S. Public Law 103-150, 103rd Congress Joint Resolution 19, Nov. 23, 1993. The resolution acknowledges "the 100th anniversary of the January 17, 1893 overthrow of the Kingdom of Hawaii" and apologizes "to Native Hawaiians on behalf of the United States for the overthrow of the Kingdom of Hawaii."

7. Kelly 1956.

8. The three most important trusts are the ones tied to the Kamehameha Schools (the Bishop Estate), Queen's Health Systems, and Queen Liliuokalani Trust, which together account for about 5 percent ($6.5 billion) of the state's total assessed land value (Trifonovitch 2001).

9. Kelly 1956.

10. U.S. Bureau of the Census 1932.

11. U.S. Department of Agriculture 2004. The statistics for Native Hawaiian–owned farms include those where Native Hawaiians are either full or part owners. The acreage for partly owned farms is estimated.

12. Data from the Bureau of Economic Analysis 2004.

13. U.S. Bureau of the Census 2001.

14. The statistics are based on the author's tabulations of the 5 percent Public Use Microdata Sample of the 2000 census. The sample size for executives is small, but the tabulations are consistent with the statistics from Summary File 4 for the 2000 census, which is based on a much larger sample. Unfortunately, the statistics from Summary File 4 do not differentiate between public and private sector workers. A highly paid chief executive is defined as a chief executive making over $75,000 in 1999.

15. These proportions are the average of the single-race and multirace counts. Single-race White non-Hispanics account for 23 percent of the state's total population, and multirace White non-Hispanics account for 36 percent of the state's total population. The comparable statistics are 17 percent and 24 percent for Japanese Americans, and 7 percent and 20 percent for Native Hawaiians.

16. For a discussion on the 8(a) program and the data, see Ong 2001. For the eighty-four Hawaiian firms in 8(a), the correlation between net assets and sales is statistically significant ($r = .538$, $p < .0001$). Moreover, the relationship holds for both Native Hawaiian and other Hawaiian firms. In a simple regression model with net asset as the dependent variable, the independent variable for revenues is statistically significant, but a dummy variable for Native Hawaiian firms is not.

17. Department of Transportation 2004.

18. For details on the data, see U.S. Census Bureau 2003.

19. The federal government accounts for 12.7 percent of Hawai'i's economy, with the military alone accounting for 7.2 percent. The location quotation for Hawai'i's military sector is 7.2, which means that this sector is proportionately over seven times larger in the state than for the nation as a whole. These statistics are based on data from the Bureau of Economic Analysis 2004.

20. The amount and type of wealth vary by life-cycle stages. Young adults are just starting their working career and have limited discretionary income for investments. During the prime working age, individuals are earning more and investing in real and financial assets. Moreover, individuals are more willing to take on debts and make more risky investments with higher potential returns. During the last decades of life, individuals stop accumulating assets, and the existing assets tend to be in less risky investments.

21. The relation between asset income and accumulated wealth is probably not linear. Households with younger heads are more likely to invest in

growth assets that generate little in current income, while households with older heads are likely to shift their portfolio to lower-risk investments that generate more in current income to cover living expenses.

22. Aizcorbe, Kennickell, and Moore 2003.

23. The home values in the PUMS are reported as categorical data. The analysis assigned the midpoint of those categories. The top category is for values of $1 million or more, and the analysis assigned a value of $1.5 million.

24. The relation between home value and equity is probably not linear. The equity-to-value ratio is likely to vary positively with the age of the head of household. For example, the proportion of home owners who are "free and clear" of a mortgage increases with age.

25. "Earnings" are defined as the sum of wage or salary income and net income from self-employment. "Earnings" represent the amount of income received regularly for people sixteen years old and over before deductions for personal income taxes, social security, bond purchases, union dues, medicare deductions, etc.

26. Regression results are available from the author. The decomposition of the percentage point differences in outcomes is estimated in three steps. The impact of being Native Hawaiian relative to the comparison group for any given factor is calculated as $c * [p * (1 - p)] * (x1 - x2)$, where c is the estimated coefficient from the logistic regression, p is the probability for the outcome for the whole sample, $x1$ is the mean of the independent variable for Native Hawaiians, and $x2$ is the mean of the independent variable for the comparison group. The estimated impacts are then summarized into clusters of factors (demographic, location, income, education, and the residual race effect). The final step is to scale the estimates so the sum of all estimated impacts is equal to the observed (unadjusted) difference in the outcome between Native Hawaiians and the comparison group. The decomposition of the dollar differences in outcomes is calculated in two steps. The impact of being Native Hawaiian relative to the comparison group for any given factor is $c * (x1 - x2)$, where c is the estimated coefficient from the OLS regression, $x1$ is the mean of the independent variable for Native Hawaiians with reported values, and $x2$ is the mean of the independent variable for members of the comparison group with reported values. The estimated impacts are then summarized into clusters of factors (demographic, location, income, education, and the residual race effect).

27. For an example of a similar analysis of employment and home ownership, see Ong 2004.

28. In *Rice v. Cayetano,* the U.S. Supreme Court ruled in 2002 that the Office of Hawaiian Affairs could not limit its board elections to only voters of Hawaiian ancestry. The 2002 *Arakaki v. Lingle* lawsuit argued that government programs benefiting Native Hawaiians are unconstitutional. This case has been dismissed based on the grounds that Congress is still debating the legal status of Native Hawaiians. However, there will likely be more legal challenges in the future against Native Hawaiian programs.

29. The "Native Hawaiian Government Reorganization Act of 2005" (S. 147 in the 109th Congress) was introduced in the Senate on January 25,

2005 and recommended by its committee to the full Senate. It remains on the Senate calendar (No. 101) scheduled for debate, but no date has been assigned for its consideration. The official title is "A bill to express the policy of the United States regarding the United States' relationship with Native Hawaiians and to provide a process for the recognition by the United States of the Native Hawaiian governing entity."

REFERENCES

Aizcorbe, Ana M., Arthur B. Kennickell, and Kevin B. Moore. 2003. "Recent Changes in U.S. Family Finances: Evidence from the 1998 and 2001 Survey of Consumer Finances." *Federal Reserve Bulletin* 89: 1–32. http://www.federalreserve.gov.

Bureau of Economic Analysis. 2004. "Regional Economic Accounts." August 20, 2004. http://www.bea.gov/bea/regional/gsp.htm.

Department of Transportation, State of Hawaii. 2004. *Disadvantaged Business Enterprise (DBE) Directory.* August 16, 2004.

Kanaiaupuni, S. M., and K. Ishibashi. 2003. "Left Behind: The Status of Hawaiian Students in Hawai'i Public Schools." Honolulu, HI: Kamehameha Schools.

Kelly, Marion. 1956. "Changes in Land Tenure in Hawaii, 1778–1850." Master's thesis, University of Hawaii.

Office of Hawaiian Affairs. 1998. *Native Hawaiian Databook, 1998.* Available at http://www.oha.org/databook/databook1996_1998/go-chap1.98.html.

Ong, Paul. 2001. "Set-Aside Contracting in S.B.A.'s 8(A) Program." *Review of Black Political Economy* 28 (3): 59–71.

———. 2004. "Socioeconomic Status of American Indian Adults in Los Angeles." Policy Brief, United American Indian Involvement and UCLA Ralph and Goldy Lewis Center for Regional Policy Studies, June 2004.

Ong, Paul, and Loh-Sze Leung. 2003. "Asian Pacific American Demographics: Past, Present and Future." In *The New Face of Asian Pacific America,* ed. Eric Lai and Dennis Arguelles, 7–16. San Francisco and Los Angeles: AsianWeek and UCLA Asian American Studies Center.

Takai, Ronald. 1984. *Pau Hana: Plantation Life and Labor in Hawaii, 1835–1930.* Honolulu: University of Hawaii Press.

Trifonovitch, Kelli Abe. 2001. "Land Locked: You Will Be Surprised to Learn to Whom Hawaii Belongs." *Hawaii Business Online.* http://www.hawaiibusiness.cc/hb112001/ (accessed on August 21, 2004).

U.S. Bureau of the Census. 1913. *Thirteenth Census of the United States Taken in the Year 1910.* Vol. 3, *Population.* Washington, DC: Government Printing Office.

———. 1932. *Fifteenth Census of the United States, 1930: Outlying Territories and Possessions.* Washington, DC: Government Printing Office.

———. 1950. *A Report of the Seventeenth Decennial Census of the United States, Census of the Population: 1950.* Vol. 2, *Characteristics of the Population.* Washington, DC: Government Printing Office.

———. 2001. *1997 Economic Census Survey of Minority-Owned Business Enterprises.* Washington, DC: Government Printing Office.

———. 2003. *2000 Census of Population and Housing, Public Use Micro-data Sample.* United States, technical documentation.

U.S. Department of Agriculture. 2004. *2002 Census of Agriculture: Hawaii State and County Data.* Washington, DC.

7 Asian Americans & Wealth

PAUL ONG & R. VARISA PATRAPORN

This chapter has two goals: (1) to provide a statistical profile from available data of wealth among Asian Americans[1] relative to other racial groups and among Asian American ethnic groups and (2) to provide insights into the complex way immigration, race, and ethnicity interact in generating Asian American wealth outcomes. Asian Americans are widely viewed as an economically successful minority that has overcome more than a century of harsh discrimination, including state-sponsored acts of racism that at various points in time have restricted their right to immigration, citizenship, property, and family formation in the United States.* In fact, racial ghettos had their origins in the latter half of the nineteenth century, when White citizens imposed the segregation of Asians in California by enacting the first use of racially motivated land use laws. The colonization of Filipinos and the mass incarceration of Japanese during World War II stand as shameful examples of blatant acts of domestic and international racism perpetrated by this country (Takaki 1990; Chan 1991). Despite this history, contemporary Asian Americans have achieved a level of economic status that has earned them the label of being a "model minority." As with all stereotypes, this one has an element of truth.

The media hype on Asian American accomplishments has focused on education and income but has recently included popular articles on Asian American wealth. In 2000, *Forbes* heralded the entry of eight Asian Americans into the ranks of America's four hundred wealthiest

---

* A similar history of genocide, colonization, and asset stripping was experienced by Native Americans, Native Hawaiians, African Americans, and Latinos. See the group-specific chapters in this volume, as well as our "Introduction and Overview" *[Editors]*.

(DiCarlo 2004). Four years later, the *Wall Street Journal* reported that the number of affluent Asian Americans increased more than fivefold from 2002 to 2004. In the latter year, Asian Americans made up 5 percent of all affluent (those with more than $500,000 of investable assets, excluding primary residence) Americans (Frank 2004). By 2005, the *Washington Post* highlighted the emerging trend among brokerage firms to pursue wealthy Asian Americans as clients (White 2005). Clearly, Asian Americans are among the nouveau rich, which is consistent with being a "model minority."

However, this picture of average wealth is an overly simplistic one that obscures the complexity within the population. Much of the debate around the "model minority" has focused on income (Ong et al. 1993). Income statistics show, on the average, Asian American households are faring reasonably well. Nonetheless, there is more below the surface. The existing data show that even after adjusting for factors that influence wealth (e.g., education, age, and experience), Asian Americans face a racial gap relative to White non-Hispanics. The same issues may also be relevant in assessing wealth. In particular, where do Asian Americans stand on the wealth ladder? Are they faring as well as White non-Hispanics after adjusting for individual and household characteristics and how is wealth distributed among Asian Americans? Unfortunately, there is a paucity of information and studies addressing these questions.*

To fill the lacuna in the literature on Asian American wealth, this chapter presents findings from an analysis of available data and from other relevant studies. The first part examines the overall status of Asian American wealth compared with that of other major U.S. racial groups. The second part examine wealth distribution within the Asian American population and by Asian ethnicity. Next we discuss the barriers to wealth accumulation for Asian Americans, with a focus on lending in the housing market. We then return to a discussion about the larger issues that inform our analysis of Asian American wealth: within group distribution of wealth and the role of immigration policy in shaping the wealth distribution and outcomes.

In the conclusion, we explore the broader implications of our findings. One is that racial inequality is defined in two conceptually independent

---

* Dymski, Mohanty, and Li (chap. 9) also discuss the paucity of data about wealth holdings of Asian Americans and focus on regional bank ownership as an Asian American community asset *[Editors]*.

ways: where a racial group stands on the wealth ladder, and the other is how a group experiences the process of wealth accumulation differentially than White non-Hispanics. Even those Asian Americans who have achieved a level of socioeconomic status equal to or beyond that of White non-Hispanics do not consistently display equal wealth outcomes. This mismatch threatens the very ideals that this country was based on and, thus, deserves more policy and planning attention.

DATA & METHODS

This chapter analyzes wealth using data from the Survey of Income and Program Participation (SIPP) and the Public Use Microdata Sample (PUMS). Both surveys are administered by the Census Bureau but for distinctive purposes. The Census Bureau administers the SIPP primarily to track entry into and exit from participation in various government programs. In part because of its purpose, the SIPP does not accurately account for wealth held by households at the top end of the distribution (Czijka, Jacobson, and Cody 2003–4; Cobb-Clark and Hildebrand 2004; Di 2001). In comparison with the SIPP, the Survey of Consumer Finances (SCF) more accurately accounts for wealth at the high end of the wealth distribution. The Federal Reserve Bank designed the SCF specifically to examine wealth, and it takes into account those at the top end of the wealth distribution by oversampling such individuals. Despite this advantage over the SIPP, the public use version of the SCF does not identify Asian Americans as a separate racial category.*

Another commonly used data set for studying wealth is the Panel Survey of Income Dynamics (PSID). In contrast to the SCF, the PSID identifies Asian Americans and nativity status of individuals, but the sample size of Asian Americans and immigrants is too small for further examination by ethnicity and even for Asian Americans as a whole. As Leigh points to in chapter 1, the available data on Asian Americans in national samples remain a problem. The challenge to collecting data on wealth for Asian Americans is further complicated by the need for disaggregated data given the within-group disparity we see in the Asian American population. Thus, despite the limitations of the SIPP, compared with other sources of data on wealth, the SIPP provides the most comprehensive set

---

* Leigh (chap. 1) fully describes and compares six national data sets with wealth information and analyzes their strengths and weaknesses for each population *[Editors]*.

of wealth variables in conjunction with a sufficient sample of Asian Americans.

The SIPP is a longitudinal survey of households regarding the distribution of income, wealth, and poverty and the effects of federal and state programs that promote family and individual well-being. It defines a household as all the people who occupy a housing unit and does not include persons in group quarters. Family characteristics and income information were derived from the 2001 wave 3 core microdata file. Information on total and home-related wealth and debt was derived from the wave 3 topical module microdata file. Demographic characteristics including race and ethnicity were derived based on the household survey reference person. Nativity status of respondents was derived from wave 2 and matched with data from wave 3. The total sample from the SIPP 2000 data was over 17,000. There are over 13,000 White non-Hispanics in the sample, 600 Asian Americans, 2,300 Blacks, and 1,000 Latinos in the sample. The actual number of observations may differ for various analytical steps because of missing values. The sample includes the race of individuals who self-reported as White, Black, American Indian, Aleut or Eskimo, Asian or Pacific Islander, or with one of nine Latino countries. (See this chapter's appendix for more information about the SIPP survey data used.)

Although the SIPP sample is sufficient for an examination of Asian Americans as a group, the SIPP does not identify Asian Americans by ethnicity. Therefore, for purposes of examining wealth among the various Asian ethnic groups, this chapter uses the 2000 PUMS data set. While PUMS does not have the same direct measures of wealth contained in the SIPP, we are able to indirectly measure wealth through use of average income, home value, and income generated from interest, dividends, and rental income. Such proxies can provide insights into the magnitude of ethnic differences in wealth. The PUMS 2000 data had a total sample of 458,824 Asians in the United States. Among Asians, we focused on the six largest groups. There were 71,784 Asian Indians, 103,745 Chinese, 87,496 Filipinos, 36,809 Japanese, 47,681 Koreans, and 50,863 Vietnamese in the sample.

WEALTH DISTRIBUTION AMONG MAJOR RACIAL GROUPS

Asian American household income is higher than that of all major racial groups, including White non-Hispanics. However, Asian American wealth lags behind that of White non-Hispanics. The income pattern for Asian American households is consistent with statistics from the 2000 census, which also shows high income among Asian Americans. However, it appears that such income is not translating into wealth. Table 7.1 shows the mean and median wealth held by Asian Americans. Because the SIPP underestimates those at the top end of the wealth distribution (sampling as well as top coding; see this chapter's appendix for discussion), the median is reported to provide a more accurate picture of the typical household for each racial group. The SIPP variables on wealth that are reported and included in this analysis are household income, total net worth, total debt, housing equity, and housing debt.

Compared with other racial groups, Asian Americans have a wealth status closer to that of White non-Hispanics, but they remain consistently behind White non-Hispanics on all wealth measures. White non-Hispanics have the highest mean and median net worth at $221,000 and $101,700, respectively. The net worth gap between Asian Americans and White non-Hispanics is a difference of close to $30,000 in median net worth and over $40,000 in mean net worth. The Black-White gap is largest, with a mean difference of over $170,000 in net worth and a median difference of close to $95,000. The Latino-White gap is similar to the Black-White gap, but slightly smaller.

Household income is the one measure in which Asian Americans not only are equal to White non-Hispanics but exceed the White non-Hispanic value. The difference in wealth between Asian Americans and White non-Hispanics despite a higher household income implies that

TABLE 7.1. Wealth Distribution, Major Racial Groups (in dollars)

	Asian	White non-Hispanic	Black	Latino
Mean				
Household income	71,600	63,500	42,300	46,700
Net worth	178,200	221,000	50,900	75,900
Debt	89,800	76,600	38,400	50,700
Housing equity	84,500	87,700	29,800	37,400
Housing debt	66,900	52,900	26,100	36,800
Median				
Household income	55,600	51,100	33,300	36,700
Net worth	73,600	101,700	7,100	10,400
Debt	40,400	40,400	8,500	15,600
Housing equity	28,000	54,000	0	0
Housing debt	0	20,000	0	0

Source: Tabulations by authors using SIPP 2000 Wave 3 data.

Asian American income is not translating into wealth at equal levels to White non-Hispanics' levels. Such a difference has meaning in our society because we value socioeconomic achievement as a way to secure societal rewards.

A closer examination of debt and housing equity also emphasizes differences between achievement and rewards. As a group, Asian Americans hold at least as much mean and median total debt as White non-Hispanics, but they have less wealth in housing (mean and median) compared with White non-Hispanics (see table 7.1). The difference in housing equity is even larger when we compare the median (as opposed to the mean) home value among Asian Americans and White non-Hispanics. Overall, our findings suggest that despite a household income that exceeds that of White non-Hispanics, Asian Americans do not have a corresponding wealth status equal to White non-Hispanics.

BARRIERS TO WEALTH

Oliver and Shapiro (1995) describe the racial gap between Blacks and Whites as one between achievement and rewards. The reason they use this description is because once they controlled for differences in education, age, and other factors important to understanding wealth, Blacks continued to lag behind Whites in wealth status. Our findings suggest that the same description can be applied to Asian Americans. While the gap between Black and White wealth is larger, it is clear from figure 7.1 that a racial gap exists between Asian Americans and Whites. Figure 7.1 displays the gap between Asian Americans and White non-Hispanics before and after controlling for numerous factors (e.g., education, family structure, income, and age), including nativity status. After adjusting for such factors, the linear model shows a $26,086 mean wealth gap between Asian Americans and White non-Hispanics.

We also transformed the dependent variable by taking the square root of the wealth to attenuate the impact of outliers in the model.[2] In comparison with the linear model, the nonlinear transformation of the dependent variable shows a smaller wealth gap between White non-Hispanics and Asian Americans. Nonetheless, a significant gap remains at $18,516 even after adjusting for key variables and using a nonlinear dependent variable. The gap identified by these models may be partially explained by differential access to financial capital, a key component to wealth building. Studies on access to financial capital indicate that there

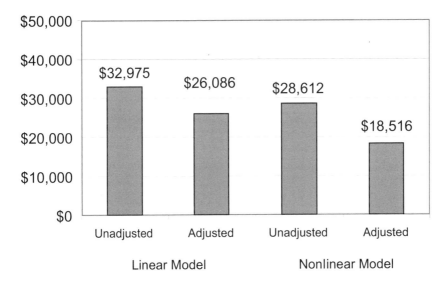

Fig. 7.1. Racial wealth gap (in mean dollars) between White non-Hispanics and Asian Americans. (Based on SIPP 2000 Wave 2 and Wave 3 data.)

remain hurdles to both housing and small business lending for Asian Americans.

For the most part, studies on lending for home purchasing have examined the difference between Whites and Blacks and to a lesser extent Latinos and Asian Americans. More recent studies (Krivo 2004; Dymski 2001; Turner and Ross 2003; Zonta 2004) consistently include Asian Americans. These studies report mixed and complicated findings that demonstrate that access to financial capital varies by geography, time period, ethnicity, financial institution type, and location of financing entity. Dymski (2001) examined denial rates for mortgage lending in eighteen cities in the 1990s for all major racial groups, including Asian Americans. His findings point to the relevance of place in the Asian American experience. He found that Asian Americans have a higher probability of home loan approval in Los Angeles relative to other California metropolitan areas and states outside of California.

Zonta (2004) also found that credit approval for Asian Americans varies depending on location (enclave neighborhood versus nonethnic neighborhood) and type of financial institution (ethnic versus nonethnic traditional financial institution). Zonta concluded that Asian banks have a higher propensity to grant loans to Asian home mortgage seekers than do conventional banks. Thus, it appears that the existence and use of such ethnic banks by Asian Americans might work to close the racial gap between Asian Americans and White non-Hispanics. Chapter 9 in this volume, by Dymski, Mohanty, and Li, also points to the significance of ethnic banks in Los Angeles County and their relevance to addressing capital access issues.

Much less is known about small business lending, but one study by Cavalluzzo and Wolken (2002) found that credit history and personal wealth significantly influenced the probability of being denied a loan. The average predicted probability of being denied credit at least once in the last three years was 44 percent if all firms are treated as Asian owned compared with 26 percent if the firms had been owned by Whites. In addition, Cavalluzzo and Wolken found that more than 10 percent of the difference in credit denial rates for Latino-/Asian-owned firms relative to those owned by Whites could be explained by personal wealth. They found that personal wealth was the most important factor in explaining the differences in denial rates between Asian and White firms. Their findings illustrate the importance of personal wealth for other asset building, including small business development particularly for Asian Americans. Since most wealth in the United States is held in a primary residence, the results from Cavalluzzo and Wolken point to the importance of home ownership for Asian Americans relative to White non-Hispanics.

WITHIN-GROUP DISTRIBUTION OF WEALTH

The SIPP data also show that Asian American wealth is far more unevenly distributed than White non-Hispanic wealth (table 7.2). The bottom half of Asian American households have less wealth than their White non-Hispanic counterparts, especially for wealth not held in housing. In addition, the gap between Asian Americans and White non-Hispanics becomes larger as we move up the wealth distribution.

Overall, the gap between "the have and the have nots" is larger among Asian Americans than among White non-Hispanics. Table 7.2 compares total net worth and other net worth of Asian Americans and White non-Hispanics by percentile ranking. Asian Americans hold less total net worth and other net worth than White non-Hispanics at all levels of wealth. This gap is larger for other net worth (wealth not held in housing) compared with total net worth. The one exception is Asian Americans at the twenty-fifth percentile, who have a total net worth of about half of White non-Hispanics. In comparison, Asian Americans at the twenty-fifth percentile have other net worth which is 67 percent of White non-Hispanics' other net worth.

Table 7.2 also includes a normalized spread, which tells us the amount of difference in wealth between those at the extreme ends of the wealth distribution normalized by those at the fiftieth percentile. The normalized spread is used instead of the Gini coefficient because the SIPP top codes those at the high end of the wealth distribution and has an inadequate sample of the wealthiest households. The normalized spread for Asian American total net worth and other net worth exceeds that of White non-Hispanics. This is particularly true for other net worth, where the normalized spread is 17.9 for Asian Americans and 13.1 for White non-Hispanics.

Much of the variation in wealth within the Asian American population can be attributed to ethnic disparities. This can be seen in the indirect wealth measures derived from the 2000 census. Table 7.3 uses a parity index to determine the relative difference between each Asian ethnic group as compared with the average for all Asians. To calculate the ratios in the parity index, we took the mean value of each wealth indicator for each Asian ethnic group and divided that by the average for all Asians. For example, the mean home value for all Asians is $158,000. The parity index shows that Other Southeast Asian mean home value is 37 percent of $158,000. Other Southeast Asians include historically refugee populations, including individuals of Cambodian, Hmong, and Laotian descent.

TABLE 7.2   Wealth Distribution, Asians and White Non-Hispanics

	Total Net Worth			Other Net Worth (nonhousing)		
	Asian	White non-Hispanic	Asian/ White non-Hispanic	Asian	White non-Hispanic	Asian/ White non-Hispanic
Percentile						
90th	$443,000	$561,400	0.79	$283,900	$369,900	0.77
75th	$222,800	$271,900	0.82	$91,200	$135,500	0.67
50th	$73,600	$101,700	0.72	$16,300	$27,600	0.59
25th	$6,900	$13,400	0.51	$1,800	$2,700	0.67
10th	−$400	−$200	NA	−$8,000	$7,100	NA
Normalized spread						
(75th−25th)/50th	2.9	2.5	NA	5.5	4.8	NA
(90th−10th)/50th	6.0	5.5	NA	17.9	13.1	NA

Note: Tabulations by authors using SIPP 2000 Wave 3 data.

Our results are consistent with other studies that document that, on the average, Asian Indians, Chinese, and Japanese have a higher socioeconomic status, while Southeast Asian refugees typically have a lower socioeconomic status. Asian Indians, Chinese, and Japanese have higher levels of mean income, interest, dividends, and rental income, as well as home value, compared with other Asian American groups. On the other end, Southeast Asians fall below the average for all Asians on all three measures. The most significant difference is between Japanese and Other Southeast Asians. For instance, Other Southeast Asian mean interest, dividend, and rental income makes up less than one-tenth of the mean amount of interest, dividend, and rental income held by Japanese. These findings demonstrate the magnitude of differences and disparity within the Asian American population.

Some groups fall in between those above the average of all Asians and those below the average for all Asians. The groups include: Filipinos, Koreans, and the Vietnamese. These Asian groups have a higher wealth status relative to Other Southeast Asians, but a lower status relative to Asian Indians, Chinese, and Japanese. In addition, their position varies by wealth measure. For Filipinos, mean income is equal to the average for all Asians, but the income held in interest, dividend, and rental income is substantially lower than the average for all Asian Americans. Similar to Filipinos, Vietnamese also fare better in terms of mean income

TABLE 7.3. Mean Household Income and Assets in the United States by Asian Ethnicity

	Mean Income	Mean Interest, Dividend, and Rental Income	Mean Home Value
All Asians	$77,300	$2,800	$158,00
	Parity Index (relative to all Asians)		
Asian Indian	1.21	1.26	1.00
Chinese	1.02	1.43	1.24
Filipino	1.01	0.41	0.94
Japanese	1.14	1.70	1.39
Korean	0.86	0.97	0.81
Vietnamese	0.80	0.34	0.68
Other Southeast Asian	0.61	0.16	0.37
Other Asian	0.93	1.01	0.94

Source: U.S. Bureau of the Census, Public Use Microdata Sample, 2000.

Note: "Mean income" and "mean interest, dividend, and rental income" include negative and zero dollar amounts. "Mean home value" includes those who do not own their own home—those with zero mean value. Other Southeast Asian includes historic Southeast Asian refugee populations to the United States, including Cambodians, Hmong, and Laotians. All data reported for single race/ethnicity.

relative to the other measures of wealth, yet they remain more closely aligned with Other Southeast Asians on home value and interest, dividend, and rental income. Finally, Koreans are slightly below the average of all Asians for all three measures of wealth, while Other Asians are a bit closer to the average of all Asians.

The largest variance across ethnicity is in mean interest, dividend, and rental income. For this measure of wealth we see the largest spread, with Japanese, Chinese, and Asian Indians holding significantly more wealth in mean interest, dividend, and rental income as compared with Other Southeast Asians and Vietnamese. Mean home value also is substantially spread out, but to a lesser extent than mean interest, dividend, and rental income. While the size of the interethnic disparities varies by the wealth proxy, the overall conclusion is that ethnic differences play a signficant role in the unequal distribution of wealth among Asian Americans.

DISCUSSION

Our findings indicate that, despite a high socioeconomic status, Asian Americans continue to experience barriers to wealth accumulation compared with White non-Hispanics. While the gap between White non-Hispanic and Black and Latino wealth is greater, Asian Americans continue to lag behind their White non-Hispanic counterparts in wealth accumulation. We found that even after controlling for factors that contribute to wealth (e.g., education, income, age, and life stage), including nativity status, a wealth gap remained between Asian Americans and White non-Hispanics.

Previous work on lending (Dymski 2001; Zonta 2004), particularly in housing markets, points to the importance of the type of financial institution and the location of such institutions (e.g., ethnic enclave versus nonethnic enclave) for Asian American access to credit. Such variations in access by location of institution and type of institution highlight the complexity of understanding barriers to accessing capital and accumulating wealth for Asian Americans.

Not only do Asian Americans as a group experience barriers but various groups within the population appear to have specific disadvantages. Our results show that Asian American wealth is more unevenly distributed than for White non-Hispanics. In addition, the difference between those with significant wealth holdings and those at the bottom of the distribution is greater for Asian Americans compared with White non-Hispanics as well. This finding holds true even for other types of wealth, including assets not held in housing. Much of the unequal distribution in wealth among Asian Americans can be attributed to noted ethnic differences. Using indirect measures of wealth (mean income; interest, dividend, and rental income; and home value), we found that Japanese, Chinese, and Asian Indians consistently held more wealth at the top end, while Other Southeast Asians settled at the bottom end. The most significant gap is between Japanese and Other Southeast Asians, where the mean Japanese household income is almost twice that for Other Southeast Asians, at $88,122 and $47,153, respectively.

The Asian American experience in the United States is complicated by a number of factors, including economic diversity, a variety of cultural and ethnic differences, and varying historical treatment in both immigration and settling in the United States. These experiences point to three lessons from which we can better understand wealth and race in the United States: (1) how immigration policy shapes wealth accumulation and distribution, (2) how ethnicity alone can create differential economic outcomes, particularly as it relates to immigration, and (3) how we need to move beyond establishing racial gaps and understanding the process by which wealth accumulation occurs.

IMMIGRATION POLICY

Asian American wealth has been most influenced by immigration policy, which determines not only who enters and settles in the United States but the demographic characteristics of the individuals who enter. As a result, such policies have significantly shaped the wealth distribution we see today (Hao 2003; Ong and Liu 2000). The most influential policies in shaping the distribution we see today are (1) economic selection (2) refugee policy, and (3) family reunification.

The United States prefers and selects individuals who are more highly educated and wealthy. Many immigrants have come and continue to enter the United States by bringing capital investment or by filling highly skilled occupations. These Asian immigrants arrive ready to ride the wave of the new economy, contributing their skills, knowledge, and dollars to the United States (Tseng 1995, 2000; Zhou and Kim 2003). For the most part political refugees from Southeast Asia have come with few economic resources, to escape war and political persecution. These individuals have not been necessarily highly educated and/or skilled.

The last influential immigration policy is family reunification. Family reunification has facilitated a chain migration of individuals of the same socioeconomic standing, reinforcing class differences and reproducing the same patterns and distribution of wealth among Asian Americans (Ong and Liu 2000). This policy makes it possible for an uneven distribution of wealth to exist and be maintained as individuals bring over family members who are most likely to have similar socioeconomic status as them.

The role of immigration policy and ethnicity in shaping Asian American wealth also applies to other highly immigrant populations to the United States, such as Latinos. However, Asian Americans relative to other immigrant populations demonstrate a greater number of cultural and linguistic differences in the United States. Furthermore, there is not one single dominant ethnic group as in the case of Latinos, with immigrants from Mexico.

ETHNICITY

Immigration policy also shapes the ethnic distribution of Asians we see in the United States. Immigration policies help us understand that wealth distribution among Asian Americans is also associated with particular ethnic groups and countries. For instance, previous studies (Tseng 1995, 2000; Zhou and Kim 2003) have documented the role of Taiwanese and Chinese immigrants investing in the United States. Similarly, scholars (Liu, Ong, and Rosenstein 1991) have identified occupations in health and science being filled by Filipino and Asian Indian immigrants.

Most Cambodians, Hmong, Laotians, and Vietnamese came to the United States to escape war and political persecution. Such refugees continue to be a reminder of the tragic legacy of our misguided intrusion into Southeast Asia. This population has a disproportionate share of individuals with lower levels of education and higher welfare participation rates (Le 1993; Ong and Blumenberg 1994). In some California counties, Southeast Asian refugees have the highest number of adults and children who have reached the maximum time limit to be receiving assistance. In Santa Clara County, California, alone, that number is significantly higher than the sum of all other groups who have "timed out" of welfare (Gustafson 2002). This fact demonstrates the vulnerability of specific Asian ethnic groups and the degree of economic disparity within the population.

BEYOND SIMPLE WEALTH STATUS

On the whole, Asian Americans have achieved a high wealth status, yet our results suggest that they are not being rewarded for this achievement.

The evidence from this chapter demonstrates that, on the average, Asian American wealth status is close to White non-Hispanics' but that barriers to wealth accumulation remain and that a racial wealth gap exists for Asian Americans. This finding suggests that we need to move from examining where racial groups lie in the wealth hierarchy to an examination of how such processes of wealth accumulation differ by race. The Asian American experience highlights how race is interconnected with immigration and ethnicity in ways that clarify and enrich our understanding of race and wealth in the United States. Immigration is particularly important as U.S. immigration policy determines not only who comes but with what resources. Ultimately, understanding Asian American wealth means understanding how race, ethnicity, and immigration interact to produce varying wealth outcomes.

CONCLUSION

This chapter highlights the complex effects ethnicity and immigration can have on wealth and race. The diversity within the Asian American population in terms of ethnicity, culture, language, and immigration influences wealth and can create barriers to accumulating it. Our findings suggest that there is some truth to the popular image of Asian Americans as a "model minority." Asian Americans have higher median and mean household income compared with all racial groups, including White non-Hispanics. However, having a higher household income has not translated into equal or more wealth as compared with White non-Hispanics.

While Asian Americans hold greater wealth than Blacks and Latinos, they lag behind White non-Hispanics in total net worth even after controlling for socioeconomic factors and nativity status. Our findings suggest that barriers to wealth indeed exist for Asian Americans and that such barriers may vary by ethnicity. Such ethnic variation can be explained mostly by examining immigration policies that have greatly influenced the wealth distribution we see today, a distribution that continues to be reinforced through current policies. Ultimately, the Asian American experience refines our understanding of wealth and race by highlighting the interaction between race, ethnicity, and immigration.

Future studies of wealth and race should examine not only the overall wealth status of groups but also whether group members experience disadvantages in the process of wealth accumulation that White non-Hispanics do not. Examining this process not only provides a more refined understanding of wealth accumulation but informs policy and planning. If we understand how various racial groups experience wealth accumulation differently than with White non-Hispanics, policies and planning can be specifically designed to address such barriers.

APPENDIX: SURVEY OF INCOME & PROGRAM
PARTICIPATION (SIPP) DATA

One of the uses of the SIPP is assessing wealth. The SIPP is a "longitudinal multi-panel survey primarily of adults in households in the United States, interviewed at least nine times at four-month intervals and followed over the life of the panel. It provides data that afford a better understanding and analyses of the distribution of income, wealth, and poverty in the society, and of the effects of federal and state programs on the well-being of families and individuals" (ICPSR 2005).

Information on the distribution of wealth across racial/ethnic groups was derived from wave 3 of the 2001 panel of the SIPP, which contains information on family assets, liabilities, and mortgages of households in the U.S. civilian population in the period of February 2001 through September 2002. The SIPP is a longitudinal survey of households regarding the distribution of income, wealth, and poverty and the effects of federal and state programs that promote family and individual well-being. It defines a household as all the people who occupy a housing unit and does not include persons in group quarters. Family characteristics and income information were derived from the wave 3 core microdata file. Information on total and home-related wealth and debt was derived from the wave 3 topical module microdata file. Demographic characteristics including race and ethnicity were derived based on the household survey reference person. These files were merged based on SSUID and STATE. In thirteen cases, an SSUID was associated with two different states in the merged data. In order to avoid having duplicate records for a given SSUID in the analysis, we assigned SSUIDs with any record in California as a California SSUID.

This chapter analyzes wealth distributions among family households using the U.S. Census definition of a family. A family includes a householder with one or more persons living in the same household who are related by birth, marriage, or adoption. Family households can include households in which the householder is married or a single male or female. Family households may contain people not related to the household. Although these individuals may not be part of the "family" based on the census definition, we include their income and wealth in our analysis of household income and wealth. That is, we use household income and wealth rather than family income or wealth. This approach more closely corresponds with asset pooling at a household level. For instance, nonfamily household members often contribute to monthly housing or mortgage costs. Household racial/ethnic status is based on the reference person even though households could contain persons of another race or ethnicity.

Since some households had one survey response due to data collection and other issues, we defined a reference person's income, wealth, and debt based on the maximum value for each amount from all surveys. We converted monthly income levels reported in the SIPP data to annual measures by multiplying by twelve. Results differentiate wealth distributions by racial/ethnic groups. Although nativity status is available in wave 2 of the 2001 panel data, we were unable to subcategorize racial/ethnic groups by nativity due to the small sample size.

Czijka, Jacobson, and Cody (2003–4) found that the limitations of the SIPP mostly affected the survey's estimate of high-income families and the assets that they hold. The SIPP underestimates both the number and average wealth of the wealthiest families in the survey by top coding, essentially "dropping off," or removing, assets from those families who exceed the value at the top. The SIPP underestimates net worth relative to estimates based on the SCF. The SIPP is more in line with the SCF on some assets as opposed to others. For instance, an estimate of home value is more accurate than that of other real estate.

NOTES

This research was supported in part by a grant from the U.S. Department of Housing and Urban Development and the UCLA Asian American Studies Center. The authors are grateful to Don Nakanishi for his support on this project and Douglas Houston and Hiroyuki Iseki for their research assistance.

1. Asian Americans include individuals of East Asian, Southeast Asian, and South Asian descent, including the six largest groups in the United States: Asian Indian, Chinese, Filipinos, Japanese, Koreans, and Vietnamese.

2. We calculated the square root of the absolute value of the wealth variable and then assigned a positive sign if wealth is greater than zero and assigned a negative sign if wealth is less than zero. An alternative is using the natural log of the absolute value of wealth, but this transformation is not ideal given the large number of zero values for wealth.

REFERENCES

Cavalluzzo, Ken, and John Wolken. 2002. *Small Business Loan Turndowns, Personal Wealth and Discrimination.* Washington, DC: Federal Reserve Board.

Chan, Sucheng. 1991. *Asian Americans: An Interpretive History.* Twayne's Immigrant Heritage of America Series. Boston: Twayne.

Cobb-Clark, Deborah A., and Vincent Hildebrand. 2004. "The Wealth of Mexican Americans." IZA Discussion Paper no. 1150, May.

Czijka, John L., Jonathan E. Jacobson, and Scott Cody. 2003–4. *Survey Estimates of Wealth: A Comparative Analysis and Review of the Survey of Income and Program Participation.* Baltimore, MD: Social Security Administration.

Di, Zhu Ziao. 2001. "The Role of Housing as a Component of Wealth." Northwestern Joint Center for Poverty Working Paper Series no. 16, January. http://www.jcpr.org/.

DiCarlo, Lisa. 2004. "Forbes 400 Richest in America (2000): Nine Foreign Born Americans Added to Forbes 400." http://www.forbes.com/.

Dymski, Gary. 2001. "Is Discrimination Disappearing? Residential Credit Market Evidence, 1992–1998." *International Journal of Social Economics* 28 (10–12): 1025–45.

Frank, Robert. 2004. "Affluence Rises for Asian Americans: Group Now Accounts for 5% of U.S. Wealthy Investors; A New Market for Advisors." *Wall Street Journal,* February 25. http://www.asianscomingtogether.com/news/2004/.

Gustafson, Kaaryn. 2002. "Welfare Time Limits to Disproportionately Cut Immigrants." *AsianWeek,* December 19. http://www.asianweek.com/.

Hao, Lingxin. 2003. "Wealth Inequality in the U.S.: Does Nativity Play a Role?" Russell Sage Foundation Working Paper no. 202, February. http://www.russellsage.org/publications/.

ICPSR (Inter-university Consortium for Political and Social Research). 2006. "Survey of Income and Program Participation (SIPP) Series," 2001 Panel Study No. 3894. http://webapp.icpsr.umich.edu/cocoon/ICPSR-SERIES/00135.eml (accessed March 20, 2006).

Krivo, Lauren Joy. 2004. "Housing and Wealth Inequality: Racial-Ethnic Differences in Home Equity in the United States." *Population Association of America* 41 (3): 585–605.

Le, Ngoan. 1993. "The Case of Southeast Asian Refugees: Policy for a Community 'At Risk.'" In *The State of Asian Pacific America: Policy Issues to the Year 2020.* Los Angeles, CA: LEAP Asian Pacific American Public Policy Institute and UCLA Asian American Studies Center.

Liu, John, Paul Ong, and Carolyn Rosenstein. 1991. "Dual Chain Migration Post 1965 Filipino Immigration to the United States." *International Migration Review* 25 (3): 487–513.

Oliver, Melvin L., and Thomas M. Shapiro. 1995. *Black Wealth/White Wealth: A New Perspective on Racial Inequality.* New York: Routledge.

Ong, Paul, and Evelyn Blumenberg. 1994. "Welfare and Work among Southeast Asians." In *The State of Asian Pacific America: Economic Diversity, Issues and Policies.* Los Angeles, CA: LEAP Asian Pacific American Public Policy Institute.

Ong, Paul, and John Liu. 2000. "U.S. Immigration Policies and Asian Migration." In *Contemporary Asian America: A Multidisciplinary Reader,* ed. Min Zhou and James V. Gatewood, 155–74. New York: NYU Press.

Ong, Paul, Dennis Arguelles, Susan Castro, Theresa Cenidoza, Bruce Chow, Chanchanit Hirunpidok-Martorell, Tarry Hum, Winnie Louie, Erick Nakano, and Roderick Ramos. 1993. *Beyond Asian American Poverty: Community Economic Development Policies and Strategies.* Los Angeles, CA: LEAP Asian Pacific American Policy Institute and the UCLA Asian American Studies Center.

Takaki, Ronald T. 1990. *Strangers from a Different Shore: A History of Asian Americans.* New York: Penguin Books.

Tseng, Yen-Fen. 1995. "Beyond 'Little Taipei': The Development of Taiwanese Immigrant Businesses in Los Angeles." *International Migration Review* 29 (1): 33–58.

———. 2000. "The Mobility of Entrepreneurs and Capital: Taiwanese Capital-Linked Migration." *International Migration* 38 (2): 143–66.

Turner, Margery, and Steven Ross. 2003. "Discrimination in Metropolitan Housing Markets Phase 2, Asians and Pacific Islanders: Final Report." Urban Institute, Metropolitan Housing and Communities Policy Center, Washington, DC. http://www.hud.gov/.

White, Ben. 2005. "Following the Money: Brokerage Firms Are in Pursuit of a Diversified Client Base, Looking to Keep up with a Demographic Shift in U.S. Wealth." *Washington Post,* May 10, E01. http://www.washingtonpost.com/.

Zhou, Min, and Rebecca Kim. 2003. "The Tale of Two Metropolis." In *New York and Los Angeles: Politics, Society and Culture; A Comparative View,* ed. David Halle. Chicago: University of Chicago Press.

Zonta, Michela. 2004. "The Role of Ethnic Banks in the Residential Patterns of Asian Americans: The Case of Los Angeles." PhD diss., University of California Los Angeles.

8 Financial Marketplace Participation & Pension Holdings over the Life Course

NGINA CHITEJI, ELENA GOUSKOVA, & FRANK STAFFORD

Anyone familiar with the financial marketplace knows that it presents many options for families seeking to store savings. It is possible to choose from a variety of assets, some of which are highly functional—for example, housing, which provides a consumption flow in addition to serving as a store of value, and bank accounts, which provide a way to make payments. Other assets are purely financial, assuming there is no inherent pleasure in holding stocks or bonds—other than their monetary return. Still others—such as a family business—have financial returns and are complementary to employment. And further, there are pensions, which can be seen as assets to employees but as a compensation mode for employers seeking to retain a workforce.

How do U.S. families allocate their wealth across so many different asset types? The choices that families make are important because they can have bearing on how much wealth is accumulated over the life course, a particularly important issue for families nearing retirement. While one might think that a family's wealth position at retirement would largely reflect its earnings over the life course, research shows that income and wealth holdings are related but do not march in lockstep. One study of income and household wealth growth shows the importance of both long-run income and saving. Yet the same study shows that for those families in the top one-tenth of family income, 1984–94 household wealth growth ranged all the way from −$270,000 (in 1996 dollars) at the tenth percentile to $929,000 at the ninety-fifth percentile (conditional on income in the top 10 percent) (Juster, Smith, and Stafford 1999). Portfolio and saving behavior also can have implications for macroeconomic policy-making because families may react differently to specific changes in the tax code, to inflation, and to unemployment depending upon the way that their portfolios are structured (Bertraut and Starr-McCluer 2002; Poterba 2001).

This chapter examines the wealth portfolios of families in their pre-retirement years, examining both the number of assets held in families' portfolios and the different combinations of assets that are held. Additionally, it looks at the place of pensions in families' strategies for saving. Standard economic theory suggests that a pension may serve as a substitute for other forms of saving. Yet empirical research has shown that participation in certain types of pension programs appears instead to generate new saving and to actually increase the total amount of wealth that a family has, perhaps by building financial knowledge, or because of peer effects, or by reducing transaction costs associated with the saving process (Poterba, Venti, and Wise 1996, 2004; Maki 2001; Duflo and Saez 2000; Hong, Kubik, and Stein 2004). In line with earlier studies of pension and wealth patterns (Cagan 1965), one would not necessarily expect having a pension to provide evidence of a substitution effect at work.[1] Instead, because greater wealth has been shown to be associated with more complex portfolios (Guskova, Juster, and Stafford 2004), it is possible that pensions would instead appear simply as yet another element of a complex, diversified portfolio, with more of a "scale of portfolio effect" and little evident displacement effect on other assets. That is, one might observe that those participating in a pension program have greater savings and nonpension wealth because families with higher wealth tend to spread their wealth over a greater number of assets, even if a pension is not the cause of a family's higher wealth level.

EXISTING RESEARCH

The literature examining the magnitude of wealth held by American families clearly and unequivocally demonstrates that net worth, or household wealth (not including pensions or the present value of future Social Security payments), is unevenly distributed in the United States. As shown in the chapters of this volume and in research published elsewhere, families differ greatly in terms of the total amount of wealth that they possess and in their rates of ownership of individual assets (Leigh, chap. 1; Hurst, Luoh, and Stafford 1998; Oliver and Shapiro 1995). Across all families, some have sizeable resources, while others have little, none, and even negative net worth. The gaps by race are particularly pronounced, with Black families being found to posses only about one-fifth of the wealth that White families have, on average (chap. 1). And, while smaller, a net gap remains even when one takes factors such as income, educational levels, and health condition of the family members into account. Because these gaps in levels of wealth held have been discussed extensively elsewhere in the literature, we do not document them here. Instead, we simply remind the reader of their existence because they offer one way of analyzing family wealth. We offer another perspective by focusing on the specific structure of the elements in families' wealth portfolios.

While the aforementioned research examining wealth inequality has focused primarily on nonpension wealth, other scholarship analyzes the distribution of pension wealth and differences in pension coverage rates. Because the research covering the U.S. pension system has evolved somewhat separately from the literature on racial wealth inequality, we present a selection of the results found in this literature in table 8.1.

One of the primary conclusions drawn in this literature is that pension wealth is distributed more evenly than is nonpension wealth and this carries over to differences by race. In part, this is from the equalizing effect of defined benefit, or "formula," plans. The U.S. pension system features two types of pensions: defined benefit (DB) plans and defined contribution (DC) plans.[2] As the data in table 8.1 indicate, the Black/White pension wealth ratio ranges from about 0.52 to 0.85, depending upon the age range studied, the data set used, and—apparently—whether Latinos are included in the non-White category. For example, using data from the 1992 Health and Retirement Study (HRS), McGarry and Davenport (1998) find that, when looking at families in the 51–61 age range, non-White families have, on average, $68,420 in pension wealth, while White families hold $129,630. This gap is much smaller than the gap they find for net worth excluding pensions, where the authors find that the typical older non-White family has a net worth of $75,633 compared with the typical older White family's $206,330. Even and MacPherson's analysis of the pension wealth of individuals suggests an even smaller difference between Blacks and Whites.

TABLE 8.1. Comparison of Findings about Pension Wealth in the Literature

Author	Data Set	Proportion of Households or Individuals with Pension Coverage (%)		Mean [median] Pension Wealth of Households		Mean [median] Nonpension Wealth of Households		Mean [median] Pension Wealth Conditional on Holding	
		Whites	Nonwhites	Whites	Nonwhites	Whites	Nonwhites	Whites	Nonwhites
		Households		*Households*		*Households*			
Choudhury 2002	1992 HRS	79	66 (Blacks) 47 (Latinos)	$100,865 [$37,721]	$65,897 (Blacks) [$24,076—Blacks] $32,581 (Latinos) [$0—Latinos]	$273,847 [$127,000]	$78,444 (Blacks) [$30,500—Blacks] $79,751 (Latinos) [$36,000—Latinos]	NA	NA
		Individuals		*Households*		*Households*		*Individuals*	
McGarry and Davenport 1998	1992 HRS	69	54	$129,630 [NA]	$68,420 [NA]	$206,330 [NA]	$75,663 [NA]	$114,437 [$86,971]	$67,061 [$55,532]

		Individuals	Individuals	Individuals
Even and MacPherson 2003	1992 SCF	60.7 59.3 (Blacks) 36.6 (Latinos)	$38,226 $34,527 (Blacks) $16,784 (Latinos)	$17,661 (Average benefit level among Whites) $11,664 (Average benefit level among Blacks)
Even and MacPherson 2003	1994 CPS	33.5 26.1 (Blacks) 18.6 (Latinos)		
Wolff 2003	1998 SCF	73.7 (All households)	$105,086 (All households) [$34,483—All households]	

Sources: Wolff 2003, tables 4 and 5; Choudhury 2002, table 2; McGarry and Davenport 1998, tables 4 and 5; and Even and MacPherson 2003, tables 1, 2, 3, and 7. McGarry and Davenport (1998) do not report median values for the household information. Choudhury (2002) and McGarry and Davenport (1998) both rely on data from the 1992 HRS. This is a sample of individuals and households ages 51–61. The 1994 CPS is used to provide information about individuals age 55 and older who are retired and receiving pension income. The coverage rates are for the entire sample, while the averages reported for pension income are for former public sector employees. Even and MacPherson also use the 1992 SCF to produce estimates for working individuals ages 21–55. In table 8.1, all data from years after 1992 have been converted into 1992 dollar values using the consumer price index CPI-U.

Using a sample of working individuals ages 21–55 from the Survey of Consumer Finances (SCF), Even and MacPherson (2003) estimate that average pension wealth among Blacks was about $34,527 in 1992, while the average amount of pension wealth held by White individuals was $38,226. Analysis of pension income received by retirees echoes this result that the differences between Blacks and Whites in the realm of pensions are smaller than they are for nonpension wealth. Even and MacPherson also examine data from the 1994 Current Population Survey (CPS), and using a sample of individuals age 55 and older, who are in their retirement phase and who were once employed in the public sector, the authors find that the average level of pension income for Blacks is $11,664, while the typical older White person receives $17,661 in pension benefits.[3] This represents a Black/White ratio of 0.66, far narrower than the gaps for household wealth.

Table 8.1 also shows estimates of pension coverage rates by race. While different authors find somewhat different results, taken together, the data suggest that, on average, the percentage of Blacks with pensions is at least slightly smaller than the percentage of Whites who have them. For example, McGarry and Davenport (1998) find a 15 percent gap between Whites and non-Whites at the *individual* level. Using the same data set, but focusing on *households* and disaggregating further by race, Choudhury (2002) finds that 66 percent of Black families have pension coverage, while 79 percent of White families do. And, using a sample of individuals age 55 and older who are not in the labor force, Even and MacPherson find that 33.5 percent of older Whites are currently receiving pension benefits, while the comparable figure for Blacks is 26.1 percent. The one instance in which it is not clear that Whites are advantaged is among women. Here, Even and MacPherson (2003) find that the proportion of Black women with pension coverage sometimes equals or exceeds that of White women. This result is consistent with the pattern of Black women as more likely to be full-time, primary earners.

While the literature on nonpension wealth inequality indicates that racial differences remain even when factors such as income, education, and age are taken into account, the multivariate analyses conducted in the literature covering pensions contain mixed results. For example, McGarry and Davenport (1998) find that, among those with positive pension wealth, non-Whites have about 17 percent *more* wealth than Whites do, ceteris paribus. When looking at coverage rates, McGarry and Davenport (1998) find a small net gap—on the order of 2 percent—in their analysis of coverage rate differences between Whites and non-Whites. However, Even and MacPherson (forthcoming) find that demographic and economic factors related to individual and job characteristics explain virtually all of the gap in coverage rates between Black and White men. What each of these papers has in common is that it takes an employment perspective toward analyzing pension coverage. Such a perspective does not take into account financial or portfolio factors and thereby ignores the influence that families' other wealth holdings can have on their desire to have a pension. Our work examines participation in pension programs in conjunction with other forms of financial market participation.

How does including pension wealth affect the distribution of wealth among U.S. families? In their study of HRS data McGarry and Davenport (1998) analyze the size distribution of wealth and find that including pension wealth reduces overall wealth inequality somewhat.[4] They do not find much effect for the distribution of wealth by race however.[5] Wolff's work echoes the finding: incorporating pension wealth has some, though modest, effect on the distribution of wealth (Wolff 2003). Using 1998 data from the SCF to examine mid-age households (ages 47–64), Wolff finds that the Gini coefficient for net worth (excluding pension wealth) is 0.817, while the Gini for total private wealth is 0.753. The author also finds that the inferences that one draws can depend upon pension type. Wolff finds that DB plans play a more equalizing role than do DC plans. DC pension wealth is more unevenly distributed, among those who have DC plans, than DB pension wealth is (conditional upon having that type of coverage). This is an interesting finding to contemplate in the context of the changes that have occurred in the U.S. pension system over the past two decades. In the past, DB pension coverage was standard among companies offering pensions. However, in the past twenty-five years, DC coverage has increased, partly because some firms have shifted away from DB plans toward DC plans (Wolff 2003; Friedberg and Owyang 2002, 2003). For example, Friedberg and Owyang (2002) report that about 46 percent of full-time employees had DB pensions in 1983 but that this number fell to about 23 percent by 1998, while the percentage of full-time workers with DC plans rose from about 30 percent to 46.5 percent over the same period.[6] Debates abound about whether this trend will continue, about whether it signals a decreased commitment by companies to providing benefits, and about what the changes will mean for the adequacy of savings when workers reach retirement (Hewitt Associates 2004; Friedberg and Owyang 2002, 2003; Wolff 2003; Bloom and Freeman 1992).

DATA & METHODS

Our chapter focuses on characterizing the portfolios held by preretirement households. Following Guskova, Juster, and Stafford (2004), we represent portfolio choice in two ways. We first examine the number of assets that families typically hold, or "portfolio span." We then describe the exact types or specific combinations of assets held, or "portfolio composition." This allows us to provide a better characterization of the participation in different asset markets by U.S. families. From this characterization of the household wealth portfolio, we then examine the form of net worth holdings in relation to pension coverage. This facilitates a more thorough understanding of family financial behavior. A comprehensive analysis of portfolio behavior that includes a look at pension coverage should provide helpful information that can enrich policy discussions. There has been a continuing dialogue over the prospect of partially privatizing social security, the adequacy of retirement savings, and the ongoing shift from DB to DC plans in the pension system. These all raise questions about the ability of individual families to make good judgments in planning for sufficient resources for retirement.

We use data from the Panel Study of Income Dynamics (PSID). The PSID is a nationally representative survey of U.S. individuals and families that includes information about their wealth holdings, their pension coverage, and a variety of other sociodemographic and economic characteristics. While the PSID contains information about individuals of all age ranges, including children, and about families headed by married and unmarried individuals, we focus on married couples in the 30–59 age range. This allows us to focus on a group that will be old enough to have started working, accumulating wealth, and participating in retirement plans, but young enough to not yet be in the retirement phase of their life cycle.

The PSID asks questions about seven different asset categories in addition to pensions. These are (1) equity in owner-occupied housing, (2) equity in other real estate, (3) business equity, (4) autos and other vehicles, (5) stocks, (6) bank accounts, including checking accounts, savings accounts, certificates of deposit, money market funds, savings bonds and treasury bills, and (7) other assets, which include bond funds, the cash value of life insurance policies, rights in a trust or estate, and valuable collections. The information that is collected about pensions includes whether the head or spouse of the family currently has a pension, whether the head/spouse will have pension coverage at the job if he or she simply continues to work there,[7] and whether the employer offers its employees a DB or DC plan (or both). Additionally, there is information indicating whether the DC plan is one in which the employer makes contributions, as well as how the funds in the employee's DC account are invested.

HOUSEHOLD PORTFOLIOS & PENSIONS

Why do we emphasize portfolio behavior? We believe that it is important to provide a broad view of financial market participation—one that looks at the entire portfolio, rather than focusing on the likelihood of owning a single asset, or on the total amount of wealth held, or on the overall saving rate. While analyses of individual asset-ownership rates will indicate whether a family has a specific asset and identify some of the co-variates driving ownership and lack of ownership, looking at a single asset in isolation will not tell us whether the individual holds another asset in its place, or whether he or she holds any other assets at all. When one thinks about answering a question about "what resources people have," it is apparent that the question is not simply about whether they have one specific asset. To fully understand the choices families make, one needs information covering the entire portfolio.

PORTFOLIO SPAN

One way to view a family's portfolio is to look at the *number of elements* that it contains, or the number of assets over which the portfolio spans. As indicated in table 8.2, the span of portfolios varies, ranging from zero assets to more than six. In the population at large one finds that many households—about half—have portfolios that are very basic, with no more than three elements. However, the number of elements in families' portfolios varies by age, race, education levels, and gender of the household head. For example, young families have fewer elements in the portfolio than middle-aged families do, as might be expected given their position in the life cycle. The median or typical young family has a portfolio with three assets, while the typical middle-aged family's portfolio has four.

The difference between African American and White families is greater than the difference found between the young and the middle-aged. The median White family holds a portfolio with four elements, while the median Black family has only two assets in its portfolio. These data echo the story of racial wealth inequities seen elsewhere in the literature. For race, the three-asset portfolio represents a clear dividing line. About 79 percent of White families have portfolios with three or more different assets. Among Black families one finds that about 80 percent of families have three elements or fewer. Additionally, among African Americans, about 16 percent of families actually hold no assets at all. Given the functional nature of many assets, no-asset status might be viewed as a sign of considerable disadvantage. Bank accounts provide means for making and receiving payments for example, and automobiles provide transportation services. Families that do not own these types of assets that many take for granted will obviously have to turn elsewhere for these services.

There is also a noticeable difference between the portfolios of college graduates and those of household heads who did not finish high school. For both groups about 20 percent of families hold portfolios with three elements. Among college graduates, about 66 percent of families have more complex portfolios, with four or more elements. However, among those without a high school degree, the majority of families (about 57 percent) actually have fewer than three elements in their portfolios.

TABLE 8.2. Distribution of Portfolio Span (percent)

	Portfolio Span						
	0	1	2	3	4	5	6 up
Total	3.5	8.8	17.1	24.7	23.0	15.8	7.1
Age of head							
30–44	4.7	10.8	20.3	27.2	20.5	11.8	4.8
45–59	2.2	6.6	13.6	22.1	25.8	20.2	9.6
Race of head							
White	1.1	5.4	14.5	25.4	25.7	19.0	8.9
Black	16.5	23.4	23.0	21.2	9.8	4.7	1.4
Years of education							
No high school degree	10.2	17.1	29.5	21.9	13.7	4.9	2.8
High school degree	4.1	11.3	19.8	27.6	18.6	12.8	5.8
Some college	2.9	7.4	14.6	28.8	23.2	17.1	6.0
College degree or more	0.1	2.2	10.8	20.0	31.9	23.1	11.8
Gender of head							
Male	1.9	6.5	13.7	25.6	25.4	18.1	8.9
Female	8.2	15.6	27.1	22.2	16.1	9.0	1.8
Marital status							
Married	0.7	3.6	11.3	25.3	28.1	20.7	10.3
Not married	7.5	16.3	25.2	23.9	15.8	8.8	2.5
Number of observations	276	553	904	1,201	989	604	269

Gender and marital status also appear to be associated with portfolio span. Female-headed households and unmarried people tend to hold less diversified, or less complex, portfolios than married households and those headed by men.

While examining the span of the household portfolio is not the same as measuring by the total amount of wealth a family has, wealth clearly increases with span. Table 8.3 shows that families who hold more complex portfolios tend to be wealthier than other families. Means and medians both rise as one moves from left to right in any row of table 8.3.

TABLE 8.3.   Mean (median) Net Family Wealth (in thousands)

	Portfolio Span						
	0	1	2	3	4	5	6 up
	Mean (median)	Mean (median)	Mean (median)	Mean (median)	Mean (median)	Mean (median)	Mean (median)
Total	−3.0	4.0	25.0	98.0	210.0	485.0	1,196.0
Age of head							
30–44	−4.0	1.0	15.0	82.0	187.0	335.0	1,028.0
	(0.0)	(1.0)	(6.0)	(40.0)	(120.0)	(203.0)	(401.0)
45–59	−1.0	9.0	41.0	121.0	229.0	580.0	1,288.0
	(0.0)	(2.0)	(12.0)	(63.0)	(152.0)	(309.0)	(550.0)
Race of head							
White	−6.0	2.0	23.0	106.0	219.0	489.0	1,224.0
	(0.0)	(1.0)	(6.0)	(52.0)	(141.0)	(255.0)	(493.0)
Black	−2.0	8.0	34.0	79.0	101.0	258.0	472.0
	(0.0)	(2.0)	(12.0)	(35.0)	(64.0)	(250.0)	(423.0)
Years of education							
No high school degree	−5.0	6.0	23.0	49.0	118.0	362.0	362.0
	(0.0)	(1.0)	(12.0)	(34.0)	(78.0)	(250.0)	(299.0)
High school degree	−1.0	5.0	24.0	81.0	159.0	301.0	656.0
	(0.0)	(2.0)	(6.0)	(50.0)	(127.0)	(200.0)	(408.0)
Some college	0.0	4.0	26.0	91.0	161.0	396.0	1,398.0
	(0.0)	(1.0)	(9.0)	(49.0)	(108.0)	(248.0)	(368.0)
College degree or more	−10.0	−1.0	27.0	158.0	284.0	647.0	1,457.0
	(−18.0)	(1.0)	(6.0)	(57.0)	(189.0)	(337.0)	(600.0)
Gender of head							
Male	0.0	6.0	24.0	111.0	223.0	525.0	1,154.0
	(0.0)	(2.0)	(9.0)	(52.0)	(145.0)	(294.0)	(480.0)
Female	−4.0	2.0	26.0	54.0	149.0	244.0	1,817.0
	(0.0)	(1.0)	(6.0)	(39.0)	(95.0)	(132.0)	(493.0)
Marital status							
Married	0.0	6.0	24.0	109.0	228.0	521.0	1,171.0
	(0.0)	(2.0)	(12.0)	(51.0)	(147.0)	(291.0)	(517.0)
Not married	−3.0	4.0	25.0	83.0	163.0	362.0	1,344.0
	(0.0)	(1.0)	(6.0)	(45.0)	(110.0)	(208.0)	(455.0)
Number of observations	276	553	904	1,201	989	604	269

Interestingly, among families that hold three or more elements in their portfolios, White families have greater mean and median wealth, but among families holding smaller, less-diversified portfolios, Black families appear to have slightly more wealth than Whites, on average.

PORTFOLIO COMPOSITION

An alternative way to view a family's portfolio is to examine the portfolio type or the specific combination of assets that the family holds. Table 8.4 presents such information. It lists the five most commonly held portfolio types for different population subgroups. Among married families, the five most commonly held portfolio types are a portfolio with a bank account (C), home (H), and vehicle (T). The next most commonly held portfolio combination includes stock (SI). The third most common portfolio is one with "bonds and valuables" (V) in addition to the above assets. The fourth most popular combines only a bank account and a vehicle. And the fifth most common type includes real estate (R), bank accounts, stock, a home, and a vehicle. The portfolios held by unmarried individuals tend to be much simpler. The portfolio composition data reveal that the most commonly held portfolio includes only a bank account and a vehicle; the second most popular adds a home to this bundle. The third most commonly held portfolio among single people includes only a vehicle. Tied for fourth are the portfolio that includes stocks, a home, a vehicle, and a bank account and the portfolio with zero elements.

Again, there are interesting differences by race. Regardless of family

TABLE 8.4. **Distribution of the Five Most Popular Portfolio Types**

	Rank	All Households	%	Cum. %	White Households	%	Cum. %	Black Households	%	Cum. %
Married	1	(C)(H)(T)	18	18	(C)(SI)(H)(T)	17	17	(C)(H)(T)	23	23
	2	(C)(SI)(H)(T)	16	34	(C)(H)(T)	17	34	(H)(T)	10	33
	3	(C)(SI)(V)(H)(T)	7	41	(C)(SI)(V)(H)(T)	8	43	(C)(T)	9	42
	4	(C)(T)	5	47	(R)(C)(SI)(H)(T)	5	48	(C)(SI)(H)(T)	8	50
	5	(R)(C)(SI)(H)(T)	5	51	(B)(C)(SI)(H)(T)	5	53	(T)	6	56
Single	1	(C)(T)	17	17	(C)(T)	18	18	None	21	21
	2	(C)(H)(T)	12	29	(C)(H)(T)	13	31	(T)	16	37
	3	(T)	9	38	(C)(SI)(H)(T)	10	41	(C)(T)	12	49
	4	(C)(SI)(H)(T)	8	46	(T)	6	47	(C)(H)(T)	10	59
	5	None	8	53	(C)(SI)(T)	5	52	(C)	8	66

Note: C—transaction account(s), SI—stocks (IRAs included), B—business, V—other assets, H—housing (primary residence), T—vehicle.

type, the portfolio composition data echo findings in the analysis of portfolio span: Black families tend to hold much more basic portfolios than White families, with bank accounts, homes, and vehicles being the specific assets that appear most often. This indicates not only that Black families' portfolios are smaller in number of elements, on average, but that the assets held are ones that can be thought of as providing day-to-day services, or a consumption flow, rather than serving solely as a store of value over time. This is a marked difference from the portfolios that are common among White families. With the exception of the C-H-T portfolio, the top portfolios among White families always include stocks, and portfolios of White families commonly include bonds/valuables, real estate, and business equity.

PENSIONS

While economists do not typically speak of a market for pensions, pensions (as in the case of the assets discussed in the preceding) do represent a store of savings—one that is targeted specifically at the saving-for-retirement motive.[8] Additionally, pensions represent a form of savings that not all families have. Accordingly, this section turns to an analysis of patterns of participation in pension programs. As shown in table 8.5, among married couples, about 30 percent of families are ones in which neither the head nor the wife has a pension. For Blacks and Whites, the number of families without a pension is comparable; however, more

TABLE 8.5. Pension Ownership Rates among Married Couples

	Pension Position			
	No Pension	Only Head Has Pension	Only Wife Has Pension	Both Have Pension
Total	31.2	31.3	14.7	22.8
Age of head				
30–44	31.5	33.7	13.6	21.2
45–59	30.9	28.7	15.8	24.6
Race of head				
White	27.7	33.3	15.3	23.7
Black	26.4	21.4	17.3	35.0
Years of education				
No high school degree	62.6	13.6	13.7	10.2
High school degree	28.3	33.1	17.2	21.4
Some college	24.3	32.6	16.0	27.1
College degree or more	23.9	37.0	12.3	26.8
Number of observations	905	854	405	678

Black families than White are ones where wives have pensions or where both spouses have pension coverage. (Forty percent of White families fall into this category—of a wife with a pension or both the head and wife have a pension—while the majority, 52 percent, of Black families do.) Additionally, as might be expected, lack of coverage declines with levels of education. Among single people, we find that the majority of Blacks are without pension coverage.[9]

What are the features of families' pension plans, for those with pension coverage? As might be expected, given the changes that have occurred in the pension system over the past two decades, a somewhat smaller proportion of younger families has heads with DB coverage and a larger proportion has heads with DC plans than is the case for middle-aged families. (See table 8.6.) The same pattern holds for wives. For Blacks and Whites, the total percentage of families whose head has some involvement in DC plans is comparable (about 57 percent if one adds the proportion of heads with DC coverage only and the proportion with both a DC and a DB plan). However, the proportion of White families whose head solely has a DC plan—where the individual chooses whether his or her retirement funds will be invested in stocks, bonds, or mutual funds

TABLE 8.6.   Distribution of Head's Pension Plan Type

	Pension Type		
	DB	**DC**	**Both**
Total	41.3	37.5	21.1
Age of head			
30–44	38.8	41.7	19.5
45–59	44.0	33.2	22.9
Race of head			
White	41.5	37.9	20.7
Black	42.3	30.7	27.0
Years of education			
No high school degree	38.2	50.4	11.4
High school degree	40.1	36.9	23.0
Some college	41.0	38.6	20.4
College degree or more	42.2	35.2	22.6
Gender of head			
Male	40.8	36.3	22.8
Female	43.0	41.2	15.8
Marital status			
Married	40.0	36.6	23.4
Not married	43.4	39.0	17.6
Number of observations	800	709	453

and bears the risk of ensuring that the fund grows large enough to meet his or her retirement needs—is somewhat greater (about 38 percent compared with 31 percent for Blacks).

There are also differences in types of coverage for household heads by education level, as well as some minor differences by marital status and gender. Among wives, conditional on having a pension, the proportion of Black wives that have DB plans is greater than the proportion of White wives that do.[10] And a larger fraction of White wives has DC plans than is true for Black wives. There are also differences in the type of pension a wife has based on her level of education.

INTERACTIONS BETWEEN HOUSEHOLD PORTFOLIOS & PENSIONS

What connections does one see between family portfolios and pensions? To answer this question, we first present descriptive data covering the relationship between household portfolios and pensions. Several interesting patterns are noted. Then, we show results from multivariate regression analysis.

THE PLACE OF PENSIONS IN THE PORTFOLIO

How do families integrate pensions into their portfolios? One does not find many sizeable differences in whether a family has a pension or not based on its portfolio type. There is a slight suggestion that those with the more complex, four-element portfolio that includes stocks have a greater tendency to also have a pension, which is consistent with a scale effect rather than a substitution effect. However, among families holding the even more complex five-element portfolio, C-SI-V-H-T, one does not find a similar effect.

Table 8.7 partitions the universe of portfolio types into six groups. The first three, C-H, C-H-T, and C-SI-H-T, are the most popular types of portfolios among all households (Gouskova, Juster, and Stafford 2004). In addition to these types, the table identifies households that have stocks in their portfolios (though not in the form of the C-SI-H-T portfolio discussed in the preceding) and households who report the presence of other valuable assets (V) in their portfolios. The category "rest" contains all the remaining families. This table first indicates that among families with the simple, most basic portfolio types, a greater percentage of Black families has a pension in their family portfolios than do Whites. For

Black families we find about 66 percent of C-T holders and about 87 percent of C-H-T holders also have at least one pension in their portfolios. The comparable numbers are about 52 percent for C-T White families and about 77 percent for C-H-T White families.

Particularly striking is the fact that 50.8 percent of Black families holding the C-H-T portfolio are those with two pensions (despite the simplicity of their portfolio otherwise). Second, it is interesting to note that the proportion of families in which *both* spouses have a pension (35 percent) is greater than the proportion of White families for which this obtains (23.7 percent). This suggestion of greater "double-coverage" in Black families is noteworthy. It may indicate a tendency of some Black families to do really "well" relative to other Blacks (those with pension coverage being able to have two pensions, not just one), while White families exhibit less contrast within the group.[11] Another finding is that

TABLE 8.7. Pension Ownership Rates by Household Portfolio Type (percent)

		Pension Position			
	Portfolio Type	No Pension	Only Head Has Pension	Only Wife Has Pension	Both Have Pension
All households	Total	31.2	31.3	14.7	22.8
	(C)(T)	51.5	23.8	9.7	15.0
	(C)(H)(T)	26.0	34.2	9.7	30.1
	(C)(SI)(H)(T)	18.3	41.0	13.9	26.8
	SI, not above	28.5	30.7	17.6	23.2
	V, not above	24.1	29.3	17.7	28.9
	Rest	51.3	23.4	14.9	10.4
White households	Total	27.7	33.3	15.3	23.7
	(C)(T)	47.8	26.2	8.6	17.3
	(C)(H)(T)	23.3	37.6	8.9	30.3
	(C)(SI)(H)(T)	17.0	42.2	14.6	26.2
	SI, not above	29.4	30.4	16.9	23.3
	V, not above	22.0	29.8	19.3	28.9
	Rest	40.1	29.4	18.5	12.0
Black households	Total	26.4	21.4	17.3	35.0
	(C)(T)	34.0	19.3	14.3	32.4
	(C)(H)(T)	13.1	21.3	14.8	50.8
	(C)(SI)(H)(T)	19.6	24.0	12.1	44.4
	SI, not above	4.6	29.3	35.2	30.9
	V, not above	14.7	23.5	8.5	53.3
	Rest	53.3	16.0	13.8	16.9
Number of observations					
All households		905	854	405	678
White households		547	611	290	461
Black households		184	175	85	178

if one examines the portfolio groups for Whites, there is more of a suggestion of substitution effect than one sees for Blacks. For example, among White families with the SI portfolio, 29.4 percent do not have a pension, yet among Black families holding this portfolio, only 4.6 percent do not have a pension in the family. This may be evidence of the presence of a substitution effect operating for Whites, while it is the wealth scale effect that mostly operates for Blacks. Stocks are likely to be held primarily to build retirement savings, since one typically must hold them long-term in order to realize substantial gains.

THE RELATIONSHIP BETWEEN NONPENSION WEALTH & PENSION COVERAGE

How much nonpension wealth do families have conditional on pension coverage? Table 8.8 allows us to answer this question. Across all married couples, those without a pension tend to have greater mean wealth than

TABLE 8.8.   Mean (median) Net Wealth among Married Couples (in thousands)

| | Pension Position | | | |
	No Pension Mean (median)	Only Head Has Pension Mean (median)	Only Wife Has Pension Mean (median)	Both have Pension Mean (median)
Total	324.0	387.0	259.0	291.0
	(87.0)	(136.0)	(128.0)	(123.0)
Age of head				
30–44	192.0	206.0	171.0	212.0
	(45.0)	(90.0)	(63.0)	(90.0)
45–59	462.0	606.0	338.0	362.0
	(159.0)	(182.0)	(197.0)	(175.0)
Race of head				
White	410.0	430.0	285.0	316.0
	(143.0)	(154.0)	(144.0)	(134.0)
Black	45.0	79.0	134.0	132.0
	(5.0)	(39.0)	(70.0)	(52.0)
Years of education				
No high school degree	83.0	85.0	178.0	77.0
	(29.0)	(31.0)	(82.0)	(39.0)
High school degree	216.0	180.0	175.0	147.0
	(88.0)	(73.0)	(85.0)	(97.0)
Some college	277.0	432.0	323.0	207.0
	(94.0)	(97.0)	(160.0)	(105.0)
College degree or more	742.0	549.0	345.0	462.0
	(305.0)	(259.0)	(200.0)	(210.0)
Number of observations	905	854	405	678

families in which both spouses have a pension and families in which only the wife has a pension. This provides some suggestion of a substitution effect across the holdings of married couples.[12] It suggests that families who hold savings in a retirement asset (a pension) substitute this form of saving for other forms. The story does not hold consistently by race, however. For Whites, families with no pension tend to have greater wealth holdings than families with pension coverage (though when compared with families in which only the head has coverage, the level of wealth is close to even). This is somewhat consistent with the presence of a substitution effect. For Blacks however, families with no pension in the portfolio have a substantially lower level of wealth than those with pension coverage, particularly those families in which both spouses have pensions. This is more suggestive of a wealth scale effect than a substitution effect. Further, this scale effect for Blacks fits with an interpretation of more intragroup inequality among Blacks than among Whites. It may simply be just another reflection of the way that Blacks who do "poorly" really fare badly. We also see evidence consistent with a substitution effect for the high-school-educated families and the families in which the head has at least a college degree.

At the median, the patterns change somewhat. Table 8.8 shows that the median level of wealth for married couples with no pension is smaller than the median level of wealth for those that have pensions. When disaggregating by race, one finds that median White wealth among married couples with no pension ($143,000) is slightly lower than it is for those in which the head (only) has a pension ($154,000). However, it is comparable to that held by married families in which it is only the wife that has a pension. Among Black families we continue to see evidence of a scale effect. That is, even at the median, Black families with no pension have substantially less wealth than those that do have pensions.

MULTIVARIATE REGRESSION ANALYSIS

To isolate the effects of different aspects of families' portfolio structure on whether a family has a pension, we present results from logistic regression models analyzing pension participation at the family level. The first set of results come from an ordered logistic regression model in which the dependent variable takes on a value of zero if neither the head nor the wife has a pension, a value of one if only one spouse has a pension, and a value of two if both the head and the wife have pensions. Four different specifications of the model were implemented. The results are presented in the first four columns of table 8.9. The final column of table 8.9 reports the results from a binomial logistic model of pension plan participation for family heads.

Table 8.9 shows that Black families appear to have a higher propensity to participate in pension plans compared with White families. However, the difference progressively decreases as one adds controls for portfolio composition, as well as job characteristics of the head and wife. The variables that are most important in bringing about the reduction are whether the head or wife is self-employed, whether the head or wife has

TABLE 8.9.   Logistic Models

Variable	A. Dependent Variable: 0 = Neither Have Pension 1 = Either Head or Wife Have Pension 2 = Both Have Pension				B. Dependent Variable Head's Pension 0/1
Intercept 1	−9.128***	−9.390***	−9.456***	−9.362***	−8.105***
Intercept 2	−6.984***	−7.157***	−7.037***	−6.720***	
D White	−0.604***	−0.576***	−0.410***	−0.309**	−0.441**
D Other	−1.101***	−1.222***	−1.177***	−1.020***	−1.089***
Log of income	0.863***	0.765***	0.702***	0.632***	0.711***
Log of wealth	−0.083**	0.024	0.068	0.091**	0.118**
Age (head)	0.006	0.005	0.002	−0.002	−0.008
D No high school degree (head)	−0.778***	−0.799***	−0.645***	−0.507**	−0.912***
D High school degree (head)	−0.103	−0.134	−0.238*	−0.255*	−0.625***
D Some college (head)	0.170	0.128	0.123	0.083	−0.208
D Business		−0.994***	−0.406***	0.048	−0.256
D Real estate		−0.049	0.005	0.033	0.216
D Stocks (including stocks in IRA)		−0.196*	−0.152	−0.249**	−0.198
D Other valuable assets		0.045	0.033	0.103	0.042
D Checking/savings		0.533***	0.529***	0.587***	0.515**
D Self-employed (head)			−0.922***	−1.362***	−2.224***
D Government job (head)			0.792***	0.638***	1.675***
D Job is union covered (head)			0.986***	0.995***	2.125***
D White collar (head)			−0.063	−0.033	−0.126
D Construction industry (head)			−0.214	−0.150	−0.485**
D Part-time (head)			−0.379	−0.415	−1.213***
D Self-employed (wife)				−0.937***	0.510**
D Government job (wife)				0.867***	−0.283*
D Job union covered (wife)				0.727***	−0.471**
D White collar (wife)				0.400***	−0.282*
D Construction industry (wife)				−0.922**	−0.397
D Part-time (wife)				−0.711***	0.599***
D Wife has pension					0.624***

Note: Sample for table includes married couples with both head and wife employed. In the column for variable names, D stands for "dummy."

*Denotes significance at 10% level
**Denotes significance at 5% level
***Denotes significance at 1% level

a government job, and whether the wife is employed part-time. While a priori one might expect Black families to be disadvantaged relative to Whites in terms of having a pension, perhaps because one sees so much disadvantage elsewhere—in lower rates of bank account ownership, stock ownership, and other forms of saving, for example—the finding that Blacks have slightly greater likelihood of having pension coverage than Whites do is consistent with a job selection story. It may be the case that Black families are more likely than Whites are to seek out or choose "good" jobs with pensions when all other characteristics of the job are comparable. Note, however, that because pension benefits are usually proportional to income, the fact that Blacks, compared with Whites, appear to have a comparable or higher probability of pension plan *participation* is not expected to translate into a higher level of pension *wealth* for Blacks relative to Whites. Instead, the value of pension holdings for Black families is likely to be lower than it is for White families because of the underlying income gap that exists between Black and White families.

Table 8.9 also indicates that Black families have higher rates of pension coverage than families in the "other" category, which is predominately made up of Latino families. This is consistent with the findings in the existing literature that suggest that Latinos lag behind both Blacks and Whites in terms of pension coverage. (See table 8.1 for example.) Table 8.9 also reveals that the pension participation decision appears to be related to aspects of household portfolio structure. The presence of a checking or savings account in the family portfolio appears to be a strong predictor of pension coverage. This may due to a learning effect, as a bank account may indicate a high level of financial awareness in a household. Or the association between pension coverage and having a bank account may suggest that technological changes have created a situation in which having a bank account is akin to a job attribute, as many employers pay wages and salaries mostly or exclusively through direct deposit. Employers who use this system of payment may be the ones who are also more likely to offer pension plans (particularly DC plans, which also are based on technological developments—those allowing automatic payroll deductions).

The apparent relation between pensions and transaction account ownership also raises interesting questions about whether the workplace might be starting to become a sphere in which economic learning occurs (i.e., a place for financial education and socialization). In recent years there has been a growing body of research on peer effects and learning, as scholars seek to determine why participation in company-sponsored DC plans appears to raise aggregate saving. A natural question to ask is whether companies' policies toward direct deposit might have similar educational effects. Discussion of an employer's direct deposit policy may occur and raise an employee's understanding of the banking sector.

Another portfolio element that is related to pension participation is stocks. The *negative* sign for the coefficient on this variable suggests possible substitution between stocks and pension holdings in household portfolios. Finally, job characteristics have a particularly strong effect on pension participation, as one might expect. The inclusion of the self-employment variable (D SELF-EMPLOYED) changes the coefficient on owning a business (D BUSINESS) from significantly negative to small and insignificant. This suggests that pensions may be more an aspect of employment and less subject to as much choice as holding traditional elements of a household portfolio.

The final column of the table reveals that the head's and wife's pensions appear to be complements in household portfolios. A head is *more* likely to have a pension when the wife has one, as seen in the positive coefficient on "D WIFE HAS PENSION." Interestingly however, the coefficients on the measures of a wife's job characteristics point to some substitution between head and wife pensions. A wife's having a unionized job, or a government job, or a white-collar job—all instances in which pension coverage is likely to be present—reduces the head's probability of having a pension.

CONCLUSION

This chapter examines the ways that families structure their wealth portfolios and the degree to which pensions are part of families' strategies for saving. In analyzing household wealth holdings by focusing on the different forms in which wealth is held, the chapter presents a novel perspective on racial differences, and by merging in information about pensions, it presents a broader view of family holdings than is typically presented in the literature. The existing literature's finding that Black families have less wealth, on average, than White families is *echoed* in our finding that Black families also have a tendency to hold fewer assets and less complex portfolios than White families, on average. However, we find that when one considers pensions as another device for saving, one finds that the portrait of disadvantage is less clear. While analyses of individual asset-ownership rates (such as for bank accounts or stock) routinely find that Blacks are less likely to own any given asset than Whites are, such disparity is not so apparent with pensions. Our findings indicate that among married couples Black families are not less likely to possess pensions than White families are.

We also find some evidence that Black and White families incorporate pensions into their portfolios in different ways. For White families there is evidence suggesting the presence of a substitution effect between pensions and nonpension wealth holdings. For Black families there appears to be more of a scale effect, with families that have pensions also having a tendency to have greater nonpension wealth than those without pensions (rather than trading off pensions and other forms of saving).

While our regressions accounting for the role of job characteristics and other variables in predicting pension coverage cannot address the relationship between firm size and pension coverage—a relationship that is complex and that might be expected to lead to a somewhat wider net Black/White differential if firm size were included as a predictor—they do shed light on the connection between different elements of the household portfolio and having a pension. Bank account ownership is positively correlated with pension coverage, and as one might expect, owning a business or being self-employed is negatively associated with having a pension, though accounting for the latter subsumes the effect of the former. For stocks there is limited evidence suggesting that families view pensions and stocks as substitutes for each other. Future research will examine the relationship between directly held stock and stock held as part of DC pension plans to further investigate the hypothesis that there might be substitution between pensions and other elements of the household portfolio.

Our finding that Black families typically hold simpler portfolios than White families do has interesting potential policy implications. If a more basic portfolio structure implies a lack of financial sophistication, particularly if it means that some groups have less experience navigating the terrain of the stock market, one has to wonder how the ongoing switch toward DC pension plans (which shift primary responsibility for asset selection and risk onto the worker) is likely to affect families' prospects for accumulating sufficient retirement savings and, ultimately, their retirement outcomes. Additionally, one has to wonder how families that currently hold simple portfolios are likely to be affected if social security is privatized, and whether it would be necessary to accompany any privatization efforts with educational or information programs designed to raise financial literacy.

NOTES

1. In his analysis of data from the Consumer Union Survey, Cagan (1965) found that those covered by pensions had a nonpension saving rate of 8.7 percent, while those not covered by pensions had a saving rate of only 7.7 percent.

2. Under a DB plan, the employer promises to pay the worker a fixed percentage of his or her annual earnings during retirement. In the typical DC plan, the employer makes contributions to a fund set up on behalf of the employee provided that the employee also contributes to it, and the amount of resources that the employee has available for the retirement years depends upon the employee's investment decisions. The employee bears the responsibility for investing the funds wisely and for ensuring that the funds grow large enough that the total value of accumulated sums is adequate to meet his or her needs during retirement. (See Wolff 2003 for additional details about the structure of pensions.)

3. Even and MacPherson's 1994 data have been converted into 1992 dollars using the consumer price index for urban consumers.

4. McGarry and Davenport (1998) find that the fraction of wealth held by the bottom 30 percent increases by 1 percentage point, while the fraction held by the top 30 percent falls by about 5.5 percentage points when one compares the distribution of net worth with the distribution of total private wealth. (Total private wealth is the sum of pension wealth and nonpension net worth.)

5. In tables presenting the wealth distribution by decile, the authors show that the addition of pension wealth does not substantially change the percentage of non-White households at the bottom, top, or middle of the distribution.

6. In a more recent analysis of data from the National Compensation Survey, Purcell (2004) reports that in 2003, among those with pension coverage, 24 percent of full-time *private sector* employees had DB plans, while 40 percent participated in DC plans. And analyses from the Bureau of Labor Statistics (BLS) indicate that in 2003 about 40 percent of private industry workers participated in DC plans, while 20 percent participated in DB plans. These figures can be compared with the situation in 1991, at which time the BLS's analysis indicates that about one-third of private industry workers participated in each type of plan (see BLS 2004).

7. Many companies require employees to work for the company for a certain period of time before they become eligible for pension coverage.

8. Economic theory identifies four primary motives for saving: (1) saving for retirement or consumption-smoothing purposes, (2) the precautionary motive, (3) saving to acquire an indivisible good, and (4) the bequest motive. For additional discussion of these theories see Browning and Lusardi 1996.

9. Our findings here are consistent with findings elsewhere in the literature in analyses of coverage at the individual level. Our findings at the

family level show somewhat smaller race differences in possessing pensions than is found by others. This may be due to the fact that many of the papers in the existing literature focus on older families and are therefore analyzing a generation that entered the workforce in the early 1950s and 1960s when pensions were beginning to become a staple of compensation packages. Because our sample includes families headed by younger individuals, we may be capturing the effects of increased coverage once pensions became standard. For example, the studies by McGarry and Davenport (1998) and Choudhury (2002), discussed earlier, use HRS data covering families with heads or wives ages 51–61 in 1992. These are people who are likely to have begun their work lives sometime between about 1950 and 1960.

10. This table is available from the authors upon request.

11. Research in other areas finds that there is significant intragroup in equality among Blacks (chap. 3 and Wolff 1994, for example).

12. Families in which only the head has a pension have a net worth of about $387,000, on average, which is slightly higher than the $324,000 held by families with no pension, so here the aforementioned pattern does not hold.

REFERENCES

Aizcorbe, Ana, Arthur Kennickell, and Kevin B. Moore. 2003. "Recent Changes in U.S. Family Finances: Evidence from the 1998 and 2001 Survey of Consumer Finances." *Federal Reserve Bulletin,* January, 1–32.

Bertraut, C. C., and Martha Starr-McCluer. 2002. "Household Portfolios in the United States." In *Household Portfolios.* Cambridge, MA: MIT Press, 181–217.

Bloom, David, and Richard Freeman. 1992. "The Fall in Private Pension Coverage in the United States." *American Economic Review* 82 (2): 539–45.

Browning, Martin, and Annamaria Lusardi. 1996. "Household Saving: Micro Theories and Micro Facts." *Journal of Economic Literature* 34 (4): 1797–1855.

Bureau of Labor Statistics. 2004. "Chart: Percent of Private Industry Workers Participating in Retirement Plans, Selected Periods, 1990–2003," *Compensation and Working Conditions Online.* July 28, 2004 posting http//:www.bls.gov/opub/cwc (accessed October 14, 2004).

Cagan, Philip. 1965. "The Effect of Pension Plans on Aggregate Saving: Evidence from a Sample Survey." Occasional Paper no. 95, National Bureau of Economic Research. New York and London: Columbia University Press.

Choudhury, Sharmila. 2002. "Racial and Ethnic Differences in Wealth and Asset Choices." *Social Security Bulletin* 64 (4): 1–15.

Duflo, Esther, and Emmanuel Saez. 2000. "Participation and Investment Decisions in a Retirement Plan: The Influence of Colleagues' Choices." National Bureau of Economic Research Working Paper no. 7735, June.

Even, William, and David MacPherson. 2003. "Racial and Ethnic Differences in Pension Wealth." *Research in Labor Economics* 22: 205–27.

———. Forthcoming. "Why Do Black and Hispanic Workers Have Low Pension Saving?" *Quarterly Review of Economics and Finance.* (Manuscript July 2003, Florida State University.)

Friedberg, Leora, and Michael T. Owyang. 2002. "Not Your Father's Pension Plan: The Rise of 401(k) and Other Defined Contribution Plans." *Federal Reserve Bank of St. Louis Economic Review,* January/February, 23–34.

———. 2003. "Explaining the Evolution of Pension Structure and Job Tenure." Federal Reserve Bank of St. Louis Working Paper no. 2002-022C.

Guskova, Elena, F. Thomas Juster, and Frank P. Stafford. 2004. "Trends and Turbulence: Allocations and Dynamics of American Family Portfolios, 1984–2001," Paper presented at the Jerome Levy Economics Institute's Conference on "International Perspectives on Household Wealth," October 17–18, 2003.

Hewitt Associates. 2004. "Hewitt Study Shows Most U.S. Employees May Need to Work Longer and Save More for Retirement." Press release, June 28.

Hong, H., J. D. Kubik, and J. C. Stein. 2004. "Social Interaction and Stock Market Participation." *Journal of Finance* 59 (1): 137–63.

Hurst, Erik, Ming Ching Luoh, and Frank P. Stafford. 1998. "The Wealth Dynamics of American Families, 1984–94." *Brookings Papers on Economic Activity* 1: 267–337.

Juster, Thomas, James Smith, and Frank Stafford. 1999. "The Measurement and Structure of Household Wealth." *Labour Economics* 6 (2): 253–75.

Kennickell, Arthur, and Annika Sunden. 1997. "Pensions, Social Security, and the Distribution of Wealth." Board of Governors of the Federal Reserve Bank Working Paper no. 1997-55, October.

Maki, Dean. 2001. "Financial Education and Private Pensions." In *Private Pensions and Public Policies,* ed. William Gale, John Shoven, and Mark Warshawsky. Washington, DC: Brookings Institution Press.

McGarry, Kathleen, and Andrew Davenport. 1998. "Pensions and the Distribution of Wealth." In *Frontiers in the Economics of Aging,* ed. David Wise. Chicago: University of Chicago Press.

Oliver, Melvin, and Thomas Shapiro. 1995. *Black Wealth/White Wealth: A New Perspective on Racial Inequality.* New York: Routledge.

Poterba, James. 2001. "Taxation and Portfolio Structure: Issues and Implications." In *Household Portfolios,* ed. Guiso Luigi, Michael Haliassos, and Tullio Jappelli, 103–42. Cambridge, MA: MIT Press.

Poterba, James, Steven Venti, and David Wise. 1996. "How Retirement Savings Programs Increase Savings." *Journal of Economic Perspectives* 10 (Fall): 91–112.

———. 2004. "The Transition to Personal Accounts and Increasing Retirement Wealth: Macro and Micro Evidence." In *Perspectives on the Economics of Aging,* ed. David Wise. Chicago: University of Chicago Press.

Purcell, Patrick. 2004. *Pension Sponsorship and Participation: Summary of Recent Trends.* CRS Report for Congress no. RL30122, September. Washington, DC: Congressional Research Service.

Wolff, Edward. 1994. "Trends in Household Wealth in the United States, 1962–1983 and 1983–1989." *Review of Income and Wealth* 40 (2): 143–75.

———. 2003. "The Devolution of the American Pension System: Who Gained and Who Lost." *Eastern Economic Journal* 29 (4): 477–95.

IV Wealth Effects & Communities

9 Banking & Wealth Accumulation in the Asian American Community

Questions & Evidence from Los Angeles

GARY DYMSKI, LISA MOHANTY, & WEI LI

Several recent studies (Conley 1999; Massey and Denton 1993; Oliver and Shapiro 1997) have highlighted the dramatic inequality in wealth between Blacks and Whites in the United States and have argued that this wealth divide is fundamental in the dynamics of Black/White inequality and discrimination. As dramatic as this gap is, it represents only a partial racial/ethnic wealth mapping for the nation as a whole, for many regions in the United States are well into a transition from being a nation with bipolar racial-ethnic divides to regions with a multiethnic tableau.

This transition reflects, in part, the growth of individuals and families with multiple ethnic and racial affiliations. It is also due to the rapidly growing numbers of Latino and Asian Americans. The growing Hispanic-origin, or Latino, population has attracted more attention, in part because of this community's larger size—33 million persons, or 11.7 percent of all Americans recorded in the 2000 census. But the Asian American population has also become a significant component of the national population—10.2 million persons, 3.6 percent of the 2000 total. And between the 1990 and 2000 censuses, the growth rate of the Asian American population was faster than that of any other—48.3 percent, slightly ahead of the 47.8 percent growth rate for Latinos.[1]

These statistical trends suggest that a broader framework of information on wealth disparities is overdue; in particular, Latinos and Asian

Americans need to be brought into the analysis. This chapter focuses on the role of Asian-owned banking in wealth accumulation in Asian American communities. We begin with an initial survey of the data resources currently available regarding Asian Americans and wealth relative to other racial/ethnic groups in the United States. Not only are Asian Americans prominent in the transformation of the U.S. racial/ethnic context but their situations are significant because they are often viewed as a "model minority," showing the way for other ethnic groups.

The data on Asian American wealth holdings, unfortunately, are fragmentary. The data required for an overall evaluation are not yet in hand. Many of the standard measures used to examine Black-White wealth disparities cannot be calculated for Asian Americans because the samples drawn are not large enough to permit the calculation of reliable and publishable statistics.

In the case of Asian Americans (as, indeed, for other racial/ethnic groups), this limitation is worsened by the remarkable diversity of the Asian American population. Contrary to the model minority myth, Ong (1993) has shown that poverty is an especially serious problem for some subpopulations among Asian Americans. And as his work illustrates, Asian Americans are made up of a complex set of subpopulations.[2] The histories and backgrounds of Vietnamese, Chinese, Japanese, Korean, and other groups are extremely disparate. Further, even the circumstances of members of individual ethnic groups can vary widely. Note, to take one example, the varieties of Vietnamese American experience: from Texas fishing communities to District of Columbia émigrés to Southern California multitiered communities.

Unfortunately, the fragmentary data on Asian American wealth are not rich enough to permit us to even begin capturing this complexity in statistical terms. Instead, this chapter explores wealth and wealth building for the Asian American community broadly, particularly examining home-purchase-loan approval, the development of Asian American banking, and Asian-owned banks as a collective asset.

The following section sets out, as a point of reference, a framework specifying what data would ideally permit a deep and detailed analysis of wealth and wealth building in any given racial/ethnic community. The next section of this chapter reviews existing statistical data on the income/wealth circumstances of Asian Americans in the United States. This chapter then discusses the one area in which substantial research about wealth accumulation in the Asian American community has been done: the development of the Asian American banking sector in Los Angeles County. This portion of our exploration begins with brief discussions of the role of banks in community economic development and, in turn, of ethnic banks' specific contributions in this area. We then report some specifics on Asian American banking in Los Angeles, with particular attention to the Chinese American banks in this metropolis. Los Angeles County is a privileged location for this closer look, both because of the density and dynamism of its Asian population (second highest to San Francisco, in absolute numbers, among U.S. counties).[3] The chapter ends with a comparison of non-White-owned banks in the Asian American and African American communities.

CONCEPTUALIZING WEALTH BUILDING IN A U.S. ETHNIC COMMUNITY

Given the overwhelming data limitations that affect the other portions of this chapter, we begin by spelling out very schematically what data we would like to have, in order to understand the situation of different ethnic communities with respect to their members' wealth and wealth accumulation. What is it that we would like to know?

To begin, we would like detailed information about the structure of the ethnic community's wealth holdings at any point in time; the links between income generation in the community and wealth accumulation or decumulation therein; and the interactions between individuals, firms, and institutions in income-wealth processes. While information about these items is now unavailable for any ethnic community in the United States, it is worthwhile to elaborate on these different elements of prospective knowledge.

First, consider what we would like to know about the structure of wealth for members of a given ethnic group. Keep in mind that residential segregation—whether involuntary or voluntary—is a defining element for virtually every U.S. ethnic non-White population. Consequently, we can conceptualize an ethnic community—a spatial area in which members of any given ethnic group are concentrated—on the one hand, and individual members of an ethnic group, on the other hand. The members of a given ethnic group all possess wealth assets (or liabilities) to a greater or lesser extent. These wealth assets have two crucial characteristics: first, they are held in either liquid or illiquid forms; second, they are based either in the ethnic group area of principal spatial concentration or elsewhere (that is, "offshore"). Assets are liquid when they can be converted into cash quickly, at little cost, and with certainty; illiquid assets are by contrast not readily convertible into cash, can only be converted into cash on demand at a deep discount (in most cases), and may fluctuate in value widely from the price for which they were purchased. Investment in illiquid assets is generally considered irreversible because only a portion of the funds put into these assets can be recaptured, and then at substantial cost in value and time.

At any point in time, there is a definite distribution of wealth assets for members of any ethnic group, paralleling (but not reducing to) its income distribution. This distribution is what is captured in the statistics summarized in the following section. However, the wealth accumulation and decumulation processes moves through time. So in addition to snapshots at a point in time, we ideally like to know about the movement of asset values through time. This element of economic processes is even more poorly captured than the point-in-time measurement of wealth assets, if that is possible. Gains or losses from holding assets are either excluded from calculations or included in net calculations of income or loss.

However, this hides the problem of what happens to the value of different types of assets as they move through time. This problem is interlinked with that of the movements of population and money into (or out of) the community, which includes the linked problem of the extent to which income circulates within the community when it is respent. Further, because individuals with specific racial/ethnic backgrounds are tied by family, by residential choice or constraint, or by business location to areas with concentrations of the same racial/ethnic population, and because most individuals hold some amount of illiquid assets linked to their communities of origin and/or residence, then the time trajectory of specific racial/ethnic individuals is not independent of the broader trajectory of those individuals' racial/ethnic communities.* Can individuals in a community generally improve their rates of return by investing their assets in illiquid, community-based assets whose value is linked to the values of other assets owned by other, independent economic agents? Or is the only "rational" choice to shield one's assets from such neighborhood effects, as these are likely to merely detract from asset value?

These are questions that arise when analyzing wealth building in

---

*Robles, in chapter 10, also explores a community-based model to understand Latino wealth accumulation [Editors].

communities of color. Most of them remain unanswered because we lack reliable, robust data about wealth holdings, particularly of Asian Americans. In addition, it is important to note that simply an accurate listing of the dollar value of the assets owned by every individual at every point in time will not tell investigators everything they would ever want to know about racial/ethnic wealth creation. Some mysteries will remain, with keys to unlock them appearing only when more complete and imaginative data collection and analysis are undertaken.

MEASURING ASIAN AMERICANS' INCOME & WEALTH: AVAILABLE EVIDENCE

As noted, available data on the economic circumstances of Asian Americans either at present or over time are fragmentary, at best. Changes in ethnic/racial classifications make it impossible to accurately assess changes over time.[4] Statistically, according to the 2000 decennial U.S. Census, the Asian American population is younger than Whites, but older than African Americans; the Hawaiian and Pacific Islander population, by contrast, has an age profile more like that of Blacks.[5] Only 53 percent of Asian households are home owners, versus 71 percent of White households; by contrast, approximately 45 percent of both Black and Hawaiian/ Pacific Islander households are home owners. Both Asians and Hawaiian/ Pacific Islander households are larger, on average, than Black and White households (the averages for household size are, respectively, 3.1, 3.6, 2.7, and 2.5). Further, available data reveal that the situation of Asian Americans varies tremendously across regions and even within subareas in the United States.[6] Ong (2004) has pointed out other aspects of these changing demographic circumstances: Asian Americans are more likely to be foreign-born and are more dispersed across the nation.

Table 9.1 (subdivided into *A, B,* and *C*) summarizes recent aggregate statistics for Asian Americans regarding income, home ownership, and business ownership. In *A,* data for the 1990 and 2000 decennial U.S. censuses suggest a substantial gap between Whites and Asian Americans (as for Latinos and Blacks) in the percentage of home owners. The data for 2000 suggest that homes owned by Asian Americans are often worth more than those owned by Whites. Asians' median household income is higher than that for Whites as of 2000, and well above the income levels for other non-Whites. At the same time, Asian American per capita income has been below that for Whites in both 1990 and 2000. The difference is

TABLE 9.1. Summary Census Data on Income, Home Ownership, and Business Ownership, 1990–2000

A: Income and Home Ownership Comparisons by Race

	Whites	Blacks	% of Whites	Hispanic Origin	% of Whites	Asian	% of Whites
				1990 Decennial Census			
Number of individuals (U.S.)	199,827,064	29,930,524	15.0	21,900,089	11.0	7,226,986	3.6
Number of households (U.S.)	76,959,531	9,919,313	12.9	5,822,000	7.6	1,982,867	2.6
% Home owners	68.2	43.3	63.5	42.4	62.2	52.2	76.5
Per capita income	$15,687	$8,859	56.5	$8,400	53.5	$13,638	86.9
				2000 Decennial Census			
Number of individuals (U.S.)	211,460,626	34,658,190	16.4	35,305,818	16.7	10,242,998	4.8
Number of households (U.S.)	83,764,021	12,055,082	14.4	9,222,402	11.0	3,130,263	3.7
% Home owners	71.3	46.3	64.9	45.7	64.1	53.4	74.9
Median household income (1999)	$44,687	$29,423	65.8	$33,676	75.4	$51,908	116.2
Per capita income	23,918	14,437	60.4	12,111	50.6	21,823	91.2
Median house value (home owners)	$122,800	$80,600	65.6	$105,600	86.0	$199,300	162.3

B: Median Income of Asian Americans, by Country of Origin, 1999

	China	Korea	Vietnam	India	Filipino	Japanese	Other
Median household income (1999)	$51,444	$40,037	$45,085	$63,669	$60,570	$52,060	$47,716
% of White household income	115.1	89.6	100.9	142.5	135.5	116.5	106.8

C: Business Ownership and Race, 1992 and 1997 Economic Censuses

	Nonminority[a]	Blacks	% of Non-minority	Latin	% of Non-minority	Asian/ Pacific Islander	% of Non-minority
				1992 Economic Census			
Number of businesses (U.S.)	15,166,187	620,912	4.1	862,605	5.7	603,439	4.0
Average revenue per business	$205,690	$51,900	25.2	$89,100	43.3	$159,200	77.4
				1997 Economic Census			
Number of businesses (U.S.)	17,598,644	823,499	4.7	1,199,896	6.8	1,199,896	6.8
% Growth in businesses, 1992–97	13.5	32.6		39.1		98.8	
Average revenue per business	$1,016,687	$86,500	8.5	$155,200	15.3	$336,200	33.1
	394.3	66.7		74.2		111.2	
Number of firms with paid employees	4,700,034	93,235	2.0	211,884	4.5	289,999	6.2
Average employees per business	21.6	7.7	35.6	6.6	30.3	7.6	35.1
Businesses per 10,000 households	2,286.7	830.2	36.3	2,061	90.1	6,051	264.6
Businesses with paid employees per 10,000 households	610.7	94.0	15.4	363.9	59.6	1,462.5	239.5

Source: All data are taken from published data for the 1990 and 2000 decennial censuses and the 1992–97 Economic Censuses.

[a]The "nonminority" business data shown in the first column of 1C have been generated by subtracting the three categories of minority business shown here from the "all business" total for the Economic Census. The resulting figures contain some minority businesses, notably those owned by Native Americans. However, the vast majority of businesses reported here are not minority owned.

explained by household size, which is larger for Asian Americans than for Whites.

In table 9.1, C presents data for White and non-White businesses in the 1992 and 1997 U.S. Economic Censuses and reveals that Asian/Pacific Islander firms tend to have larger revenue totals than those owned by African Americans and Latinos; they also are more likely to have paid employees. However, Asian/Pacific Islander firms are substantially smaller than those owned by Whites in terms of revenues and employees per firm. Combining Census 2000 data with 1997 Economic Census data suggests that Asian/Pacific Islander households have twice as many businesses as do White households, three times as many as Latino households, and seven times as many as Black households. Further, they are four times as likely as Latino households to have businesses with paid employees, and sixteen times as likely as Black households. And the number of Asian Pacific Islander businesses grew more quickly than did other businesses between 1992 and 1997.

Generally, the data shown in A and B in table 9.1 suggest that Asian Americans are prosperous on average and that their income and business-ownership levels have been rising. However, these data do not pertain directly to wealth. The national data sets and published literature that provide wealth statistics do not report much, if any, information on Asian American wealth. The data are not reliable, in great part because sample sizes are too small—far short of the number of observations obtained for other non-White populations to be statistically significant.[7] Increasing Asian American sample sizes in some of the 2001 surveys appears promising for future use of national data sets to analyze Asian American wealth, if the numbers increase. The general picture that has begun to emerge is that wealth levels are higher for Asian households than for other ethnic groups, sometimes including Whites.[8] These levels of advantage are approximately the same when the home equity value is excluded. Asian Americans have a slightly higher mean rate of home ownership than do Blacks or Latinos, but a lower rate than Whites. Ong and Patraporn (chap. 7) use information on the distribution of wealth from wave 3 of the 2001 panel of the Survey of Income and Program Participation (SIPP), which for the first time has a sufficient number of Asian American participants. They find that Asian Americans have the second-highest median net worth of $73,600 and median housing equity of $28,000 compared with levels of $101,700 and $54,000, respectively, for White non-Hispanic populations. The Ong and Patraporn chapter investigates the puzzling phenomenon that high Asian American household income has not translated into levels of wealth comparable to White Americans'.

Income levels appear to be more tightly bunched than wealth levels for Asian Americans, as is true for Blacks and Latinos. This suggests large differences in economic status among Asian Americans as a group. The available census data suggest that there is considerable diversity in economic status among Asian Americans (also noted by Ong and Patraporn). In table 9.1, *B* shows, first, that median household incomes are very different for different Asian American subgroups (Chinese, Japanese, Korean, Pacific Islanders, etc.). For several economic-status variables, table 9.2 depicts ratios of these variables for Asian/Pacific Islanders relative to the values of these same variables for Whites (shown, in every case, as percentages). Table 9.2 shows, for example, that Asian/Pacific Islander median home value in Los Angeles County was 95.3 percent of that for Whites in the 2000 census. This table reveals several points about the Asian/Pacific Islander community economic status. First, there is remarkable county-to-county variation in California (a state in which approximately four of every ten Asian Americans in the United States reside). In San Francisco, Asian/Pacific Islander median home value is just 79 percent of that of Whites, whereas in Sacramento this ratio equals 98.8 percent. In five of the six counties for which data are shown, median household incomes of Asians/Pacific Islanders are equal to (or even above) that of Whites; San Francisco is the exception, at 78 percent. Per capita incomes tell a different story: these are substantially below those for Whites in every case. This is consistent with the stylized fact mentioned above—Asian Americans have larger household units than the national average; further, it is consistent with the fact that this population has high rates of labor force participation. Home ownership rates are in most cases close to those for Whites; the San Francisco Asian/Pacific Islander community has by far the highest relative rate of home ownership. Interestingly, the relative percentage of Asian/Pacific Islander households who own homes (compared with Whites) declined slightly between 1990 and 2000 in three of the six counties depicted.[9]

ETHNIC BANKING & WEALTH BUILDING IN NON-WHITE COMMUNITIES

The fragmentary data reviewed here provide only hints of the point-in-time situation of Asian Americans relative to members of other ethnic groups in the United States. As noted in the preceding pages, however, extensive exploratory research has been done on the process of wealth building in the Asian American community—focusing specifically on the remarkable concentration of ethnic banks in Los Angeles County. This section and the next discuss non-White-owned banking as one potentially critical component of processes of wealth building in American ethnic communities.

Access to credit is widely recognized as vital for the development of lower-income communities. Credit markets link the past and future levels of income and wealth generated by a community's individuals and firms (Dymski 1995). Banks, in turn, are the key to ensuring that robust and sustainable levels of credit are available in any community.

There are several arguments for the special role of banks (that is, formal financial institutions whose charters permit them to accept deposits and make loans). First, every individual requires basic financial services such as cashing checks, making long-distance payments, and protecting savings. Financial institutions can provide their customers with liquidity services, allowing customers to conduct transactions more easily and cheaply; banks can also permit small savers and borrowers to avoid liquidity constraints and hold more optimal sets of financial and nonfinancial assets.

The presence of a bank contributes to community economic stability, while creating positive externalities by encouraging other retail business to locate there (Vaughn 1989). Banks increase the pedestrian flows sought by other businesses and can specialize in evaluating the credit risks of neighborhood businesses and individuals. Conversely, communities in which banks are absent are likely to have higher transactional and

TABLE 9.2. Ratio of Asian/Pacific Islander Values to Whites' Values, Selected California Counties, 2000 Census (percent)

	Los Angeles	Orange	Sacramento	San Diego	San Francisco	Santa Clara
Median value of home, for homeowner households	95.3	93.0	98.8	89.7	79.0	86.3
Median household income (1999 dollars)	98.0	94.3	95.5	103.0	78.4	108.3
Per capita income	75.3	67.9	70.4	69.9	46.2	74.4
Home ownership rate						
All households, 1990	95.5	96.4	96.9	92.8	129.7	97.7
All households, 2000	100.2	92.6	89.7	94.8	152.4	94.2

informational costs for local firms and residents. One key credit-market barrier is the greater difficulty of local residents in obtaining mortgage credit, leading to fewer home sales and lower home ownership. When fewer homes are owned and sold in an area, they become less liquid, and their value as collateral decreases, making it harder for small business owners to secure bank financing (Dymski 1995). So in the absence of a robust financial infrastructure, community asset values are jeopardized.

In this context, non-White banks historically emerged as a response to the inadequate banking infrastructure in communities of color and to the unfair credit practices of other banks and lenders, including discrimination and redlining.[10] African Americans and members of other racial/ethnic minorities began creating their own banks in the nineteenth century in response to their exclusion from mainstream financial markets (Dymski and Weems 2005).

ASIAN AMERICAN BANKING IN LOS ANGELES

Asian American–owned banks were first created in California in the 1890s, during a period in which White-owned banks were reluctant—or refused—to conduct banking business with Asians. These banks, established by Japanese Americans, all failed in the wake of the financial panic of 1907. In the 1960s, the story of Asian American banking began anew in California: some Japanese American credit associations were created, and the first Chinese American bank in Los Angeles, Cathay Bank, opened its doors in 1962. This first wave of Asian American banks was founded for the same category of reasons that has led to the founding of most African American–owned banks: that is, the exclusion of potential customers from participation in banking practices, because of either exclusionary rules or culturally insensitive practices (or both). Like Black-owned banks across the country, the institutions comprising this first wave of Asian American banks were small in the banking marketplace and operated in markets that usually operated under adverse economic conditions. In all these varieties of ethnic bank, customers were largely community-based, and these institutions primarily gathered deposits from, and lent to, members of the same ethnic community.

The Asian American banking sector in Los Angeles underwent renewed expansion as of the 1980s due to two reinforcing trends that especially impacted the Asian American community (and not other racial/ethnic communities in California): (1) the increasingly dense trans-Pacific trade in goods and services, which was accompanied by an increasing volume of cross-Pacific financial flows, and (2) a surge in immigration from Asia. Large numbers of Asians moved to California and to other locations in the United States—in some cases to work, earn money, and return home; in most cases to settle down and make a new life. Los Angeles became the leading gateway city for two of the most robust new flows of immigrants and economic migrants.

This new population surge was accompanied by the newcomers' financial capital inflows. The result was the creation of a new stage of economic development for much of the Asian community. The transformation has been most profound in Los Angeles County. The first expansion of Asian banking in Los Angeles involved a surge of Japanese-owned banks. While these banks were established as commercial banks under U.S. law, they largely represented the domestic arms of the huge, multinational Japanese banks that dominated global banking in the 1980s. During the same decade, a similar phenomenon occurred on a much smaller scale for the Korean community: a wave of Korean American banks was created, most of them owned by parent banking corporations in Korea. The Japanese banks were focused on the mainstream U.S. market and on the large Japanese multinationals engaged in trade with the United States. Korean banks opened offices in the heart of the Los Angeles Koreatown community and helped to orchestrate the growth of a vibrant commercial/industrial area. The Chinese American banking sector also exploded in size. Some institutions were created as stand-alone (FDIC-insured) banks in the United States by parent corporations in Taiwan (or elsewhere). Other institutions were created by immigrants from various points of the Chinese diaspora in East and Southeast Asia. Many overseas Chinese foreign banks opened nonbank offices in Los Angeles as well.[11]

The literature on Asian American urban economic development has focused primarily on these communities' marginal status, as exemplified in the sociological "ethnic enclave" model (see, for example, Light and Bonacich 1988). Lending circles and informal financial arrangements among ethnic minorities are well-known—they suggest the idea of ethnic economic development at the margins of the broader economy, orchestrated by members of lower-income ethnic communities.

However, contemporary Chinese communities are no longer confined to enclaves, and their financial institutions are formal banks, not "fringe banks." This shift from informal practices to the formation and expansion of formal institutions is attributable to shifting global movements of human and financial capital, the heterogeneity of this ethnic population and its businesses, and this population's increasingly dense transnational ties. The Asian American banking sector has continued to grow strongly in the past decade. This sector now encompasses eight Korean and twenty-four Chinese banks. Together with other ethnic banks in Los Angeles, this banking sector has grown into a sizeable financial force in Los Angeles.

Table 9.3 describes some aspects of the recent growth of the Los Angeles ethnic banking sector in the period 1994–2003. In 1994, ethnic bank branches made up 16 percent of all FDIC-insured bank branches in Los Angeles County; by 1999, this total had grown to 21 percent, before declining slightly to 19 percent of all Los Angeles bank branches at the end of 2003. Deposits at ethnic banks constituted a much smaller share of the countywide total in 1994 (12 percent), but by 2003 the ethnic-bank deposit total equaled 17 percent of that for all banks. Table 9.3 also depicts the composition of ethnic-bank deposits and bank branches by

TABLE 9.3. Ethnic and Nonethnic Bank Branches and Deposit Totals, Los Angeles County, 1994–2003, FDIC-Insured Banks Only

	1994 Data (12/31)		1999 Data (12/31)		2003 Data (12/31)	
	Branches	Deposits ($M)	Branches	Deposits ($M)	Branches	Deposits ($M)
All bank branches, LA County	1,643	128.4	1,475	132.1	1,536	179.5
All ethnic bank branches	270	15.1	307	24.5	288	30.1
			Percentage of Total			
All ethnic banks	16.4	11.7	20.8	18.6	18.8	16.8
Japanese banks	8.6	7.2	7.3	9.9	4.5	6.4
African American banks	0.7	0.2	0.9	0.3	0.7	0.2
Latino banks	0.5	0.3	1.4	1.2	1.3	1.1
Chinese banks	5.0	3.2	8.7	5.9	9.2	7.3
Korean banks	1.5	0.8	2.4	1.3	2.9	1.8

	Branches			Deposits		
	1994–99	1999–2003	1994–2003	1994–99	1999–2003	1994–2003
			Percentage of Growth			
All bank branches, LA County	−10.2	4.1	−0.1	2.9	35.9	0.4
All ethnic bank branches	6.7	−12.3	0.1	62.6	16.5	0.7
Japanese banks	−25.3	−83.9	−0.9	−3.4	−80.6	−0.8
African American banks	18.2	−15.4	0.0	14.5	4.5	0.2
Latino banks	122.2	0.0	1.2	276.7	18.3	3.5
Chinese banks	56.1	10.9	0.7	89.2	69.2	2.2
Korean banks	50.0	22.2	0.8	81.2	81.7	2.3

subcategory. Initially, Japanese-owned banks were by far the largest sector (9 percent of the county total), but closures and buyouts during the 1990s reduced this total to less than 5 percent by 2003. Chinese American banks grew from 5 percent of the Los Angeles County total in 1994 to 9 percent in 2003. Korean banks grew at approximately the same rate, climbing from 1.5 percent of all branches in 1994 to 3 percent in 2003. African American banks experienced significant growth between 1994 and 1999 but lost all of this gain by 2003, ending where they began a decade earlier, with 0.7 percent of all branches and just 0.2 percent of all deposits.

The articles cited in note 11 use extensive quantitative evidence and information derived from interviews to show how the Chinese American banks, in particular, have helped to coordinate and finance robust and sustained Asian American commercial and residential development in Los Angeles County, particularly in the Asian "ethnoburbs" (Li 1998) of the San Gabriel Valley.

Dymski and Mohanty (1999) contrast several subareas within Los Angeles County to evaluate the impact of ethnic bank behavior. One contrast involves differences between the two predominantly Asian American "ethnoburb" areas of San Gabriel Valley and the largely Latino area between them. The two Asian areas have a remarkably large concentration of bank branches, half of which are Asian ethnic banks; the Latino area in the middle has a paucity of branches and, instead, a large population of informal financial offices (check cashers, pawnbrokers, and loan offices). The two Asian areas have a high volume of applications for home-purchase loans, most registered by Asian American applicants, with a high proportion at Asian American banks and disproportionately few denials; by contrast, the Latino area has many fewer home-purchase-loan applications (relative to the available stock of single-family housing) and a much higher denial rate. The Dymski and Mohanty paper goes on to evaluate some portions of South Los Angeles in which African American banks are active.

There are some similarities between the activities of the Asian American banks in the San Gabriel Valley and the African American banks of South Los Angeles: both sets of banks focus on making loans in or near their areas of concentration, and both disproportionately accept applications from and loan to members of the same ethnic community. The difference is one of scale. As table 9.3 shows, the African American banks lack the size to move the market. Some of the ideas set out in the sec-

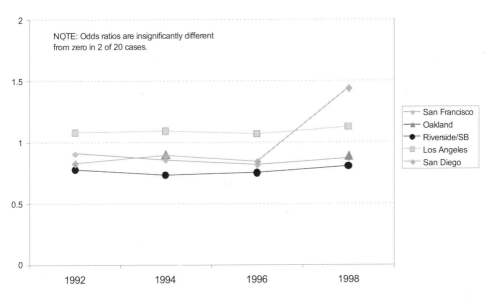

Fig. 9.1. Odds ratios for home-purchase-loan approval, Asian Americans, selected California cities, 1992–98

tion "Conceptualizing Wealth Building in a U.S. Ethnic Community" are pertinent here; for example, financing illiquid, irreversible assets is problematic when the lender lacks the capacity to affect the risk characteristics of those assets' neighborhood. Lenders in such a case—African American banks in South Los Angeles, in this instance—instead focus on picking winners within a relatively adverse (high-unemployment, slow-growth) environment; by contrast, the Asian American banks are able to focus on transforming their market environment.

Figure 9.1 provides some evidence in support of this last point. Figure 9.1 depicts the outcomes for one independent variable used in a model of mortgage-loan approval. Specifically, Dymski (2001) develops a probit model that assesses the impact of several variables on the probability of being approved for a home-purchase loan and applies this model to several metropolitan areas, including several in California.[12] Among the variables included in this model are dummy variables for applicant ethnicity. Since there are significant numbers of applicants of all racial/ethnic categories in California credit markets, Asian American applicants were given a separate designation. The impact of this racial designation on the probability of loan approval was then evaluated for four separate years (1992, 1994, 1996, and 1998), on a city-by-city basis. Figure 9.1

shows the results obtained for the Asian American dummy variable, using odds ratios derived from the estimated coefficients. An odds ratio depicts the impact of any given variable (in this case, Asian American status) on the probability being estimated. An odds ratio equal to one indicates that the variable in question has no effect on the outcome, an odds ratio of less than one (if statistically significant) indicates this variable has a negative impact (in this case, on the probability of loan approval), and an odds ratio greater than one indicates a positive impact.

In figure 9.1, eighteen of twenty odds ratios for the impact of being Asian American on loan approval are based on statistically significant coefficients. Only these eighteen odds ratios are shown (the two missing odds ratios are for Oakland in 1992 and 1996). Note that five odds ratios are positive, indicating a statistical advantage for Asian American loan applicants, and the remainder are negative, indicating a statistical disadvantage. Four of the five positive odds ratio scores are recorded for Los Angeles—the home of the robust Asian American banking sector depicted in table 9.3. Except for one San Diego coefficient, these equations find that in the other four cities depicted—none of which have numerically significant Asian American banking sectors—Asian American applicants are at a statistical disadvantage.

The same paper from which this figure is taken, as well as hundreds of others by many authors, finds that African Americans also are at a systematic statistical disadvantage in a model of home-purchase-loan approval. This finding, of course, is inconsistent with the notion of Asian Americans as a relatively prosperous racial/ethnic group. The difference for Los Angeles odds ratios suggests that, in some cases, ethnic banks may be a source of racial/ethnic wealth: in Los Angeles, Asian American banks arguably function as a collective asset that is maintained through the financial behavior of the rapidly growing Asian American residential and business communities. Whether this is a transitional phenomenon or a permanent feature of the growing Asian American community of Los Angeles remains to be determined.

CONCLUSION

This chapter necessarily concludes with a series of open questions and challenges. The data regarding Asian Americans and wealth are preliminary, fragmentary, and contradictory, in great part because of the small sample sizes. Examination of census statistics at the aggregate level similarly provides no consistent information about the relative economic circumstances of Asian Americans. Disaggregated data from the census only amplify the idea that Asian Americans' economic circumstances evidently vary widely from place to place within the United States. These differences may be traced to national differences within the Asian American grouping, differing amounts of time living in the United States, differing levels of education and skill, differences in opportunity structures in different regions, and so on.

One challenge emerges clearly from this chapter concerning statistical evidence about the relative income levels of Asian Americans in the United States. A second challenge concerns statistical evidence about the relative wealth of Asian Americans. In short, there is a clear need for much more substantial evidence about the economic and social circumstances of Asian Americans. This explosively growing portion of the U.S. residential population is heterogeneous and rapidly evolving. In the aggregate, statistics suggest that Asian Americans are a prosperous community, with high house values, high household incomes, and a high rate of business ownership. However, other fragmentary evidence suggests that some Asian Americans—including some proper subsets within this grouping—are worse off in income terms than other Americans. Both conclusions may well be true. Ong (2004) also concludes that 2000 census data lead to ambiguous conclusions regarding the relative socioeconomic status of Asian Americans.[13] In any case, publicly available statistics do not make it possible to illuminate the true extent of the socioeconomic circumstances of the entire Asian American population.

Another set of open questions concerns the current and potential role of ethnic banks in community economic development. A decade ago, Brimmer (1992) argued that African American–owned banks might be unable to finance sustained community economic development within the Black community. The research summarized here, to the contrary, suggests the opposite for Asian American banks in Los Angeles. It seems that this latter banking sector is able to underwrite wealth creation and asset accumulation for the communities it serves at a scale that is beyond the reach of the much smaller African American banking sector. In effect, one banking sector is primarily a place for storing wealth, and the other a place for financing wealth creation.

There are important, if fuzzy, implications of the ethnic banking scenario in Los Angeles for understanding wealth, inequality, and ethnicity. Following the discussion in the section "Conceptualizing Wealth Building in a U.S. Ethnic Community," one implication is that size matters. This point is illustrated in table 9.4. Table 9.4 contains some summary data on the ethnic business, residential, and banking populations for a selection of U.S. cities. Note first that the situation in Los Angeles is unique in several respects: its Asian American residential population is numerically large, and its Asian American ethnic banking sector is large relative to

TABLE 9.4.   Chinese and African American Residential, Business, and Bank Populations, Selected Metropolitan Areas, 2000

	New York CMSA	San Francisco CMSA	Los Angeles CMSA	San Diego MSA
Chinese American Data				
Population	503,347	468,736	408,239	166,382
Business establishments	58,767	42,525	53,623	1,915
Sales and receipts ($M)	18,548	23,011	27,859	669
Number of businesses per 1,000				
population	117	91	131	12
Bank branches	13	23	49	2
Chinese foreign bank offices	19	5	20	0
Chinese American population per				
Chinese American branch	38,719	20,380	8,331	83,191
African American Data				
Population	3,638,570	118,590	1,245,039	96,216
Bank branches	9	0	6	0
African American population per				
African American branch	404,286	0	207,507	0

	Chicago CMSA	Philadelphia CMSA	Houston CMSA	Atlanta MSA
Chinese American Data				
Population	68,879	42,959	48,537	22,564
Business establishments	5,703	3,732	5,657	2,625
Sales and receipts ($M)	5,121	620,666	3,033	1,097
Number of businesses per 1,000				
population	83	88	117	116
Bank branches	20	0	24	3
Chinese foreign bank offices	1	0	1	0
Chinese American population per				
Chinese American branch	3,444	0	1,941	7,521
African American Data				
Population	3,638,570	1,210,846	789,489	1,189,179
Bank branches	9	8	2	21
African American population per				
African American	404,286	151,356	394,745	56,628

Source: Population—Census 2000 Summary File 2 (SF 2) 100 Percent Data (single-race only); business establishments—1997 Economic Census; bank branch data—Federal Reserve Board list of minority-owned bank branches, March 31, 2004.

that of the residential population (as measured by ethnic bank branches per ethnic resident).[14] Two of the three cities in table 9.4 whose Asian American residential population is, like Los Angeles, very large (New York and San Diego) lack Asian American banking sectors of a similarly large scale, and two of the other cities in table 9.4 have a relatively large Asian American banking sector (Chicago and Houston) but a much smaller Asian American residential population.[15]

In addition to the point about scale, which itself requires further investigation, many additional questions crowd in: is the rise of the ethnic banking sector in Los Angeles linked exclusively to that city's status as an immigration gateway? Can this sector maintain its growth once the pace of immigration from Asia slows and/or once the pace of Asian nations' economic growth declines?

In conclusion, this chapter has reviewed the fragmentary data that currently exist on wealth and income and the Asian American community. Far more questions have been raised here than conclusions reached. Intriguing questions have been posed about the implications of the Los Angeles Chinese American banking experience for other groups' asset accumulation and wealth building. Only a great leap forward in the amount and quality of information about this rapidly growing and remarkably diverse racial/ethnic population will open the way to systematic progress on these important questions.

NOTES

1. These percentage-change figures are derived from official Census Bureau figures. They are computed only for persons who listed a single race for themselves in the 2000 census count (since the multiple-race option was not available in the 1990 census). Between 1990 and 2000, the overall population of the United States, as recorded in official census counts, grew 13.2 percent; the population of (single-race-only) Whites grew 5.9 percent; the population of Blacks, 15.6 percent; Hawaiians and Pacific Islanders, 9.3 percent.

2. Takaki (1994) has described the complex roots and substantial economic inequality among people. Discussion in this chapter sometimes refers to Asian Americans and sometimes includes Pacific Islanders as well. These two aggregates are often grouped together in statistical reporting. For convenience, the term *Asian American* will be employed, not *Asian Pacific Islander*. Since the Asian American population outnumbers that of Hawaiians and Pacific Islanders by twenty-five to one, the former term represents a more satisfactory shorthand term of reference.

3. The authors of this chapter have examined the dynamics of the Asian American and other non-White populations in Los Angeles from various perspectives: the shift of the Asian population base from downtown enclaves to

suburban communities (Li 1998), the interaction of gender and race/ethnicity in mortgage markets (Mohanty 2001), and the growth of ethnic banks in Los Angeles (see references in n. 11).

4. For example, Vietnamese Americans were classified as "other" (not Asian) in the 1970 census, while Asian Indians were classified as "White." Six response categories were used for Asians in the 1980 and 1990 census counts; the 2000 census included an additional category, "other Asian." Further, the 2000 census questionnaire asked respondents to report one or more races when this designation applied. See Barnes and Bennett 2002.

5. These statistics exclude census respondents who report multiple racial categories.

6. For example, Asian Americans' median income in Forsyth County, Georgia (the county with the largest percentage increase in Asian American population in the 1990–2000 period, 139 percent), was 29 percent higher than that of Whites in the same county; in DeKalb County, Georgia, Asian Americans' median income was 25 percent below that for Whites. Whites' median income was 17 percent higher in Forsyth County than in DeKalb County; Asian Americans' median income was 103 percent higher.

7. Less than 25 respondents to the wealth questions in the 1994 Panel Study of Income Dynamics (PSID), for example, are identified as Asian Americans, and less than 370 in the 2001 survey. *Leigh discusses the paucity and limitations of these data in several sections of chapter 1. See her sections on the specific data sets for discussion of their limitations for studying the wealth holdings of Asian American populations. And see her discussion of Asian American wealth [Editors].*

8. The latest data from the Survey of Income and Program Participation (SIPP), reported in chapter 7 by Ong and Patraporn, confirm this. In addition, Wolff (2004, 23 and table 18) reports that the Asian subcategory (which includes the "other" categories and Native Americans) in the Survey of Consumer Finances had the second-highest rate of stock ownership at 51.2 percent of households owning stocks in 2001, and the fastest growth of stock ownership of all groups (up from 17.5 in 1989 and 46.9 percent in 1998).

9. County-by-county data on median family and household income levels also reveal the large variation in the economic status of the Asian American population. Statistical measures of dispersion show that county-to-county variance for Asian Americans exceeds that for any other racial/ethnic grouping, based on Census 2000 data.

10. Caskey (1994) finds that communities with a majority of African American residents are less likely than other communities to have a local bank branch. African American and Latino communities are also disproportionately affected by bank closings (Vaughn 1989).

11. The history and institutional details of Asian American banking in Los Angeles are set out in Li et al. 2001 and in Li et al. 2002. The operations of Chinese foreign-bank offices in Los Angeles are analyzed in Dymski and Li 2004.

12. Other independent variables include the log of applicant income, loan value, presence or absence of a cosigner, median income in the census tract of the home being sought, and so on. For details see Dymski 2001.

13. In addition, Ong (2004) remarks on the "ambiguous picture" revealed by the 2000 census. Data on earnings for Asian Americans, when adjusted for education and experience levels, do not indicate any systematic evidence of discrimination in the labor market. And while there is some recorded evidence of discrimination in the housing market against Asian Americans (Turner and Ross 2003), evidence of residential discrimination does not show up in census data. Ong concludes by suggesting that the "existing race-based paradigm of civil rights" be set aside, when analyzing the circumstances of Asian Americans, and the discussion "reframe[d] . . . around the demographic realities of Asian Americans" (124).

14. In Los Angeles the ratio of Asian-owned businesses relative to the Asian population is, interestingly, the smallest among the eight metropolitan areas depicted, so for any racial/ethnic subpopulation, the key variables seem to be the relative sizes of the residential and banking populations.

15. These two cities' Asian American banking sectors are also dominated by a small number of multibranch ethnic banks; by contrast, Los Angeles has a large number of ethnic banks, each of which (with several exceptions) has relatively few branches.

REFERENCES

Barnes, Jessica, and Claudette Bennett. 2002. *The Asian Population: Census 2000 Brief.* C2KBR/01-16, February. Washington, DC: Bureau of the Census.

Brimmer, Andrew F. 1992. "The Dilemma of Black Banking: Lending Risks vs. Community Service." *Review of Black Political Economy* 20 (3): 5–29.

Caskey, John. 1994. *Fringe Banking: Check-Cashing Outlets, Pawnshops, and the Poor.* New York: Russell Sage Foundation.

Conley, Dalton. 1999. *Being Black, Living in the Red: Race, Wealth and Social Policy in America.* Berkeley: University of California Press.

Dymski, Gary.1995. "The Theory of Credit-Market Redlining and Discrimination: An Exploration." *Review of Black Political Economy* 23 (3): 37–74.

———. 2001. "Is Discrimination Disappearing? Racial Differentials in Access to Credit, 1992–1998." *International Journal of Social Economics* 28 (10/11/12): 1025–45.

Dymski, Gary, and Wei Li. 2004. "Financial Globalization and Cross-Border Co-movements of Money and Population: Foreign Bank Offices in Los Angeles." *Environment and Planning A* 36 (2): 213–40.

Dymski, Gary, and Lisa Mohanty. 1999. "Credit and Banking Structure: Insights from Asian and African-American Experience in Los Angeles." *American Economic Review Papers and Proceedings* 89 (2): 362–66.

Dymski, Gary, and Robert E. Weems, Jr. 2005. "Black-Owned Banks: Past, Present, and Future." In *African Americans in the U.S. Economy,* ed. Cecilia Conrad, John Whitehead, Patrick L. Mason, and James Stewart, 246–51. Lanhan, MD: Rowman and Littlefield Publishers.

Li, Wei. 1998. "Anatomy of a New Ethnic Settlement: The Chinese *Ethnoburb* in Los Angeles." *Urban Studies* 35 (3): 479–501.

Li, Wei, Gary Dymski, Yu Zhou, Carolyn Aldana, and Maria Chee. 2002. "Chinese American Banking and Community in Los Angeles County: The Financial Sector and Chinatown/Ethnoburb Development." *Annals of the American Association of Geographers* 92 (4): 777–96.

Li, Wei, Gary Dymski, Yu Zhou, and Maria Chee. 2001. "Banking on Social Capital in the Era of Globalization: Chinese Ethnobanks in Los Angeles." *Environment and Planning A* 33: 1923–48.

Light, Ivan, and Edna Bonacich. 1988. *Immigrant Entrepreneurs: Koreans in Los Angeles, 1965–82.* Berkeley: University of California Press.

Massey, Douglas S., and Nancy A. Denton. 1993. *American Apartheid: Segregation and the Making of the Underclass.* Cambridge: Harvard University Press.

Mohanty, Lisa. 2001. "Access to Credit: A Study of Nonwhite Women." Dissertation, Department of Economics, University of California, Riverside.

Oliver, Melvin L., and Thomas M. Shapiro. 1997. *Black Wealth, White Wealth: A New Perspective on Racial Inequality.* New York: Routledge.

Ong, Paul M., lead author. 1993. *Beyond Asian American Poverty: Community Economic Development Policies and Strategies.* Los Angeles, CA: Asian Pacific American Public Policy Institute, LEAP.

———. 2004. "Asian American Demographics and Civil Rights." *AAPI Nexus* 2 (1): 105–28.

Takaki, Ronald T. 1994. *A Different Mirror: A History of Multicultural America.* New York: Little, Brown, and Company.

Turner, Margery Austin, and Stephen L. Ross. 2003. "Discrimination in Metropolitan Housing Markets: Phase 2—Asians and Pacific Islanders." Mimeo, Department of Economics, University of Connecticut, Storrs.

Vaughn, John. 1989. "Banks Cash out of the Ghetto," *Business and Society Review* 70: 40–42.

Wolff, Edward N. 2004. "Changes in Household Wealth in the 1980s and 1990s in the U.S." Working Paper no. 407, Levy Economics Institute, Bard College, May.

10 Wealth Creation in Latino Communities

Latino Families, Community Assets, & Cultural Capital

BÁRBARA J. ROBLES

This chapter profiles the wealth indicators of the Latino community in the United States. Wealth creation activities in working poor Latino communities rest on the presence of Latino community-based organizations (CBOs) engaged in serving Latino families and promoting asset- and wealth-building initiatives such as self-help housing, microbusinesses,[1] and nontraditional family savings vehicles. These community-based organizations have replaced many private and public sector entities that have failed to maintain a permanent presence in working poor and low-income Latino communities in the United States.

As is true for other communities of color, there are micro- and macro-dimensions to wealth creation in Latino communities. The macrodimension of wealth creation is fundamentally dependent upon the economic markets, institutions, and policies that impact communities on a daily basis. The microdimension relies inherently on family of origin and intergenerational transfers of physical assets, cultural capital,[2] and social capital. Additionally, community asset building depends upon physical, financial, human, social, and cultural capital and the degree to which each can be successfully combined to produce sustainable communities. Latino communities display cultural attributes not found in other communities while simultaneously sharing many macrodimensions of wealth creation with other communities of color.

One common theme for all communities of color is that the standard economic definition of *assets,* which emphasizes savings instruments that are held at the individual level and physical items or financial instruments to which individual property rights can be assigned, may be too narrow a conceptualization for communities of color. This chapter shows that for Latino communities the ability to own and control assets and to engage in wealth-creating activities relies on a variety of both tangible and intangible factors.[3] Biculturalism and bilingualism are attributes that can garner a higher wage premium in the labor market, especially in industries with a global market and reach. In working poor Latino communities, the ability to navigate local institutions, to understand mainstream markets, and to access affordable housing, financial services, and transportation contribute to increasing family wealth and financial stability. The chapter first presents an overview of Latinos in the United States and their asset-ownership experience. It then analyzes factors related to wealth accumulation among this group.

LATINOS IN THE UNITED STATES:
AN INTRODUCTION

Hispanic, or *Latino,* is an "ethnic-origin" term to describe Spanish-speaking-origin populations in the United States. Hispanics can be of any race. This means that Hispanics can be White, Black, Asian, American Indian, or Other, which are the official racial categories employed by the U.S. Bureau of the Census. The U.S. Census Bureau began using the term *Hispanic* during the 1980 census. Since then, it has become the "generic" term for all Spanish-speaking-origin peoples living in the United States. During the 1990s, the term *Latino,* which is largely a self-identifying or self-ascribed term, gained prominence in media reporting and is now used in governmental agency reporting. In this chapter, the term *Latino* is used interchangeably with *Hispanic.*

Currently, 68 percent of the U.S. population is White non-Hispanic. This indicates that the Latino population combined with other racial/ethnic non-White populations total 32 percent of the U.S. population (U.S. Bureau of the Census 2003). The diversity of the Latino population in the United States in terms of racial characteristics stems from a historical legacy of colonization and immigration. There is a significant Euro-Amerindian and Euro-African population among the Latino communities in the Western Hemisphere. This diversity of ethnic-racial characteristics within U.S. Latino communities has an impact on economic mobility opportunities (Darity et al. 2002; Gomez 2000).

Of the almost 40 million Latinos residing in the United States, approximately 67 percent are Mexican origin (Mexican Americans/Chicanos), 4 percent are Cuban American, 9 percent are Puerto Rican, 14 percent are Central and South American (with Central Americans more numerous than South Americans), and 6 percent are classified as Hispanic or Latino Other (Rameriz and de la Cruz 2002).

HOME & BUSINESS OWNERSHIP

Home ownership is often the most important asset a family owns and becomes an important source of "wealth," especially in leveraging education, business ownership, and retirement choices. As an intergenerational bequest, ownership of a home can contribute to the next generation's economic stability and progress. Moreover, home ownership has been found to be an important indicator of positive educational attainment rates for children of home owners regardless of neighborhood characteristics (Harkness and Neuman 2003), an important predictor of civic participation (Glaser and DiPasquale 1999), as well as an indicator of financial stability (Boehm and Schlottman 2001). Nationally, Latinos lag behind other populations in home ownership rates. In 2002, the Latino home ownership rate was 46.8 percent according to the Consumer Expenditure Survey (Paulin 2003, table 2:15). For the various Latino communities, the rate of home ownership varies with educational attainment rates, self-employment rates, median age, and immigration experience (see fig. 10.1).

Federal housing policies and agencies promoting home ownership have not encouraged two important legislative reforms needed for Latino families seeking to become home owners: (1) creating mortgage products that allow extended family workers' income to be included in home-purchase-qualifying evaluation of "family" income and (2) instituting wider criteria in underwriting assessment of credit scoring (alternative credit-scoring mechanisms). If these two legislative and industry reforms were aggressively supported by government agencies or quasi-government agencies such as Housing and Urban Development (HUD), Fannie Mae, and Freddie Mac, we would see an increase in Latino home ownership rates without a corresponding increase in subprime mortgages.[4] Moreover, evidence continues to attest to the presence of redlining in Latino

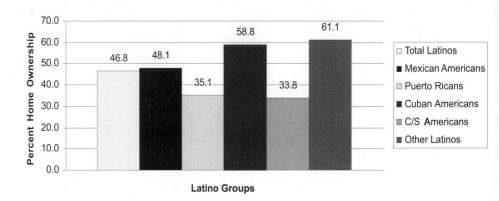

Fig. 10.1. Home ownership rates by Latino community, 2000–2001. (From Paulin 2003.)

communities by banks and other financial institutions (Ross and Yinger 2002).[5]

Self-employment rates among Latino communities indicate that push factors (inability to find work) and pull factors (high rates of self-employment in home country) are present (Light and Gold 2000; Fairlie and Meyer 1996; Wilson and Portes 1980). Latinos overall have a 9.6 percent self-employment rate (U.S. Bureau of the Census 2003a, calculations made by the author). The lowest rate of self-employment is displayed by the Puerto Rican community (5.4 percent), which parallels the self-employment rate for African Americans (5.7 percent). The highest rate of self-employment is reported by the South American community with 13.8 percent; next the Central Americans with 12.3 percent, Cuban Americans with 11.5, and the Mexican American community with 9.5 percent (U.S. Bureau of the Census 2003a, calculations made by the author).

A scarcity of data recording many Latino self-employment activities such as babysitter, lawn service provider, day laborer, maid, and seasonal cultural food vendor presents a challenge for researchers. This may indicate there is a higher self-employment rate among Latinos than the official data suggest.

Latina entrepreneurial activity has increased significantly since 1987 (U.S. Small Business Administration 1998; Center for Women's Business Research 2001). Nationally, Latina businesses employ 198,000 workers and generate $29.4 billion in receipts (Center for Women's Business Re-

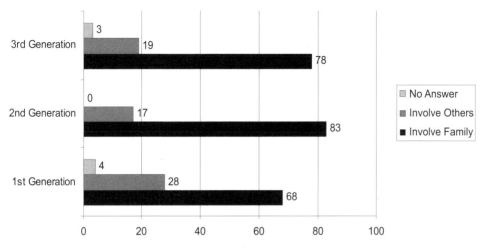

Fig. 10.2. Percentage of Latina entrepreneurs involving family members in business operations, 2000. (From Center for Women's Business Research 2000.)

search 2001). Latina entrepreneurship overwhelming involves family members (Robles 2002; Robles, forthcoming; see fig. 10.2). This alleviates many child care concerns associated with full-time wage-earning employment. Microenterprises proliferate along the U.S.-Mexican border and in Latino ethnic enclaves in urban areas. Many Latinas find barriers to entry in the general labor markets, turning to entrepreneurial activities to supplement or "patch" family income (Edgcomb and Armington 2003). These microentrepreneurs are supported by nonprofit microfinance lending organizations (community development financial institutions) that have replaced banks and credit unions as sources of capital for microbusinesses and small businesses in the Latino community.

NET WORTH, RETIREMENT PENSIONS, & INHERITANCE INDICATORS

Wealth inequality as measured by net worth is not as simple a task to uncover as income inequality.[6] Our national data collection efforts focus on the earnings capacity of different communities and indicate that only income and earnings matter. But this tends to focus our attention toward labor and job discrimination and away from barriers in the housing and real estate markets, as well as lack of financial services access such as

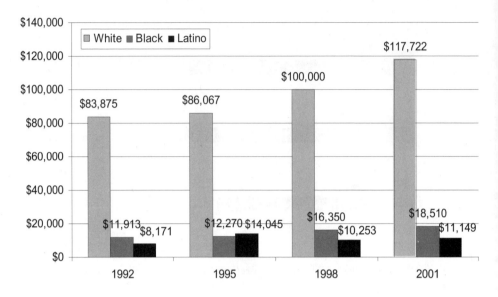

Fig. 10.3. Latino median net worth (2000 dollars). (From the Federal Reserve Board 1992, 1995, 1998, and 2001.)

credit opportunities and small business loan availability. The Survey of Consumer Finances, a national wealth survey that is released by the Federal Reserve Board of Governors every three years, tracks a variety of wealth measures for White, Black, Hispanic, and Other populations.[7] The data indicate that the net worth of our communities of color is intimately tied to educational attainment rates, occupational status, financial market sophistication and participation, home ownership, and pension participation. Figure 10.3 shows that Latino median networth was highest in 1995, at $14,045 and was $11,149 in 2001 (from the most recent survey).

Retirement income is essential for the well-being of those past their prime working years. The degree of pension gaps between the White, Black, and Latino communities in real inflation adjusted dollars is grim. Latinos and Black Americans have the lowest participation rates in private pension plans, thrifts, and IRAs (Federal Reserve Board 2001; see fig. 10.4). This lack of retirement pension income indicates that family and our national social security program play large roles in maintaining the standard of living of the elderly in communities of color.

An important aspect of wealth accumulation is the intergenerational bequests that occur from parents to children. The capacity to purchase a home (using inheritances as down payments) or begin a business

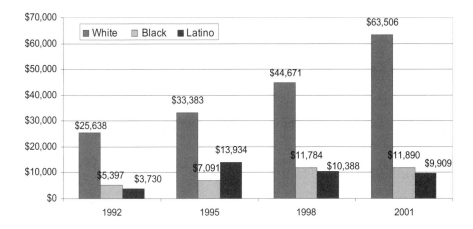

Fig. 10.4. Retirement pensions (sum of IRAs, thrifts, and future pensions, 2000 dollars). (From the Federal Reserve Board 1992, 1995, 1998, and 2001.)

(using start-up capital from a gift) often becomes possible due to transfers of wealth (in the form of income, homes, or portfolios) received from parents. The Survey of Consumer Finances asks respondents if they have been recipients of gifts and/or inheritances.[8] The data clearly map out who has benefited from such transfers. Whites receive gifts and inheritance at much higher levels than Blacks or Latinos (see fig. 10.5). In addition, intergenerational transfers in 2001 for Latinos were very small. Intergenerational transfers buffer many families from serious economic instability brought about from a loss in employment, a divorce, or a serious health crisis in the family.

Government policies that aided many families during the late 1940s and 1950s through the GI Bill and FHA/VH mortgages helped increase the probability of inherited transfers from one generation to the next. That not all Americans were able to benefit from these policies can be seen generations later in the low wealth accumulated by many families of color. As generations accumulate small wealth portfolios, family size becomes another obstacle in wealth transfers from parents to children in Latino communities.

Current asset-building policies such as Individual Development Accounts (IDAs) disqualify many working poor and low-income families from these matching savings accounts by imposing "net worth" eligibility requirements. In *colonias*,[9] many families own their land and have some

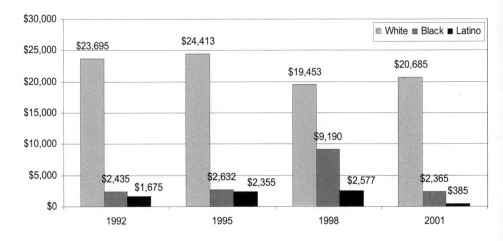

Fig. 10.5. Average gifts and inheritances (2000 dollars). (From the Federal Reserve Board 1992, 1995, 1998, and 2001.)

equity in their homes yet earn $5,000 to $14,000 dollars a year (U.S. Bureau of the Census 2000).[10] Yet these same families seek to provide opportunities for their children and are disqualified from participating in IDAs because their assets are over the $10,000 threshold set by most participating federal, state, or private foundation program funders.

EDUCATIONAL ATTAINMENT RATES

Latino educational attainment rates are intimately related to financial stability and wealth creation in Latino communities. Two Latino communities stand out among all other Latino communities in approaching White non-Hispanic educational attainment rates: Other Latinos and Cuban Americans. The Current Population Survey (Rameriz and de la Cruz 2002) indicates that 19.7 percent of Other Latinos hold a bachelor's degree or higher, while 18.6 percent of Cuban Americans have a bachelor's degree or higher. Bachelor's degrees among Mexican Americans are lower at 7.6 percent, Central and South Americans at 17.3 percent (with 49 percent of foreign-born South Americans having a high school degree or higher and 24 percent of foreign-born Central Americans having more than a high school degree), and Puerto Ricans at 14 percent. In 2002, the proportion of Hispanics born in the United States who had a bachelor's degree or more (14 percent) was higher than that of foreign-born Latinos (9 percent) (Rameriz and de la Cruz 2002).

Several state legislatures have enacted "percentage" plans in response to federal-court-mandated repeals of affirmative action programs in higher education (Hopwood, Fifth Circuit Court, 1996, Texas, and Proposition 209, 1996, California). These percentage plans have worked in large part because high schools with high Latino enrollment are de facto segregated. Moreover, no corresponding legislative response has occurred to remedy the demise of affirmative action admissions in graduate and professional programs in affected public universities. This has resulted in a lost cohort of Latino, African American, and Native American leaders in business, law, policy, medicine, and other graduate fields.

Studies indicate that low educational attainment rates are also correlated with low earnings and low median household and family income (Thomas-Brietfeld 2003; Sorensen, Carroll, Bryton 1995; Bureau of Labor Statistics 2002). For example, median income (year-round full-time) for Latinos with bachelor's degrees in 2001 was $40,162 compared with the median income (year-round full-time) for Latinos with high school degrees, $25,088 (Rameriz and de la Cruz 2002). This gap translates into a 37.5 percent differential between Latinos with a college degree and Latinos with a high school degree. Another way to interpret this earnings gap is that Latino high school graduates earn 62.5 percent of what a Latino with a college degree earns. Policies that promote a "pipeline" approach to educational opportunities are needed in the public domain. Thirty-five percent (14 million) of the Latino population is 18 years old and younger (Census 2000). In order to prepare Latino youth for a rapidly changing work and career environment, national, state, and local policies must be flexible.

Policies that create educational programs that increase apprenticeships in the arts, engineering, computer technology, crafts, health, business, and communications could be implemented in high school curricula. This would integrate Latino youth into a learning process focused on life skills and lifelong learning programs. Such an overhaul does not "track" Latino students into single-skilled employment or educational dead ends but rather prepares them for the reality of current career and work environments that require multiskilled and lifelong learning citizen-participants. Moreover, communities of color and Latino communities, in particular, bring a high degree of natural assets to the educational environment (Valenzuela 1999). If instead of "deficit" thinking policies we approach multilingual and culturally diverse children as resources in the educational process, we can then build educational spaces and places that reflect our communities, that make use of communities' "real-life" resources, and that recognize the "globally diverse" perspectives that Latino youth can bring to the local educational process.

INCOME & LATINO FAMILIES

Of the 11.4 million Latino households, 9.1 million are families (Rameriz and de la Cruz 2002). The income distribution for families indicates that 57 percent of Latino families earn zero to $40,000 annually (Rameriz and de la Cruz 2002; see fig. 10.6). Thirty percent of Latino families have five or more members (Rameriz and de la Cruz 2002). Of the almost 40 million Latinos in the United States, over half (21.5 million) reside in states along the U.S.-Mexican border (Texas, New Mexico, Arizona, and California).

Aggregate national data present a "typical" picture of a very diverse community with a variety of historical settlement and immigration experiences in the United States. The differences among Latino communities are captured by 2000 census data indicating the variation by income and origin. The European Spanish/Spaniard family income reported at $53,002 parallels that of the White non-Hispanic family ($50,046). South American family income ($42,824) is the next highest reported income and reflects the high degree of human capital maintained by many but not all South American families. The next highest reported family income is for the Cuban American population ($42,642), which reflects a unique immigration experience to the United States with federal policies enacted in the early to mid-1960s that encouraged Cuban integration into U.S. markets and institutions. The Central American ($34,150), Puerto Rican ($32,791), and Mexican ($33,516) family incomes are quite similar. For the aggregate category of Latinos in the United States, family income is reported at $34,397 and reflects the large demographic component of Mexican-origin families.

Family formation among Latinos continues to display nonnuclear and extended-kin or pseudokin arrangements. Family formation among Latinos has implications for income budgeting for necessary family expenditures and wealth-building opportunities. For example, family status plays a significant role in normalizing immigration status, in sponsoring family members, and in reunifying families. Additionally, family living arrangements and large families contribute to economies of scale, lowering the costs of housing and transportation. Finally, larger families gen-

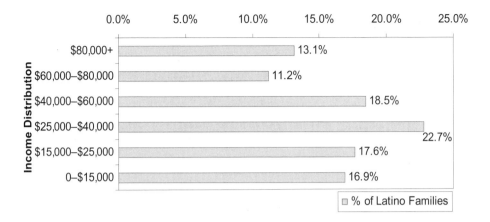

Fig. 10.6. Latino income distribution, 2001. (From the U.S. Bureau of the Census 2002.)

erally have more earners in the household, which contributes to income flow, pooling of resources, and wealth accumulation.

The downside of extended and pseudokin family arrangements in terms of mainstream institutions and data collection is the communal nature of pooling resources to acquire assets. In the United States, most binding contracts are between individuals. The emphasis on individual property rights and corresponding individual liability discourages communal asset-building activities. These communal poolings of resources are not on the radar with respect to data collection and government bureaucratic social services application forms. The collective manner in which family economic survival strategies have evolved in working poor and low-income Latino communities is not recognized by U.S. government agencies and bureaucracy, whose legal definition of family depends upon the nuclear family structure. Consequently, this poses a significant problem for Latino extended families and multigenerational families transitioning from poverty status into financially stable circumstances.

Current policies that impact the income and economic stability of Latino families center on legislation, executive orders, and judicial rulings at the federal, state, and local levels. Migrant workers, day laborers, seasonal workers, and recently arrived Latino immigrant families pool their resources in order to purchase assets as a group while listing the assets under an individual name to meet legal requirements (such as auto loans). Federal and state asset eligibility rules do not take into account the communal pooling of resources that occurs among many Latino working families and extended kin (Vélez-Ibañez 1983, 2004).

LATINO FAMILIES, CULTURAL CAPITAL, & COMMUNITY-BASED ORGANIZATIONS

The historical and cultural ties with Latino-sending countries create a unique transnational reality for many Latino families in the United States. They also contribute to the diversity of family arrangements and self-resilient economic activities in Latino communities. For many Latino families, economic mobility depends upon extended family resources and on learned economic survival strategies, which in turn depend upon class and community resources (Light and Gold 2000; Portes 1998). These social and cultural familial and community resources can be difficult to quantify but observable in effectiveness.

Cultural capital plays an important and supporting role in wealth-creating activities in working poor Latino communities. Edin (2001) explains that cultural capital consists of "intangible assets" in ethnic enclaves that are crucial to enterprise success by reflecting the cultural norms and behaviors of ethnic communities. In rural and urban ethnic enclaves, language switching between Spanish and English is one example of cultural capital.

Latino adult-adult relationships through religious marriage, baptism, communion, or confirmation rites of children known as *comadre* or *compadre* (*comadrazgo* or *compadrazgo*[11]) relationships, as well as adult-children relationships such as *madrina* (godmother) or *padrino* (godfather), also capture the notion of cultural capital. Dill (1994) explains that the system of compadrazgo creates linkages in Mexican communities that connect class and wealth resources and create opportunities to access extended social networks.[12]

Youth and young children often serve as translators and language mediators for those extended family members with limited English abilities (Dorner and Pulido 2003). Bilingualism thus becomes a cultural capital resource for extended and multigenerational families, as well as pseudo-kin, as they engage in consumer transactions, employment opportunities, or microbusiness activities

Latino family poverty rates are higher in high-Latino-population-density states and metro areas. For example, the receipt of public cash assistance income in U.S.-Mexican border states has declined significantly during the 1989–99 period: Texas, −71.1 percent; New Mexico, −50.4 percent; Arizona, −85.6 percent; and California, −60.9 percent (U.S. Bureau of the Census 1990 and 2000). The corresponding changes in median household income have not kept pace with the decline in public assistance income for these states during the same time period: Texas, 13.8 percent; New Mexico, 9.1 percent; Arizona, 13.4 percent; and California, 2.2 percent.[13]

Such stressful economic conditions generally encourage informal economic activity, and observably, this occurs with a high degree of frequency in Latino ethnic enclaves (Edgcomb and Armington 2003). In an era of nonreversible devolution, microbusinesses and self-employment activity substitute for the increasing scarcity of public assistance dollars, supplement or "patch" family income, and create additional earning opportunities for struggling families (Clark and Kays 1999). For example, in San Antonio, Texas, Cavazos (2002), using AccionTexas (a microlending CDFI) data, reports that microbusinesses increased mean monthly business activity revenues by 76.9 percent (after two microloans). For microentrepreneurs with one microloan history, average monthly revenues were $3,810, and for clients with two microloan histories, mean monthly revenues were $6,741.[14] The median monthly household income was $2,452 for the sample of microbusinesses ($n = 630$).

Both Latino and Latina entrepreneurial activities rely on family, culture, and community resources to establish their enterprises and increase the income and wealth-generating opportunities that economic survival requires. CBOs providing support services, governmental agencies administering programs, and local, state, and federal policies aimed at increasing the economic well-being of Latino families and Latino ethnic enclave communities fail to meet "outcomes" and "results-oriented" measures when they do not account for the bicultural and transnational economic environment that characterizes many Latino working poor and low-income communities. Foundation evaluations have documented that attempting to institute and replicate programs and services that have succeeded in urban and rural communities elsewhere in the United States does not result in the same successful and sustainable outcomes in Latino ethnic enclave communities (Robles, forthcoming).

Assessments indicate that cultural responsiveness and knowledge of bicultural families are the missing elements in poverty reduction programs imported into Latino communities. IDA program evaluators have found that the extremely poor save at a higher rate than do the middle-and high-poor participants (Clancey, Schreiner, and Sherraden 2002). However, attempting to implement IDA programs in Latino ethnic enclaves and in the Borderlands (the U.S.-Mexican border), even by culturally responsive community-based organizations, does not result in success. IDA programs limit eligibility through asset tests and limit withdrawals of funds saved for a limited number of family investment events: home purchase, microbusiness start-up, or tuition and expenses for education. Many Latino families refuse to participate because of these strict withdrawal rules and indicate that they are better off saving in a community *tanda*.[15] Perhaps the slow accumulation of a small amount of saved funds over time and deposited in some vague and "unconnected-with-community" bank or financial institution is not as attractive a prospect for accumulating savings as is a "communal/collective" initiative. There is a strengthening of community building and solidarity in such a collective economic activity reminiscent of mutual aid societies.

CBOs such as community development corporations (CDCs), community development financial institutions (CDFIs),[16] and community development housing organizations (CDHOs) are the source of much-needed revitalization capital, service networks, and resources for Latino communities. These organizations provide child care, health care, immigration services, affordable housing, housing rehab, support services for the elderly, food banks, entrepreneurial and microbusiness technical assistance, tax preparation and filing services, and a host of youth programs that alleviate constrained school budgets. However, the degree of "success" that many of these organizations experience in Latino communities is predicated on the degree of cultural competence present in the services they provide Latino families and Latino microbusinesses. Without understanding the manner in which many informal economic activities driven by cultural factors occur in Latino communities and become part of daily community life, many nonculturally responsive CBOs are not successful in delivering relevant or effective social services (Edgcomb and Armington 2003). Many top-down nonprofit organizations and university satellite programs fail to fully collaborate with community leaders and key community organizations, increasing the probability of service delivery failure in Latino communities.

An additional factor that arises in this context, the intersection of Latino ethnic enclave culture and class status, creates a set of behaviors that often escapes or bewilders nonprofit service providers who believe language ability is sufficient to initiate entry into low-income and working poor Latino communities. There is no substitute for time spent cultivating networks and building trust within the community (Anthony 1999). Moreover, it is insufficient to provide "mediating" employment to community members without also committing to upward mobility within the nonprofit. Clearly, for CBOs to successfully provide services in Latino communities, they must be willing to engage with Latino communities as full partners in program design, implementation, and service outreach.

La Union del Pueblo Entreo (LUPE), located in San Juan, Texas, Hidalgo County, is an example of a community-based social and economic justice organization for change.[17] Sustainability, respect for human dignity, and learning by doing are the prime pillars of the entire organizational philosophy of LUPE. The three main programs that lay the foundation for permanent and sustainable change for community members are

Mano de Apoyo: Responding to the immediate needs of people
Programa Escalera: Investing in the self-development of people
Juntos Adelante: Transforming people and their communities through participation and advocacy

LUPE is the umbrella organization for these programs. There are two affiliate, or subsidiary, organizations that provide additional resources that make Mano de Apoyo (Supporting Hands) and Programa Escalera (Ladder of Opportunity Program) especially successful: (1) Proyecto Azteca, which is a self-help, affordable home ownership program (Cascaron Program[18]) where families build their own homes (see fig. 10.7) that cost between $13,500 and $23,500 (along the U.S.-Mexican border low-cost housing is possible when no builder, developer, or realtor is involved as a middleman and families build their own homes) and (2) Azteca Community Loan Fund (CDFI), which offers emergency family loans, microenterprise loans, individual development accounts, and other financial services so that predatory lenders and pay day loans are less prevalent in the community.

Community members are also engaged in "learning by doing" through educational programs that are bundled with the asset-building services. Community members can choose from literacy classes, English as a second language, GED, citizenship classes, financial and home ownership counseling, and learning about the Earned Income Tax Credit (EITC). Finally, the leadership component is not part of the "educational" services

Fig. 10.7. Proyecto Azteca, Cascaron Self-Help Housing Program, San Juan, Texas. (Photo by Y. Robles.)

provided by LUPE. Instead, LUPE defines leadership as qualities any community member can acquire or display through engaging in activities that add to community collaboration and community development. Every community has indigenous leaders that emerge as a community coalesces around its own internally defined needs and aspirations. The key to opening asset-building opportunities for communities of color is to fully recognize every community is unique; what works in an urban northeastern ethnic enclave or inner-city community will not necessarily work in a southwestern semirural border community.

Every successful community development program must contain a flexibility and a capacity to modify elements of the program and community development initiative in order to continually incorporate the changing dynamics of community members themselves. Word of mouth, community events, and community goals all play a crucial part in creating and promoting an environment for change and proactive engagement (Gregory 2003). Here, the foundation of success is a community-created organization that becomes a resource for community members engaging in community change. The improvement in economic security for families creates more resources for sustainable change in the community.

Nonprofit, community-based microfinance lending organizations (CDFIs) in the United States have garnered nonpartisan political support. This is a clear indicator that microenterprise services and programs meant to encourage self-sufficiency and transition individuals from welfare to work are part of asset-based policies that have gained national support. Many communities of color have responded to welfare reform by simply engaging in economic survival strategies that help make ends meet. Microenterprises have grown exponentially precisely because in relevant ways they have been ignored by mainstream financial institutions.

The formal U.S. financial services sector does not find it profitable to loan money in small amounts or to "uncreditworthy" customers. Community-based organizations like CDFIs have taken over as community financial service providers. A CDFI is similar to a CDC but focuses on providing the community members with capital and other financial products and services that mainstream financial institutions do not provide to low-income communities.[19]

But just as they seek to assist individuals and families to become self-sufficient through microenterprises and other economic activities, CDFIs must remain solvent and operating in order to continue providing services to working poor and low-income communities. For many of the CDFIs, self-solvency (self-sufficiency) of their operations and organization is paramount, coupled with the need to expand services (grow to scale) in order to meet the growing demand for their expertise and culturally responsive assistance and support services.

Even as nontraditional sources of capital become available in the form of rotating credit and savings associations (tandas), for-profit and not-for-profit microlending agencies, business trade credit, the traditional banks, capital markets, and other financial institutions cannot escape the demographic shifts occurring in the United States and in particular regional markets. The financial services industry is only recently beginning to recognize the growing economic implications of the increasing presence of regional and transnational ethnic markets. The traditional finance sector is one of the most crucial sectors of the economy for regulating economic growth, and yet it appears to lag behind in terms of "inclusive incorporation" of differing needs of economic participants. The growth of the Latino community in the United States along with their purchasing power, projected to be $1 trillion by 2008 (Humphreys 2003), has provoked recent attention in the financial services industry.

COMPREHENSIVE COMMUNITY WEALTH ACCUMULATION POLICIES

Past public policies have resulted to some extent in discouraging or mitigating wealth accumulation in communities of color. These policies play a direct and powerful role in ethnic economic mobility inside and outside Latino ethnic enclaves and communities. The issues of wealth stagnation and wealth reversals during episodes of economic growth and prosperity are particularly salient to discussions of ethnic/racial entrepreneurial and economic activities and, consequently, the health of ethnic economies and enclaves.

Researchers, entrepreneurs, and public policy experts will need to craft new policies on issues addressing the increasing wealth divide among the various populations in the United States and the consequences this has for civil society. We have sufficient innovative community initiatives that, if supported by local, state, and federal policies, could rapidly decrease the economic stress currently being felt in Latino working poor and low-income communities. An example of such policies is comprehensive wealth-building programs that tie the refundable EITC to affordable home ownership and to other asset-accumulating activities, like Children's Savings Accounts, that are not included in asset tests for other welfare- and income-based programs. A very troubling part of current policies meant to increase self-sufficiency for individuals and families is the mismatch between asset development programs and income-based programs. For example, encouraging families to contribute to Children's Education Saving Accounts is considered to be a strong asset-based policy, but these accounts conflict with income-based programs (like food stamps or supplement security income) that consider the Children's Savings Accounts "family assets" and thus can disqualify families from cash assistance programs.

The lack of cultural knowledge by policy and program administrators and service providers creates confusing messages of noninclusiveness toward Latino working poor communities. If transnational working poor and low-income communities in Latino urban ethnic enclaves and rural areas are encountering government institutions (in the form of program accessibility and service provision) that are indifferent to community needs and cultural behaviors, a rational community response is to disengage from civic participation. The degree of commitment to serving our less wealthy communities at the micro level can be measured by how culturally competent, inclusive, and welcoming our government and democratic institutions behave toward working poor families. At the macro level, this is reflected in the number of family-friendly policies enacted by Congress or executive order.

Our policy debates and public conversations often occur riddled with terms such as *at risk, permanent underclass,* and *culture of poverty,* indicating a defeated attitude toward proactive policy and program outcomes. Our universities and think tanks describe struggling communities in ways that often indicate a failure to craft innovative approaches, a deficit in proactive theorizing by the very institutions that are charged with intellectual leadership. Moreover, policymakers and analysts take their cues from academic "experts" who are often disconnected from community development initiatives and innovative programs that are underway in communities of color. Because they listen to community leaders, our public community colleges appear to be doing a better job of serving our less wealthy communities than our public institutions of higher learning. What this admits to is a lack of university-community partnerships that create research agendas incorporating the voices of community members engaged in social change on the ground. Communities of color are not waiting for government policies or academic models to create positive economic change for themselves and their families.

Our reliance on "empirical data" alone to craft our policies has brought us a "deficit mentality" when crafting programs and agendas that are meant to address social and economic injustice. Dynamic community-based organizations in collaboration with community members dispel the "culture of poverty" assessment. There are many examples of communities organizing around issues they define as priorities, as opposed to "external needs assessment surveys," which do not employ many of the community's comparative advantages or account for community cultural factors that are, in essence, hidden assets. When communities engage in change, they set social change parameters with new ways of thinking about and dealing with "old" problems. If policy analysts, researchers, and policymakers spend time in working poor and low-income Latino communities, they will find that models of self-resiliency and economic survival proliferate. Our task is to document these positive initiatives, and to publicize these initiatives to dispel media-perpetuated images of a "permanent underclass." Our task is also to bring policymakers into classrooms to learn from, as well as focus the teaching on, future economic and community development leaders.

CONCLUSION

The Latino community in the United States is diverse in three significant ways: (1) Latino communities are not culturally monolithic, differing in country-of-origin out-migration, (2) every Latino community has a range of generations with different immigrant experiences, so that most Latino communities in the United States are made up of the foreign-born, the native-born with parents who were foreign-born, and those with grandparents or ancestors who were foreign-born, and (3) Latino communities are stratified by class. This creates a very dynamic community that is enriched by the country-of-origin diversity and the generational diversity that contributes to sustaining transnational ties, multilingual proficiency, and dynamic economic activity. Finally, class affiliations that are intertwined with cultural behaviors also generate new and complex dynamics that give rise to an increasingly visible Latino labor and consumer presence in the United States.

Latino communities have enriched the United States through cultural exchange, participation in labor markets and the military, and contributions to a continual economic (productive and consumption) growth throughout the history of the United States. Latinos have also brought additional multilingual and cultural assets to U.S. business during a period of rapid globalization. The continual waves of immigration become a resource for Latino communities and, consequently, for the United States. For example, many U.S. Latino families retain close ties with extended family in their home countries. This allows for a continual learning of cultural mannerisms and nuances by second- and third-generation U.S.-born Latinos, which are marketable assets that can then be translated into premium wages in a variety of U.S. occupations in the private and public sectors. This is a form of wealth and asset building in U.S. Latino communities that has not been identified as a benefit and resource to U.S. economic markets and institutions.

Aside from bicultural and bilingual assets that can be leveraged to increase family and community wealth accumulation, U.S. Latinos also serve to export democratic and cooperative ideals to extended family members not residing in the United States. This transnational "exchange" also serves as a type of "patient" capital in the form of democratizing wealth and asset-building behaviors that ultimately benefit the United States in the long run by creating strong allegiances and familiarity with U.S. customs and values.

Latino wealth inequality can easily be remedied through increased educational opportunities, financial market participation linked with financial literacy outreach, and access to home ownership counseling and mortgage markets. Government policymakers at local, state, and federal levels can contribute to wealth and asset building in communities of color by simply engaging in egalitarian actions that match stated policy and program goals. An important source of tax revenues can be had from incorporating Latino microbusiness activities and self-employment behaviors into mainstream markets and financial institutions. These activities and behaviors are present in Latino communities but are not fully documented in local, state, or national databases. Families can benefit from establishing formal relationships with private and public sector institutions and markets. Community wealth and asset-building activities can continue to occur below the "formal" radar or can be brought into the mainstream via community-based organizations serving Latino low-income and working poor communities and partnering with government, educational, and financial institutions. We have the imagination, the innovative skills, and the capacity to democratize access to financial services, products, and markets. The real question is this: Will we continue to stipulate that there is only one middle-class model leading to the American Dream? Or are we willing to recognize that there are imaginative paths and egalitarian models that provide concrete opportunities to struggling communities of color in their pursuit of the American Dream?

NOTES

1. *Microbusinesses* and *microenterprises* are defined as small businesses with fewer than five employees and requiring less than $35,000 in start-up capital. Many microbusinesses consist of the self-employed and part-time family workers.

2. *Cultural capital* takes on a distinct meaning when applied to communities of color. In this context, cultural capital is defined as the ability to navigate two cultural systems: one's own community and the mainstream institutional, social, and market systems. Each ethnic/racial community has its

own well-defined cultural milieu different from and often intersecting main-stream structures. In a nonracial/nonethnic context, economists and other researchers define cultural capital as familiarity with and attendance of symphonies, operas, museums, art galleries, and other "cultural" events. For communities of color, cultural capital is the ability to switch behavioral attributes that gain acceptance and can be leveraged in differing cultural constructs. For example, the ability to language switch and to engage in translating activities when managing consumer activities is a form of cultural capital.

3. Accordingly, a more general definition of the term *asset,* which views an asset simply as "something having value," may be a more useful construct when examining Latino communities. For example, *wealth* is defined as "all such material things, and qualities or attributes of man, as health, intelligence, etc., that increase his ability to produce" in the *World Book Encyclopedia Dictionary* (1965). While such a definition incorporates common parlance and metaphorical uses of the term *wealth,* its broader conceptualization is helpful when analyzing communities of color.

4. Subprime mortgages tend to proliferate in communities of color. These mortgages charge a higher interest rate than the prime interest rate generally awarded to creditworthy customers. For example, Fannie Mae and Freddie Mac indicate that, between 1993 and 1998, the growth in housing mortgages and refinancing for minority and low-income populations in the subprime market (the mortgage market that lends at higher rates of interest than the prime market and where predatory lending occurs) increased from 5 percent to 46 percent (Joint Center for Housing Studies 2000). This implies that home ownership among Latinos and other minorities has come at an increasing cost to overall consumer well-being.

5. The term *redlining* comes from the practice of outlining particular zip codes and areas where community members were not extended residential or personal loans by banks or by government agencies created to increase home ownership. This practice began during the New Deal creation of social programs meant to increase community revitalization.

6. *Net worth* is defined as the difference between a family's assets and total debts (liabilities). Many researchers believe that this is too wide a measure of financial well-being for communities of color since a significant amount of net worth held by households of color is in their homes. Another measure used to define accessible wealth is financial net assets. It aggregates all sources of financial wealth minus durable assets like vehicles, primary homes, business real estate, and secondary or vacation homes.

7. The Survey of Consumer Finances, Federal Reserve Board of Governors, does not publish wealth data by separate ethnic/racial categories for the non-White population. It publishes two categories: "White" and "non-White or Hispanic."

8. The Survey of Consumer Finances asks only for the amount of inheritance or gift received by respondents. I use the mean value of gifts and inheritances reported by respondents for the years 1992 to 2001.

9. *Colonia* is the Spanish term for "neighborhood." In the South and

West, where the majority of Latinos reside, unincorporated townships (colonias) are numerous. Colonias generally do not have water/wastewater facilities, paved roads, schools, health clinics, or most of the public services that taxpayers take for granted.

10. U.S. Census Bureau: State and County QuickFacts. Data derived from Population Estimates, 2000 Census of Population and Housing, 1990 Census of Population and Housing, Small Area Income and Poverty Estimates, County Business Patterns, 1997 Economic Census, Minority-and Women-Owned Business, Building Permits, Consolidated Federal Funds Report, 1997 Census of Governments.

11. *Compadrazgo* is a Spanish term used for capturing the supportive nature of "godfathering" that occurs in Latino communities. The female version of this is *comadrazgo*.

12. These pseudokin relationships are discussed in Dill (1994) in terms of Mexican-American communities but are prevalent in all Latino communities.

13. All percent change calculations are in 2002 real dollars (U.S. Bureau of the Census 1990 and 2000).

14. Calculations are in 2002 current dollars.

15. A *tanda* is a rotating credit-savings association formed by trusted members of a community. Each member is scheduled to receive the aggregate monthly "pot" (accumulated collective funds) at a specified monthly date. Each member contributes a set amount of money on a weekly basis, say $20. One trusted person holds the entire amount during the monthly accumulation. Tandas can have anywhere from five to twenty-five-plus participants. The monthly pots can be substantial, and tanda participants are quite adept at scheduling their turn to coincide with an important family expense (a family reunion in Mexico, a wedding, a baptism, the start of a school term, or other family event). For an in-depth description of Chicano and Mexican participation in tandas, see Veléz-Ibañez 1983.

16. CDFIs can be organized to target a variety of community development financial needs, such as a community development bank, a community development credit union, a community development venture capital fund, or, for my purposes in this chapter, a microenterprise development loan fund also known as *microfinance* or *microlending organizations*.

17. The LUPE state director is Juanita Valdez-Cox, and David Arizmendi is the director of Proyecto Azteca. They can be contacted at (956)782-6655 and jvaldez@lupemail.com for further information on LUPE and its programs.

18. *Cascaron* is the Spanish word for "shell." This program engages entire families in building their own homes. While building their homes, family members learn basic construction, plumbing, and electrical wiring skills that can then be used in job seeking.

19. The Community Reinvestment Act (CRA) of 1977 stipulates that mainstream banking institutions must serve all their potential customers by geographical operations. However, mainstream financial institutions have a long history of closing branch banks in low-income communities, denying ethnic and racial small business start-up capital, and not actively pursuing

low-income customers. However, the $38 billion remittance market by Latino temporary and transnational workers is creating more interest in the traditional financial services industry.

REFERENCES

Anthony, D. 1999. "The Importance of Trust in Micro-Credit Borrowing Groups." In *Business Access to Capital and Credit,* Proceedings of a Federal Reserve System Research Conference (Arlington, VA, March 8–9), ed. J. Blanton. Jackson L. Blanton, Alicia Williams, and Sherie L. W. Rhine, 547–78, http://www.chicagofed.org/cedric/files/V.%20Micro%20Lending.pdf (accessed March 19, 2006).

Association for Enterprise Opportunity. 2004. "What Is Microenterprise?" About Microenterprise. http://www.microenterpriseworks.org/about/whatis.htm. (accessed February 26, 2004).

Boehm, T., and A. Schlottman. 2001. "Housing and Wealth Accumulation: Intergenerational Impacts." Low-Income Homeownership Working Paper Series, *Joint Center for Housing,* Harvard University, LIHO-01.15, October.

Bureau of Labor Statistics. 2002. "Education Pays" *Occupational Outlook Quarterly* Online 46 (1): 52. http://www.bls.gov/opub/ooq/2002/spring/oochart.htm (accessed May 24, 2004).

Cavazos, Perla. 2002. "Measuring Asset Development among San Antonio Microentrepreneurs: An ACCION Texas Impact Study." Unpublished profession report, LBJ School of Public Affairs, University of Texas at Austin.

Center for Women's Business Research. 2000. *The Spirit of Enterprise: Latina Entrepreneurs in the United States.* Survey, September.

———. 2001. "Hispanic-Owned Businesses in the United States, 2002: A Fact Sheet." http://www.womensbusinessresearch.org/minority/hispanic.pdf.

Clancey, M., M. Schreiner, and M. Sherraden. 2002. "Saving Performance in the American Dream Demonstration—A National Demonstration of Individual Development Accounts." Final report, Center for Social Development at Washington University at St. Louis, October.

Clark, Peggy, and Amy Kays. 1999. *Microenterprise and the Poor: Findings from the Self-Employment Learning Project Five Year Survey of Microenterprise.* Washington, DC: Aspen Institute.

Darity, W. A., Jr., D. Hamilton, and J. Deitrich. 2002. "Passing on Blackness: Latinos, Race and Earnings in the USA." *Applied Economics Letters* 9 (13): 847–53.

Darity, W., Jr., and S. Myers, Jr. 1998. *Persistent Disparity: Race and Economic Inequality in the United States since 1945.* Northampton, MA: Edward Elgar Publishing.

DeFilippis, James. 2001. "The Myth of Social Capital in Community Development." *Housing Policy Debate* 12 (4): 781–806. http://www.fanniemae foundation.org/programs/hpd/pdf/hpd_1204_defilippis.pdf.

Dill, B. Thorton. 1994. "Fictive Kin, Paper Sons and Compadrazgo: Women of Color and the Struggle for Family Survival." In *Women of Color in U.S. Society,* ed. M. Baca Zin and B. Thornton Dill. Philadelphia, PA: Temple University Press.

Dorner, L., and L. Pulido. 2003. "Accessing Assets: Immigrant Youth's Work as Family Translators or 'Para-Phrasers.'" *Social Problems* 50 (4): 505–24.

Edgcomb, Elaine, and Maria M. Armington. 2003. *The Informal Economy: Latino Enterprises at the Margin.* Washington, DC: FIELD, Aspen Institute.

Edin, Kathyrn. 2001. "More Than Money: The Role of Assets in the Survival Strategies and Material Well-Being of the Poor." In *Assets for the Poor: The Benefits of Spreading Asset Ownership,* ed. T. Shapiro and E. Wolff. New York: Russell Sage Foundation.

Fairlie, R. W., and B. D. Meyer. 1996. "Ethnic and Racial Self-Employment Differences and Possible Explanations." *Journal of Human Resources* 31 (4): 756–93.

Federal Reserve Board. 1992, 1995, 1998, and 2001. *Survey of Consumer Finances,* Washington, DC.

Glaser, E., and D. DiPasquale. 1999. "Incentives and Social Capital: Are Homeowners Better Citizens?" *Journal of Urban Economics* 45: 354–84.

Gomez, C. 2000. "The Continual Significance of Skin Color: An Exploratory Study of Latinos in the Northeast." *Hispanic Journal of Behavioral Sciences* 22 (1): 94–103

Grameen Bank, USA. 2003. "Self-Employment in the United States." http://www.gfusa.org/gbrp/sel.html.

Gregory, Peggy. 2003. "The History of Latino Community Involvement: A Literature Review." Working paper, University of California, Davis, April.

Harkness, J., and S. Newman. 2003. "Effects of Homeownership on Children: The Role of Neighborhood Characteristics and Family Income." *Economic Policy Review,* Federal Reserve Bank of New York, June, 87–107.

Humphreys, J. 2003. "The Multicultural Economy, 2003: America's Minority Buying Power." *Georgia Business and Economic Conditions,* Selig Center for Economic Growth, Terry College of Business, University of Georgia, vol. 62, no. 2.

Hurlbert, J. S., J. J. Beggs, and V. A. Haines. 2001. "Social Networks and Social Capital in Extreme Environments." In *Social Capital: Theory and Research,* ed. N. Lin, K. Cook, and R. Burt. Hawthorne, NY: Aldine De Gruyter.

Joint Center for Housing Studies. 2000. "The State of the Nation's Housing: Harvard University." http://www.jchs.harvard.edu/publications/markets/son_2000_intro.html.

Light, I., and S. J. Gold. 2000. *Ethnic Economies.* San Diego, CA: Academic Press.

Office of the Advocacy. 1999. *Minorities in Business.* Washington, DC: U.S. Small Business Administration.

Paulin, G. 2003. "A Changing Market: Expenditures by Hispanic Consumers, Revisited." *Monthly Labor Review* 126 (8): 12–35. http://www.bls.gov/opub/mir/2003/08/art2full.pdf.

Portes, A. 1998. "Social Capital: Its Origins and Applications in Modern Sociology." *Annual Review of Sociology* 24: 1–24.

Portes, Alejandro, and Rubén G. Rumbaut. 1990. *Immigrant America: A Portrait.* Berkeley: University of California Press.

Rameriz, R. and G. Patricia de la Cruz. 2002. *The Hispanic Population in the*

United States: March 2002. Current Population Report, P20-545, U.S. Census Bureau, Washington, DC. http://ww.census.gov/prod/2003pubs/ p20-545.pdf (accessed March 19, 2006).

Robles, B. 2002. "Latino Microenterprise and the US-Mexico Border Economy." *Estey Centre Journal of International Law and Trade Policy* 3 (2): 307–27.

———. Forthcoming. "Latina Entrepreneurship in the Borderlands: Family Well Being and Poverty Reduction Policies." In *Transformation of La Familia on the US-Mexico Border Landscape,* ed. Raquel Marquez. Notre Dame, IN: University of Notre Dame.

Ross, Stephen L., and John Yinger. 2002. *The Color of Credit: Mortgage Discrimination, Research Methodology and Fair-Lending Enforcement.* Cambridge, MA: MIT Press.

Sorensen, D. Brewer, S. Carroll, and E. Bryton. 1995. "Increasing Hispanic Participation in Higher Education: A Desirable Public Investment." *Rand Internet Policy Brief, IP-152.* http://www.rand.org.

Thomas-Brietfeld, S. 2003. "The Latino Workforce." *National Council of La Raza,* Statistical Brief no. 3 (August). http://www.nclr.org/policy/briefs/ SB%203%20Latino%20workers-FNL.pdf.

U.S. Bureau of the Census. 1990 and 2000. "State and County QuickFacts." Online access http://www.census.gov (accessed March 16, 2004).

U.S. Bureau of the Census. 1992 and 1997. *Survey of Minority-Owned Business Enterprises.* Washington, DC.

U.S. Bureau of the Census. 2003. "Census 2000 Summary File 4." Online access http://www.census.gov (accessed March 19, 2006).

U.S. Small Business Administration. 1998. *Women in Business.* Washington, DC, October.

Valenzuela, A. 1999. *Subtractive Schooling: U.S. Mexican Youth and the Politics of Caring.* Albany, NY: State University of New York Press.

Vélez-Ibañez, C. G. 1983. *Bonds of Mutual Trust: The Cultural Systems of Rotating Credit Associations among Urban Mexicans and Chicanos.* New Brunswick, NJ: Rutgers University Press.

———. 2004. "Regions of Refuge in the United States: Issues, Problems, and Concerns for the Future of Mexican-Origin Populations in the United States." *Human Organization* 63 (1): 1–20.

Wilson, K., and A. Portes. 1980. "Immigrant Enclaves: An Analysis of the Labor Market Experience of Cubans in Miami." *American Journal of Sociology* 86 (2): 295–319.

11 Living Where the Neighbors Are Invested

Wealth & Racial/Ethnic Differences in Individuals' Neighborhood Home Ownership Rates

RACHAEL A. WOLDOFF

Family characteristics and socioeconomic resources (SES) have been central to most theories of racial and ethnic stratification in residential experiences. Additionally, there is a general consensus that discrimination occurs in the housing market. Still, many people are optimistic about the increasing percentages of African Americans and Latinos who own their homes. For instance, in an October 2002 news conference, President George W. Bush announced a goal to greatly expand non-White home ownership by the end of the decade. *However, where will these home owners live?*

The assumption is that racial/ethnic differences in neighborhood characteristics are the result of group differences in individual characteristics, especially educational and economic resources. Thus, people are thought to live in the best neighborhoods they can afford. Even though recent analyses challenge this assumption and show that racial differences in neighborhood quality remain even after taking individual levels of education and income into account (Alba and Logan 1993; Alba, Logan, and Bellair 1994; Logan, Alba, and Leung 1996), some speculate that racial/ethnic differences in neighborhood quality can be explained by other characteristics that are difficult to measure, such as wealth, family of origin, and current family characteristics (Conley 1999; Clark 1986, 1991).

Wealth, as it relates to neighborhood quality, is an understudied concept. In contrast to standard measures of SES that use a mix of education, income, and employment characteristics, wealth is a concept that takes into account accumulated assets. According to the U.S. Census Bureau, the concept of wealth refers to "the level of economic resources that a person or household possesses at any given time" (Davern and Fischer 2001). Wealth may be central to understanding racial/ethnic differences in residential outcomes because African Americans and Latinos have dramatically lower levels of wealth than Whites (Gittleman and Wolff 2000; Keister 2000; Oliver and Shapiro 1995). Data from the Survey of Consumer Finances show that these wealth disparities are present for every age group and do not disappear after controlling for differences in educational attainment (Scholz and Levine 2002). Additionally, on average, African Americans and Latinos have less wealth in their families, and this is important for housing outcomes—especially when one considers that 10–20 percent of first-time home buyers use gifts from relatives for their down payments (Charles and Hurst 2002; Mayer and Engelhardt 1996). Indeed, recent research shows that many different dimensions of socioeconomic status remain correlated across generations (Solon 1992).

These large and persistent racial/ethnic disparities in wealth may contribute to residential stratification, as the lack of economic resources available for rent, loans, and down payments renders certain housing and neighborhoods less affordable than others. Individuals with lower levels of wealth have a lower probability of home ownership (Haurin, Hendershott, and Wachter 1997). This may be because borrowers with assets and savings demonstrate their stability to lenders and show them that they have reserves of resources in case of an emergency. Wealth is so important to housing outcomes that one recent study shows that a third of renters in the sample were able to afford monthly mortgage payments but they could not buy a home because they lacked the wealth required for down payments and closing costs (Collins and Dylla 2001).

WEALTH, RESOURCES, & NEIGHBORHOOD HOME OWNERSHIP

Thus, we know that wealth is important for individuals seeking to buy a home, but what is the link to neighborhood levels of home ownership?

With a substantial body of research showing that the location of one's home is important for ensuring high-quality schools, reliable services, stable residents, controlled crime, and greater life chances for families[1], racial/ethnic differences in access to good neighborhoods are a key concern in the fight for fair housing. Understanding these differences is essential to reducing racial and ethnic social stratification. Given the desirability of neighborhoods where many residents own their homes, neighborhood home ownership is important for understanding neighborhood quality and the way of life in communities.

Neighborhood home ownership has recently become a central topic in studies covering a range of quality-of-life issues, such as housing prices, dwelling maintenance, crime rates, NIMBYism (Not in My Backyard), schools, political responsiveness, public services, political action, and social networks (see Haurin, Dietz, and Weinberg 2003 for a review). Americans view home ownership as essential to, and symbolic of, success and the achievement of the American Dream. This makes sense because, on a practical level, home ownership comes with a great deal of responsibility. When a family lives in a neighborhood where home ownership is the norm, its members can expect better property maintenance, less residential mobility, and greater property appreciation (Rohe and Stewart 1996).

While these conditions are very desirable to most citizens, not all people have equal access to neighborhoods with high levels of home ownership. Indeed, a long history of federal policies has created and maintained segregation and inequality, leaving African Americans and other people of color struggling to gain fair housing opportunities in the neighborhoods of their choice (see Yinger 1995 for a review). Massey and Denton (1993) and Hirsch (1983) summarize the role of the government in subsidizing the postwar housing boom in the United States and facilitating the segregation of American metropolitan areas. Federal policies opened many housing opportunities for Whites and closed them for African Americans.

Even with the abundance of evidence about racial discrimination in the housing market (Galster and Keeney 1988; Yinger 1995), critics tend to downplay the importance of race/ethnicity and discrimination in contemporary housing issues (Clark 1986, 1991; Patterson 1997; Thernstrom and Thernstrom 1997). This chapter deals with the consequences and manifestations of such policies in the contemporary United States of America by examining racial/ethnic differences in the way wealth, socioeconomic characteristics, and other factors translate into living in neighborhoods with higher levels of home ownership.

Studies that have compared the determinants of neighborhood outcomes among Whites and non-White racial/ethnic groups tend to be single-city analyses, with large geographic units used as "neighborhoods" (Alba, Logan, and Stults 2000; Alba and Nee 1997; Massey and Denton 1985). Further, these studies do not account for wealth and family-of-origin characteristics. Socioeconomic disadvantages in the form of educational and employment disparities contribute to wealth and income gaps and prevent African Americans and Latinos from accumulating a surplus of economic resources. For instance, research suggests that large racial/ethnic gaps exist in educational achievement in math and reading (Ralph and Crouse 1997), high school dropout rates (Kaufman, Alt, and Chapman 2001), and unemployment (McKinnon 2003) in the United States. These deficits combined with the cumulative, historical, and intergeneration effects of disadvantage can adversely affect residential outcomes.

To date, I know of only one study examining the effects of wealth on locational attainment, but the outcome is neighborhood racial composition, not neighborhood home ownership. Also, the samples are from Boston and Los Angeles rather than national samples. When combining the samples for each city, Freeman (2000) found that wealth has a positive effect on "proximity to Whites" (the percentage of Whites in one's neighborhood) for African Americans and Latinos. Examining Los Angeles and Boston separately shows differences between these two places. Wealth has a positive effect on proximity to Whites for both groups in Los Angeles. However, wealth had a negative effect on proximity to Whites for African American Bostonians and no effect for Latino Bostonians. While informative, Freeman only examined individuals in two cities. Also, he measured wealth with a net worth variable that included housing-related wealth. This can be problematic when predicting neighborhood outcomes because it can lead to circular arguments that confound independent variables (housing wealth) with dependent variables (neighborhood quality). Further, he did not have information on family of origin. In contrast, the present national-level study carefully explores the effects of family of origin, wealth, and other socioeconomic and family characteristics on neighborhood home ownership.

THE LOCATIONAL ATTAINMENT APPROACH TO
NEIGHBORHOOD HOME OWNERSHIP

This analysis assumes that residence in a high-home-ownership neighborhood is more likely for people with larger amounts of resources. Accordingly, recent explanations of racial/ethnic differences in neighborhood quality are rooted in the locational attainment approach (Logan and Alba 1993). Locational attainment research examines the relationship between individuals' background characteristics and their residential outcomes. In this literature, research examines the ways in which race/ethnicity and personal characteristics affect people's location in neighborhoods with higher or lower levels of resources and/or integration. This perspective combines two models to explain differences in group members' locational returns to socioeconomic resources and personal characteristics.

The first part of the locational attainment approach applies the spatial assimilation model (Massey 1985) to assess the degree to which individual SES levels (in the form of income, education, and employment) and cultural assimilation translate into residential locations that offer amenities—such as high levels of home ownership. Any observed racial/ethnic group differences in neighborhood home ownership are assumed to be attributable to racial/ethnic group differences in SES levels (e.g., income and education), but wealth differences may also matter. The spatial assimilation model has been very useful in examining the locational outcomes of minorities and immigrants and exploring the role of acculturation patterns for gaining access to good neighborhoods.[2]

The second part of the approach, the place stratification model, is more critical and assumes that discriminatory forces are in place and these interfere with residents' efforts to convert resources into residential outcomes. Place stratification posits that institutional variables (e.g., housing/mortgage discrimination) should prevent individuals' socioeconomic and personal characteristics from fully explaining group differences in neighborhood levels of home ownership. This model maintains that any racial/ethnic differences in neighborhood levels of home ownership that remain after modeling the spatial assimilation variables indicate a racial/ethnic gap in access to quality neighborhoods that is likely to be caused by discrimination in the housing market. Moreover, in group-specific analyses, any observed group differences in *returns* to socioeconomic characteristics also support the place stratification aspect of the locational attainment approach because these show that one group benefits from socioeconomic characteristics more than other groups. In other words, the very observation that racial/ethnic groups have different levels of return to their socioeconomic characteristics lends support to the place stratification model.

In this chapter I argue that, after controlling for geographic differences in location (urban residence and regional differences), three groups of factors predict neighborhood home ownership levels for an adult: family-of-origin characteristics, adult socioeconomic characteristics, and adult family characteristics. Additionally, I argue that African Americans are likely to get the fewest returns to socioeconomic characteristics because of the high levels of discrimination they have faced and continue to face in the housing market.

Together, the two parts of the locational attainment approach hypothesize that people from more stable families of origin, those with higher levels of socioeconomic resources and wealth, and those with more stable families as adults will be better off but that Whites and Latinos should reap more benefits than African Americans. Each set of variables is accompanied with a rationale. In examining wealth effects, it is essential to control for other factors that vary by race and may have an effect on neighborhood home ownership. It is crucial to control for geography because ethnic and racial groups are not evenly dispersed throughout the United States. The rationale for including family of origin is that social sciences have long found an influence of family-of-origin characteristics on life chances. I include other SES variables to isolate the effects of wealth. I control for current family characteristics because there are large disparities in the family structures and characteristics of African Americans, Latinos, and Whites and these could account for neighborhood quality differences.

Additionally, it is expected that Latinos and Whites will fare better than African Americans. Several studies support the place stratification model for explaining White–African American locational differences. For instance, Logan, Alba, and Leung (1996) found that African Americans receive lower locational returns to socioeconomic characteristics in their study of residential proximity to Whites. They showed that, after controlling for individual differences in SES, the White–African American disparity in proximity to Whites was the largest, while the disparities between Whites and Asians and Whites and Latinos were smaller. Also, Alba, Logan, and Bellair (1994) show that African Americans are very different from Whites, Asians, and Latinos in their ability to convert individual characteristics into safe, low-crime neighborhoods. They found that individual-level socioeconomic variables do not account for group differences in neighborhood crime between African Americans and the other groups. Logan and Alba (1993) examined racial/ethnic group differences in access to middle-class suburbs in New York and found that African Americans fare worse than other groups. They found that while Whites and Latinos receive consistent locational returns to income, acculturation, and family status, African Americans' access to suburbs is the least responsive to these variables. Finally, Krivo (1986, 1995) found that Latinos have higher housing returns to income and education than Whites and African Americans.

Accordingly, I hypothesize the following six relationships about neighborhood home ownership and family of origin (hypotheses 1 and 2), individual wealth and socioeconomic characteristics (hypotheses 3 and 4), and current family characteristics (hypotheses 5 and 6):

> *Hypothesis 1:* Adults who grew up with higher SES parents, married parents, and greater acculturation to the United States will live in neighborhoods with higher levels of home ownership.
>
> *Hypothesis 2:* The neighborhood home ownership returns to family-of-origin characteristics will be lower for African Americans than for Whites and Latinos.
>
> *Hypothesis 3:* Adults will have higher levels of neighborhood home ownership with higher levels of wealth and other SES characteristics.
>
> *Hypothesis 4:* The neighborhood home ownership returns to wealth and other SES characteristics will be lower for African Americans than for Whites and Latinos.
>
> *Hypothesis 5:* Adults who are single parents and those with a larger family size will live in neighborhoods with lower levels of home ownership.
>
> *Hypothesis 6:* The neighborhood home ownership penalties for being a single parent or having a large family size will be greater for African Americans than for Whites and Latinos.

DATA & METHODS

Relating adults' family-of-origin characteristics, wealth, SES, and current family characteristics to their neighborhood levels of home ownership requires a unique combination of information on individuals' wealth/income levels and specific residential locations. My analyses link longitudinal data from the National Longitudinal Survey of Youth (NLSY79) to census tract data for individual respondents. Because of the highly secure nature of the address-based information on tract location, the use of these secure NLSY data is limited to on-site associates of the Center for Human Resources Research (CHRR) at the Ohio State University.

The NLSY79 is a longitudinal survey of U.S. residents. This nationally representative sample includes 12,686 young men and women who were aged 14 to 22 when they were first surveyed in 1979. Respondents have completed interviews on an annual basis through 1994 and every other year after this time. Individual data for NLSY79 respondents include information on wealth, income, a wide range of demographic and family history characteristics, as well as data on various attitudes and experiences.

VARIABLES

I use census data to measure the dependent variable: neighborhood home ownership. Dating back to early research on neighborhood social disorganization at the University of Chicago, this is a proxy for neighborhood stability and a key predictor of neighborhood crime (see Sampson 1988; Sampson, Raudenbush, and Earls 1997). The NLSY79 provides detailed and disaggregated measures of central independent variables in this study: education, income, and wealth. In particular, the wealth variables include items about the ownership and value of individuals' possessions, accounts, and investments. Note that wealth in this analysis is the sum of respondents' nonhousing assets in 1998. Locational outcomes are related to the housing stock and the housing values in their locations, so I use a wealth measure that excludes housing wealth. This sample contains large racial/ethnic differences in wealth, with Whites having the most wealth ($139,260). On average, Latinos have 39 percent of the wealth of Whites ($53,818), while African Americans have merely 22 percent of White wealth ($30,181).[3]

In addition to wealth, I measure other independent variables that play a role in residential patterns, including family-of-origin characteristics, SES characteristics (education, income, and employment), and life-cycle characteristics (e.g., marital status and presence of children) and cultural variables (e.g., speaking a second language in the home as a child). All variables are listed in table 11.1 and represent factors that are important

TABLE 11.1. Measures and Descriptive Statistics for Independent and Dependent Variables

Variables	Total	Whites	African Americans	Latinos
Dependent variable				
Percentage of home owners in tract	70.41	73.44	57.42	62.17
	(20.04)	(17.92)	(23.22)	(22.86)
Race/ethnicity				
White	.79			
	(.41)			
African American	.14			
	(.35)			
Latino	.07			
	(.25)			
Family of origin				
Adjusted 1979 family income in 1,000s	48.54	53.50	28.59	32.23
(unlogged)	(36.81)	(37.74)	(24.84)	(26.31)
At least one parent had at least some	.33	.37	.18	.16
college by 1978	(.47)	(.48)	(.38)	(.36)
At least one parent worked full-time in	.86	.90	.71	.73
1978	(.35)	(.31)	(.45)	(.45)
Lived with a single parent at age 14	.13	.09	.30	.20
	(.33)	(.29)	(.46)	(.40)
As a child, spoke foreign language at home	.13	.09	.03	.89
	(.34)	(.29)	(.18)	(.31)
Wealth				
Adjusted 1998 nonhousing wealth in	11.80	13.93	3.02	5.38
10,000s (unlogged)	(42.92)	(47.49)	(13.67)	(14.11)
SES characteristics				
Respondent only had a high school degree	.42	.42	.48	.40
by 1998	(.49)	(.49)	(.50)	(.49)
Respondent had completed some college	.22	.21	.25	.26
by 1998	(.41)	(.41)	(.43)	(.44)
Respondent had completed four years of	.14	.16	.08	.06
college by 1998/BA	(.35)	(.36)	(.27)	(.25)
Respondent had completed > four years	.10	.11	.04	.05
college/post-BA by 1998	(.30)	(.31)	(.20)	(.22)
Adjusted 1998 family income in 1,000s	64.75	68.83	44.50	59.79
(unlogged)	(61.84)	(63.44)	(47.96)	(60.23)
Number of weeks worked (1997–98)	41.12	42.11	37.08	37.95
	(19.45)	(18.71)	(21.76)	(21.24)
Current family				
Respondent is a single parent	.06	.02	.22	.08
	(.23)	(.15)	(.42)	(.27)
Respondent is married without children	.09	.10	.04	.05
	(.29)	(.30)	(.20)	(.23)
Respondent is a married parent	.53	.58	.32	.51
	(.50)	(.49)	(.47)	(.50)
Family size	3.30	3.27	3.29	3.65
	(1.54)	(1.46)	(1.85)	(1.70)

(continued)

TABLE 11.1.—*Continued*

Variables	Total	Whites	African Americans	Latinos
Controls				
Urban	.68	.64	.84	.85
	(.47)	(.48)	(.37)	(.35)
Northeastern region	.17	.18	.15	.15
	(.38)	(.38)	(.35)	(.36)
Midwest region	.28	.32	.18	.08
	(.45)	(.47)	(.39)	(.27)
Southern region	.37	.33	.59	.34
	(.48)	(.47)	(.49)	(.47)
N	7,879	3,968	2,413	1,498

to neighborhood locational research: race/ethnicity, family-of-origin characteristics, wealth, SES, and adult family characteristics, and urban and regional residence.

STATISTICAL ANALYSIS

To evaluate the effects of theoretical predictors of neighborhood home ownership, I first perform ordinary least squares (OLS) regression analyses for the total sample to confirm that these factors are influential and especially to determine whether race and ethnicity are significant predictors of neighborhood levels of home ownership. Second, I perform race-specific regressions to examine the relative importance of these characteristics for each group. Finally, I test for racial/ethnic differences in the impact of each predictor on neighborhood home ownership using group-specific analyses. To review, in the regressions, I examine geographic variables, family of origin, wealth, SES, and adult family characteristics.

FINDINGS

The descriptive statistics in table 11.1 demonstrate large racial/ethnic disparities in neighborhood home ownership rates. On average, non-Latino Whites live in neighborhoods in which 73 percent of the residents are home owners compared with 57 percent for African Americans and 62 percent for Latinos. One-way ANOVA analyses reveal that these race-specific means are significantly different.

Table 11.2 presents the results of the regression models for the total sample. The model examines the effects of geographic controls, family of origin, and wealth, as well as a series of variables about SES and current family structure. In general, table 11.2 allows us to see which variables predict neighborhood levels of home ownership. Also, it allows us to learn whether gross racial/ethnic differences in neighborhood levels of home ownership can be explained by individual differences among groups. After discussing the relationships for the total sample, I present group-specific analyses of the relationships between each set of factors and neighborhood home ownership to explore whether patterns differ across the three groups.

RESULTS FOR THE TOTAL SAMPLE

Table 11.2 presents the neighborhood home ownership model estimated for the total population. Some variables had very large effects, such as urban residence, being African American, and having four years of college. Other variables had relatively smaller effects, like current income, wealth, and the income of one's family of origin. Notably, the regression coefficients show that large racial/ethnic differences remain even when compositional differences in geographic location, family of origin, wealth, SES, and adult family characteristics are controlled. Even after controlling for these, African Americans and Latinos live in neighborhoods with lower average home ownership rates than non-Latino White households. In comparison with White respondents, African Americans have 9.02 percent fewer neighbors who own their homes and Latinos have 4.3 percent fewer home owners as neighbors. Additionally, race/ethnicity is far more important in explaining the African American–White gap in neighborhood home ownership than the Latino-White gap. This is evident in comparing these findings with the descriptive statistics presented in table 11.1 that represent the gross racial/ethnic differences in neighborhood home ownership. By adding the rest of the controls and independent variables, the White–African American difference in home ownership is reduced by about 44 percent from 16.03 percent to 9.02 percent. The White-Latino difference is reduced by more—about 62 percent from 11.27 percent to 4.3 percent. This preliminary evidence partially supports the spatial assimilation theory because racial/ethnic differences in neighborhood home ownership levels are reduced after introducing these variables. However, the fact that there are remaining racial and ethnic differences in neighborhood home ownership—even after controlling for various other characteristics—lends support to place stratification theory. Also, the fact that the effect of race/ethnicity is more greatly reduced for Latinos than for African Americans also lends support to the place stratification model.

This table demonstrates that some geographic, family-of-origin, SES, and current family characteristics do have distinct effects on residential levels of home ownership. Turning to the geographic control variables,

TABLE 11.2. Results for OLS Regression Analysis for Neighborhood Home Ownership, Total Sample

Variables	Regression
Controls	
African American	−9.027*
	(.585)
Latino	−4.302*
	(.910)
Urban	−15.914*
	(.501)
Northeast region	−3.509*
	(.732)
Midwest region	4.123*
	(.679)
Southern region	3.454*
	(.619)
Family of origin	
1978–79 income ($1,000s)	.026*
	(.007)
Parent—some college	−1.912*
	(.548)
Parent—one full-time	2.448*
	(.575)
Lived with single parent	−1.997*
	(.595)
Spoke foreign language	−.163
	(.818)
Wealth (1998)	
Nonhousing wealth ($10,000s)	.015*
	(.006)
SES characteristics	
High school	1.938*
	(.701)
Some college	3.937*
	(.783)
Four years college	5.384*
	(.940)
Postcollege education	4.569*
	(1.063)
Family income, 1998	.009*
	(.004)
Number of weeks worked	.067*
	(.011)

TABLE 11.2.—*Continued*

Variables	Regression
Current family	
Single parent	−.941
	(.785)
Married without children	4.489*
	(.871)
Married with children	4.327*
	(.578)
Family size	.583*
	(.155)
Constant	67.214
Adjusted R^2	.281
N	7,879

*Significant and have a *t*-statistic greater than 1.645 (for one-tailed tests with a critical value of 5 percent).

on average, urban residents have about 16 percent fewer home owners in their neighborhoods than their nonurban counterparts. This is consistent with other research that finds that ownership is higher in rural and suburban areas than in the city (Mikesell 1998). Additionally, northeasterners have lower percentages of home owners in their neighborhoods, while midwesterners and southerners have higher percentages of home owners in their neighborhoods than those who live in the West. Specifically, northeasterners have about 3 percent fewer home owners, while midwesterners and southerners have about 4 percent more home owners in their communities than individuals living in the West. This is consistent with other findings that northerners and westerners have more similar and lower levels of home ownership than southerners and midwesterners (Mikesell 1998).

Factors related to individuals' family of origin also represent possible compositional differences across racial/ethnic groups, but these are less powerful than race and geography. This is important to model because some advantages and disadvantages may have a "trickle-down" effect across generations. Four out of five of the family-of-origin factors had significant effects on neighborhood home ownership in adulthood. Parental socioeconomic factors—income, parental education, and full-time work—are important predictors of adult neighborhood home ownership. Also, childhood family structure is related to neighborhood home ownership in adulthood, such that adults who lived with a single parent as children tend to live in less stable neighborhoods as adults. There is no evidence that cultural family characteristics, such as having spoken a foreign language in the childhood home, affect neighborhood home ownership in adulthood.

Wealth, a rarely examined concept in past research, also has effects on neighborhood home ownership rates. As expected, even after adjusting for other compositional differences, respondents with higher levels of wealth live in neighborhoods with higher levels of home ownership. This supports the spatial assimilation theory because it demonstrates that neighborhood home ownership levels are positively related to wealth. This does not mean, however, that the effects of wealth on neighborhood home ownership are the same for each group; this is explored in the group-specific analyses.

Turning to the other SES variables, not surprisingly, the results show that all are significantly and positively associated with neighborhood home ownership rates. In contrast, not all of the current family characteristics produce significant effects on neighborhood home ownership. On average, when compared with being single and childless or divorced with or without children, being married with or without children is associated with living in a more stable community. However, single parenthood is not related to neighborhood home ownership. Additionally, residents with larger families tend to live in more stable neighborhoods. This suggests that, net of other factors, larger family size is occasionally beneficial to residential outcomes. Indeed, the life-cycle model of residential mobility claims that people with children cluster into neighborhoods because certain neighborhoods have amenities that benefit children, such as schools and child care (Rossi 1955). Also, the probability of moving is inversely related to the number of children one has (Long 1972), with those with multiple children being less likely to move. Further, since zoning segregates neighborhoods by housing tenure (Shlay and Rossi 1981) and apartments and rentals are too small to accommodate larger families, those with large family size are more likely to live in owner-occupied communities and less likely to move.

In sum, even with geographic, family-of-origin, wealth, SES, and current family characteristics controlled, the disparities between Whites and African Americans and Latinos remain large (the dummy variables representing African Americans and Latinos are statistically significant in the equation). Most of the family and SES characteristics that are significant are theoretically consistent with the spatial assimilation theory.

Three unanticipated findings include the negative effect of parental education and the nonsignificant effects of being raised in an immigrant household and being a single parent as an adult.

With such large racial/ethnic differences remaining even after controlling for racial/ethnic compositional differences, the next step is to learn whether these determinants of neighborhood home ownership work in the same ways for each group. It may be that Whites and Latinos gain more in neighborhood home ownership levels from wealth and other factors than African Americans, or it may be that these factors operate similarly across groups.

COMPARING GROUPS

What are the relative effects of these sets of explanatory variables on neighborhood home ownership for each group? Are these effects race-specific? Table 11.3 presents results for regression analyses for neighborhood home ownership separately for Whites, African Americans, and Latinos. These regressions allow the effects of the predictors to vary for each group and thus provide evidence for the locational attainment hypotheses listed in the preceding section. The columns on the right (with coefficients) allow for a comparison of the relative importance of specific variables in the models for each group. The three columns on the far right side of the table allow for a comparison across groups. These columns reveal group differences in the relationships between the independent and dependent variables.

Overall, the analyses show that wealth—the topic most relevant to this book—affects neighborhood home ownership rates in a similar fashion for African Americans and Latinos, but not for Whites. This finding is consistent with the spatial assimilation theory, but not with place stratification theory.

GEOGRAPHIC CONTROLS

Of all sets of variables, this is the only one for which some variables differentially affect neighborhood home ownership levels for every group, but in most cases, Whites gain more from geographic location than other groups.

As is true with the total sample, the race-specific models show that Whites, African Americans, and Latinos who live in urbanized areas live

TABLE 11.3. Group-Specific Results for Regression Analyses for Neighborhood Home Ownership

Variables	Whites	African Americans	Latinos	W-L Difference	W-AA Difference	AA-L Difference
Controls						
Urban	−12.708*	−22.334*	−16.805*	+	+	+
	(.558)	(1.134)	(1.438)			
Northeast	4.684*	−10.222*	−15.863*	+	+	+
	(.889)	(1.884)	(1.590)			
Midwest	6.945*	1.643	2.278	+	+	
	(.781)	(1.789)	(2.052)			
Southern region	3.694*	2.633	3.074*			
	(.789)	(1.605)	(1.196)			
Family of origin						
1978–79 income	.018*	.036*	.032			
($1,000s)	(.007)	(.018)	(.021)			
Parent—some college	−2.344*	−1.740	1.893	+		+
	(.610)	(1.217)	(1.617)			
Parent—one full-time	1.437	2.000*	2.872*			
	(.879)	(.971)	(1.250)			
Lived with single parent	−2.949*	−1.606*	1.330	+		+
	(.932)	(.947)	(1.396)			
Spoke foreign language	−1.016	1.785	.162			
	(.918)	(2.355)	(1.817)			
Wealth (1998)						
Nonhousing wealth	.012*	.071*	.084*	+	+	
($10,000s)	(.006)	(.038)	(.039)			
SES characteristics						
High school	.441	.736	2.790*			
	(1.002)	(1.344)	(1.399)			
Some college	3.071*	2.974*	3.861*			
	(1.102)	(1.501)	(1.596)			
Four years college	2.174*	5.496*	10.306*	+		
	(1.193)	(1.992)	(2.499)			
Postcollege education	1.352	6.424*	9.517*	+	+	
	(1.297)	(2.469)	(2.759)			
Family income, 1998	.010*	.009	.007			
	(.005)	(.009)	(.009)			
Number of weeks	.029*	.077*	.093*	+	+	
worked	(.015)	(.021)	(.026)			
Current family						
Single parent	.325	−.237	−1.040			
	(1.730)	(1.104)	(1.956)			
Married without	4.384*	4.111*	5.222*			
children	(.961)	(2.134)	(2.432)			
Married with children	4.271*	3.430*	5.710*			
	(.793)	(1.097)	(1.354)			
Family size	.621*	.770*	−.073			+
	(.242)	(.249)	(.362)			
Constant	64.838	64.838	63.322			
Adjusted R^2	.193	.243	.260			
N	3,968	2,413	1,498			

Note: *Significant and have a t-statistic greater than 1.645 (for one-tailed tests with a critical value of 5 percent).
+ Coefficients are significantly different in analyses of each pair.

in neighborhoods with lower rates of home ownership than their nonurban counterparts. On average, African Americans who reside in urban areas live in neighborhoods that have almost 23 percent fewer home owners than the communities in which their nonurban counterparts live. Urban Latinos live in communities with an average home ownership rate that is about 17 percent lower, and urban Whites' neighborhoods have about 13 percent fewer home owners. The results reveal the effects of urban residence vary for each group. On average, urban African Americans live in neighborhoods with lower levels of home ownership than do urban Whites and Latinos. Also, Latinos in urban areas live in areas with lower home ownership than urban Whites.

Another key geographic variable, region of residence, has effects that are inconsistent across groups. Living in the Northeast is associated with residing in less stable neighborhoods for the total sample, as well as for the African American and Latino samples, but has a positive effect for Whites. The group-specific analyses show that, on average, northeastern Latinos live in less stable areas than Whites and African Americans and northeastern African Americans live in less stable areas than Whites. The effect of living in the Midwest on neighborhood home ownership is significant for Whites, but not for African Americans and Latinos. Whites who reside in the Midwest are similar to the total sample in that this variable has a positive effect on neighborhood home ownership. Also, compared with African Americans and Latinos in the Midwest, White midwesterners have higher levels of home ownership. The neighborhood home ownership rates of African Americans and Latinos in the Midwest are not significantly different from their western counterparts nor are they different from each other. As with the total sample, the within-group analyses show that southern residence has a positive effect on neighborhood home ownership for Whites and Latinos but has no effect for African Americans. However, among southern Whites, African Americans, and Latinos, there are similar neighborhood levels of home ownership.

To summarize the effects of geographical location, urban residence has a uniformly negative effect on neighborhood home ownership across groups, but the effect is most severe for African Americans. Also, the effects of region vary by group, with Latino northeasterners at the greatest disadvantage. White and Latino southerners tend to live in more stable neighborhoods than their western counterparts, but these effects are not significantly different across racial/ethnic groups. It is notable that these variables affect neighborhood home ownership even after all of the other controls are in place.

Recall that, for the total sample, residents whose parents had higher incomes, full-time employment, and intact marriages tend to live in neighborhoods with higher levels of home ownership than their less-privileged counterparts. Do these patterns hold when separately examining Whites, African Americans, and Latinos?

In general, the regressions show that the effects of family of origin on neighborhood home ownership vary by group. These variables have less relative importance in the Latino sample and are more important in the White and African American samples. The within-group findings mirror those for the total sample for Whites and African Americans, as those raised by parents with higher incomes reside in more stable neighborhoods as adults. Surprisingly, in analyses of the total sample and the White sample, parental education is negatively related to neighborhood home ownership levels, but it has a positive effect for Latinos and is nonsignificant for African Americans. Having a parent who worked full-time is a significant predictor of home ownership for the total sample and for African Americans and Latinos in the race-specific analyses. Living with a single parent is negatively associated with neighborhood levels of home ownership for the total, White, and African American samples but has no effect for Latinos. Additionally, having spoken a foreign language at home is not a significant predictor of neighborhood home ownership when the groups are combined or when they are analyzed separately.

Comparing across groups, the family-of-origin variables affect African American and White levels of home ownership in a similar fashion in every case. However, two family-of-origin characteristics have a significantly different effect for Latinos than for the other groups, although these variables are not significant in the equations for Latinos. Unlike Whites and African Americans, the effects of parental education and living with a single parent are positive, but these are not significant predictors of neighborhood home ownership rates for Latinos. This is difficult to explain, but one may speculate that Latinos' families of origin may have limited effects on adult outcomes because of their immigrant status, whereas Whites and African Americans are more affected by family backgrounds since they have had more time in this country.

Recall that, for the total sample, wealth has a significant and positive effect on neighborhood home ownership. Table 11.3 shows that this significant positive effect remains for all three groups in the group-specific analyses, meaning that, relative to the other variables in the equation, wealth is a significant predictor of neighborhood home ownership for each group. However, the analyses show that on average, for Latinos and African Americans, higher levels of wealth are more effective in facilitating residence in neighborhoods with higher levels of home ownership than for Whites. Additionally, there is not a significant difference in the effect of wealth on neighborhood home ownership for African Americans and Latinos. Considering that Latinos and African Americans tend to have far less wealth than Whites, it is notable that the effect of wealth on neighborhood home ownership is significantly different for these two non-White groups than Whites. However, the hypothesis that Latinos have greater locational returns to wealth than African Americans is not supported.

ADULT SOCIOECONOMIC STATUS

For the total sample, each level of education has a significantly positive effect on neighborhood home ownership. In the group-specific analyses, education generally affects all racial/ethnic groups, but not consistently at all levels. Relative to the other variables in the equations, education had the greatest impact on home ownership for Latinos. For all groups, completing some college or four years of college increases the home ownership levels in one's neighborhood compared with not having a high school degree. However, within groups, only Latinos benefit from completing high school and only African Americans and Latinos benefit from postcollege education. Thus, African Americans and Whites do not get locational returns at the lowest level of education, and Whites do not get locational returns at the very highest level of education.

As with the total sample, relative to the other variables, family income has a positive effect on neighborhood home ownership for Whites, but not for the other groups. Finally, for the total sample and in each of the group-specific analyses, those who worked more weeks out of the year tended to live in more stable communities.

The group-specific analyses reveal a few interesting findings. African Americans and Latinos with postcollege education and those who work a relatively high number of weeks per year have higher levels of home ownership than their White counterparts. Also, compared with Whites, Latinos with four years of college live in neighborhoods with higher levels of home ownership. However, having four years of college education does not have a different effect on neighborhood home ownership when comparing Latinos to African Americans or Whites to African Americans. It is notable that none of the effects of these variables differ when comparing African Americans to Latinos as they sometimes do when comparing these groups to Whites. This suggests that these variables operate more similarly for minorities but have weaker effects for Whites.

CURRENT FAMILY

The effects of respondents' current family characteristics on neighborhood levels of home ownership do not vary greatly across groups. In the analyses of the total sample, three of the four current family characteristics are significant. The findings for the total sample and the group-specific samples show that single parenthood is a nonsignificant predictor of neighborhood home ownership. In other words, compared with being single without children and divorced with or without children, single parents do not live in less stable communities. As with the total sample, the group-specific analyses show that all groups live in more stable communities when they are married, with or without children. Finally, the positive effect of family size that is found for the total sample is only significant for Whites and African Americans in the race-specific analyses. The group-specific analyses show that, compared with Latinos with larger families, African Americans with larger families live in neighborhoods with higher levels of home ownership, but there is no White-Latino difference in the effect of family size on neighborhood home ownership.

DISCUSSION

Many theories of racial and ethnic inequality lead one to expect that similar processes occur for various racial and ethnic groups when they have the same levels of resources, but this chapter presents regression analyses that challenge this assumption. First, even after controlling for important compositional differences—including wealth—race/ethnicity remains an important predictor of neighborhood levels of home ownership. Second, for each group, wealth is an important predictor of neighborhood levels of home ownership. Third, comparing across groups, wealth is more important for African Americans and Latinos than for Whites in gaining access to a neighborhood with high levels of home ownership.

Some of the factors that lead people to live in neighborhoods with higher levels of home owners have stronger effects for Latinos, some have stronger effects for African Americans, and some have stronger effects for both non-White groups than for Whites. This suggests that Whites with a wide range of family characteristics are able to access good neighborhoods.

Theoretically, this chapter examines the spatial assimilation and place stratification hypotheses of locational attainment by incorporating the effects of family-of-origin, wealth, SES, and current family characteristics into models of neighborhood home ownership. Results show that the spatial assimilation model is fairly effective in explaining neighborhood home ownership rates. The findings also suggest that the model fits African Americans and Latinos better than Whites.

The spatial assimilation theory argues that adults whose parents have greater SES levels, intact families, and greater acculturation to the United States should have better locational outcomes. With the exception of the geographic controls, SES characteristics are the most consistent predictors and have the greatest effects for African Americans and Latinos. These characteristics improve the chances of living in communities where more residents own their homes. For Latinos, all but one SES variable are significant. For Whites and African Americans, all SES variables are significant with the exception of two. African Americans and Latinos often get higher locational returns to these characteristics than Whites. This suggests that we may need to look at these models in a new way. Perhaps the fact that SES variables do not seem as important for predicting Whites' residential outcomes indicates that non-White racial/ethnic group members *need* to have specific characteristics to gain access and Whites do not.

Recall that hypothesis 1 predicted that adults whose parents have greater levels of SES, intact families, and greater acculturation to the United States will live in more stable neighborhoods. I find that these characteristics do not improve the chances of living in more stable neighborhoods for all groups. There is not one consistent finding about the effects of family of origin on neighborhood home ownership that holds for every group. In general, in the within-group analyses, Whites and African Americans are more likely to convert socioeconomic and structural familial characteristics into neighborhood home owner-ship. Latinos convert parental socioeconomic variables into neighbor-hood home ownership to a far lesser extent since only parental work is significantly related to home ownership for them.

Hypothesis 2 predicted that locational returns to family-of-origin char-acteristics will be lower for African Americans than for Latinos and Whites. The group-specific analyses show that only two childhood family variables differently affect home ownership rates across groups: parental education and having a single parent. Whites and African Americans are similarly negatively affected by these characteristics, but Latinos are pos-itively affected by these factors. Yet, relative to other variables, family-of-origin characteristics are less important for Latinos than Whites and African Americans.

Moving to adult SES, hypothesis 3 predicted that those with higher SES levels will live in more stable neighborhoods. In four cases, this is true for all groups. Wealthier people, those with some college, those with four years of college, and those who work more weeks in a year live in neighborhoods that are more stable. However, Latinos, but not Whites and African Americans, translate the lowest level of education into loca-tional attainment. African Americans and Latinos also benefit from hav-ing postcollege education, but Whites do not.

Hypothesis 4 predicted that African Americans will have fewer loca-tional returns to SES characteristics than Whites and Latinos, but I find no support for this. In contrast, African Americans and Latinos have greater returns to wealth, postcollege education, and number of weeks worked than Whites, and Latinos also have greater returns to a four-year degree than Whites. It is notable that African Americans and Latinos do not have greater returns to their SES when compared with each other.

Overall, the results show that for all groups, when aspects of respon-dents' geographic location, family of origin, SES, and current family are controlled, wealth remains a significant predictor of neighborhood home ownership. However, in examining the model as a whole and how well it fits each group, it is noteworthy that African Americans are still behind Latinos in getting access to neighborhoods that fit their socioeconomic profiles.

Finally, regarding adult family characteristics, hypothesis 5 predicts that adults with less stable family structures and larger families will live in neighborhoods with lower levels of home ownership. The results for the total sample show mixed support for this hypothesis, with two of the four variables having the predicted effect: those who are married with children and without children live in areas with high levels of home ownership. In the within-group analyses, we see that these two factors are relatively good predictors of neighborhood home ownership for all groups. This is true for all groups with respect to two variables: people who are married with or without children live in more stable neighborhoods. The remaining effects of family structure are varied—but more consistent for African Americans and Whites than Latinos. None of the groups' neighborhood home ownership levels are significantly affected by single parenthood, and Whites and African Americans with larger families actually live in more stable communities.

Hypothesis 6 argues that the locational returns to having a stable family structure will be greater for Whites and Latinos than for African Americans. The group-specific analyses show that this hypothesis is not supported. Being a single parent, married with children, or married without children has similar effects across groups. Additionally, compared with Latinos with large families, African Americans with large families actually live in neighborhoods with higher levels of home ownership.

Looking at all sets of factors, the analyses show that Latinos are the group most likely to get the greatest returns to individual characteristics, although in one case (family size) African Americans get higher returns. Whites have greater returns than both non-White groups in the case of geographic location variables like urban residence, northeastern residence, and midwestern residence.

Overall, the spatial assimilation model is best supported in the model for Latinos. It is clear that wealth, education, and employment help all groups gain access to stable areas, but these characteristics are essential for African Americans and Latinos and have a major impact on residential stability. Yet the place stratification model still applies. In the end, compared with African Americans and Latinos, Whites seem to be able to live in stable neighborhoods, regardless of who they are and what they have.

NOTES

1. Brooks-Gunn et al. 1993; Curry, Schwirian, and Woldoff 2004; Massey 1996; Sampson and Groves 1989; Sampson and Morenoff 2000; Shaw and McKay 1942; Wilson 1987; Woldoff 2002

2. Alba and Logan 1991; Alba, Logan, and Bellair 1994; Alba, Logan, and Stults 2000a, 2000b; Alba and Nee 1997; Logan and Alba 1993; Logan, Alba, and Leung 1996; Rosenbaum and Friedman 2001; White and Sassler 2000.

3. Nonresponse on the value of wealth is a common problem in wealth surveys (Fries, Starr-McCluer, Sundén 1998). I correct for nonresponse in 1998 wealth and 1979 income items by using random regression imputation to handle missing data on wealth and income. Random regression imputation replaces missing values with predicted values from an estimated regression and adds an error term to predicted values to correct an underestimated variance (Seastrom 2002).

REFERENCES

Alba, Richard D., and John R. Logan. 1991. "Variations on Two Themes: Racial and Ethnic Patterns in the Attainment of Suburban Residence." *Demography* 28: 431–53.
———. 1993. "Minority Proximity to Whites in the Suburbs: An Individual Analysis of Segregation." *American Journal of Sociology* 98 (6): 1388–1427.
Alba, Richard D., John R. Logan, and Paul E. Bellair. 1994. "Living with Crime: The Implications of Racial/Ethnic Differences in Suburban Location." *Social Forces* 73 (2): 395–434.
Alba, Richard D., John R. Logan, and Brian J. Stults. 2000a. "The Changing Neighborhood Contexts of the Immigrant Metropolis." *Social Forces* 79 (2): 587–621.
———. 2000b. "How Segregated Are Middle-Class African Americans?" *Social Problems* 47 (4): 543–58.
Alba, Richard D., and Victor Nee. 1997. "Rethinking Assimilation Theory for a New Era of Immigration." *International Migration Review* 31 (4): 826–74.
Brooks-Gunn, Jeanne, Greg J. Duncan, Pamela Kato Klebanov, and Naomi Sealand. 1993. "Do Neighborhoods Influence Child and Adolescent Development?" *American Journal of Sociology* 99 (2): 353–95.
Charles, Kerwin Kofi, and Erik Hurst. 2002. "The Transition to Home Ownership and the Black-White Wealth Gap." *Review of Economics and Statistics* 84 (2): 281–97.
Clark, W. A. V. 1986. "Residential Segregation in American Cities: A Review and Interpretation." *Population Research and Policy Review* 5: 95–127.
———. 1991. "Residential Preferences and Neighborhood Racial Segregation: A Test of the Schelling Segregation Model." *Demography* 28 (1): 1–19.
Collins, J. Michael, and Doug Dylla. 2001. "Mind the Gap: Issues in Overcoming the Information, Income, Wealth, and Supply Gaps Facing Potential Buyers of Affordable Homes." Local Initiatives Support Coalition (LISC) Center for Home Ownership, Washington, DC.
Conley, Dalton. 1999. *Being Black, Living in the Red: Race, Wealth, and Social Policy in America.* Los Angeles: University of California Press.
Curry, Timothy J., Kent P. Schwirian, and Rachael A. Woldoff. 2004. *Big Time Sports, and Downtown Redevelopment.* Columbus: Ohio State University Press.

Davern, Michael E., and Patricia J. Fisher. 2001. "Household Net Worth and Asset Ownership: 1995." In *U.S. Census Bureau, Current Population Reports, Household Economic Studies,* series P70–71. Washington, DC: U.S. Government Printing Office.

Freeman, Lance. 2000. "Minority Housing Segregation: A Test of Three Perspectives." *Journal of Urban Affairs* 22 (1): 15–35.

Fries, Gerhard, Martha Starr-McCluer, and Anika E. Sundén. 1998. "The Measurement of Household Wealth Using Survey Data." Federal Reserve Board of Governors.

Galster, George C., and Mark W. Keeney. 1988. "Race, Residence, Discrimination, and Economic Opportunity: Modeling the Nexus of Urban Racial Phenomena." *Urban Affairs Quarterly* 24 (1): 87–117.

Gittleman, Maury, and Edward N. Wolff. 2000. "Racial Wealth Disparities: Is the Gap Closing?" Economics Working Paper Archive, Jerome Levy Economics Institute.

Haurin, Donald R., Robert D. Dietz, and Bruce A. Weinberg. 2003. "The Impact of Neighborhood Homeownership Rates: A Review of the Theoretical and Empirical Literature." *Journal of Housing Research* 13 (2): 119–51.

Haurin, Donald R., Patric H. Hendershott, and Susan M. Wachter. 1997. "Borrowing Constraints and the Tenure Choice of Young Households." *Journal of Housing Research* 8 (2): 137–54.

Hirsch, Arnold R. 1983. *Making the Second Ghetto: Race and Housing in Chicago.* New York: Cambridge University Press.

Kaufman, Philip, Martha Naomi Alt, and Christopher Chapman. 2001. "Dropout Rates in the United States: 2000." National Center for Education Statistics, U.S. Department of Education, Washington, DC.

Keister, Lisa A. 2000. *Wealth in America: Trends in Wealth Inequality.* New York: Cambridge University Press.

Krivo, Lauren J. 1986. "Home Ownership Differences between Hispanics and Anglos in the United States." *Social Problems* 33 (4): 319–34.

———. 1995. "Immigrant Characteristics and Hispanic-Anglo Housing Inequality." *Demography* 32 (4): 599–615.

Logan, John, and Richard Alba. 1993. "Locational Returns to Human Capital: Minority Access to Suburban Community Resources." *Demography* 30 (2): 243–68.

Logan, John R., Richard A. Alba, and Shu-Yin Leung. 1996. "Minority Access to White Suburbs: A Multiregional Comparison." *Social Forces* 74 (3): 851–81.

Long, Larry H. 1972. "The Influence of Number and Ages of Children on Residential Mobility." *Demography* 9 (3): 371–82.

Massey, Douglas. 1985. "Ethnic Residential Segregation: A Theoretical Synthesis and Empirical Review." *Sociology and Social Research* 69: 315–50.

———. 1996. "The Age of Extremes: Concentrated Affluence and Poverty in the Twenty-first Century." *Demography* 33: 395–412.

Massey, Douglas S., and Nancy A. Denton. 1985. "Spatial Assimilation as a Socioeconomic Outcome." *American Sociological Review* 50: 94–106.

———. 1993. *American Apartheid: Segregation and the Making of the Underclass.* Cambridge: Harvard University Press.

Mayer, Christopher J., and Gary V. Engelhardt. 1996. "Gifts, Down Payments, and Housing Affordability." *Journal of Housing Research* 7 (1): 59–77.

McKinnon, Jesse. 2003. "The Black Population in the United States: March 2002." *Current Population Survey Reports* Washington, DC: U.S. Census Bureau.

Mikesell, James J. 1998. "Federal Housing Assistance Promotes Homeownership." *Rural Conditions and Trends* 9 (1): 25–31.

Oliver, Melvin L., and Thomas M. Shapiro. 1995. *Black Wealth/White Wealth: New Perspectives on Racial Inequality.* New York: Routledge.

Patterson, Orlando. 1997. *The Ordeal of Integration: Progress and Resentment in America's "Racial" Crisis.* New York: Civitas/Counterpoint.

Ralph, John, and James Crouse. 1997. "Reading and Mathematics Achievement: Growth in High School." National Center for Education Statistics, Washington, DC

Rohe, William M., and Leslie S. Stewart. 1996. "Homeownership and Neighborhood Homeownership." *Housing Policy Debate* 7 (1): 37–46.

Rosenbaum, Emily, and Samatha Friedman. 2001. "Differences in the Locational Attainment of Immigrant and Native-Born Households with Children in New York City." *Demography* 38: 337–48.

Rossi, Peter H. 1955. *Why Families Move.* New York: MacMillan.

Sampson, Robert J. 1988. "Local Friendship Ties and Community Attachment in Mass Society: A Multi-Level Systemic Model." *American Sociological Review* 53: 766–79.

Sampson, Robert J., and W. Byron Groves. 1989. "Community Structure and Crime: Testing Social-Disorganization Theory." *American Journal of Sociology* 94(4): 774–802.

Sampson, Robert J., and Jeffrey D. Morenoff. 2000. "Public Health and Safety in Context: Lessons from Community-Level Theory on Social Capital." In Institute of Medicine, ed. 366–89. *Promoting Health: Intervention Strategies from Social and Behavioral Research.* National Academy Press, Washington, D.C.

Sampson, Robert J., Stephen Raudenbush, and Felton Earls. 1997. "Neighborhoods and Violent Crime: A Multilevel Study of Collective Efficacy." *Science* 277: 918–24.

Scholz, John Karl, and Kara Levine. 2002. "U.S. Black-White Wealth Inequality: A Survey." Institute for Research on Poverty, working paper.

Seastrom, Barbara. 2002. "National Center for Education Statistics (NCES) Statistical Standards." Publication no. 2003601.

Shaw, Clifford R., and Henry D. McKay. 1942. *Juvenile Delinquency and Urban Areas.* Chicago: University of Chicago Press.

Shlay, Anne B., and Peter H. Rossi. 1981. "Keeping Up the Neighborhood: Estimating the Net Effects of Zoning." *American Sociological Review* 46: 703–19.

Solon, Gary. 1992. "Intergenerational Income Mobility in the U.S." *American Economic Review* 82 (3): 393–408.

Thernstrom, Stephan, and Abigail M. Thernstrom. 1997. *America in Black and White: One Nation, Indivisible.* New York: Simon and Schuster.

U.S. Bureau of the Census. 2000. *Census of Population and Housing, 2000.* Summary File 3. Washington, DC: U.S. Bureau of the Census.

White, Michael J., and Sharon Sassler. 2000. "Judging Not Only by Color: Ethnicity, Nativity, and Neighborhood Attainment." *Social Science Quarterly* 81 (4): 1015–31.

Wilson, William J. 1987. *The Truly Disadvantaged: The Inner City, the Underclass, and Public Policy.* Chicago: University of Chicago Press.

Woldoff, Rachael A. 2002. "The Effects of Local Stressors on Neighborhood Attachment." *Social Forces* 81 (1): 87–116.

Yinger, John. 1995. *Closed Doors, Opportunities Lost: The Continuing Costs of Housing Discrimination.* New York: Russell Sage Foundation.

12 Wealth, Civic Engagement, & Democratic Practice

JESSICA GORDON NEMBHARD &
ANTHONY A. BLASINGAME

Wealth holding is an important dimension to understanding civic engagement and political efficacy. In a preliminary working paper (2002), we examine the literature and explore many of the ways in which economic status and interests, as well as political-economic relationships, impact the extent and quality of individual civic participation, including the political behavior and political influence of individuals. We also examine the ways that group activity in the pursuit of primarily economic interests impact the level or quality of civic engagement and political influence of members (and in some cases the consequences for nonmembers). The broad category of civic engagement includes charitable giving; volunteering; membership and leadership in community, religious, political, and other civic organizations; and voting, political participation, and other such activities encompassed in good citizenship. The types of organizations given specific consideration in the 2002 working paper are labor unions, cooperatives and/or democratically organized workplaces, local community groups that are primarily concerned with the costs or benefits resulting from the provision of local public goods and services, competing socioeconomic status groups (i.e., city versus suburban groups or wealthy versus low-income groups in competition for economic and political power), and corporations, particularly in the United States.

In our 2002 paper we find that economic democracy, socioeconomic diversity, and interest-group membership (especially as collective ways to counter or balance prevailing influences and monied interests) en-

294   - ✿ -

hance or facilitate positive civic engagement and political participation. Wealth inequality and, particularly, corporate hegemony diminish or restrict civic engagement and political participation. However, there are few conclusive findings about the magnitude of the impact of socioeconomic status, social capital accumulation, interest-group participation, wealth, or corporate influence on individual civic engagement. Only a small number of academic empirical studies directly address these issues, and a majority of them explore the relationships to voting rather than the other aspects of civic engagement. Most studies do not delineate the relationships in ways that expose, measure, or explain the magnitude of the impact, although these studies do indicate the direction of impact. More longitudinal data and analysis are needed, along with innovations in appropriate outcome measurement instruments and case study designs. The most promising of the research is that which finds relationships between (1) participation in democratic ownership and governance of economic enterprises and (2) increased civic and political participation of members.

Our previous findings suggest that it is important to consider the impact of substantial inequality in wealth and economic power on the civic engagement of individuals. Ideally this should be studied across class, gender, race, and ethnicity. While some studies of community development attempt to connect economic power with political efficacy and political empowerment, few studies have considered how wealth, and inequality in wealth and economic power, affect the degree of civic engagement, using a range of types of participation—particularly among communities of color and low-income communities. The acknowledged connection between socioeconomic status and participation in civic life may be directly related to levels of individual educational attainment and in part related to family income levels. Much of the existing empirical work on this issue focuses on educational attainment rather than wealth and accumulated economic power.

This chapter examines the role of socioeconomic and wealth status on civic participation for Whites and African Americans. We expand our previous investigation with a specific empirical study—a study of the relationship between (1) wealth and (2) charitable giving and volunteering—using data from the Center of Philanthropy Panel Study (COPPS) of the 2001 Panel Study of Income Dynamics (PSID) among Whites and African Americans. Much more empirical analysis needs to be done; however, it is difficult to find the necessary data. This study only begins to investigate some of the issues that arise. We hope it paves the way for more sophisticated and comprehensive explorations.

In this chapter, we first review what is known about the relationship between socioeconomic inequality and civic engagement. We look briefly at the debate about wealth and political participation. Next we discuss ways that democratic economic participation, particularly membership in democratic economic institutions such as cooperatives, increases wealth and civic engagement. We then present our empirical analysis of the relationship of wealth to charitable giving and volunteering. We deepen the analysis by comparing White and African American charitable giving and volunteering, by distinguishing between the incidence and amounts of giving and volunteering, and by disaggregating between the kinds of charitable organizations that receive donations. We end with a summary of our findings and a discussion about strategies that increase wealth, civic engagement, and democratic practice.

SOCIOECONOMIC STATUS

One of the important debates in the civic participation literature centers around the impact of socioeconomic status on political participation in the United States. Conventional wisdom suggests that individuals with more education and income have more resources—disposable income, leisure time and interest, and human capital—and accumulate greater levels of social capital (social facility, status, connections, contacts, leadership, etc.) and therefore are more likely to participate in civic life. Given that participation in civic life has been observed to be in decline over the last several decades (according to Putnam 2000 and others), at the same time that educational attainment and earnings have increased for many in the United States, the conventional wisdom has come under criticism.

Oliver's (1999) work points out that during the last several decades the United States experienced a marked segregation along socioeconomic class, with high-income, highly educated individuals migrating to suburbs, leaving cities predominantly low income and relatively less educated. This development of a new city versus suburbs dichotomy has been accompanied by what Oliver describes as a decline in "'norms and networks of civil engagement' that sustain their democratic processes." Oliver contends that the observed increase in economic segregation is the source of the decline in civic structures. This phenomenon creates separate, less diverse low-income and high-income areas with fewer of the more racially diverse middle-income neighborhoods characterized by diversity in educational attainment and class (also see Wilson 1987).

Wilson's (1987) study suggests that socioeconomic inequality and segregation threaten the health of civic life. He does not specifically address individual civic engagement, but he proposes that the geographic concentration of the economically disadvantaged erodes the civic structure and social organization necessary for healthy communities to develop. He argues that concentrated, severe urban poverty severely disrupts or destroys institutions like families and churches.[1] The issue of socioeconomic segregation is important to our understanding of economic power, or lack of, and the health of key civic institutions. Public policies have played a role in increasing socioeconomic segregation and isolation, particularly for African Americans, as well as the existing segregation limiting African American participation and involvement in civic and political activities (see Massey and Anderson 2001; Thomas and Ritzdorf 1997; Gregory 1998; McDougall 1993).

Another perspective suggests that, given economic segregation, the level of civic participation in specific areas will be determined by its level of social need. Affluent areas have less civic engagement because their social needs are less, while poorer areas with great social needs will have the highest level of civic engagement. This contrasts with the view that the homogenous higher-income community with a greater level of social capital will have higher civic participation. Oliver (1999) finds that the evidence does not support either of these views. He finds that civic engagement is higher in middle-income areas. He explains that the greater economic diversity found in middle-income communities generates much more group competition for local government budgets than occurs in either low-income or wealthy communities. As a result of group competition for shares of local budgets, residents of middle-income neighborhoods participate more in local politics. With perceived competition, special interest groups feel more compelled to be active in order to secure their own interests.

WEALTH, ECONOMIC POWER, & POLITICAL ENGAGEMENT

As the chapters in this volume attest, distributions of income and wealth have become significantly more unequal in the late twentieth and early twenty-first centuries. For example, in a comparison of the distribution of aggregate income earned by different percentages of the population, the lowest fifth of the population (20 percent who have the lowest incomes) earned only 3.5 percent of aggregate, or total, U.S. income, while the top fifth earned half of all income in 2001. The top 5 percent of all income earners hold 22.4 percent of aggregate income or 4.5 times their share (U.S. Census Bureau 2002b). For the top earners (highest fifth) these percentages have been increasing since the 1960s (from a low of 42.8 percent of the aggregate in 1968 to the high of 50.1 in 2001). For all other fifths of the population, their shares of aggregate income have been declining over the same period. In addition, the U.S. Gini ratios measuring income inequality of households have increased almost steadily from 0.388 in 1968 (when income distribution was most equal; Left Business Observer 1993) to 0.466 in 2001 (the highest level since the ratio has been calculated) (U.S. Census Bureau 2002a).[2] Between 1980 and 1998, average CEO pay compared with average factory worker pay increased from 42:1 to 531:1 (United for a Fair Economy 2004).

Wealth inequality in the United States is more severe than is income inequality, and increasing. Wolff (2004), for example, summarizes that the wealthy continue to increase their privilege as the poorest continue to lose. The average wealth of the poorest 40 percent, for example, decreased by 44 percent between 1983 and 2001, while the number of households worth $1 million, $5 million, and $10 million surged during the same period (Wolff 2004, 23). The average wealth of the poorest 40 percent fell to only $2,900 by 2001. The levels of net worth, financial wealth, and income of the top 1 percent of wealth holders continued to grow disproportionately during the same period (33 percent, 53 percent, and 28 percent, respectively, Wolff 2004, 23). In addition, the chapters in this volume all report persistently large gaps in wealth between Whites and other ethnicities and races, and between men and women, which we do not repeat here. The data we use in the following from the COPPS 2001 PSID indicate that White wealth is more than five times that of Black wealth.

Some observers argue that the rise in economic inequality contributes directly to the decline in civic engagement and political participation (see, for example, Greider 1992; Phillips 2002; Hill 2002; Green 2002). While many scholars readily admit that socioeconomic status affects individual civic engagement and have addressed this relationship, there is little empirical research examining the impact of wealth and economic power on political participation and civic engagement. This means that there are also no longitudinal studies of the possible changes over time, which would help us better understand these relationships.

Generally, individuals engage in civic activities because they want to help themselves and/or others, and in order to affect the decisions and decision-making processes of their government in the hope of securing public policy initiatives that are consistent with their individual and/or their group interests. Some political and economic researchers suggest that wealthy individuals in the United States make use of their considerable economic power to obtain disproportionate levels of political power. Wolff (2004) notes that "in a representative democracy, the distribution of power is often related to the distribution of wealth" (1). Greider (1992) argues that "interest-group bargaining" has become the norm, with the ultimate effects being undemocratic: "People with limited resources, with no real representation in the higher levels of politics, are bound to lose in this environment" (28). An example of the power of the monied class is that this group has steadily reduced its tax burden over the past twenty-five years more than any other group (Greider 1992). Phillips (2002) notes:

> The erosion within the United States of popular and national sovereignty, some of it tied to corporate behavior, also crystallized as a concern between 1995 and 2000. Public influence shrank as unelected experts became ever more prominent in national decision-making. Judges and Federal Reserve Boards enlarged their roles while corporate and bank influence over Congress and the White House climbed in tandem with the dollar totals of huge federal campaign contributions and lobbying outlays. Voters began to understand themselves to be on a seesaw—popular influence fell as that of the economic elites rose. (413)

Similarly, more than sixty years ago, W. E. B. Du Bois's concerns about wealth inequality led him to observe that the monopolization of wealth was increasing the power of the ruling oligarchy and severely curtailing prospects of using meritocracy to gain social and political influence and power.

> Many assume that an upper social class maintains its status mainly by reason of its superior culture. It may, however, maintain its status because of its wealth and political power and in that case its ranks can be successfully invaded only by the wealthy. In white America, it is in this direction that we have undoubtedly changed the older pattern of

social hierarchy. Birth and culture still count, but the main avenue to social power and class domination is wealth: income and oligarchic economic power, the consequent political power and the prestige of those who own and control capital and distribute credit. This makes a less logical social hierarchy and one that can only be penetrated by the will and permission of the ruling oligarchy or the chances of gambling. Education, thrift, hard work and character undoubtedly are influential, but they are implemented with power only as they gain wealth; and as land, natural resources, credit and capital are increasingly monopolized, they gain wealth by permission of the dominating wealthy class. (Du Bois 1986 [1940], 692–93).

Powerful economic interests determine the limited choices that people have at the polls, for example, because those with resources and money to spare pay for the campaigns of those they choose. They also have money to pay lobbyists who press certain issues and flood representatives with misinformation and threats about money for the next campaign. Candidates need money to run for office. In our system with limited public funding for campaigns, corporate money and private wealth pay for this. Once candidates assume office, reelection campaigns and the policy development require money, information, and time (to get their points known and win over public opinion or the opinion of other legislatures). Here again corporations and the wealthy have the time and money to lobby, finance their own research favorable to their position, and put out disinformation. In a system where people vote with their dollars, democracy is held hostage by those who can pay the most for information, its dissemination, and the reputation of those supporting or opposing it. Greider (1992) suggests that the real issues are in the "politics of governing," not the elections themselves. Those who make it on the ballots may already be handpicked, and the decisions they make once in office are heavily influenced by those who had the most resources to get them in office and to convince or threaten them to vote a certain way.

Much of the debate surrounding recent campaign finance reform in the United States consisted of proponents of this reform proposal arguing that wealthy interests, particularly big corporate interests, could purchase more influence in Congress and negate the efforts of less financially influential individuals and groups who compete with corporations for economic and political power.[3] Green (2002) documents, for example, that "while in 1976 it cost an average of $87,000 to win a House seat and $609,000 a U.S. Senate seat, those amounts grew by 2000 . . . to $842,000 for the House and $7.2 million for the Senate—a tenfold leap (or more than threefold in current dollars)." No politician can afford to ignore this reality. Green argues,

> The scandal of strings-attached money corrupting politics and government is the most urgent problem in America today—because it makes it harder to solve nearly all our other problems. How can we produce smart defense, environmental, and health policies if arms contractors, oil firms, and HMOs have such a hammerlock over the committees charged with considering reforms? How can we adequately fund education and child care if special interests win special tax breaks that deplete public resources? How can we attract the best people to be public servants if those who run and serve are increasingly either special-interest or self-financing multimillionaires?

Green cites a study from the Center for Responsive Politics, which finds that 20 percent of the members of Congress admitted that campaign contributions affected their voting. Half claimed contributions had no effect, and 30 percent responded that they were not sure.[4]

Thus, the political power of those with little economic wealth significantly decreases along with their ability to obtain greater economic power. Wealthy individuals and the organizations they control possess greater resources with which to lobby government officials, contribute campaign donations to candidates for elections, and also shape public opinion. In so doing, they are often able to maintain and increase their economic power as they buy more political influence. Economic inequality in the United States, especially wealth inequality, therefore threatens the ability of members of society, particularly the economically disadvantaged, to affect the decisions of their governments and institutions through civic participation.

WORKPLACE DEMOCRACY, WEALTH
ACCUMULATION, & CIVIC ENGAGEMENT

On a more positive note, workplace democracy seems to correlate with both wealth accumulation and civic engagement. There are several types of democratic workplaces, which range from formal legal cooperative businesses to businesses where employees own shares, to businesses run democratically, particularly by the employees, or as a collective.[5] Although not

studied widely, a few scholars have investigated the relationship between cooperative ownership, workplace democracy, and civic and political participation in the United States. A few scholars are also beginning to find that cooperative and democratic ownership facilitate wealth
accumulation.

Equity in a business is one of the major components of a household's
wealth (see Leigh, chap. 1, in this volume, for example). Expanding, encouraging, and facilitating business ownership and broader business
ownership, as well as people's equity in a business, must necessarily contribute to wealth accumulation and enhance wealth portfolios. While traditional business wealth has been well studied, wealth from cooperative
enterprise ownership and employee stock ownership plans (ESOPs) has
not—particularly not for their wealth-producing abilities or potential.

Ownership Associates (2003) reports on two studies that explore
wealth accumulation through ESOPs. Based on ESOP asset values in 1995
and 1996, both studies find that the wealth held per employee in ESOPs
was higher than in non-ESOP companies. In the Washington State example, employees of ESOP firms had almost 2.5 times the retirement
wealth of similar non-ESOP firms. Wages were also about 12 percent
higher in the ESOP companies than the non-ESOP companies. According
to these studies, average asset accounts in ESOPs range from $24,620 to
over $100,000.

Gordon Nembhard (2002) has begun to investigate the relationship
between democratic ownership and wealth accumulation. Housing cooperatives, for example, provide home ownership opportunities, particularly for low-income people who might not otherwise be able to own a
home on their own. Home ownership provides equity accumulation and
tax advantages. Recent research suggests that home owners accumulate
more wealth in general than renters (see Gordon Nembhard 2002). Cooperative business ventures and employee ownership provide investment and business ownership opportunities, particularly to people who
might not otherwise be able to afford such opportunities as individuals.
Most of the little existing "evidence" comes in the form of anecdotal information and case study surveys of individual enterprises. Cooperatives
tend to reduce costs both for members and patrons, pay living wages,
generate income, and return patronage refunds—and in those ways help
members accumulate wealth. Gordon Nembhard (2002) finds that successful cooperatives provide monetary returns to their members through
annual dividends (patronage refunds), equity appreciation, and experi-

ence. In addition, although often not publicly traded, even initial owner-ship shares appreciate. Since 1987, worker-owners of Cooperative Home Care Associates in the South Bronx, New York, for example, have earned annual dividends of between 25 and 50 percent on their initial invest-ment (see http://www. paraprofessional.org/Sections/chca.htm). The co-op also maximizes wages and benefits for members, providing paid vaca-tions and health insurance and stable employment—all unprecedented in this sector. Many of these women were formerly receiving public as-sistance before joining the cooperative. Surveys and interviews with CEOs and directors about the history of patronage refunds and distribu-tion systems will help give a picture of individual member wealth cre-ation and asset ownership through ownership in cooperative businesses.

Successful cooperative corporations have increasing assets and return surplus to their members. While data about cooperatives are scarce, par-ticularly because government statistics include cooperative businesses in the category "Other" (along with a host of other kinds of nontradi-tional businesses), we do have basic statistics about the revenues and as-sets of some cooperatives. The National Cooperative Bank analyzes the wealthiest one hundred cooperative companies annually. Total assets of these companies ranged from a high of $38.12 billion to a low of $31 mil-lion in 2003, a steady increase over previous years. The average value of the assets of the "Co-op 100" in 2003 was almost $2.85 billion (NCB 2004).[6] As cooperatives these assets belong to the members but are dis-tributed in a variety of ways according to their charters. Looking at total assets only gives us a glimpse of how these companies contribute to the wealth of their owner-members.

In terms of farmer-owned co-ops, the total asset value was $27 billion in 1998 (Chesnick 2000, the most recent study). Total investment (in other cooperatives and other businesses) was $3.5 billion, an increase of 21 percent in 1998. The "members payable" accounts give an idea of the funds that members have tied up in these cooperatives. These include "cash patronage refunds, dividends and revolving equity that have been declared but not yet paid" (Chesnick 2000, 4). Of the $27 billion in com-bined assets, $1.3 billion belongs directly to individual member ac-counts, and total member equity increased to a record high of $9.9 bil-lion in 1998 (Chesnick 2000, 5). All commodity groups showed an increase in equity certificates ($6 billion total). The total of members payable accounts, total member equity, and total equity certificates ($17.2 billion) combined constitute 63.7 percent of total assets,[7] which suggests that individual co-op members do share in the wealth of these companies.

The stability of the income, experiences gained, and the opportunities provided by the ownership share are all additional forms of wealth from cooperative ownership. The value of the pooled resources gives a picture of communal/co-op wealth, which, in addition to individual members' assets, which also has a positive impact on quality of life and civic participation. Much more research is warranted in this area. Much of what little we know is anecdotal, or industry-specific, or at the company level rather than the individual level. Too few studies exist, and the data are quite limited. Therefore, we continue to have little data on or understanding about the range of contributions workplace democracy and cooperative ownership make to wealth accumulation and/or civic life and political efficacy, even as we have many hints that there is a strong positive relationship.

Regardless of its form, some theorists predict that a democratization of workplaces promotes exactly the political learning that is necessary for greater participatory democracy in the wider society. Spear (1999), for example, contends that cooperatives create "social efficiency," in addition to achieving economic efficiency. This social efficiency is derived from the self-help, self-management, empowerment, and concern for community principles upon which cooperatives are based. Gordon Nembhard (2000), in a review of the literature on democratic economic participation, concludes,

> Research in this area finds not only traditional economic benefits from economic democracy—productivity, efficiency, and increased skills and profitability—but also socioeconomic benefits (for lack of a better term)—improved working conditions and quality of employment, job and economic security, concern for the environment and community development in general, increased self esteem, and empowerment in many areas of the participants' lives. (28)

From interviews with women worker-owners, Weiss and Clamp (1992) find that cooperatives "afford women a number of important benefits, including empowerment, leadership training, learning opportunities not available in traditional work settings, and increased self-esteem" (225).

Much of the relevant empirical existing literature, though small, builds upon Pateman's study (1970), which finds that greater employee control over his or her own work is positively correlated with political

participation. Elden (1981) empirically demonstrates the positive relationship between workplace democracy and the involvement of workers
in civic life outside of the workplace. Elden tests the correlations of various aspects of work life with political participation outside of work and
obtains findings exactly consistent with Pateman's theory. He cites similar studies that are also consistent with the hypothesis that political
skills and political efficacy obtained within the democratic workplace are
transferable to life in the civic arena outside of work. Similarly, Greenberg's (1986) study of the Plywood Cooperatives examines the relationship between workplace democracy and political participation. Based on
his analysis of worker-shareholders in the Plywood Cooperatives and
their counterparts in conventional work settings, Greenberg finds that
while no differences are found in voting, "worker-shareholders were significantly more active in all phases of political life than workers in conventional firms" (131). This difference increased over time so that the
advantage of political learning continued to grow.

Democratic ownership in general is also being found to be a positive
influence on civic engagement. Members of housing cooperatives are
found to be more civically engaged (see Cooperative Housing Coalition
2000; Saegert and Winkel 2000). Anecdotal data indicate that many cooperative businesses are very community minded and contribute to job
creation and community development, monetarily and in other ways
(Gordon Nembhard 2004b). Gordon Nembhard (2004a, 2004b) is beginning to find similar results in studies of African American–owned cooperatives: member-owners help develop their communities, engage in
high levels of education and training, increase their leadership skills, and
become leaders in other organizations and civic pursuits (also see Federation of Southern Cooperatives/Land Assistance Fund 2002). Most cooperatives also engage in charitable giving.

In a relevant study, though conducted in Italy, Erdal (1999) finds that
social health and civic participation are positively related to measures of
democratic ownership and/or employment in a democratic workplace.
He conducted an empirical study comparing social health and participation in three towns in northern Italy with different levels of cooperative
ownership. In the town with the highest level of the workforce employed
in cooperatives (25 percent), citizens had a higher quality of life than in
the other towns. This town, Imola, scored highest (positively) on seven-
teen of the nineteen combined measures about quality of life. Experience of crime, police activity, cardiovascular mortality, perception of the

gap between rich and poor were all lowest in Imola. Positives such as confidence in government, perceiving politicians to be on your side, posteducation training rates, and physical and emotional health were all highest in Imola. Interestingly, those who reported good physical health were more likely to also report being members of voluntary organizations. There were slight but not significant differences between the towns on the social networks residents felt they had (the majority had them; a few more said they had them in Imola). Imola had the highest number of respondents in one or more voluntary organizations (about 41 percent). However, the frequency of involvement in voluntary associations, mean hours in volunteer work, and committee membership were all not significantly different between the towns, and the number of positive responses on all the volunteering questions was too low for any meaningful statistical results. Sassuolo (with no cooperatives) scored highest only on time children spent in school and importance of education for happiness, while in the other two towns the population was actually better educated and the truancy rates were lower.

We do not yet know how much of the increased well-being and civic participation of members of cooperatives and democratic workplaces are due to increased income and economic security, increased participation in enterprise governance, or increased wealth—or some combination. This is an area that needs much more research.

WEALTH & CHARITABLE GIVING & VOLUNTEERING—EMPIRICAL ANALYSIS

We investigate the relationship, across racial and ethnic groups in the United States, between household wealth (net worth) and civic and political participation. Since most studies on civic engagement do not include wealth data, we possess scarce direct empirical evidence of the relationship between wealth and civic engagement. In addition, most of the research that does exist focuses on political participation rather than other forms of civic engagement. We also know little about the relationship between race and civic engagement. Frasure and Williams (2002) examine ethnoracial civic engagement, focusing mostly on political participation. They find that no generalizations can be made about the civic participation of African Americans mostly because of the paucity of empirical research about racial and ethnic civic participation. Data problems include the small samples of people of color, particularly in national samples, and lack of disaggregation. The data sets assume all people of color are homogeneous—nuances of the different kinds of participation by different sectors in a racial or ethnic group, qualitative issues such as trust or distrust of government, are ignored.

One study by Musick, Wilson, and Bynum (2000) examines race, class, and religious differences in formal volunteering. This is a comprehensive study of volunteering across those dimensions, and the closest study we could find to our own investigation. While they do not use wealth as a variable, their study does compare White and Black volunteering according to socioeconomic and human capital indicators (income, functional health, and education). They find that Whites do volunteer more than Blacks, in part because of existing educational and income inequalities. However, after controlling for personal resources, Blacks have more social resources than Whites, which help to close the volunteer gap. In addition, church attendance is more significant for Black than White volunteering. Musick, Wilson, and Bynum find that Black volunteering is more influenced by church attendance than White volunteering, a reflection of the more prominent role of the Black church in African American communities.

The COPPS of the 2001 PSID does allow us to investigate the relationship between wealth and charitable giving and volunteering for Whites and African Americans. The study asked 7,406 household heads or wives detailed questions about their donations of cash and time to formal charitable and nonprofit organizations. The data provide extensive information about the incidence of giving to a variety of formal charitable organizations, including religious, health, educational, environmental, international, youth, culture and the arts, local community, and need-based causes, but they do not include information about political donations or campaign volunteer activities. In addition, the dollar amounts of charitable donations and the volunteer hours of heads and wives are available. We analyze the empirical relationships between race, wealth, and civic engagement, as measured by charitable giving and volunteering.

We estimate several models of charitable giving and volunteering using information from the COPPS 2001 PSID. Descriptive statistics from the sample are presented in table 12.1. The sample we use to estimate equations consists of 5,833 households, whose head was either White (3,924) or Black (1,909).[8] The data have been weighted to yield statistics that are representative of the U.S. population. Summary statistics in table 12.1 indicate significant racial differences in the level of wealth (including home ownership), family income, and formal giving and volunteering.

Mean family permanent income of Whites, for example, is $69,958 compared with $36,154 for Black households. Mean wealth (total net worth including home equity) is $286,133 for White households and only $54,777 for Black households. Comparing the distribution across wealth quintiles by race further illustrates the level of wealth inequality across race in the United States. Thirty-five percent of the Black households participating in the 2001 PSID study, for example, are in the lowest wealth category compared with 14 percent of the White households. Almost 6 percent of the Blacks are in the wealthiest quintile (quintile 5) compared with 32 percent of Whites. Only 21 percent of Blacks compared with 56.5 percent of White households are in the top two wealth quintiles. This also shows that the Black population is much less wealthy than the White population and that intragroup wealth inequality is more

TABLE 12.1. PSID 2001 Descriptive Statistics

Variables	Both Races	White	Black
White head	0.865	1.000	—
Black head	0.135	—	1.000
Married	0.528	0.567	0.280
Male head	0.691	0.726	0.472
Age of head	49.280	49.760	46.250
Education (years)	13.360	13.530	12.260
Head works	0.696	0.706	0.634
2000 Permanent family income	65,422	69,958	36,154
Wealth (including home equity)	254,967	286,133	54,777
Wealth quintile 1	0.171	0.143	0.352
Wealth quintile 2	0.142	0.129	0.230
Wealth quintile 3	0.168	0.163	0.206
Wealth quintile 4	0.232	0.244	0.154
Wealth quintile 5	0.285	0.321	0.058
Number of children	0.552	0.517	0.777
Poor health	0.157	0.146	0.228
Giving incidence	0.687	0.718	0.485
Amount of total giving	1,474	1,597	689
Giving to religious organization	824	870	530
Protestant (last reported)	0.576	0.548	0.758
Catholic	0.211	0.235	0.055
Jewish head	0.037	0.043	0
Other religion head	0.056	0.053	0.079
Volunteering incidence	0.329	0.351	0.189
Volunteer hours	62	68	26
Observations	5,833	3,924	1,909

Note: The data are weighted by 2001 PSID family weights.

significant in the Black community. For charitable giving and volunteering, however, it appears that disaggregating wealth provides little additional information.

Just as Whites have more income and are wealthier than African Americans, we find that White households give more and volunteer more than Black households. In terms of giving to charity, almost 72 percent of Whites and 48.5 percent of Black households give to charity. White households' average total giving is $1,597 compared with Black averages of $689 per year. White households give an average of $870 per year to religious organizations. Black households give an average of $530 per year to religious organizations. White households volunteer an average of sixty-eight hours compared with twenty-six hours that Black households volunteer per year. Thirty-five percent of Whites volunteer their time to charitable organizations compared with almost 19 percent of Blacks. How does wealth impact these behaviors?

We estimate several race-specific probit and Heckman selection models of formal giving and volunteering behavior to determine the impact of wealth after controlling for a number of other variables. For White and Black households, we estimate bivariate probit models of giving and volunteering behavior. In addition, we use Heckman selection models to estimate the impact of household wealth on charitable gifts of money and time. Our primary interest is to determine how household wealth impacts philanthropic behavior, particularly whether there are any differences in the way that household wealth affects the giving and volunteering behavior of White and Black households. Table 12.2 reports the results for White households, and table 12.3 reports the results for Black households.

First, household decisions to make charitable contributions, either money or time, or both, can be seen as separate, independent decisions, or alternatively, they can be viewed as highly correlated (i.e., joint decisions). If the decisions are independent, then we can obtain consistent estimates with separate probit equations of the incidence of giving and volunteering. If the decisions to donate money and time to charity are joint decisions (i.e., the errors of the two separate probit equations are correlated), then a bivariate probit model provides the best estimates of philanthropic behavior.

Table 12.2 indicates that wealth (in units of $100,000) is not a significant factor in the giving decisions of White households but is mildly significant in the decision to volunteer, with the marginal effect of a $100,000 increase in household wealth resulting in a small increase in the probability of volunteering (less than a 1 percent increase). The variables that have the strongest influence on the giving incidence of White households include permanent family income, the head's age, employment status, marital status, education, and religious affiliation (all positive) and health

TABLE 12.2.   Probit Models of the Incidence of Charitable Giving and Volunteering for Whites

Variable	Single Probit Equations		Bivariate Probit Estimates	
	Coefficient	Marginal Effect	Coefficient	Marginal Effect
Giving incidence equation				
Wealth	0.0098	0.0032	0.0054	0.0020**
Permanent family income	0.0016***	0.0005***	0.0016***	0.0002**
Head's age	0.0552***	0.0180***	0.0549***	0.0078***
Age squared	−0.0004***	−0.0001***	−0.0003***	−0.00004*
Head works	0.2536***	0.0858***	0.2434***	0.0386*
Marital status	0.4130***	0.1390***	0.4130***	0.1301***
Years of education	0.1321***	0.0430***	0.1340***	0.0429***
Male head	−0.0497	−0.0160	−0.0425	−0.0339
Head religious	0.3918***	0.1381***	0.3853***	0.0775***
Hispanic	−0.1323	−0.0448	−0.1522	−0.0722
Number of children	−0.0002	−0.00005	0.0074	0.0351***
Age of youngest child	0.0023	0.0007	0.0027	0.0073***
Metro population > 1 million	0.1039**	0.0335**	0.1014**	−0.0159
Head in poor health	−0.3307***	−0.1153***	−0.3339***	−0.0863***
Constant	−3.741***	—	−3.760***	—
Volunteering incidence equation				
Wealth	0.0053**	0.0020**	0.0053**	
Permanent family income	0.0003	0.0001	0.0003	
Head's age	0.0109	0.0041	0.0116	
Age squared	−0.00005	−0.00002	−0.0001	
Head works	0.0661	0.0245	0.0626	
Marital status	0.3270***	0.1194***	0.3363***	
Years of education	0.1078***	0.0403***	0.1071***	
Male head	−0.0891	−0.0336	−0.1000	
Head religious	0.1594**	0.0581**	0.1589**	
Hispanic	−0.2134	−0.0762	−0.2132	
Number of children	0.1155***	0.0431***	0.1143***	
Age of youngest child	0.0236***	0.0088***	0.0235***	
Metro population > 1 million	−0.0728	−0.0271	−0.0778*	
Head in poor health	0.2127***	−0.0769***	−0.2010***	
Constant	−2.6476***	—	−2.6486***	
ρ (std. error)	0.000 (0.0000)		0.4294 (0.0271)	
Log L	−4,260.5956		−4,158.9722	

Note: Marginal effects are calculated at sample means.
*** .01 level of significance   ** .05 level of significance   * .1 level of significance

status of the household head (negative). The strongest influence, in magnitude of the marginal effect, is marital status: White married households are nearly 14 percent more likely to give to charity compared with single households. As for the incidence of volunteering, the strongest factors in White household volunteering decisions include marital status, education, number of children, and age of the youngest child (all positive) and health status of the household head (negative). Again, married White households are 11 percent more likely to volunteer than single households.

The bivariate probit model in table 12.2 reports the combined direct and indirect effects (the effects of volunteering on giving) of variables on the giving decision of White households. It indicates that the combined marginal effect of wealth on the giving incidence of White households is both positive and somewhat significant (at the .05 level). Yet the magnitude of the combined marginal effect of wealth on the giving incidence is very small. A $100,000 increase in wealth results in less than a 1 percent increase in the likelihood of making a monetary donation to charity. The reported correlation for this White bivariate probit equation, $\rho = 0.4294$ with a standard error of 0.0271, indicates that the giving and volunteering decisions are highly correlated and, therefore, the bivariate probit estimates are the most reliable.

The probit models for Black households appear in table 12.3. The results indicate that the marginal effect of wealth (in units of $100,000) is highly significant and positive in the giving equation. A $100,000 increase in wealth results in a nearly 4 percent increase in the incidence of giving. Other highly significant variables in the incidence of giving for Black households include permanent family income (in units of $10,000), marital status, years of education, and number of children. Black married households are 13 percent more likely to donate to charity than single Black households. The univariate probit of Black household volunteering incidence indicates that wealth is not a significant factor. The marginal effects of permanent family income and years of education are positive and highly significant to African American volunteer behavior. Black households are nearly 10 percent more likely to volunteer as the head's level of education increases by one year.

The bivariate probit equation for Black households in table 12.3 indicates that the combined marginal effect of wealth on giving is positive and somewhat significant (at the .05 level). A $100,000 increase in wealth results in a 1 percent increase in the likelihood of giving to charity. It also indicates that married households are 5 percent more likely to give to charity than unmarried households. The employment status of Black household heads is also a significant factor in their giving decisions. The reported correlation between the giving and volunteering decisions of Black households, $\rho = 0.4355$ with a standard error of 0.0271, also indicates that these decisions are highly correlated.

TABLE 12.3. Probit Models of the Incidence of Charitable Giving and Volunteering for Blacks

Variable	Single Probit Equations		Bivariate Probit Estimates	
	Coefficient	Marginal Effect	Coefficient	Marginal Effect
Giving incidence equation				
Wealth	0.0922***	0.0367***	0.0876**	0.0110**
Permanent family income	0.0114***	0.0046***	0.0110***	0.0014***
Head's age	0.0072	0.0029	0.0074	0.0025
Age squared	0.00007	0.00003	0.00007	0.0000
Head works	0.1877***	0.0745**	0.1900**	0.0469***
Marital status	0.3302***	0.1311***	0.3384***	0.0581**
Years of education	0.1017***	0.0405***	0.1048***	0.0240***
Male head	−0.2055**	−0.0818**	−0.2000**	−0.0193
Head religious	0.1827*	0.0722*	0.1807**	0.0203
Hispanic	−0.1899	−0.0748	−0.1492	0.0569
Number of children	−0.1102***	−0.0439***	−0.1085***	0.0024
Age of youngest child	−0.0062	−0.0025	−0.0066	−0.0004
Metro population > 1 million	0.1083*	−0.0431*	−0.1101*	−0.0175
Head in poor health	−0.0996	−0.0396	−0.0939	−0.0147
Constant	−2.3031***	—	−2.3365***	—
Volunteering incidence equation				
Wealth	0.0309	0.0084	0.0303	
Permanent family income	0.0035***	0.0010***	0.0035***	
Head's age	0.0010	0.0026	0.0116	
Age squared	−0.00003	0.0000	−0.00006	
Head works	0.2241**	0.0589***	0.2054**	
Marital status	0.1926*	0.0536	0.1902	
Years of education	0.0962***	0.0263***	0.0959***	
Male head	−0.0405	−0.0111	−0.0310	
Head religious	0.0473	0.0127	0.0458	
Hispanic	0.3961	0.1255	0.3986	
Number of children	0.0597**	0.0163**	0.0569*	
Age of youngest child	0.0002	0.00007	0.0002	
Metro population > 1 million	−0.0499	−0.0136	−0.0564	
Head in poor health	−0.0448	−0.0121	−0.0483	
Constant	−2.8291***	—	−2.8398***	
ρ (std. error)	0.0000 (0.0000)		0.4355 (0.0271)	
Log L	−1,991.1697		−1,943.6247	

Note: Marginal effects are calculated at sample means.
*** .01 level of significance   ** .05 level of significance   * .1 level of significance

The implications from tables 12.2 and 12.3 are that as wealth increases among White families, they tend to volunteer hours to charities and perhaps donate cash to charity, while Black families tend to make modest cash donations to charities as their wealth increases, but they do not necessarily decide to volunteer. The magnitude of wealth's influence is relatively small for both races, but the impact of wealth on the incidence of giving is many times greater in magnitude for Black households than for Whites. Family income, marital status, and education matter consistently for Black households for both charitable giving and volunteering.

Table 12.4 provides the results from the Heckman selection model of total cash donations to charitable organizations. The Heckman selection estimates correct for sample selection bias in which the total amount of household giving is estimated using information about the probability that each household would make a contribution greater than zero. The univariate probit models estimated for White and Black households in tables 12.2 and 12.3 are the selection models, providing information about the likelihood that each household will make a nonzero contribution to

TABLE 12.4. Heckman Selection Model of Total Amount of Giving to
Charitable Organizations

Models/Variables	Whites	Blacks
Maximum Likelihood Estimates		
Total charitable giving		
Wealth	45.64***	44.93
Head works	345.63	−5.54
Years of education	340.66***	96.74***
Permanent family income	12.59***	8.49***
Marital status	1,093.89***	519.11**
Head's age	101.32***	−23.74
Age squared	−0.48**	0.30
Male head	−137.30	42.06
Hispanic	−329.32	2,612.73***
Age of youngest child	38.46**	27.37*
Number of children	21.18	−136.73*
Head in poor health	−655.81***	−96.90
Head religious	1,145.98***	−163.24
Metro population > 1 million	−17.41	17.79
Constant	−10,717.93***	938.72
Selection model	See table 12.2: single-equation probit of giving incidence	See table 12.3: single-equation probit of giving incidence
Log Likelihood	−26,768.65	−9,060.016
ρ (rho)	1	−0.5120
σ (sigma)	3,986.66	2,214.648

*** .01 level of significance   ** .05 level of significance   * .1 level of significance

charity. The reported estimates can be interpreted as the marginal effects on the total amount of giving for those households that do make charitable contributions. The results indicate that wealth is a significant determinant of the amount of White household donations but not for Black donations. A $100,000 increase in White household wealth results in an estimated increase in donations to charities of $46. While wealth is not a significant factor in total dollar amounts of Black charitable donations, it must be remembered that wealth is a significant variable in the Black household decision to make a donation. The significant variables for Black households in giving totals are income, education, and marital status. For Whites the significant variables, in addition to wealth, are education, income, marital status, head's age, age of youngest child, religiousness of the head, and (negative) the health status of the head.

Is there a difference in the kinds of organizations to which Black and White households give? We take a closer look at the giving decision and disaggregate the kinds of organizations—religious, educational, and multipurpose organizations. Since the largest category of charitable donations is giving to religious organizations, and religious giving is very important to African Americans, we estimate probit models of the religious giving behavior of Blacks and Whites. The results (table 12.5) indicate that wealth and income are significant to African American giving to religious charities but wealth and income do not factor significantly for White households. Education, marital status, head's age, number of children, and religious affiliation (or lack of religiousness) of the head are all variables that matter for White donations to religious organizations. Head in poor health is a negative significant variable. Controlling for marital status, which is positive and significant for both racial groups, Black single males are less likely to give to religious organizations, as are households with an atheist head. Two other strong determinants for both groups are education and number of children, except that additional children increase the propensity of White households to give and decrease the incidence of giving by Black households (perhaps an indirect wealth effect for Blacks).

In terms of the amount of giving to religious organizations, the Heckman selection estimates in table 12.6 indicate that wealth is not a significant determinant of the levels of religious donations for Blacks and is significant only at the weakest level of significance (.1) for White households. Income is a strong determinant of contributions to religious organizations for both races. The marginal effects of a $10,000 increase in income equals $5 for White contributions and $8 for Black households. Income therefore contributes more powerfully to the amount of African American donations to religious charities than to the amount of White religious giving. After controlling for the selected samples (i.e., determining the probability that each household will give money to a religious organization), we find that education and marital status are significant positive variables for White but not Black households. In fact, it appears from these results that there is very little that helps us to distinguish those Black households that make religious contributions from one another, yet we do know, from table 12.5, that wealth, income, education, and marital status help us to distinguish the contributors to religious charities from the noncontributors.

Finally, we report Heckman selection models of total volunteer hours of heads and wives for White and Black households. For both Blacks and Whites, the results in Table 12.7 indicate that household wealth is not a significant factor in the volunteer hours decision once the decision to volunteer has been correctly controlled. Again, the univariate probit models of tables 12.2 and 12.3 indicate how wealth affects the volunteering decision in general (i.e., significant for White households and not for Black households). In terms of how many hours Black households report

TABLE 12.5. Probit Analysis of the Incidence of Giving to Religious Organizations

Variables	Whites (marginal effects)	Blacks (marginal effects)
Wealth	0.0011	0.0473***
Head's age	0.0137***	0.0034
Age squared	−0.00006**	0.00002
Marital status	0.1708***	0.1955***
Male head	−0.0204	−0.9233**
Years of education	0.0354***	0.0389***
Permanent family income	0.00009	0.0026***
Age of youngest child	0.0003	−0.0010
Number of children	0.0282***	−0.0406***
Head in poor health	−0.1134***	−0.0514*
Atheist head	−0.2962***	−0.1285***
Catholic head	0.0097	−0.8130
Jewish head	−0.1400***	—
Other religion head	−0.0808**	0.0367
Log L	−2,346.6389	−1,081.4026
Pseudo R-square	0.1158	0.1256
Observations	3,833	1,859

Note: Marginal effects are calculated at sample means.
*** .01 level of significance   ** .05 level of significance   * .1 level of significance

that they do volunteer, the only significant variable is number of children in the household.

We did estimate models of giving to educational charities and to multipurpose charitable organizations as well, but the results are not appreciably different from what we have reported already for charitable giving in general. We therefore do not report on those results. One point of interest, though probably not surprising, is that, in terms of giving to educational organizations, education and income are stronger variables than wealth for Black households. We also considered the impact of the wealth quintiles (instead of total wealth) on these models, hoping we could find more nuances in how wealth matters to charitable giving. Using the middle quintile as the comparison group, there are no significant findings to report. Black households in the middle wealth quintile, for example, do not give significantly more or less to religious organizations than their counterparts in the higher wealth (fourth and fifth) quintiles.

TABLE 12.6. Heckman Selection Model of Total Amount of Giving to Religious Organizations

Variables	Whites	Blacks
Maximum Likelihood Estimates		
Total charitable giving		
Wealth	11.57*	−23.07
Years of education	280.84***	52.11
Permanent family income	5.22***	8.10***
Marital status	1,643.61***	252.66
Head's age	115.90***	20.74
Age squared	−0.59**	−0.23
Male head	−193.34	233.55
Hispanic	−0.21	2,126.04***
Age of youngest child	33.54*	25.27*
Number of children	76.09	−154.84**
Head in poor health	−749.64***	−170.06
Atheist head	−2,810.60***	252.00
Catholic head	−656.50***	−596.88
Jewish head	−1,186.20***	—
Other religion head	−535.60	−85.39
Constant	−9,794.27	648.34
Selection models	See table 12.5: probit models of incidence of religious giving	
Log Likelihood	−18,795.62	−7,436.469
ρ (rho)	1	−0.49075
σ (sigma)	3,812.21	2,013.249

*** .01 level of significance   ** .05 level of significance   * .1 level of significance

The results of these econometric estimations are somewhat surprising. They indicate that the magnitude of the effect of wealth on White giving and volunteering behavior is small and that an increase in wealth results in only modest increases in money and time contributions to charity. Interestingly, the impact of wealth on the African American households' decision to give monetary donations to charity is many times greater than for their White counterparts—wealth does matter to the incidence of Black giving. Once we control for the decision to give, however, the amount of wealth has little impact on the total amount of Black household monetary giving, particularly religious giving. Wealth does not affect Black household volunteering or the number of volunteer hours at all. The number of hours Blacks report for volunteering is not directly related to their wealth holdings, though it is related to the number of children in the household.

Musick, Wilson, and Bynum (2000) find that socioeconomic differences have a smaller impact on the volunteering of African Americans, which may be a similar finding. However, our findings suggest that income

TABLE 12.7. Heckman Selection Model of Total Volunteer Hours to Charitable Organizations

Variables	Whites	Blacks
Maximum Likelihood Estimates		
Total charitable giving		
Wealth	1.24	−6.36
Years of education	35.03***	0.732
Permanent family income	−0.033	0.363
Marital status	111.92***	−65.43*
Head's age	4.501	−0.34
Age squared	−0.0078	0.028
Male head	−4.50	53.28
Hispanic	−73.58	226.53***
Age of youngest child	6.79***	1.93
Number of children	42.78***	29.41***
Head in poor health	−86.27***	18.12
Head religious	66.62***	5.80
Metro population > 1 million	−20.33	25.48
Constant	−1,026.79***	14.11
Selection models	See table 12.2: single-equation probit of volunteering incidence	See table 12.3: single-equation probit of volunteering incidence
Log Likelihood	−11,653.83	−3,494.133
ρ (rho)	1	−0.06795
σ (sigma)	417.0074	207.1453

*** .01 level of significance   ** .05 level of significance   *.1 level of significance

and education have the greatest impact on the incidence of African American volunteering and are quite significant to African American giving to religious charities. While Musick, Wilson, and Bynum do not have a direct wealth measurement, their socioeconomic indicators might have enough of a wealth effect to lessen the significance of the combined category on Black volunteering, as wealth does on ours. On the other hand, some of the other variables that do affect Black volunteering (and giving) may be related to wealth, such as level of education, number of children, poor health, and being married (see Conley 1999 and Chang, chap. 4, in this volume, for example). Thus, for African Americans, the wealth effect on volunteering appears to be less significant, and volunteering is a much more complicated behavior for Blacks than Whites.

It is not surprising that religious giving is important to African Americans, though it is interesting that wealth seems to matter in terms of whether or not Black households will make a contribution, but not in terms of how much the contribution will be. Several studies show that religious organizations are important to Blacks. Musick, Wilson, and Bynum (2000) do find that church attendance is more significant for Black volunteering than for White and that the "Black church" plays a more prominent role in African American communities. Frasure and Williams (2002) note that the civil rights movement drew upon the strength of the accumulated social capital in many Black churches to support protest politics. Here affiliation with and the prominence of the attachment to religious institutions arises but needs more study so that the nuances of the relationship with wealth holding can be understood.

One of the lessons we learn from this investigation is that it is important to explore indirect effects of wealth and to better understand where and when wealth and income matter, how they intersect and diverge in relation to explaining aspects of civic participation. It is helpful to disaggregate categories in order to understand both when wealth matters and Black and White differences.

Also more research is needed about the relationship between wealth inequality and civic participation. We investigated the influence of wealth holding on civic engagement, but research on wealth inequality suggests that including a wealth inequality variable would also yield interesting results. While Black households have approximately five times less wealth than White households, for example, differences in giving and volunteering show up even more in amounts than incidence (except in religious giving). Yet wealth does not matter directly for Black volunteering. Several questions arise. Do Blacks compensate for not having much income or wealth, or are the other significant variables affecting Black giving and volunteering just proxies for wealth? Does income inequality better explain the differences in formal giving and volunteering behavior for Black and White households than wealth? When and how does wealth matter? Also, if wealth does matter, how does the skewed distribution of wealth impact such behaviors in the aggregate? Will changes in wealth and economic stability increase or positively impact civic engagement, and what kind of engagement? Are there certain levels of income where wealth kicks in and begins to matter, or vice versa? While we still do not have answers to questions such as these, empirical study is beginning to show us that including wealth in the equation and understanding how wealth relates to other variables is important to our understanding of giving and volunteering, and presumably other aspects of civic engagement.

Although we would like better and more data sets, and more research in this area in general, we can conclude that wealth matters to civic engagement—sometimes in combination with income, employment, education, number of children or age of youngest child, and health, among other variables. Specifically, wealth is significant to African American charitable giving but not significant to African American volunteering. In contrast, wealth is mildly significant to White volunteering, though not to the number of volunteer hours. Wealth is not significant to White charitable giving, although is significant to the total amount that White households give to charity.

CONCLUDING POLICY REFLECTIONS

Our investigation has found that alternative forms of wealth creation, particularly democratic and cooperative business ownership and employee participation, increase wealth and civic engagement. We therefore end by briefly indicating areas where public policies can change, be augmented, or be initiated, which would impact on economic democracy and other opportunities for wealth accumulation.

There is little contention that the rich are getting richer, so the direction of our suggestions for alternative policies focuses on policies that are promising ways to increase the wealth of low-income individuals, families, and communities and thus increase civic participation and democracy.

Public policy needs to focus on wealth creation and accumulation opportunities, as well as asset development. Since equity in a home is a major component of household wealth, particularly for communities of color, affordable housing policies such as the housing trust fund,[9] policies to end mortgage discrimination, and policies to encourage cooperative housing options are indicated. Home ownership does appear to be related to civic engagement. Equity in a business is another important component of household wealth, also for communities of color. Policies to facilitate business ownership and help to mitigate its riskiness, policies to end discrimination in credit markets and financial institutions and increase financial services in low-income communities,[10] and policies that encourage and facilitate the development of cooperatively owned businesses, worker ownership, and credit unions would be helpful. Individual Development Accounts and Children's Savings Accounts would help low-income people to save more, reward them for their savings behavior, and provide them with funds to invest in education, home ownership, and business ownership.[11] Living wage ordinances allow cities to guarantee above-poverty wages with benefits to residents, which would help lift them out of poverty and could contribute to their ability to invest rather than consume all their income.[12] Scholars who discuss wealth inequality in general also suggest policies such as a wealth tax to help distribute wealth more equally (Wolff 2002).

While increasing civic participation in local communities is not the expressed goal of most of the preceding policies, these policies address the disparities in wealth and economic power that decrease or threaten civic participation at the local level in the United States. In addition, democratic economic enterprises and the democratization of ownership and the workplace reduce economic and wealth inequalities and the power of corporations. There is some emerging analysis that suggests that increased democratic economic alternatives, for example, help to distribute wealth more evenly and change the power dynamics in localities (make them more equal). The research about the impacts of democratic economic enterprises is becoming substantial, and the results are quite promising for better understanding the relationships between economic and political democracy, as well as economic democracy and civic engagement.

NOTES

The authors thank Democracy Collaborative–Knight Foundation Civic Engagement Project (codirected by the Democracy Collaborative, University of Maryland, College Park, and the Center for the Study of Voluntary Organizations and Service, Georgetown University) for some of the initial funding for this research. Thanks also to Nigel Greaves for research support, Patrick Mason for asking the right questions and providing technical advice, Steve Dubb for helpful comments, and Ngina Chiteji for encouragement and support.

1. Wilson's contention that social isolation in inner cities has increased as middle-class Blacks have moved to the suburbs is contested. See Darity and Myers (2000), for example, who demonstrate that social isolation has not increased and that income inequalities between Blacks and Whites, and between Blacks in central cities and Blacks outside central cities, have not worsened or appreciably changed during the period Wilson studied (between 1970 and 1988). On the other hand, as a theoretical concept and where the empirical reality is not in question, the notion that socioeconomic isolation decreases civic engagement and the social health of a community appears to have validity, though it needs more testing.

2. The Gini ratio measures income inequality by how much current inequality differs from the ideal of perfectly equal income distribution (each share of the population has an equal share of income). A ratio of zero (0) means no deviation from the ideal or no inequality, and a ratio of one (1) means total inequality.

3. Some groups in competition with corporate interests, such as labor unions, do provide means by which individuals may compete with corporations for political and economic power. Therefore, opponents of campaign finance reform insist that the campaign donations of labor unions also need to be limited by campaign finance reform. However, the resources (and thus influence) of labor unions and other countervailing forces are often much less than those of large multinational corporations and wealthy individuals.

4. Greider (1992), Hill (2002), Kelly (2001), Palast (2002), and Phillips (2002), among others, also discuss and document the corruption of campaign contributions and the power of wealthy individuals and corporations.

5. Democratic ESOPs (employee stock ownership plans) and worker cooperatives are the most common of democratic workplaces. The democratically organized ESOP is a variation of the more common ESOPs, which are defined as legal structures designed to enable employees to buy stock in their companies through payroll deductions (Krimerman and Lindenfeld 1992, 1; also see Williamson, Imbroscio, and Alperovitz 2002). Democratic ESOPs give employees a role in governance as well as ownership of stock. They are majority owned and democratically operated by their employees. In worker cooperatives employee-members own and control the enterprise cooperatively, with each worker/owner having an equal vote. Some are even self-managing. A cooperative enterprise in general is a business collectively owned and operated by the producers, consumers, residents, or workers who have organized to provide or procure particular goods and services through an alternative structure that better meets their needs. Worker-owned cooperatives allow workers to collectively offer a service or good and control the quality of the good or service as well as the working conditions, compensation, and benefits. Cooperatives are governed democratically according to the principle of "one person, one vote." Continuous education and concern for community are among the other cooperative business principles.

6. Calculated by us from figures reported in NCB 2004.

7. Gordon Nembhard's calculations reported in Gordon Nembhard 2002.

8. The sample includes all households in the 2001 PSID survey, dropping the 1997 New Immigrant Sample and the Latino Sample, which were discontinued in 1996. We also dropped approximately eleven households for which the heads were identified as being both Black and White, and we dropped households where the race of the head could not be determined.

9. States and municipalities pass legislation to establish housing trust funds to provide funding to support affordable housing, particularly through community development corporations (CDCs).

10. The Community Reinvestment Act (CRA) was adopted by the federal government in 1977 to mitigate some of the effects of the lack of bank branches and banking services in low-income communities. Under this law, financial institutions have the obligation to identify and make an effort to meet the credit needs of the communities they were chartered to serve. It is unclear if Congress will reauthorize the CRA before it expires.

11. Individual Development Accounts (IDAs) are savings programs where government agencies or philanthropic groups match the private savings of low-income individuals.

12. See Neumark and Adams 2000, for example.

REFERENCES

Chesnick, David S. 2000. "Asset Growth for Largest Co-ops Shows Reliance to Declining Revenues." U.S. Department of Agriculture, Rural Development, Washington, DC, January. http://www.rurdev.usda.gov/rbs/pub/jan00/asset.htm.

Collins, Chuck, and Felice Yeskel (with United for a Fair Economy). 2000. *Economic Apartheid in America: A Primer on Economic Inequality and Insecurity.* New York: New Press.

Conley, Dalton. 1999. *Being Black, Living in the Red: Race, Wealth, and Social Policy in America.* Berkeley: University of California Press.

Cooperative Housing Coalition. 2000. "People Building Communities: Affordable Cooperative Housing." Washington, DC.

Couto, Richard A. (with Catherine S. Guthrie). 1999. *Making Democracy Work Better.* Chapel Hill: University of North Carolina Press.

Dahl, Robert A. 1985. *A Preface to Economic Democracy.* Berkeley: University of California Press.

Darity, William A., Jr., and Samuel L. Myers, Jr. 2000. "Languishing in Inequality: Racial Disparities in Wealth and Earnings in the New Millennium." In *New Directions: African Americans in a Diversifying Nation,* ed. James S. Jackson, 86–118. University of Michigan, Program for Research on Black Americans; National Policy Association.

Du Bois, W. E. B. 1986. *Dusk of Dawn: An Essay toward an Autobiography of a Race Concept* (1940). Reprinted in *W.E.B. Du Bois Writings,* 549–802. New York: Library of America.

Elden, J. Maxwell. 1981. "Political Efficacy at Work: The Connection between More Autonomous Forms of Workplace Organization and a More Participatory Politics." *American Political Science Review* 75 (1): 43–58.

Erdal, David. 1999. "The Psychology of Sharing: An Evolutionary Approach." Ph.D. dissertation, University of St. Andrews, UK.

Federation of Southern Cooperatives/Land Assistance Fund. 2002. "35th Anniversary—2002 Annual Report." East Point, GA.

Frasure, Lorrie, and Linda Faye Williams. 2002. "Civic Disparities and Civic Differences: Ethno-Racial Civic Engagement in the United States." Civic Engagement Working Paper no. 3, Democracy Collaborative–Knight Foundation Civic Engagement Project, December 17.

Gordon Nembhard, Jessica. 2000. "Democratic Economic Participation and Humane Urban Redevelopment." *Trotter Review,* 26–31.

———. 2002. "Cooperatives and Wealth Accumulation: Preliminary Analysis." *American Economic Review* 92 (2): 325–29.

———. 2004a. "Cooperative Ownership and the Struggle for African American Economic Empowerment." *Humanity and Society* 28 (3): 298–321.

———. 2004b. "Non-Traditional Analyses of Cooperative Economic Impacts: Preliminary Indicators and a Case Study." *Review of International Co-operation* 97 (1): 6–21.

Gordon Nembhard, Jessica, and Anthony Blasingame. 2002. "Economic Dimensions of Civic Engagement and Political Efficacy." Civic Engagement Working Paper no. 3, Democracy Collaborative–Knight Foundation Civic Engagement Project, December 17.

Green, Mark. 2002. *Selling Out: How Big Corporate Money Buys Elections, Rams through Legislation, and Betrays our Democracy.* New York: Regan Books.

Greenberg, Edward S. 1986. *Workplace Democracy: The Political Effects of Participation.* Ithaca and London: Cornell University Press.

Gregory, Steven. 1998. *Black Corona: Race and the Politics of Place in the Urban Community.* Princeton, NJ: Princeton University Press.

Greider, William. 1992. *Who Will Tell the People: The Betrayal of American Democracy.* New York: Simon and Schuster.

Hill, Stephen. 2002. *Fixing Elections.* New York: Routledge.

Imbroscio, David L. 1997. *Reconstructing City Politics.* Thousand Oaks, CA: Sage Publications.

Kelly, Marjorie. 2001. *The Divine Right of Capital: Dethroning the Corporate Aristocracy.* San Francisco: Berrett-Koehler Publishers.

Kraenzle, Charles A. 1994. "Full-Time Employees, Sales and Assets of Selected Farmer Cooperatives: 1981, 1986, and 1991." ACS Research Report 129, U.S. Department of Agriculture, Washington, DC, March.

Krimerman, Len, and Frank Lindenfeld, eds. 1992. *When Workers Decide: Workplace Democracy Takes Root in North America.* Philadelphia: PA: New Society Publishers.

Left Business Observer. 1993. "Gini Says: Measuring Income Inequality." *Left Business Observer,* October 18. http://www.panix.com/~dhenwood/Gini_supplement.html.

Massey, Douglas S., and Elijah Anderson, eds. 2001. *Problem of the Century: Racial Stratification in the U.S.* New York: Russell Sage Foundation.

McDougall, Harold A. 1993. *Black Baltimore: A New Theory of Community.* Philadelphia, PA: Temple University Press.

Musick, Marc A., John Wilson, and William B. Bynum, Jr. 2000. "Race and Formal Volunteering: The Differential Effects of Class and Religion." *Social Forces* 78 (4): 1539–70.

National Cooperative Bank. 2004. "The NCB Co-op 100." Washington, DC. http://www.co-op100.coop (accessed October 21, 2004).

Neumark, David, and Scott Adams. 2000. "Do Living Wage Ordinances Reduce Urban Poverty?" NBER Working Paper no. 7606.

Oliver, J. Eric. 1999. "The Effects of Metropolitan Economic Segregation on Local Civic Participation." *American Journal of Political Science* 43 (1): 186–212.

Ownership Associates. 2003. "ESOPs and Employee Wealth." Employee-Ownership Briefing Paper, Research Highlights 2, Brief 7.2. (May 20) http://www.ownershipassociates.com (accessed September 25, 2004).

Palast, Greg. 2002. *The Best Democracy Money Can Buy.* London: Pluto Press.

Pateman, Carol. 1970. *Participation and Democratic Theory.* Cambridge, UK: Cambridge University Press.

Phillips, Kevin. 2002. *Wealth and Democracy.* New York: Broadway Books.

Putnam, Robert D. 2000. *Bowling Alone: The Collapse and Revival of American Community.* New York: Simon and Schuster.

Saegert, Susan, and Gary Winkel. 2000. "Limited Equity Housing Cooperatives: An Alternative to Abandonment and Displacement." Paper presented at the Co-op Housing Summit, Washington, DC (City University of New York Graduate Center), October.

Shipp, Sigmund C. 2000. "Worker-Owned Firms in Inner-City Neighborhoods: An Empirical Study." *Review of International Co-operation* 92–93 (4/99–1/00): 42–46.

Spear, Roger. 1999. "The Co-operative Advantage." Paper presented at the International Co-operative Alliance Research Conference, "Values and Enterprise for Co-operative Advantage," Quebec City, Canada, August 28–29.

Thomas, June Manning, and Marsha Ritzdorf, eds. 1997. *Urban Planning and the African American Community: In the Shadows.* Thousand Oaks, CA: Sage Publications.

Uhlaner, Carole J. 1989. "Rational Turnout: The Neglected Role of Groups." *American Journal of Political Science* 33 (2): 390–422.

United for a Fair Economy. 2004. "The Growing Divide: Inequality and the Roots of Economic Insecurity." United for a Fair Economy, March. http://www.faireconomy.org.

U.S. Census Bureau. 2002a. "Gini Ratios for Households, by Race and Hispanic Origin of Householder: 1967 to 2001." Table H-4 in "Historic Income Tables—Households," Washington, DC, last revised, September 30, 2002. http://www.census.gov/hhes/income/histinc/h04.html.

————. 2002b. "Household Shares of Aggregate Income by Fifths of the Income Distribution: 1967 to 2001." Table IE-3 in "Historic Income Tables—Income Equality," Washington, DC, last revised, September 30, 2002. http://www.census.gov/hhes/income/histinc/ie3.html.

Weiss, Chris, and Christina Clamp. 1992. "Women's Cooperatives: Part of the Answer to Poverty?" In *From the Ground Up: Essays on Grassroots and Workplace Democracy by C. George Benello,* ed. Len Krimerman, Frank Lindenfeld, Carol Korty, and Julian Benello, 229–32. Boston: South End Press.

Williamson, Thad, David Imbroscio, and Gar Alperovitz. 2002. *Making a Place for Community: Local Democracy in a Global Era.* New York: Routledge.

Wilson, William Julius. 1987. *The Truly Disadvantaged: The Inner City, the Underclass, and Public Policy.* Chicago: University of Chicago Press.

Wolff, Edward N. 2002. *Top Heavy: The Increasing Inequality of Wealth in America.* Updated and expanded edition. New York: New Press.

————. 2004. "Changes in Household Wealth in the 1980s and 1990s in the U.S." Working Paper no. 407, Levy Economics Institute, Bard College, May.

Afterword

Trends & Trappings, Research & Policy Implications: An Unorthodox Policy Guide

JESSICA GORDON NEMBHARD

When this project first began (in some ways more than six years ago), the purpose was to understand racial wealth inequality better and highlight current research. There had been some preliminary pathbreaking studies, and we wanted to generate more data, and provide better data analysis, to deepen the understanding of African American wealth holdings and low levels of wealth, particularly compared with White Americans. There was also a little bit of information about Latino wealth and beginning speculation about other communities of color. Gordon Nembhard convened a conference in April 2000, with the late Rhonda M. Williams. "Wealth Accumulation—Global Impacts and Local Prospects: How Race and Ethnicity Matter" was the first of its kind along several dimensions: located on a college campus and sponsored by an African American studies department, convening scholars—social scientists—who work on issues of racial economic inequality to focus on wealth inequality and share information about wealth accumulation in communities of color, and consisting mostly of economists of color. Our tasks were to explore aspects of research in this area, to find out why some groups and institutions develop the capacity to generate wealth while others do not, and to propose a policy agenda. We focused on the United States because there was so little information about wealth holdings in communities of color in general. We thought it important to begin in our own backyard.

The first version of this volume was to be a compilation of the papers presented in April 2000. That version was never completed, in part because the original publisher fell through, and Williams succumbed to lung cancer in late 2000, but also because the theme was slightly ahead of its time. We did not yet have the breadth of studies necessary for the kind of volume envisioned. It became increasingly apparent that to do this volume correctly, studies of all the major non-White groups in the country should be included. At that time there was very little written and not enough data about smaller populations such as Native Americans and Asian American Pacific Islanders. Several of the potential authors went ahead and published their articles elsewhere—increasing the existing canon. In 2003, while she was a visiting scholar at the Democracy Collaborative, I was able to enlist Chiteji to join me in this project as coeditor. Between 2000 and 2003, literature about wealth had proliferated, and research on wealth in communities of color had begun to blossom so that we were able to put together the kind of volume originally intended and sorely needed. You have just read the results, the fruit of that labor.

Wealth Accumulation and Communities of Color in the United States is a compilation of research and scholarship that fills in the gaps in our knowledge and understanding of wealth creation and asset ownership in communities of color and among women in the United States. In addition to analyzing individual/household wealth holdings, these chapters add wealth as a variable in understanding and explaining many related phenomena: economic inequality, differential business and home ownership, location of where one owns a home, civic participation, and community development. Many of our authors find similar patterns of influence and significance—for example, not only portfolio composition and historical discrimination in credit, employment, and real estate markets but also the variety in the wealth portfolio, marital status, number of children, and community assets all matter to wealth accumulation in communities of color. In sum they find that the net worth of households in communities of color is interrelated with educational attainment rates, occupational status, family composition, financial market sophistication and participation, pension participation, and home ownership—which are also all affected by various public policies, economic and educational opportunities, residential segregation, and racial/ethnic discrimination.

The chapters all begin with the same understanding of wealth—the standard economic definition. In addition, some authors expand the concept of wealth in order to better illuminate issues related to wealth and well-being for specific communities of color. Some of the authors also expand the notion of family and community. They explore mechanisms and institutions that not only aid people in storing wealth but also help them to create wealth, and they point out these differences.

This afterword summarizes and discusses some of the remarkable trends and complexities revealed in these chapters. I use the word *trappings* to indicate that the trends, issues, and findings are complex, multidimensional, and sometimes paradoxical and thus get us into and out of intellectual and empirical "traps"—some that illuminate and others that complicate our understanding. In the following I reiterate what we hope readers have learned and indicate future research challenges and policy implications under topics that capture some of the trends and trappings. I also muse about where we go from here.

DATA SOURCES, SCOPE, & LIMITATIONS

While there are essentially six relevant national data sets that measure wealth in some capacity (Leigh, chap. 1), the challenge remains to combine a high level of detail about wealth holdings with enough racial and ethnic information that one data set can be used to study a variety of dimensions for each population. None of the national surveys provide that level of information for Native Americans, and only one survey so far is adequate for initial findings about Asian Americans in general, for example, but not about subgroups of Asian Americans. All the national sets have some limitations for the kind of research undertaken in this volume, and the authors have addressed this. The authors, however, heroically, rigorously, and innovatively address and compensate for the incomplete data and the lack of data about some groups or some kinds of assets. Almost every chapter exemplifies the existence of a variety of official sources of data on wealth, the variety of scope of the data sets, how a data survey can be used, and why a particular one was chosen and used for a particular study. Each chapter illustrates strategies to use in the face of limited data. Some authors use one data source to give a general snapshot of the entire population and another source to show dynamics, such as changes over time, and/or to disaggregate the population (chaps., 5, 6, 7, and 10, for example).

Actual wealth values also vary throughout each chapter depending on the data source used. This means that while every chapter documents large wealth gaps between and within groups, the exact values depend on the year and the data source. Also while absolute numbers are different across data sets, as Leigh (chap. 1) points out, the general distribution of assets and portfolio allocation percentages are similar for each group regardless of the data source. Each of the differences in the data sets and their reporting can be important in ways that unseasoned readers may not automatically recognize. Data from the Survey of Consumer Finances show a higher concentration of wealth in the top wealth classes than other sources, for example, partly because this survey oversamples families at the upper end of the wealth distribution. The authors explain and illustrate these differences. Additionally, the time periods for which data are available also differ across the data sources. There is also variation across surveys in the extent to which they can be used to examine populations other than Blacks and Whites. These are issues that individuals may be unaware of, if they are not wealth researchers themselves. Yet they represent issues that need to be acknowledged and discussed in order to help readers be certain that they fully understand any given author's results and in order to think about directions that future empirical work and data collection efforts might take.

Interpretations of data also can be affected by what measure of wealth one uses—net worth versus financial wealth, for example, or median versus mean wealth ratios. This volume provides a comprehensive discussion of the ways researchers measure wealth and wealth inequality (chaps. 1 and 2). Furthermore, the complex empirical-methodological issues that affect wealth research are addressed directly by Chiteji and Hamilton (chap. 2). These empirical-methodological issues typically have been left to technical journals or appendixes despite their relevance for truly understanding why certain authors choose the data sources and methods that they employ, as well as for what differences one might expect to observe if different choices had been made. Note that our authors use a variety of techniques to tease out the greatest meaning. This helps the readers to be critical of the methodologies used and to better understand the results of any analysis. One implication is that we need to do a better job of educating and training people about these subtleties.

Another lesson is the importance of knowing enough about the data and methodologies being used to capitalize on each data set's and methodology's strengths and minimize each weakness. There is still a need for more wealth data and different kinds of measures at the national and local levels. In addition, while we focus on national-level surveys and the need for them to be more comprehensive and to increase the numbers of people of color interviewed, there are also important regional effects and urban effects on the value of a home, quality of education, and access to capital, for example, that are equally important and will be obscured or missed by national-level data (see chaps. 9 and 12, for example). Another challenge, therefore, is to figure out where and when, as well as how, national data are important and where, when, and how regional and local data can be more illuminating.

THE IMPORTANCE OF FAMILY CHARACTERISTICS

While not a major theme, but a recurring melody, family characteristics turn out to matter a lot in wealth accumulation for women and communities of color. Chang (chap. 4) finds that the married, or a household with two income earners, have more wealth than never-married men and women. Also never-married women have much less wealth than never-married men. While marriage is associated with wealth, divorce and widowhood have strong negative impacts on the accumulation of assets. Chang finds that "being a custodial parent most likely affects women's wealth by impacting the ability to save and by affecting earnings." In addition, some women may invest in lower-risk investments in part because they feel more economically vulnerable due to their status as single parents. She finds reciprocal relationships between many of these causal factors.

Elmelech (chap. 3) also finds that family structure explains many of the intragroup differences existing within communities of color. Populations with high numbers of single parents and/or unmarried individuals experience high intragroup wealth inequality. Several of the chapters note, for example, that Black families with two earners (and thus more general resources, or more variety of resources, and more employment benefits) do "well" relative to other Blacks, while the contrast is much less among White families. This is particularly true for pension ownership (see Chiteji, Gouskova, and Stafford, chap. 8).

Because child rearing puts a burden on wealth accumulation, policies that would reduce this burden would make a difference. If child rearing were seen as a public good, there could be more cost sharing between families, communities, and the state. Affordable social services for children, health care, child care, food or food service, educational supplies, and higher education could be part of a package of family-sustaining and wealth-enhancing policies. In addition—since education has been found to enhance wealth accumulation—higher-quality education, education finance reform, and resources and opportunities for families to provide more supplemental education opportunities to their children would take some of the burden off families and increase resources that could impact wealth accumulation. The payment of child support and better mechanisms for collecting child support and making sure it reaches the actual child for whom it was intended are also important. Child savings accounts are another strategy to help lower the burden of child rearing on parents and to give all children a savings base. In some cases such accounts can compensate for lack of inheritance and intergenerational transfers.

In the past social welfare programs (such as those in the New Deal policies) have been acceptable because they were necessary to support social reproduction—to maintain a healthy and educated workforce—as well as for some moral reasons (so that not too many women and children were left to starve). While those arguments seem to be losing their persuasiveness, we are now armed with an understanding of how important providing supports for children is to their families' asset-building strategies and wealth creation, particularly since the costs of child rearing in this society interfere with wealth accumulation.

On the other hand, some communities use their extended families as a source of social capital and economic support, which aids wealth accumulation. Robles (chap. 10) finds this true in Latino families and suggests that the expansion of social networks is likely to play a critical role in determining wealth accumulation among Latinos. Extended families are also important in Native American, Asian American and Native Hawaiian, and African American communities. They can be another mechanism to reduce the burden of child rearing on one family or a single parent and also are an economic resource and a source of additional finances. Policies that recognize and empower extended family networks are therefore also wealth-enhancing policies.

THE COMPOSITION OF THE PORTFOLIO & THE VARIETY OF ASSETS

Several chapters demonstrate the importance of the choices made about wealth portfolio composition and the lack of choice that some groups face (particularly Chiteji, Gouskova, and Stafford, chap. 8, and Leigh, chap. 1). African Americans tend to hold fewer assets and less complex portfolios than Whites. Blacks are also less likely to own any given asset than Whites and in particular have less diverse portfolios, own more consumable wealth, and own fewer stocks and bonds. In the case of pension holdings, however, among married couples Black families are not less likely to possess pensions than White families are, although the value of their retirement accounts is lower (related to income differences). Similar results hold for the other groups as well.

The finding that African American families hold simpler portfolios than White families (chap. 8) leads one to wonder how the less sophisticated will handle pension plans that are increasingly "defined contribution" rather than "defined benefit," as well as privatized Social Security accounts. These trends shift primary responsibility for asset selection and risk onto the worker and may affect families' prospects for accumulating sufficient retirement savings. Chiteji, Gouskova, and Stafford suggest it may be necessary to accompany any privatization efforts with educational or information programs designed to raise financial literacy. They also suggest that this may propel the workplace into a site for financial education and socialization. Robles (chap. 10) also highlights the importance of financial literacy and the role community institutions can play. There may be a lack of financial sophistication among non-Whites, and some groups have less experience navigating the terrain of the stock market.

This volume includes discussion of assets that sometimes do not receive much emphasis, such as pensions (chap. 8), land ownership (chap. 6), and neighborhood stability (chap. 11), as well as nontraditional assets, such as bilingualism (chap. 10), international community (chaps. 9 and 10), access to banking (chaps. 1, 9, and 10), entrepreneurship (chaps. 9 and 10), and community cooperative ownership (chaps. 6 and 12).

The land issue is very important. Land is often the building block for wealth accumulation. Land loss, confiscation, and theft are salient issues for African Americans, Native Americans, and Native Hawaiians. Gordon Nembhard and Chiteji mention these issues in the introduction, and they are underlying issues throughout the volume. Ong (chap. 6) notes that sovereignty and independence issues are important for Native Hawaiians as well as Native Americans. For both communities there is a disconnection between tribal assets (historic and current) and economic well-being (also see Zagorsky, chap. 5). This is often a political disconnection first because of the political alienation from tribal assets, particularly land, the lack of ownership, and the lack of control over assets. It is also an economic disconnection: lack of profit sharing, no trickle-down effect, and bureaucratic mismanagement of assets. For African Americans there has also been a history of White violent and bureaucratic land theft, and family lands in the South are often difficult to retain, particularly by urban and northern owners, if they are not willed properly.

On the other hand, home ownership has increased for each group we have studied, and programs continue to help increase home ownership. While home ownership may not be viable for everyone, and some people will need a strong support system to remain a home owner, we know that home ownership is the most important asset in most people's wealth portfolio, especially the moderately wealthy and people of color. Home ownership is also a building block for wealth accumulation, helps to stabilize neighborhoods (Woldoff, chap. 11), and can increase owners' civic participation (Gordon Nembhard and Blasingame, chap. 12). If the largest value of wealth comes from home ownership, there is a Catch-22 if wealth is also required to enable one to purchase a home. A vicious cycle exists: some level of wealth, savings, or credit rating is needed to make a down payment, yet the major way that most people of color hold wealth is through a home.

Entrepreneurship is also an asset since business equity is an important component of the wealth portfolio. Black or ethnic capitalism policies popular in the President Nixon era had limited success. Clearly all groups studied here benefit from business ownership and would benefit from more entrepreneurship and ownership opportunities (Ong, chap. 6, and Robles, chap. 10, discuss this in some detail). A question is how to close the entrepreneurship gap. Robles proposes community solutions and notes that current policies to increase self-sufficiency are contradictory because the income-based programs still restrict significant asset development—enrollment in one precludes or limits enrollment in the other program. Gordon Nembhard and Blasingame (chap. 12) discuss cooperative ownership as a way to promote entrepreneurship and ownership while spreading the risks and sharing the profits. Cooperatives have benefits for wealth creation and civic participation. More research is clearly needed, but there also needs to be an expansion of successful programs in this area.

Access to banking facilities, access to capital, and predatory lending are huge issues that these chapters are not able to address in much detail, although Dymski, Mohanty, and Li (chap. 9) do find that ethnic banks increase both access to banking services (storing of wealth) and access to loans and credit (creating financial wealth). Predatory lending and mortgage and credit discrimination, which hinder wealth accumulation, have been written about in the literature in much detail. Here I'll just add that clearly there is a need for better and fairer access to check-cashing and payment facilities and to financial services in general. Reauthorization and expansion of the Community Reinvestment Act is an important policy, but also shoring up community development financial institutions would go far in increasing access to banking and credit services, which facilitate wealth accumulation.

International connections or interconnections with international communities and markets are also a nontraditional asset for wealth accumulation. While immigrant populations are some of the poorest in the United States, immigration and connections back to the country of origin bring some benefits. Dymski, Mohanty, and Li (chap. 9) point out that the shift from informal practices to the formation and expansion of formal Asian-owned banking institutions in Los Angeles is attributable to shifting global movements of human and financial capital— internally, Asian Americans used the banks to make remittances back home and, externally, foreigners contributed equity to the banks in the United States, which strengthened and stabilized them. The transnational ties strengthened the Asian-owned banks in the United States, which allowed them to help facilitate Asian American financial wealth creation by providing access not just to banking services but to small business loans and home mortgages. Robles (chap. 10) similarly notes that the transnational exchange of remittances "also serves as a type of 'patient' capital in the form of democratizing wealth and asset-building behaviors that ultimately benefit the United States in the long run by creating strong allegiances and familiarity with U.S. customs and values."

THE ROLE OF INCOME

Zagorsky (chap. 5) finds that low Native American incomes are the primary reason why their wealth holdings are smaller than their White cohorts'. What appeared to be a savings gap was really an income issue— savings were low because incomes did not even cover daily costs of living. This suggests that in order to increase wealth, particularly for low-income populations, income must first increase. Incomes must be high enough so that it is realistic for them to save and invest. Then they can be encouraged to save and helped to consider investments that might be safe and lucrative. This means that an analysis of wealth without an analysis of unequal labor market outcomes is only a partial analysis. Benefits to labor and stable incomes appear to be almost as important to wealth accumulation as business ownership. Livable wages increase income and bring working class families above poverty. Benefits such as health insurance, child care, and retirement plans remove obstacles such as catastrophic health costs, and out-of-pocket expenses for child care, and increase retirement savings. Steady work and stable incomes also help families plan ahead and put money aside for savings and investment.

Labor policies, however, are not enough for women. Women are discriminated against in the labor market. They earn lower wages, are segregated in certain occupations, often have less job tenure, and are less likely to work in situations that provide benefits (or better benefits) and high wages, such as full-time, unionized jobs at large firms (Chang, chap. 4). This gender discrimination is similar to the racial discrimination experienced by many African American and Latino/Latina workers. It is not just a matter of needing policies to create better jobs, but also of reducing gender and racial discrimination and inequality in hiring, retention, and promotion. Women are also less likely to be covered by pensions and thus have less pension wealth.

In addition, in the discussion about income, what Zagorsky does not address for Native Americans, but Ong addresses for Native Hawaiians (chap. 6), is that low incomes and lack of resources to invest are not just a result of the lack of good prospects in the labor market (which also has a historic dimension), lack of access to credit, and lack of intergenerational wealth transfers but also because of the continuous history of colonization and asset stripping by the U.S. government. For Native Americans who have sovereignty status, there is also an issue of asset mismanagement by the U.S. federal government, which holds assets in trust on behalf of the tribes. Native Hawaiians, Native Americans, and even African Americans (during slavery) and Asian Americans (during internment) have been disassociated from their land and stripped of assets they once owned as tribes/groups and as individuals. During enslavement African Americans were stripped of ownership of their own bodies. Each of these groups experienced periods in the United States where members were denied opportunities to own and gain new assets and/or manage their own assets. This limits wealth accumulation drastically. This history is extremely important to our understanding of wealth accumulation and "decumulation" (a term Dymski, Mohanty, and Li use) in these communities and to our understanding of viable wealth accumulation strategies. Remuneration, reparations, and other policies to compensate for those historical atrocities are in order and may be the only effective remedies (though highly contested).

Finally, a paradox exists in the difference between the Native American and Asian American wealth-income relationship, similar to the paradox for never-married women. In the Native American case, low income levels explain much of the lower wealth accumulation, not surprisingly, but in the Asian American case incomes are high but wealth levels are not commensurate. For never-married women, Black or White, income levels are near parity with never-married men, but the wealth gap between the two groups is huge (see Chang, chap. 4). In the preceding section I state that child-rearing costs may account for a lot of the discrepancy. High Asian American incomes are not translating into wealth equal to that of high-income-earning non-Hispanic Whites. Ong and Patraporn (chap. 7) note that socioeconomic achievement in this case does not secure societal rewards. In particular, access to credit is not the same for Asian Americans and Whites, and home values are lower for Asian Americans. The Asian American case explodes the meritocracy myth. Low income and income differences therefore do not explain all the wealth inequality. Discriminatory policies, past and current government actions, and other disadvantages provide a fuller explanation. Ong (chap. 6) concludes that "the impact of race is further complicated by the fact that overt and institutionalized discrimination in the school system and labor market also creates race inequalities in education and income and thus has an indirect adverse impact on asset accumulation." Finally, for Asian Americans and Latinos intragroup differences, particularly because of differential immigration patterns and statuses, also matter in understanding asset accumulation. New immigrants and immigrants who come as refugees bring fewer, if any, assets with them and have fewer opportunities to accumulate assets.

A WORD ABOUT SAVINGS & CONSUMPTION

Even though we understand that income effects on wealth are more important than savings per se, we cannot ignore issues about savings and consumption. Low levels of income do limit savings capacity, and asset poverty is of growing concern. In addition, of the four most frequently held assets in a person's wealth portfolio, two are consumable: a motor vehicle (which depreciates over time) and housing equity (which is not particularly liquid). This is significant because a large part of most people's wealth, when they have it, is functional—actually being used. On the one hand a car and a house are important assets that support employment and other activities and can be the base for future accumulation, but on the other hand these are not the kinds of assets that contribute to high wealth levels and they can even be a drain on future savings. It is certainly understandable that these would be the types of assets held, given that the majority of any population only holds moderate to low levels of wealth and almost a third of African Americans and Latinos have zero or negative levels of wealth. What wealth they do have would be held in assets that serve a function. The third most frequently held asset is interest earning accounts—but many fewer hold this. While this is another low-level asset, it is extremely important because of the high cost of alternative services.

Those who study individuals' wealth-holding behavior do recognize the need to help people balance between consumables, liquid assets for emergencies, and cash for everyday expenses, in addition to saving enough to use for investment and the accumulation of wealth. Savings adequacy for retirement is also increasingly important. Encouraging savings among the poor to facilitate asset ownership is an emerging strategy that has had some success. There are many examples of successful Individual Development Account programs, as well as education and training to encourage or lay the base for savings and entrepreneurship. However, Robles (chap. 10) points out that such programs often have conflicting goals and asset limitations that can be self-defeating. Financial education and other education programs will continue to be helpful and necessary but not sufficient.

INTRAGROUP INEQUALITY

In addition to the Elmelech and Chang chapters about intragroup inequality, Ong and Patraporn (chap. 7), Dymski, Mohanty, and Li (chap. 9), and Robles (chap. 10) all find that ethnic differences and immigration status are important contributors to intragroup wealth inequality. When members of a certain ethnic group immigrated to the United States, the skills and resources they brought with them and the economic conditions in the United States when they arrived are some of the factors explaining intragroup inequality. These studies suggest that it is very important to understand subgroup differences in order to understand the subgroup's mechanisms of wealth accumulation and prospects for increasing wealth. We must be sure that we do not put in place strategies and policies that continue to help the rich in any group just get richer while continuing to further polarize the rest of the population. Strategies and policies are going to have to be proactive and affirmative action will have to be taken to ensure that those who need the help and the targeting get it. Whatever strategies have helped the upper wealth class of each group reach that level may not be strategies that will help the middle or lower levels increase their wealth. One thing to look at is the kinds of assets and strengths that lower-income people have and figure out how to capitalize on these, using these as resources to accumulate more and more traditional kinds of wealth.

A NOTE ON MICRO- VERSUS MACRODIMENSIONS

The studies in this volume note different processes and dimensions of wealth accumulation, particularly individual versus group wealth accumulation. It becomes apparent in these pages that, too often, individual behavior plays a minor role in the face of adverse policies and historic barriers—it is overshadowed by them and the consequences of continual racial discrimination and class inequality. The cumulative effects of discrimination, adverse policy, and asset stripping are staggering. Many of the studies suggest that there is a complex interaction between the many micro- and macrodimensions of wealth accumulation, which feed on one another. In some ways every group has a "historic legacy of colonization and immigration" that can be different among the various groups but is a powerful contributor to the wealth accumulation or decumulation path.

The studies in this volume find that there is no one behavior we can tell a person or group to adopt that is a foolproof way to riches and there is no one policy that by itself will close the wealth gap for a population. We learn from Ong and Patraporn (chap. 7), for example, that access to financial capital is a key component to wealth building. However, access to financial capital varies by geography, period of time, ethnicity, financial institution type, and location of financing entity. This list does not even address an individual borrower's behavior or habits—which is often the first place we look to explain a problem with financing. A focus on the microlevel can obscure what is happening on the macrolevel. Neither should be ignored. In terms of policy, the macrolevel is the first line of offense. Our authors detail a host of barriers, inequalities, and discrimination at the macrolevel. Some individual members of each group have managed to overcome or overcompensate for these barriers, but most get caught in the web of multiple levels of discrimination and economic marginalization.

Michael Sherraden's new anthology (*Inclusion in the American Dream: Assets, Poverty, and Public Policy,* New York: Oxford University Press, 2005) addresses issues of asset poverty in particular and provides descriptions and analyses of a comprehensive array of asset-building policies past and present. In addition, Dollars and Sense Magazine's anthology of articles from various issues of their magazine on economic justice and writings from United for a Fair Economy on wealth and wealth inequality also provides examples of wealth inequality and policies to address it. *The Wealth Inequality Reader* (edited by Dollars and Sense and United for a Fair Economy, Boston, 2004) provides introductory and summary information with policy recommendations for the less sophisticated reader. Finally, the United for a Fair Economy's newly published *The Color of Wealth: The Story behind the U.S. Racial Wealth Divide* (by Meizhu Lui, Barbara Robles, Betsy Leandar-Wright, Rose Brewer, and Rebecca Adamson, New York: New Press, 2006) will also be of interest, particularly for the less sophisticated reader.

There are many different behaviors and policies that are personal and local, communal and organizational, and national that together can begin to change the wealth accumulation trajectory. The challenge is to first identify all the combinations of actions, to assemble the resources and strategies needed to change ineffective and adverse ones, and then to implement the positive micro- and macrolevel actions/behaviors. A culturally and historically sensitive, multipronged approach is necessary.

COMMUNITY

One of the unique discussions in this volume is the conversation about community-level wealth building and the way that community supports are a mechanism of wealth accumulation. An issue arises about community wealth and whether community wealth enhances individual wealth. Gordon Nembhard studies this and is working out a theory of community wealth accumulation (see chap. 12). Robles (chap. 10) focuses on this in her attempt to understand Latino wealth accumulation. Dymski, Mohanty, and Li. (chap. 9) remind us that residential segregation—whether involuntary or voluntary—is a defining element for virtually every U.S. ethnic non-White population. Consequently, we can conceptualize an ethnic community—a spatial area in which members of any given ethnic group are concentrated—on the one hand, and individual members of an ethnic group, on the other.

Robles finds that wealth creation activities in working poor Latino communities rest on the presence of Latino community-based organizations (CBOs) engaged in serving Latino families and promoting asset- and wealth-building initiatives such as self-help housing, microbusinesses, and nontraditional family savings vehicles. These CBOs have replaced many private and public sector entities that have failed to maintain a permanent presence in working poor and low-income Latino communities in the United States. The emphasis on individual property rights and corresponding, individual liability discourages communal asset-building activities. These communal poolings of resources are literally not on the "radar" with respect to data collection and government bureaucratic social services application forms. The collective manner in which family economic survival strategies have evolved in working poor and low-income Latino communities is missing or trivialized.

We have sufficient innovative community initiatives that, if supported by local, state, and federal policies, could rapidly decrease the economic stress currently being felt in Latino working poor and low-income communities. Gordon Nembhard and Blasingame (chap. 12) similarly find that democratically owned and community-based enterprises bring economic and wealth benefits to their owner-members that spill over to their communities—aiding in creating wealth, economic stability, and other economic as well as political and social benefits. We need ways to translate such models into effective policy and to support those successful efforts with appropriate policies.

WHERE DO WE GO FROM HERE?

In many ways, the implications from the research in this volume are quite discouraging and depressing. Life-cycle theory assumes that wealth accumulation increases over time and stabilizes by retirement, but for the groups discussed in this volume, this is a narrative that is complicated at every stage in the life cycle—even if one barrier is overcome, another arises. A part of the explanation in the United States is the legacy of racism (which every group covered here has experienced), but also, contemporary processes maintain and reproduce race-based wealth inequality (Ong, chap. 6). There are secondary and tertiary effects of racial discrimination, and of previous economic decisions and conditions that come into play, that are difficult to discern and to separate. In general the barrier to wealth accumulation is not individual behavior, though there are some things that individuals can do that will help. While individual agency does matter, to tackle the entire problem and increase wealth and well-being for every household, a comprehensive set of policies, programs, and behaviors (public as well as private) will need to be put in place.

We need to continue to gain a better and fuller understanding of the process of wealth accumulation and all its nuances. Therefore, there is no magic bullet, no one prescription. We can't just give everyone more income or force everyone to marry—it will still not be enough. There are multiple levels that need to be targeted and many different kinds of policies to explore, and these will need to work in conjunction with each other.

The issues are not just about measurement—what we can measure and how well we can measure wealth holding, who holds the wealth, the history of wealth accumulation, cumulative effects of wealth inequality, and asset stripping—but also about how we conceptualize wealth, how we understand the dynamics of wealth holding and the points along the continuum (trajectory) of asset building, and our recognition of wealth accumulation as a social and community process. Dymski, Mohanty, and Li (chap. 9) suggest that "it is important to note that simply an accurate listing of the dollar value of the assets owned by every individual at every point in time will not tell investigators everything they would ever want to know about racial/ethnic wealth creation. Some mysteries will remain, with keys to unlock them appearing only when more complete and imaginative data collection and analysis are undertaken." It will be important to identify nontraditional attributes and resources that can help produce assets or are assets in and of themselves. We need to better understand the role they play, their strengths and weaknesses, and how they can be further harnessed in the asset-building strategy.

About the Authors

Anthony A. Blasingame is an assistant professor at the School of Public and Environmental Affairs at Indiana University. He was assistant editor of the special issue "Tribute to Rhonda M. Williams," of the *Review of Black Political Economy* (Spring 2002). His fields of specialty include public finance, labor economics, poverty, and political economy. He received his Ph.D. from the University of Maryland at College Park in 2002.

Mariko Lin Chang is an associate professor of sociology and of social studies at Harvard University. Dr. Chang earned her Ph.D. from Stanford University. Her interests include social stratification, gender, social policy, economic sociology, and the sociology of work and occupations. She is currently involved in two lines of research: the first involves frameworks for understanding cross-national differences in patterns of occupational sex segregation, and her second line of research investigates the ways in which financial knowledge influences the distribution of wealth across race, class, and gender lines. She has published in scholarly journals such as the *American Sociological Review,* the *American Journal of Sociology,* and *Contemporary Sociology.*

Ngina Chiteji is an associate professor in the Department of Economics at Skidmore College. Dr. Chiteji's research examines intergenerational connections, family wealth, and asset-ownership patterns. Her research has appeared in publications such as *African American Research Perspectives,* the *American Economic Review Papers and Proceedings,* the *Social Science Computer Review,* the *Review of Black Political Economy,* and the *Journal of International Development.* Dr. Chiteji has held positions as a research analyst at the Congressional Budget Office, as a visiting scholar at the Democracy Collaborative at the University of Maryland, and as a fellow at the Poverty Research and Training Program at the University of Michigan. Dr. Chiteji holds a Ph.D. in economics from the University of North Carolina.

Gary Dymski is a professor in the Department of Economics at the University of California at Riverside. Professor Dymski also serves as the director of the University of California Center, Sacramento (UCCS). He is the author of several books, including *The Bank Merger Wave* (1999), and he has published widely in scholarly journals on the topics of banking, financial fragility, urban development, credit market discrimination, housing finance, and the Asian financial crisis. His many professional activities include time spent as a fellow at the Brookings Institution; time spent as a visiting scholar at Tokyo University and at the Bangladesh Institute for Development Studies; and advising roles for several city administrations, community-based organizations, and government agencies in South Korea and Japan. Professor Dymski has a B.A. from the University of Pennsylvania, an MPA from Syracuse University's Maxwell School of Public Policy, and a Ph.D. in economics from the University of Massachusetts, Amherst.

Yuval Elmelech is an assistant professor in the Department of Sociology and a research associate at the Jerome Levy Institute, all at Bard College. His current areas of research are social stratification, the distribution and intergenerational transmission of wealth, and issues related to poverty, housing, race, and immigration. He has authored or coauthored articles that have appeared in scholarly journals and in book chapters. Dr. Elmelech received his Ph.D. at Columbia University.

Jessica Gordon Nembhard is an assistant professor and political economist in the African American Studies Department and a founding principal of the Democracy Collaborative, at the University of Maryland, College Park. She was formerly research director at the Preamble Center, Washington, D.C. She has served as a senior economist at Morgan State University's Institute for Urban Research and was economic development analyst for the Black Community Crusade for Children of the Children's Defense Fund from 1993 to 1996. Dr. Gordon Nembhard specializes in economic development policy and Black political economy, with a focus on democratic community-based economic development, cooperative economics and worker ownership, alternative urban economic and educational development strategies, racial wealth inequality, and popular economic literacy. She is the author of *Capital Control, Finan-*

cial Regulation, and Industrial Policy in South Korea and Brazil, among other books. Her research also appears in journals such as the *American Economic Review Papers and Proceedings,* the *Review of International Co-operation, Humanity and Society,* and the *Review of Black Political Economy* (including guest editor of the special issue "Tribute to Rhonda M. Williams," June 2002). Dr. Gordon Nembhard earned M.A. and Ph.D. degrees in economics from the University of Massachusetts after receiving her B.A. degree from Yale University.

Elena Gouskova is a research investigator at the Survey Research Center at the University of Michigan. Dr. Gouskova's main fields of interest include financial economics, household portfolio finance, and applied econometrics. She received a Ph.D. in economics from the Rutgers University in 2003.

Darrick Hamilton is an assistant professor at the Robert J. Milano Graduate School of Management and Urban Policy and an affiliated faculty member in the Department of Economics, both at New School University. Dr. Hamilton earned his Ph.D. from the Department of Economics at the University of North Carolina, Chapel Hill, in 1999. He has held several fellowships, including a Robert Wood Johnson Foundation Health Policy Scholars Fellowship at Yale University from 2001 to 2003. His research examines the welfare of less "privileged" groups and ethnic/racial group competition for preferred economic and health outcomes, and he has published numerous articles on ethnic and racial disparities in wealth, home ownership, and labor market outcomes. Dr. Hamilton's articles have appeared or are scheduled to appear in the following publications: *African American Research Perspectives, American Economic Review, Applied Economics Letters, Challenge: The Magazine of Economic Affairs, Housing Studies, Journal of Economic Psychology, Review of Black Political Economy,* and *Social Science Quarterly.* His research agenda has been supported by grants from the Ford Foundation, National Institutes of Health, National Science Foundation, and Robert Wood Johnson Foundation.

Wilhelmina A. Leigh is a senior research associate at the Joint Center for Political and Economic Studies in Washington, D.C. Dr. Leigh has conducted policy research in the areas of health, housing, employment, and income security. Prior to joining the Joint Center in 1991, she was a principal analyst at the U.S. Congressional Budget Office and had worked for the Bureau of Labor Statistics (U.S. Department of Labor), the U.S. Department of Housing and Urban Development, the Urban Institute, and the National Urban League Research Department. Dr. Leigh also has taught at Harvard University, Howard University, the University of Virginia, and Georgetown University and has been an elected member of the National Academy of Social Insurance since 1997. She received her Ph.D. in economics from the Johns Hopkins University and her A.B., also in economics, from Cornell University.

Wei Li received her Ph.D. in geography at the University of Southern California and currently serves as an associate professor at the Asian Pacific American Studies Program at Arizona State University. Dr. Li also is affiliated with the Department of Geography, School of Justice and Social Inquiry, Center for Asian Studies, and Women's Studies Department. Her foci of research are urban ethnicity and ethnic geography, immigration and integration, and financial sector and minority community development, with particular emphasis on the Chinese and other Asian groups in the Pacific Rim and Europe. Her scholarly articles have appeared in journals such as *Annals of the Association of American Geographers, Environment and Planning A, Urban Studies, Urban Geography, Social Science Research,* and *Journal of Asian American Studies.* Dr. Li recently received funding for a comparative research project entitled "Global Banks and Immigrant Community Development in Canada and the United States" from the government of Canada. Among her many book projects, Dr. Li has an edited volume forthcoming on new suburban Asian immigrant communities in the United States, Canada, Australia, and New Zealand from the University of Hawaii Press. She was appointed as a member of the U.S. Census Bureau's Race and Ethnic Advisory Committees (REAC, Asian Population) in 2003.

Lisa Mohanty is an assistant professor of economics at the City University of New York–College of Staten Island. She received her Ph.D. from the University of California, Riverside, in 2001. Her research examines the inequalities in the distribution of wealth in the United States based on gender, minority, and immigration status.

Paul Ong is a professor of urban planning, social welfare, and Asian American studies and director of the Ralph and Goldy Lewis Center for Regional Policy Studies at the University of California at Los Angeles. Professor Ong has conducted research on the labor market status of minorities and immigrants, displaced high-tech workers, work and welfare, and transportation access. He is currently engaged in several projects, including studies on the effects of neighborhood economies on welfare and work, community economic development in minority communities, and the labor market for health care workers. Dr. Ong has served as an adviser to several organizations, including the U.S. Bureau of the Census, the California Department of Social Services, and the California Department of Employment Development. He is the author of several books, and his research also has appeared in scholarly journals such as the *Journal of Policy Analysis and Management,* the *Journal of Economic Issues, Economic Development Quarterly, Housing Policy Debate,* and the *Review of Black Political Economy.*

R. Varisa Pataporn is a doctoral student in the Department of Urban Planning at the University of California, Los Angeles. Her current work focuses on understanding minority access to financial capital, particularly in the area of mortgage and small business lending, and nonmainstream financial institutions. She has worked and consulted for the White House Budget Office, the Treasury Department's Community Development Financial Institutions Fund, and the Nonprofit Finance Fund. She holds a master's degree in public policy from the University of California, Los Angeles.

Bárbara J. Robles is an associate professor at Arizona State University's School of Social Work and at the Center for Community Development and Civil Rights. Her research analyzes Latino family and community financial needs and behaviors, asset-building policies, Latino/Latina entrepreneurship, family economic security, the Earned Income Tax Credit (EITC), and community-based organizations. Her research has appeared in scholarly journals such as the *Review of Economics and Statistics, Applied Economics,* and *Aztlan: International Journal of Chicano Studies Research.* She also is the author of several policy reports and book chapters and is coauthor of *The Color of Wealth: The Story Behind the U.S. Racial Wealth Divide* (New Press, forthcoming Spring 2006). Dr. Robles received her Ph.D. in economics from the University of Maryland.

Frank Stafford is a professor of economics at the University of Michigan and director of the Panel Study of Income Dynamics. His active research areas include issues of time allocation, the economics of child care, family wealth, pensions, and savings. He is the author of numerous articles and book chapters, and his research has appeared in scholarly journals such as the *American Economic Review, Brookings Papers on Economic Activity,* the *Journal of Human Resources,* the *Journal of Economic Literature,* the *Journal of Money, Credit and Banking,* and the *Review of Economics and Statistics.* Professor Stafford also has served as a special assistant for economic affairs at the Office of the Assistant Secretary for Policy, Evaluation, and Research at the U.S. Department of Labor and as a visiting professor at the University of Stockholm. Dr. Stafford holds a B.A. from Northwestern University, an MBA from the University of Chicago, and a Ph.D. in economics from the University of Chicago.

Rachael A. Woldoff is an assistant professor of sociology at West Virginia University. She received a Ph.D. in sociology from Ohio State University, specializing in race, crime, and community issues. Dr. Woldoff's research and publications have focused on neighborhood crime and disorder, neighborhood redevelopment, and racial/ethnic differences in residential outcomes. Her work has appeared in *Social Forces* and *Sociological Focus.* Her recently coauthored book, *High Stakes: Big Time Sports and Downtown Redevelopment,* investigates sports facilities as a form of urban redevelopment. Dr. Woldoff has a long-standing interest in race/ethnicity and urban sociology, especially neighborhood life in African American and White communities. Her recent research on Whites, African Americans, and Latinos examines racial/ethnic differences in the effects of individuals' wealth on their neighborhood characteristics.

Jay L. Zagorksy has been one of the National Longitudinal Survey's research scientists at Ohio State University since 1995. His research focuses on understanding personal wealth issues, and it has been published in scholarly journals such as the *Eastern Economic Journal,* the *Review of Income and Wealth, Economic Letters,* and the *Journal of Socio-Economics.* In addition to his research he currently teaches MBAs and undergraduates at Boston University's School of Management. He received his Ph.D. in economics from Boston University.

Index

cash holdings, 44
casinos, 133–34, 148–50
Casky, J., 238n10
Cathay Bank, 229
Cavalluzzo, L., and J. Wolken, 180
Census Bureau. *See* U.S. Census
 Bureau
Census of Agriculture, 157–58
Center for Human Resources Re-
 search (CHRR), 30, 50, 274
Center for Responsive Politics, 301
Center for the Study of Wealth and
 Inequality, 106
Center for Women's Business Re-
 search, 244–45
Center of Philanthropy Panel Study
 (COPPS), 295, 298, 307
Central American/s, 243–44, 248,
 250
charitable giving/donations, 10–11,
 305, 306–16, 317
 to religious organizations,
  314–16, 317–18
Charles, K. K., and E. Hurst, 17n4,
 268. *See also* Barsky, R., J.
 Bond, and K. K. Charles
checking accounts. *See* accounts
Cherokee, 136
Chesnick, D., 303
Chicago, 237
child
 care, 280, 335
 rearing, 330
 support, 123, 331
children, 14, 123, 125–26, 127n9,
 280, 327
Children's Savings Accounts, 16,
 258, 320, 331
Chinese, 48, 220–21, 227, 229–32,
 236–37, 238n11
 American banks, 9, 229–32, 236,
  237
 banks, 230, 238n11
Chiteji, N., 327
 and D. Hamilton, 17n4
 and F. Stafford, 17n4
Choudhury, S., 23, 25, 32–33, 55
church attendance, 307

citizenship, 173
civic
 engagement, 10–11, 294–98, 301,
  305–7, 318–20, 321n1
 organizations, 294
 participation, 243, 259, 305, 318,
  333
Clark, W. A. V., 268, 269
Clinton, W. J., 167
closing cost, 268
coefficient
 group, 78
 OLS, 75, 80
 race, 70, 85n11
 regression, 77–78, 86n21
colonization, 157, 173, 242
Columbia University, 106
comadre/compadre, 252
communal land tenure, 157
community, 3, 4, 5, 280, 339–40
 assets, 327, 340, 341
 international, 332, 334
community-based organizations
 (CBOs), 241, 252–55, 257, 259,
  261, 294, 332, 339, 340
community development
 corporations (CDCs), 254, 257,
  322n9
 financial institutions (CDFIs),
  253–55, 257, 263n16, 334
 housing organizations (CDHOs),
  254
community economic development,
 9, 157
Community Reinvestment Act,
 263n19, 322n10, 334
concentration camps, 17n2
conditional mean function, 73
Congress, 133, 157, 167, 168,
 168n6, 170nn28–29, 299, 300,
 301
Conley, D., 14, 219, 268, 318
*Consumer Expenditure Survey
 (CEX)*, 26–31, 47, 50, 53, 58
 Interview Survey, 53, 58
Consumer Union Survey, 213n1
consumption flow, 191, 203
control of capital/assets, 300, 333

economic
democracy, 294
mobility, 243, 252, 258
power, 295, 297–301, 320, 321n3
segregation, 296–97
status, 112–13, 121–22, 125, 227, 238n9
Edgcomb, E., and M. M. Armington, 245, 253, 254
Edin, K., 252
education, 91–94, 96–98, 101–3, 106, 156, 164, 166–67, 170n26, 193, 196, 199–201, 203–5, 207, 210–11, 213, 267–68, 270–71, 273–74, 278–79, 281–82, 284–86, 288, 295–97, 300–301, 305–8, 310–20, 321n5, 330–31, 336
educational
achievement, 270
attainment, 91, 104, 105, 138, 156, 168n4, 243, 246, 248–49, 268, 295–97, 327
Elden, J. M., 305
Eller, T. J., and W. Fraser, 23, 32–33
employee stock ownership plans (ESOPs), 302, 321n5
democratic, 321n5
employer pensions, 3, 11
entrepreneurship, 244–45, 332, 333, 337
equity in business or profession, 26–27, 39–42, 198, 203, 302, 333
Erdal, D., 305
error term, 73, 75
estate tax, 15
estimation techniques, 80–83
ethnic enclave, 230, 245, 252–54, 258–59, 339–40
expenditures, 28, 30, 53, 69
extended family, 243, 252, 260–61, 331

401 (k) and 403 (b) plans, 26, 40–42, 55, 118–20, 124n4, 126n4

family
characteristics, 252, 268, 270, 272–73, 276–78, 280, 282–89, 330
extended. *See* extended family
of origin, 268, 270, 272–80, 282, 284, 287–88
survival strategies, 340
Fannie Mae, 243, 262n4
FDIC-insured bank, 230–31
Federal Housing Administration (FHA), 60
Federal Reserve Bank, 175
Federal Reserve System, Board of, 31, 58, 114, 133–34, 246, 248, 262n7, 299
Federation of Southern Cooperatives/Land Assistance Fund, 305
Feminist Economics (journal), 17n3
financial
assets, 26, 143
capital, 178–79, 230–31, 338
institutions, 26, 36–38, 52, 54, 62n9, 179, 183, 228, 244–45, 254, 257, 261, 261n2, 263n19
literacy/education, 255, 261, 332, 337
market participation, 197, 199
market sophistication, 212, 327, 332
Florida, 30, 51, 54
Forbes, 173
Ford Foundation, 106
forty acres and a mule, 24
Foxwoods Casino, 148
Frasure, L., and L. F. Williams, 306, 318
Freddie Mac, 243, 262n4
Freeman, L., 270

Gallagher, M. *See* Waite, L. J., and M. Gallagher
gaming, 8
gender
earnings gap, 122, 125, 335
income gap, 120–22, 125

single-female-headed, 113
U.S., 29–30, 32, 34, 36, 48, 53
White, 23, 31, 35–38, 40–44, 49,
    51–52, 60–61, 223–24, 226
widowed, 113, 116, 118–19
housing, 10, 24–25, 27, 46–49,
    51–54, 59–61, 69, 95, 105, 119,
    143, 146, 149, 156, 161–66,
    174, 176–81, 183–84, 187, 191,
    198, 202, 226, 232, 239n13,
    241–43, 245, 250, 254–56,
    262n4, 263n10, 267–74, 280
discrimination, 271
equity, 25–27, 52, 60, 177–78,
    226, 337
nonhousing equity, 25–27
self-help and, 241, 255, 256, 340
trust funds and, 320, 322n9
Housing and Urban Development
    (HUD), 243
Houston, 237
human capital, 92, 93, 96, 105, 123,
    125, 156, 168n4, 250
Hurst, E., M.-C. Luoh, and F.
    Stafford, 3, 17n4, 71, 76.
    See also Charles, K. K., and
    E. Hurst

Illinois, 51
immigrants, 24, 27–28, 44, 46, 48,
    52, 57, 94, 104, 184, 230, 284,
    336
immigration, 173–74, 184–85,
    242–43, 250, 254, 260, 336
policy, 174, 184–86
status, 94, 96, 103, 105, 336, 337
Imola, Italy, 305–6
inclusive incorporation, 258
income
    asset, 162, 165–66, 169n21
    asset-based, 162, 165
    bracketed, 53
    definition, 2
    family, 56
    high, 58, 59
    inequality, 15, 112, 125, 319,
        321n1, 334–36

labor, 70–71, 73, 85n8, 335
low. See low income
pension, 195–96
permanent, 52, 61
policy, 333, 334–35
PSID. See Panel Study of Income
    Dynamics
rental, 176, 182–84
retirement, 246
SIPP. See Survey of Income Pro-
    gram Participation
Indian American/s. See Native
    American/s
Indian Gambling Regulatory Act, 133
indigenous population, 155–59,
    166–68
individual behavior, 338–39, 341
Individual Development Accounts
    (IDAs), 13, 16, 247–48, 253–55,
    320, 322n11, 337
Individual Retirement Accounts
    (IRAs), 26, 28–42, 54–55, 61,
    118–20, 126n4, 246, 248
inheritance, 15, 24, 50, 147–48,
    245–46, 248, 262n8
Institute for Social Research, 31, 57
institutional discrimination. See
    under discrimination
interest-earning accounts. See
    under accounts
interest-earning assets. See under
    assets
intergenerational
    bequests, 243, 246
    differences, 260
    transfers. See transfers
    transmissions, 95, 102, 105
international connections. See
    community
internment, 335
intragroup differences, 91–105,
    180–83, 186, 220, 227, 242,
    260, 330, 336, 337
intragroup wealth inequality. See
    wealth
investment, 134, 147, 152n20, 335,
    337

stocks, 26, 38–42, 52, 54, 62n5, 114, 118–20, 142–43, 152n20, 191, 198, 202–5, 207, 209, 211–12
substitution effect, 192, 205, 207–8, 212
suburbs, 296
Summers, L. H. *See* Kotlikoff, L. J., and L. H. Summers
Sunden, A. *See* Munnell, A. H., and A. Sunden
supplemental education opportunities, 331
Supplemental Security Income (SSI)
Survey of Consumer Finances (SCF), 13, 15, 16–17n1, 26–27, 31–33, 92, 114–17, 119, 126n2, 126n4, 134, 156, 175, 188, 195–97, 246, 248, 262nn7–8, 268, 329
Survey of Economic Opportunity (SEO), 23, 43, 52, 57
Survey of Income Program Participation (SIPP), 14, 16n1, 27–29, 31–35, 37–38, 45, 50 59, 71, 79, 175–77, 179–81, 188, 226, 238n8
Survey of Minority-Owned Businesses (SMOB), 159–60
Survey Research Center, 30, 54

Taiwan, 230
Takaki, R. T., 173, 237n2
tanda, 254, 257, 263n15
tangible asset. *See under* assets
tax code, 13, 192
Temporary Assistance to Needy Families (TANF), 138
Texas, 51, 220, 249–50, 253, 255–56
Thomas, J. M., and M. Ritzdorf, 297
Thrift Savings Plans, 16, 26, 41, 246, 248
tobit. *See under* regression
transaction account. *See under* accounts
transfers, 146–49
  cross-generational, 105

intergenerational, 49, 52, 56, 93, 95, 97, 99, 101, 104–5, 241, 247
  wealth, 247
transnational, 252–53, 257, 258, 260–61, 264n19
tribal assets, 17n2
Trinidad, 46, 62
Turner, M. A., and S. L. Ross, 239n13

UCLA, 188
unadjusted gap, 67–68, 71, 79
uncontrolled. *See under* variables
unemployment, 94, 112, 192, 233, 270
United for a Fair Economy, 339
United States, 23, 26, 27, 29, 31–32, 34, 43, 45–46, 48, 50–52, 57, 59–60, 173, 176, 180, 182, 184–87, 219–21, 223, 227–28, 230, 235, 237n1, 241–43, 248, 250–53, 257–58, 260–61, 269–70, 272–73, 287, 296, 298–302, 306, 308, 320
University of Chicago, 30, 55, 58, 274
University of Michigan, 30, 54, 57
USA accounts, 16
U.S. Census Bureau, 24, 30, 46, 48, 53, 55, 112–13, 123, 126, 156, 168n2, 168n4, 169n10, 169n13, 175, 242, 244, 248, 251, 253, 263n10, 263n13, 268, 298
U.S. Department of Labor, 30, 53, 55–57
U.S. Economic Censuses, 225–26, 236
U.S. General Accounting Office, 46
U.S. pension system, 193, 197
U.S. savings bonds. *See under* bonds
U.S. Virgin Islands, 28

Valenzuela, A., 249
variable
  continuous, 67, 84n2
  control, 70, 72, 77, 85n7, 113

variable (*continued*)
cultural, 274
dependent, 100–101, 107, 178,
  208–9, 270, 274–75, 281
dichotomous, 68, 74
dummy, 68, 77–78, 106, 233–34,
  280
explanatory, 74, 77–78, 80, 83,
  86n20, 96, 281
geographic, 276, 283
independent, 69–70, 72–78, 233,
  238n12, 270, 274, 277
institutional, 271
latent, 107
outcome, 68–69, 73–74, 76, 83,
  85n12
SES, 272, 280, 287
Vaughn, J., 228, 238n10
vehicle ownership, 144, 146, 150,
  153n29
Vélez-Ibañez, C. G., 252
Veteran Administration (VA), 60
Vietnamese, 48, 185, 188n2, 220,
  238n4
voluntary organizations, 306
volunteering, 10–11, 306–16, 317,
  318, 319

Wachter, S. M. *See* Haurin, D. R.,
  P. H. Hendershott, and S. M.
  Wachter
Waite, L. J., and M. Gallagher, 94
Wall Street Journal, 174
war babies, 54
Washington, D.C., 220
Washington State, 302
Washington Post, 174
wave, 54–55, 59
wealth. *See also* net wealth; net
  worth
  accumulation, 3, 27, 47–48, 51,
    67, 71, 80, 82, 85n8, 93, 97,
    123–26, 219–22, 242, 246, 251,
    258, 261, 301–2, 304, 319, 335,
    338, 339, 340–41
  assets and, 221–22, 335
  building of, 178, 220–22, 227–28,
    232, 235, 237

creation of, 241, 248, 303, 319,
  328
data on, 24, 27–28, 30–34, 37,
  44–45, 47–48, 50, 52–53,
  57–58, 61, 161–62, 164,
  174–75, 183–84, 186–87
definition of, 2, 327, 341
disparity, 71
distribution of, 3, 92, 94, 113,
  114
financial, 329
holdings of, 2, 25, 27–29, 32–33,
  44–45, 47, 51–52, 67, 70,
  134–35, 141, 146, 155–56,161,
  174, 183, 191, 197–98, 208,
  211–12, 220–21, 223, 238n7,
  317–18, 341
income and, 34
inequality, 3, 15, 71, 91–96,
  99–100, 102, 104–5, 112, 114,
  117, 121, 125–26, 193, 196–97,
  245, 261, 295, 298–99, 301,
  308, 318, 320, 338, 341
intragroup inequality in, 7, 8, 10,
  51, 91–93, 96, 100, 102–5, 128,
  208, 214n11, 308, 337–38
ladder to, 174
levels of, 2, 34, 268, 273, 280,
  285
marginal effects of, 309–14
mean, 70–71, 82, 308
measurement of, 24, 341
median, 115–18, 124
nonpension, 192–94, 196, 207,
  212
outcomes, 173, 175, 186
pensions and, 335
portfolios and, 192–93, 211
proxy, 183
and race-based inequality, 164,
  338, 340
scale effect and, 207–8
status and, 177–78, 182, 185–86
tax and, 320
transfers of. *See under* transfers
variables in, 176
wealth gap
  adjusted, 70–71

Black-White. *See* Black-White/White–non-White wealth gap; racial

gender. *See under* gender

gross, 70

net, 70, 72

unadjusted, 67–71, 79

wealth-income relationship, 336

Weems, R. *See* Dymski, G., and R. Weems

Weiss, C., and C. Clamp, 304

well-being, 1, 2, 3

West Indies, 46

White House, 299

White household. *See under* household

White–non-White gap. *See* Black-White/White–non-White wealth gap

widowed individuals/households, 113–21, 124

Williams, L. F. *See* Frasure, L., and L. F. Williams

Williams, R. M., 326

Williamson, T., D. Imbroscio, and G. Alperovitz, 321n5

Wilson, W. J., 91, 297, 321n1

Winbush, R., 17n2

Winkel, G. *See* Saegert, S., and G. Winkel

Wolff, E. N., 2, 3, 15, 23, 26, 47, 59, 61, 92, 93, 238n8, 298, 299, 320. *See also* Shapiro, T., and E. Wolff

Wolken, J. *See* Cavalluzzo, L., and J. Wolken

women, 112–30

of color, 125

divorced, 113, 116, 120

economic status of, 1, 7, 17n3, 112–13, 121–22, 335

human capital and, 122, 124–25

married, 113, 120, 124, 127n8

never married, 113, 115–22, 124–25, 127n10, 336

widowed, 115, 120 124

women's wealth, 17n3, 112–27, 335

worker ownership, 320

working poor, 241–42, 247, 251–53, 257–59, 261

workplace democracy, 301–2, 304–5

World War II, 17n2, 60, 173

Yinger, J., 269. *See also* Ross, S. L., and J. Yinger

Zhou, M., and R. Kim, 184, 185

Zonta, M., 179, 183